P9-CCC-495

The Russian Enterprise in Transition

The Russian Enterprise in Transition

Case Studies

Edited by Simon Clarke
Professor of Sociology
Centre for Comparative Labour Studies
University of Warwick
Coventry, UK

MANAGEMENT AND INDUSTRY IN RUSSIA SERIES

Centre for Comparative Labour Studies, Warwick
Institute for Comparative Labour Relations Research, Moscow

Edward Elgar
Cheltenham, UK • Brookfield, US

Published by
Edward Elgar Publishing Limited
8 Lansdown Place
Cheltenham
Glos GL50 2HU
UK

Edward Elgar Publishing Company
Old Post Road
Brookfield
Vermont 05036
US

A catalogue record for this book
is available from the British Library

Library of Congress Cataloguing in Publication Data
The Russian enterprise in transition / edited by Simon Clarke.
(Management and industry in Russia series)
"Centre for Comparative Labour Studies, Warwick [and] Institute for Comparative Labour Relations Research, Moscow" —P. 1 of cover.
Includes bibliographical references and index.
1. Industrial management—Russia (Federation)—Case studies.
2. Industrial relations—Russia (Federation)—Case studies.
3. Business enterprises—Russia (Federation)—Case studies.
4. Privatization—Russia (Federation)—Case studies. I. Clarke, Simon, 1946– . II. Centre for Comparative Labour Studies (Warwick, England) III. Institute for Comparative Labour Studies (Moscow, Russia) IV. Series.
HD70.R9R863 1996
338.7'0947—dc20 96–15888
CIP

ISBN 1 85898 341 X

Printed in Great Britain at the University Press, Cambridge

Contents

1. The Enterprise in the Era of Transition

Simon Clarke

This book is the fourth in a series written on the basis of a research project on the restructuring of management, labour relations and worker organisation in Russia which has been underway since 1991. The research has been conducted collaboratively by the Centre for Comparative Labour Studies (CCLS), University of Warwick, and teams of researchers from four regions of Russia, who have now come together to establish the inter-regional Institute for Comparative Labour Relations Research (ISITO), based in Moscow.[1] Industrial enterprises in four regions of Russia have been monitored continuously since the beginning of reform, with a period of intensive ethnographic research in twelve enterprises at shop level lasting from the beginning of 1992 to the summer of 1994. We have kept in touch with our case study enterprises since the end of the intensive fieldwork, and have monitored a significant number of other enterprises in our selected regions and elsewhere. Other research findings and press reports have also been monitored to give us a broader perspective on

1 The previous books in the series, also edited by Simon Clarke and published by Edward Elgar, are *Management and Industry in Russia: Formal and Informal Relations in the Period of Transition* (1995); *Conflict and Change in the Russian Industrial Enterprise* (1996); and *Labour Relations in Transition: Wages, Employment and Industrial Conflict in Russia* (1996). An earlier book, Simon Clarke, Peter Fairbrother, Michael Burawoy and Pavel Krotov, *What About the Workers?*, Verso, London and New York, 1993, was based in part on early research for this project. Two of the enterprises described in this volume were also discussed in an early report of the research: Simon Clarke, Peter Fairbrother Vadim Borisov and Petr Bizyukov, 'The Privatisation of Industrial Enterprises in Russia: Four Case Studies', *Europe-Asia Studies*, 46, 2, Glasgow, 1994, pp.179–214. This research has been funded by the British Economic and Social Research Council and INTAS and the project was directed by Simon Clarke and Peter Fairbrother. Our research programme is continuing with two major projects, one on the restructuring of the Russian coal-mining industry, the other on the restructuring of employment and the development of local labour markets in Russia. Further details, papers and research materials can be obtained from our WWW site:
http://www.warwick.ac.uk/WWW/faculties/social_studies/complabstuds/complab.htm

the restructuring of industrial enterprises under the impact of liberal market reform.

The previous three volumes in this series have brought together thematic papers written on the basis of our case study research, covering a wide range of substantive issues. This volume completes the set by providing detailed accounts of five of our case study enterprises, so setting the earlier thematic analyses into a wider context. In putting together this volume we have had to decide not so much what to put in, as what to leave out. The uniqueness of our project lies in the depth of the research, so that we have enough material to write a substantial volume on each of our enterprises. To cover all of our enterprises in one volume would be to reduce each account to a level of superficiality and generality which would deprive all of much of their value. We have therefore decided to limit ourselves to five of the enterprises, which are presented in some depth and cover a range of experiences of and responses to reform. Every enterprise has its own unique features, but there is a process of diminishing returns and in our view the selection offered here optimises the mix of depth and diversity. The case study reports which make up this volume have been translated and more or less extensively edited by Simon Clarke on the basis of reports and research materials prepared by the indicated authors. The reports have been discussed with the original authors at every stage.

The distinctive feature of our case studies has been the focus on the qualitative changes in the social organisation of production at all levels of the enterprise and, correspondingly, the use of ethnographic and qualitative methods of sociological research. The vast majority of the growing number of case studies of enterprises under restructuring in the former Soviet bloc have been conducted by economists and have been concerned to collect quantitative enterprise-level data, supplemented with interviews with senior managers about their investment, employment and marketing strategies, ownership patterns and so on. While we have collected a large amount of such data ourselves, we are very sceptical of its usefulness and its validity. The collection and reporting of enterprise-level data is severely constrained by the use of such data for planning, financial and fiscal purposes and distorted by the extent to which management at various levels within and beyond the enterprise seeks to use such data to conceal or misrep-

resent enterprise activities. Aggregate employment data gives little indication of the real processes of employment restructuring, financial data gives little indication of the real financial position of the firm,

production data tells us little about production trends. We quote such data at appropriate points in our exposition, but do not give it much credence.

It is well-known that Russian industrial enterprises are deeply embedded in informal networks of politicians, bureaucrats and financial and commercial structures, many of whose activities border on illegality or are straightforwardly criminal. The economic fate of many enterprises has been determined as much by their external connections as by their internal processes, and our case study enterprises are no exception in this. Rumours always circulate about such activity, and sometimes surface in press and court reports, but rumours themselves play a commercial and political role so it is impossible to know how much credence or significance to give to them, while prudence dictates that we do not investigate these too closely.

The five enterprises described in this book are all former state enterprises, but embrace a wide range of experiences. The first two enterprises, a chemical enterprise in Kemerovo and a light engineering enterprise in Moscow, were selected for study because they were two of the 'pioneers of privatisation', breaking free from the state system at a relatively early stage in the transition to a market economy, with a management positively oriented to the 'transition to a market economy' and keen to adopt Western management practice. Both enterprises prospered in the initial stage of reform, but in both cases a radical programme of restructuring ran into serious internal and external barriers, provoking internal conflicts which undermined the more radical initiatives.

The next two enterprises, both heavy engineering enterprises within the military-industrial complex in Samara, were selected for study because they represented the industrial pillars of the old system, gargantuan enterprises which were highly privileged and lived primarily off military orders and so could be expected to be the most resistant to reform, but also the hardest hit by the transition to the market economy. Both enterprises pursued management strategies which we characterise as 'balancing conservatism', attempting as far as possible to respond to external changes while preserving the internal structures of power and status intact. The two enterprises have enjoyed distinct and fluctuating fortunes but, following an initial phase of passivity, senior management in both has embraced the opportunities presented by privatisation and the market.

The final enterprise selected for case study is not strictly an industrial enterprise, but a municipal transport enterprise in the northern Komi Republic which remains a state enterprise, although a part of its activity has been privatised. We selected this enterprise for study in part because it had already been the object of a case study in 1989, but primarily because it was one of the very few enterprises that we had managed to find in Russia (at least outside the coal-mining industry) in which the trade union had consistently opposed the enterprise director not as representative of an opposing faction in management, but apparently as a representative of the labour force. This case study should enable us to see the extent to which independent workers' organisation is an effective constraint on enterprise restructuring, although in practice, as we will see, things turned out rather differently.[2]

We do not seek to generalise or to draw conclusions about the Russian enterprise in transition on the basis of our five, or even our twelve, case studies. Our primary purpose in presenting the case studies is to paint a picture of the Russian enterprise as a living social organism which unites hundreds, thousands or tens of thousands of people in a complex social structure which defines the economic, social and cultural framework for the lives of wider local communities. The fate of the enterprise is not merely a matter of profit and loss, it is the fate of people and their communities, people and communities whose lives have been built around work to a degree that has been forgotten in the capitalist West. These people, managers and workers alike, have different values, different expectations, different ways of living and working from those who have been brought up under the rule of money and the market. They bear within themselves and within their social networks the legacy of seventy years of Soviet power, practice and ideology. The values and lifestyle of liberal individualism are so deeply embedded within the Western intelligentsia, and have brought the latter such generous rewards, that they imagine them to be a natural emanation of the human essence, the epitome of reason,

[2] Independent workers' organisations have been most active in those branches of production which have remained in state ownership (predominantly transport, energy and metallurgy). Conventional wisdom is that it is state ownership which enables workers to exercise power by pressing the state for subsidies. On the other hand, industries in which workers have some independent power are not good candidates for privatisation. Thus it may be as much that privatisation is impeded by workers' power as that workers derive their power from state ownership. The experience in the West, particularly in Britain, is that the state breaks the power of workers as the prelude to privatisation.

seeing other values as artificial ideologies imposed by totalitarian power and religious or political fanaticism. If our case studies do nothing else, we hope that they will stand as testimony to the resilience of the Russian labour force in the face of the unholy alliance of Soviet and neo-liberal totalitarianism embodied in the programme of 'market Bolshevism'.

Although we do not seek to generalise about the fate of the Russian enterprise on the basis of our case studies, there is a clear convergence in their course over the first five years of reform as the most radical ambitions have been reigned in and the most conservative forces swept aside. This convergence is also apparent in our other case studies, and in the large number of other enterprises whose fate we have monitored on a less systematic basis. Moreover, this convergence is clearly feeding back into the broader economic and political changes which are taking place in Russia as the failure of enterprises to accept the fate decreed by the unfettered rule of the market subverts the attempt to subject them to the requirements of global capitalism. To present our case studies outside this broader context is to misrepresent their experience: to look at one enterprise in isolation is to depict it as the victim of changes unfolding outside its control. But those wider changes do not come from nowhere, they are aspects of the development of a social, political and economic system of which the enterprise is itself a part. The 'transition to a market economy' is a process which expresses tendencies already inherent within the Soviet system and which continue to unfold in its further development. In the rest of this chapter I will try briefly to contextualise our case studies by discussing this wider context, and by contrasting it with the dominant Western liberal characterisation of transition.[3]

THE DYNAMICS OF TRANSITION AND THE MICRO-ECONOMICS OF REFORM

The processes of marketisation and privatisation were unleashed in Russia in January 1992 with a programme more radical than that of any other former state socialist country. It is important not to under-

[3] Part of the following sections recapitulates and revises the theoretical discussion in Simon Clarke et al., *What About the Workers?*, op. cit., Chapters 1 and 2, where the contradictions of the Soviet system are discussed more fully.

estimate the impact of this programme, but its results have matched neither the hopes of radical reformers nor the fears of their critics. Capitalist activity flourishes, but productive investment has collapsed. The traditional system of central planning has disintegrated, but traditional economic relationships are maintained. Production has fallen, but we still await the predicted mass unemployment. The majority have incomes below the breadline, but there is no starvation.

At a superficial view it appears that the traditional system has been dented, but that it has an enormous inertia that makes it resistant to rapid change. The advocates of liberal market reform conclude that the reform programme has not been sufficiently radical and, in particular, that enterprises should be more rigorously subjected to the discipline of the market by being confined within a 'hard budget constraint'.

Reformers differ in their assessment of the efficacy of market adjustment, but their diagnoses rest on a common theoretical foundation, which one might call the 'neo-classical' model. According to this model the twin processes of marketisation and privatisation should lead to the transition to an efficient and dynamic capitalist economy. Marketisation is the process by which the prices of goods and services come to be determined by competitive pressures, and resources correspondingly reallocated on the basis of opportunity cost. Privatisation is the means by which productive assets are constituted as private property (this might well be corporate property), so that they can be allocated on the basis of an evaluation of discounted flows of monetary costs and benefits. Marketisation and privatisation require the development of a legal system which can guarantee the security of property and the person and the enforceability of contracts; a banking system which can guarantee free monetary circulation while preserving the integrity of the currency; a financial system which can allocate financial resources on the basis of prospective returns; and a fiscal system which is characterised as far as possible by neutrality, with predictable and reasonable levels of taxation. Depending on one's point of view, these processes require a greater or lesser degree of directive intervention from national and international state bodies.

This ideal model of a capitalist economy provides the theoretical foundations for a dualistic model of the economics of transition. According to this model the transition is not theorised as an evolutionary development of the existing system under the impact of the development of market structures. For this model the existing system has no dynamic of its own. It is defined purely negatively as a barrier to change which must be transformed, overcome or destroyed, so that a new system can be created out of its fragments.

Reformers from different camps differ in their assessment of the pace of change and the means by which the transition should be regulated. For the advocates of the neo-liberal reform package the processes of marketisation and privatisation, if carried through sufficiently rigorously and consistently, provide the necessary and sufficient condition for both destruction and regeneration. The critics of neo-liberal reform believe that, particularly in the framework of a world recession, the liberal package leads to an irrevocable spiral of decline without providing any basis for recovery, but the critics look not to the dynamics of the existing system, but to the 'outside' forces of the state or international agencies to mobilise the regenerative process. Locked into their rhetorical debate, neither side attempts to explain the specific features of the dynamics of the Russian transition.

The idea that the inertia of the existing system is a barrier to radical change is not one that is borne out by the facts. The first thing to strike anyone researching the Russian industrial enterprise is the extraordinary diversity, flexibility and originality of managerial strategies for adaptation to the pressures and opportunities created by the collapse of the Soviet system. The Russian economy since the beginning of 1992 has seen a staggering amount of change, at a pace far more rapid than one could observe in a capitalist economy. There have been enormous fluctuations in relative prices; very substantial changes in the structure of production; colossal redistributions of income and wealth; massive fluctuations in the money supply and in the terms of bank credit; rapid shifts in government fiscal and credit policies and practices; very substantial regional price differences and sectoral profit differences; large movements of labour and changes in relative wages. Unfortunately, while anything can be explained by *ad hoc* adjustment of lags and coefficients, none of these changes correspond in any obvious way to the predictions of our existing models. Russian enterprises have been responding vigorously to the stimuli of the market, but not in the ways that the neo-classical model tells them that they should.

It cannot be stressed too strongly that this failure to respond according to the dictates of the neo-classical model is an indicator of the failure of the model, not of the failure of reality, and it is the model and not reality that we have to adjust. In particular, it is not the case that the deviations from the ideal path can be explained simply by institutional and ideological barriers to change, which are underpinned by the 'soft budget constraint' that is supposed to protect Russian enterprises from the discipline of the market. The absence of a developed financial and monetary system has meant that Russian enterprises have been subjected to budget constraints far harder than anything experienced by a capitalist enterprise, while Russian managers have shown an extraordinary flexibility and adaptability in the face of changes in relative prices and in market and supply conditions which would reduce a capitalist manager to impotent despair. The Russian economy has been changing extraordinarily rapidly, and Russian managers have been responding very rationally to those changes. The problem is that economists are unable to understand, or even to identify, these changes because they are not those which they had anticipated.

If we are to understand the dynamics of transition we have to get away from the dualistic model of the ideal path which is distorted by real world barriers, to try to understand the specific dynamics of the Russian enterprise on the basis of which to develop an appropriate micro-foundation for our theories of transition. It is time that we admitted, among ourselves if not to the outside world, that we simply do not understand the dynamics of adjustment in the transition from state socialism to a market economy.[4] We do not understand where we are coming from, where we are going to, or how we are getting there.[5]

It hardly needs to be said that any economic theory rests on a micro foundation which is an abstract and greatly simplified model of the real world. Nominalists and realists can argue endlessly about the basis of evaluation of the micro foundations, realists insisting that the micro model should correspond to real processes, while nominalists insist that the model should be judged only by its predictive results. If

4 Some of us think that we do not understand the dynamics of adjustment of a mature capitalist economy either, but that is another matter.

5 The most striking failure is in our understanding of the role of money in the Russian economy. The cash rouble is still largely limited to mediating exchange between workers and the enterprise sector, with cash shortages leading to various measures designed to reduce the circulation time of cash. Relations between enterprises are mediated primarily by money-of-account, but this does not function as credit money since there is no expectation that debts will be repaid. Through 1992 this meant that cost-plus pricing was validated primarily by the expansion of inter-enterprise debt. Levels of production and purchases of supplies were adjusted to sales, and unsold stocks periodically cleared as inflation ran ahead of marked prices. Cash shortages and attempts at credit restriction in the early summer of 1992 and again from 1993 led to the suspension of wage payments and the threatened cessation of supply deliveries, with no discernible impact on inflation. Inflation was curbed not by a restrictive monetary policy but by an aggressive exchange rate policy (of which restrictive monetary policy was the underpinning).

the existing models could provide convincing results the boot would perhaps be on the nominalist foot. However, existing models have recently proved distinctly wobbly even in predicting short-term movements in the mature capitalist economies, while their predictions in the former state socialist world have proved no more than guesses based on wishful thinking. If we are to develop a more adequate model of the dynamics of adjustment, whether for prediction or understanding, we have to develop a more adequate micro foundation. Such a foundation will be a theoretical abstraction, but we can only develop such an abstraction on the basis of the real processes and real institutions of the transitional economies.

The neo-classical model is marked by a profound disregard for the reality on which it imposes its prescriptions, because that reality is irrelevant to the outcome of its prescribed reforms. Reality is no more than a barrier to the realisation of the ideal. The dominance of the neo-classical model has accordingly been accompanied by very limited research into the real developments which have been taking place within the Russian economy, and in particular within the industrial enterprises which were and remain its bedrock. The failures of reform, and the inadequacies of official statistics, have led to an increase in the number of 'case studies' commissioned or conducted by economists, but these have remained superficial, usually amounting to no more than the collection of enterprise-level data, as reported by senior management, and interviews with managers about their company's strategy. To the best of our knowledge our research programme is unique in the former Soviet Union, and probably in the former Soviet block as a whole, in providing intensive longitudinal research, using sociological and ethnographic methods of interview and observational research at all levels of the enterprise, from boardroom to shop floor. In short, our research is unique in analysing the enterprise as a social institution.

THE SOVIET INDUSTRIAL ENTERPRISE

The Western model of the Soviet enterprise

The dominant Western model of the Soviet enterprise has tended to treat it as an irrational variant of the capitalist enterprise, in which the exercise of pure economic (i.e. capitalist) rationality is constrained by political and bureaucratic pressures from outside, which are the result of the inherent irrationality of state ownership and central planning, and by the extraneous social and welfare functions assumed by the enterprise.[6]

Within the Western model the peculiarities of the Soviet enterprise are explained as the result of the rational responses of individual economic actors to an irrational economic system. The enterprise had no regard for costs, for which it was not responsible, nor did it benefit from the services it provided. The strength and prosperity of the enterprise depended not on its efficiency but on its ability to negotiate a favourable plan with the Ministry. The resulting incentive structure led to the familiar evils of the Soviet system: the hoarding of labour, the maximisation of costs, over-investment, and the neglect of maintenance and repair, health and safety, and ecological consequences. The enterprise concealed its resources and its potential from the ministry, which could only pressure the enterprise by methods of taut planning and ratcheting, which reinforced attempts of the enterprise to negotiate favourable allocations and conceal resources. The chronic shortages and disruption of supply which arose as a result of taut planning and a lack of quality control led to an uneven rhythm of production, tendencies to enterprise autarchy, and so on.

The endemic labour shortage, taut planning, and irregularity of supply inherent in the administrative-command system underlay the considerable power supposedly enjoyed by workers on the shop-floor.[7] On the one hand, the administration depended on the co-operation of the workers if it was to meet the plan. On the other hand, the administration had very little power to dismiss or discipline workers. This was the basis of the informal bargaining with workers and the high degree of shop-floor control which they supposedly enjoyed, the cost of which was poor 'labour discipline' and low productivity.

The implication of the orthodox analysis is that, once the enterprise is freed from its subordination to the administrative-command system and subjected to the pressure of competition, these distortions will all

6 David Granick, *Management of the Industrial Firm in the USSR*, New York: Columbia University Press, 1954. Joseph Berliner, *Factory and Manager in the USSR*, Cambridge: Harvard University Press, 1957.

7 Hillel Ticktin, 'The Political Economy of Class in the Transitional Epoch', *Critique*, 20–21: 7–26. Don Filtzer, *Soviet Workers and Stalinist Industrialisation*. Armonk, NY: M. E. Sharpe, 1986. Don Filtzer, *Soviet Workers and de-Stalinisation*, Cambridge: Cambridge University Press, 1992.

disappear as economic rationality prevails, while any resistance on the part of the workers will be dissolved as enterprises shed surplus labour, and job insecurity enables the administration to impose labour discipline and raise the wages of the workers who remain.

This model is very persuasive, and it is very reassuring, assimilating the Soviet enterprise to our familiar theoretical categories. Moreover it shows a clear way forward: the Soviet enterprise is just like a capitalist enterprise, except that the exercise of capitalist rationality is impeded by the imposition of political and administrative controls. Once the Soviet enterprise is freed from the system within which it is embedded, and the economic rationality of the individual given free expression, it will become just like our own capitalist enterprises.

Unfortunately, this model bears only a superficial relationship to Soviet reality. First, the deficiencies of enterprise management were not simply a matter of inappropriate incentives, as the failure of every attempt to reform the system by reforming such incentives has shown. Second, the inadequacies of the planning system were not a result of the inadequacy of information at the centre. The ministerial staff were highly professional and extremely well-informed, and knew very well what was going on in the enterprises under their control.[8] Third, although management had little control over the labour process, and was constrained by the problem of labour shortage, it did not lack for power over the workers: collective resistance was ruthlessly repressed, and workers were often forced to work extremely hard, in appalling conditions, for derisory wages. Fourth, the neo-liberal programme in 1992 foundered primarily because liberalisation did not bring about the anticipated change in the behaviour of enterprises, but if anything reinforced the existing social form of production.

From a capitalist point of view the Soviet enterprise appears profoundly irrational (just as, from a socialist point of view, capitalism appears profoundly irrational), but within the context of the Soviet system of exploitation it has its own rationality. The deficiencies of the system did not derive from its 'socialist' features of collective ownership and central planning, nor as the contingent result of a particular strategy of planning, but were the result of a specific form of exploitation, in which the ruling stratum at the centre sought to extort a surplus by maintaining control of supplies. Chronic shortages

[8] Paul R. Gregory, *Restructuring the Soviet Economic Bureaucracy*, Cambridge: Cambridge University Press, 1990.

of labour and means of production were not the result of inadequate central planning, but were rather the self-reinforcing condition of central control as the basis of the system of exploitation. The endemic supply shortage was the basis on which the dependence of enterprises on the centre was maintained.

The Politburo and the military determined the set of use-values demanded as the surplus, and Gosplan turned this into a 'plan', attempting through negotiation with ministries and enterprises to reconcile the inflated demands of the Politburo with the productive potential of the system. The system of surplus appropriation then took the form of bargaining for resources between enterprises and ministries, in which ministries used their control of supplies to induce enterprises to deliver the surplus demanded of them by the centre, while the enterprises used the need of the ministry for their product to bargain for a favourable allocation of scarce resources. The general director of the enterprise, backed up by his team of book-keepers and engineers, fought for the plan. Large enterprises in strategic sectors with good political connections could be in a fairly strong position in this bargaining relationship, but no enterprise was able to escape the problem of shortages. The enterprise administration therefore sought to protect itself against shortages, and minimise its dependence on the centre, by maximising its reserves of means of production and by controlling its own supplies through vertical integration and by developing alternative supply channels.

What appears as production without regard to costs from the centre is perfectly rational from the point of view of the enterprise. The labour, parts and raw materials claimed by the enterprise are not costs but means to the expanded reproduction of the enterprise as a social organism at the heart of the local community. The more resources the enterprise can claim the more it can produce not only for the plan, but also for its own needs. It can produce new plant and machinery for its own use, goods for local consumption, better housing, social, welfare and cultural facilities for the local community, maintain the productive and social infrastructure. It can thereby raise the prestige of the enterprise and its community and attract skilled workers and specialists. In short, the tendency to the maximisation of costs is not an economic irrationality, it is merely the view of the exploiting class of the tendency for the enterprise to expand the production of things for its own benefit: it is a drain on the surplus to the benefit of the needs of the direct producers, a subversion of the system of surplus appropriation.

To understand the Russian enterprise in transition, we first have to understand how the enterprise functioned within the Soviet system of exploitation. We can then see that the Russian enterprise was not simply an imperfect realisation of the capitalist enterprise, but was a distinctive social organism which had its own rationality. This rationality defines the basis on which the enterprise continues to develop in the wake of the collapse of the Soviet system.

The Soviet system of surplus appropriation

The principal features of the Soviet system of central planning are reasonably well known, although perhaps not so well understood. The key feature of the system was that it was not based on the maximisation of profit to the benefit of a dominant class, nor was it based on planned provision for social need, but it was a system of surplus appropriation and redistribution subordinated, even seventy years after the Great October Revolution, to the material needs of the state and, above all, of its military apparatus. This subordination of the entire socio-economic system to the demands of the military for men, materials and machines dictated that it was essentially a non-monetary system.[9] The development of the system was not subordinated to the expansion of the gross or net product in the abstract, an abstraction which can only be expressed in a monetary form, but to expanding the production of specific materials and equipment – tanks, guns, aircraft, explosives, missiles – and to supporting the huge military machine. The strategic isolation of the Soviet Union meant that no amount of money could buy these military commodities, so the Soviet state had to ensure that they were produced in appropriate numbers and appropriate proportions, and correspondingly that all the means of production required to produce them were available at the right time and the right place.

The system of central planning was developed in Stalin's industrialisation drive of the 1930s in a framework of generalised shortage, including an acute shortage of experienced (and politically reliable) managers and administrators. The system as it developed was an

[9] The Soviet Union was by no means isolated from the world market. Throughout its history the Soviet Union has relied on exports of primary products to purchase (non-strategic) foreign machinery and equipment, but the system of international trade was insulated from the domestic economy. Within the domestic economy money served as money of account, but not as a universal equivalent (Simon Clarke et al., *What About the Workers?*, op. cit., Chapters 1 and 2).

extremely complex cybernetic system, but it could hardly be called a system of planning: it was driven by the demands of the state for a growing physical surplus with scant regard for the material constraints of skills, resources and capacities on production. The strategic demands of the five-year plan would be determined by the priorities of the regime, and ultimately by the demands of the military apparatus, which would then be converted into requirements for all the various branches of production. These requirements would be determined in a process of negotiation between the central planning authorities, ministries and industrial enterprises in which the latter would trade demands for increased output for entitlements to increased resourcing. During the 1930s the system was based on exhortation, backed up with large sticks and small carrots, in which the impossible demands of the plan paid almost no regard to material constraints since shortages were to be overcome by revolutionary will and patriotic effort. To the extent that will was not enough, the plan would be constantly modified by the redirection of resources, by campaigns and 'storming' to fill the gaps. The 'plan' was a mobilising vision, not an attempt to achieve a rational allocation of resources. Indeed, the very concept of a rational allocation of resources was counter-revolutionary in regarding the revolutionary project as being constrained by immutable material constraints.

The formation and implementation of the plan was a political task which could not be entrusted to technocrats. The need regularly to condone failures of plan fulfilment, to divert resources, to demand above-plan deliveries in order to overcome bottlenecks and keep the system moving meant that decisions about priorities had to be taken daily at all levels, and since these were ultimately political priorities, the decisions were political decisions. This meant that a semblance of rationality was imposed on the system not through the framework of the plan and its administrative apparatus but through the parallel structures of the Party which provided the 'glue' that held the system together.

The ad-hoc and highly politicised character of the Soviet system of planning was reinforced by the pressures of war and immediate post-war reconstruction, where everything had to be subordinated to a single priority, and was carried through into the more bureaucratised and technocratic system which formed in the post-war period. The system remained essentially a system of bargaining for resources between enterprises and ministries, within the framework of the demand for a growing surplus product handed down from the Politburo of the CPSU. This system was dominated not by any economic rationality, but by political power and political priorities in the struggle over the extraction of the surplus.

The bureaucratisation of the planning system from the 1950s represented a significant and progressive shift in the balance of power from the centre to the periphery as the negotiated element in plan determination increased, at the expense of its exhortatory power and repressive reinforcement. Alongside this, the single-minded orientation to production was tempered by a growing concern for the material needs of the mass of the population: the expansion of housing and social consumption from the 1950s and of individual consumption from the 1960s. Ministers, department chiefs and enterprise directors could still achieve glory by undertaking superhuman commitments, usually on behalf of their subordinates, and risked dismissal or redeployment in the case of failure, but they could now defend themselves against exorbitant demands by reference to the accumulated experience of the past. Revolutionary commitment was no longer expressed by building something from nothing, but by 'planning from the achieved level': demanding proportionate increases in inputs as the price of promising increased output, less a small percentage representing increases in productivity. Priority allocation of resources to strategic industries was systematised so that it was the low priority enterprises, particularly light industry, consumer and municipal services and so on, which bore the brunt of shortages, defects and poor quality and whose workers enjoyed lower wages and social and welfare benefits.

The industrial enterprise in the system of surplus appropriation and redistribution

The system of enterprise management was adapted to the system of planning within which it was inserted. The basic task of the enterprise administration within this system was to negotiate the plan and deliver its plan targets, and the main barrier it faced was the shortage of supplies of labour and means of production. Basically the plan laid down the quantity of each product to be delivered month by month, and defined the sources and quantity of supplies, the size of the wages fund, the allocation of financial resources, and the size and skill composition and rates of remuneration of the labour force. However, even if the supplies allocated in the plan were adequate, securing these supplies was a major problem for the resolution of which enterprises came increasingly to draw on the services of unofficial intermediaries, the so-called 'pushers'.

The enterprise was subject to supervision from two directions. The system of planning operated through the ministerial system, imposing its various (inconsistent) targets, indicators, rules and regulations on the enterprise, and these defined the primary constraints within which the enterprise had to work. However, the enterprise was also supervised by Party bodies which in turn had a dual responsibility: on the one hand, higher Party bodies were responsible for combating 'formalism' – ensuring that the enterprise not only met its formal plan indicators, but also actively implemented Party policy in defining its substantive priorities. On the other hand, and in practice more effectively, local Party bodies made specific substantive demands on the enterprise to meet the social and economic needs of the locality. While the ministry disposed of economic levers of influence over the enterprise, the appropriate Party bodies disposed of political levers.

It is important to emphasise that these were constraints imposed on the enterprise from above. However demanding they might have been, and however rigorously they might have been enforced, they did not represent the purpose of the enterprise itself as a social organism: the purpose of the enterprise was the expanded reproduction of the enterprise itself. The aim of the plan was to maximise the physical surplus extracted from the enterprise by maximising its planned output and minimising its planned inputs. The interest of the enterprise, from general director down to casual labourer, was to minimise plan deliveries and to maximise the resources obtained by the enterprise.[10]

The interest of management at every level of the system was contradictory. On the one hand, the manager sought to minimise the demands imposed and maximise the resources obtained from above. Thus the general director of the enterprise was primarily concerned with representing the enterprise in its negotiations with superior bodies and with municipal and regional authorities. On the other hand, once the plan targets and resource entitlements had been defined, the manager had to ensure that those resources were actually obtained and those targets achieved. Thus the central administration of the enter-

10 Above the enterprise, the ministry similarly had an interest in minimising the exactions imposed on the enterprises under its jurisdiction and in maximising its share of resources.

prise was primarily concerned, on the one hand, with securing supplies of raw materials and equipment from partner enterprises and recruiting sufficient labour of an appropriate quality to be able to maintain production and, on the other hand, with transmitting the demands of the plan to the production units which made up the enterprise.

The central administration of the enterprise acted as a lower-level planning body in its relations with the production subdivisions of the enterprise, disaggregating the indicators imposed on the enterprise and transmitting them to the enterprise's factories, shops and departments. The accounting departments were responsible for ensuring that every part of the enterprise met the demands of the plan indicators and adhered to the network of regulations which constrained it. However, this was essentially a formal task concerned with maintaining accounts for submission to higher bodies and ensuring that appropriate forms were appropriately completed by the service personnel in the enterprise's sub-departments. The departments which were formally concerned with registering plan fulfilment: the accounts department, economics department, department of labour and wages, had very little authority within the enterprise. This was expressed in and reinforced by the fact that the staff of these departments was predominantly female.

The chain of authority within the enterprise traditionally passed from the general director, through the chief engineer to the shop chiefs, chiefs of sections and then foremen and brigadiers. This was the traditional career progression in the Soviet Union, not only for industrial managers but also for many ministerial officials and Party post holders. While (predominantly female) specialists and technical workers would be qualified primarily through the system of post-school further and higher education, managers would be qualified by work experience and by supplementary training by correspondence, evening classes and special courses.

Soviet production technology was marked by specific features which were in part an historical legacy, in part a consequence of the irrationalities of the planning system. A new factory would typically be built in a location determined by political and military rather than economic considerations. Its senior management and specialists would be drawn from an established enterprise, which would thereby be the parent of the new plant. Key workers would also be transferred from the parent, most of the rest of the labour force being trained on the job. The technology of the new plant would be determined by a combination of plans drawn up by specialists, the experience of the parent factory, and the resources available. The unavailability of appropriate equipment meant that the factory would frequently acquire some of its plant from its parent or build its own machinery on site. Shortages and delays in supply meant that a plant often had to enter production before it was fully equipped, so that even a brand new factory would enter production not as an integrated and up-to-date facility, but as a patchwork of production units put together in an ad hoc way ('something old, something new, something borrowed, something blue') to meet the pressing demands of the plan within the constraints of inadequate supply. Once installed, the basic technology would remain unchanged until the factory underwent a major reconstruction, which would typically not be for twenty or even thirty years. In the meantime new machines would be installed as and when they could be acquired or built in the factory itself, plant would be modified, unobtainable spare parts would be produced in the factory's own workshops. Machines would rarely be scrapped, even in a major reconstruction, which would normally involve the integration of old and new equipment in yet another synthesis of heterogeneous technology. The result was that every factory and every shop had a unique technology which was a legacy of its past and which bore the mark of the creative ingenuity of its workforce. This 'untechnological character of Soviet production' was a fundamental barrier to any rational system of production planning or production management since only those in direct contact with the technology could possibly know its capacities and its potential.[11] This also put an enormous premium on the acquired skills of the labour force and production managers.[12]

The production process within the Soviet system of production

The enterprise administration had remarkably little control over the process of production. Even in the most capitalist of privatised enterprises in Russia today the concept and practice of production management still does not exist. Specialists are involved in setting up a new production line, defining staffing levels and norms and so on,

[11] Sergei Alasheev, 'On a Particular Kind of Love and the Specificity of Soviet Production', in Simon Clarke, ed., *Management and Industry in Russia*, op. cit.

[12] This is reflected in a number of distinctive features of the Soviet enterprise: the paramount importance of holding on to key production workers; the limited relevance of formal, as opposed to on-the-job, training; the very narrow definitions of skill; the high degree of autonomy of direct production workers.

and then revising norms and production targets for individual shops in accordance with the plan, although norms can often go for years without revision. They may be brought in to adjudicate in the event of a conflict over norms or payment between workers and line managers, but they have little or no involvement in the management of production.

The basic unit of production in the enterprise is the shop, to which many powers and responsibilities are devolved. Workers expected the general director to negotiate a good plan with the ministry, and they equally expected their shop chief to negotiate an acceptable plan for the shop. The shop chief, whose bonuses (unlike those of the workers) depended directly on plan fulfilment, had an interest in pressing for plan tasks which he or she could be sure to fulfil. Thus the relationship between superior and subordinate typical of the Soviet system of planning was reproduced at shop level, the shop chief representing the interests of the shop as a whole in his or her relations with superior levels and those of the system in his or her relations with the shop.

The main barriers to production at shop level were shortages of supplies and labour, and the main tasks of shop chiefs and even foremen were accordingly to chase supplies, recruit and retain labour, resolve conflicts between shops, sections and brigades, fix breakdowns and monitor performance in relation to targets, so that even they had very little authority over workers in the process of production itself. The direct production workers expected line managers to supply them with parts and materials, repair machines and so on, but they were largely left to get on with the job of production as best they could, with very little managerial intervention, and were generally expected to overcome problems themselves (or often take on the responsibility to avoid delays).

Day-to-day responsibility for the supervision of production was in the hands of the foreman or the elected brigade leader. Although the foreman and shop chief had nominal authority over and responsibility for production according to the principles of delegation and one-man-management, in practice production management was based on understandings and informal negotiation, typically on a personal and individual basis, between line managers, brigadiers and workers.[13]

[13] On informal relations see Sergei Alasheev, 'Informal Relations in the Process of Production', Simon Clarke, 'Informal Relations in the Soviet System of Production', and Pavel Romanov, 'Middle Management in Industrial Production in the Transition to the Market', all in Simon Clarke, ed., *Management and Industry in Russia*, op. cit.

Soviet workers had a high level of control over production not because they had won a battle to seize control from the management, but because they had been given a high degree of responsibility for ensuring that they achieve the tasks assigned to them.[14]

The fact that Soviet workers had a high degree of control over the way in which they produced does not mean that they had power: the limits of their autonomy were set by the norms and targets imposed on them and embodied in the incentives and penalties built into the payment system. Workers were willing to accept the authority of the foreman and shop chief, within the limits imposed on him or her from above. A good chief defended his or her shop in bargaining for plan targets and resource allocation, secured supplies, did not seek to drive the workers above the demands of the plan in order to advance him or herself, and was fair in the distribution of penalties and rewards. Workers would then identify with their chief in competition with other shops and in struggles with the administration. If things were not going so well, if supplies were short, norms unfulfilled, bonuses lost, the workers would blame their shop chief. Workers attributed their relative good or bad fortune to the personality of the chief, and restricted any collective expressions of their grievances to complaints against this or that individual. There was therefore a high degree of collusion by the workers in their own exploitation, and class conflict was displaced and diffused into individual and sectional conflicts within the hierarchical structure.

Workers had to show a great deal of initiative to overcome the regular dislocation of production through breakdowns, defective parts and materials or the absence of supplies, and often had to work all hours in the regular 'storming' at the end of the month. This made it impossible for management to impose its will on the workers by purely repressive means. Although labour shortages and the demands of the plan apparently put a great deal of power in the hands of the production workers, they did not, in general, exercise this power to resist the demands made on them by their line managers, although in

[14] In this respect the Soviet enterprise was not unlike the nineteenth century capitalist factory, in which traditional forms of organisation of craft production persisted, with the foreman or gang boss sub-contracting the work and taking on responsibility for its execution. The attempt of employers to bring the labour process under the direct control of management has advanced in waves through the twentieth century, but has never been complete. Moreover, the militant resistance to such attempts on the part of the labour aristocracy should be enough to explain why the 'workers' state' has never sought to confront the workers' control of production.

extremis they might show their strength by deliberately failing to meet the plan.[15]

The labour collective

The ambiguous position of management within the Soviet system of production was reflected in the conception of the production unit as a labour collective. This representation has become increasingly important with the disintegration of the administrative-command system, within which the labour collective of the enterprise was merely a part of a wider whole. Within the system of state monopoly socialism the labour collective was the collective producer, its achievements, particularly since the 1960s, measured not simply by the growing volume of its production but by the size, education and skill composition of the labour force, the number of houses built, kindergartens supported, the scale of its cultural and sporting facilities, all of which dominate the iconography of the Soviet enterprise and of the achievements of socialism.

The ideological representation was one in which production was the means to increasing the technological, cultural and educational level and material well-being of the labour collective. The reality was that the needs of the labour collective were subordinated to the production and appropriation of a surplus product, and were determined by the need to secure the expanded reproduction of the collective labourer as an object of exploitation. Nevertheless, this ideological representation expressed a real contradiction: it was in the name of the labour collective that the administration ruled the enterprise and pressed its interests against higher authorities, and it was in the name of the labour collective that individual workers were subjected to managerial authority. The members of a brigade, a shop or an enterprise, workers and managers alike, really did have a common interest in the struggle for the appropriation and redistribution of the surplus. The director really did represent the interests of the labour collective in the battle for the plan, the shop chief in negotiating the targets for the shop, the foreman in seeking to achieve slack norms for his or her workers. Once the plans, targets and norms were set, these defined the determinate limits of the exploitation of the labour collective, within which limits it could subordinate the process and the results of production to

15 Marina Kiblitskaya, 'We Didn't Make the Plan', in Simon Clarke, ed., *Management and Industry in Russia,* op. cit.

its subjective needs; the resources which remained within the enterprise could be devoted to meeting the needs of the collective: to building new housing, sports and cultural facilities and so on, while the workers could rest once the plan tasks were completed. The shop chief or enterprise director really could pose as the paternalistic guardian of 'his' labour collective, a pose expressed in a variety of powerful symbolic representations; the director was expected periodically to 'go to the people', touring his shops and greeting veteran workers by name. He (rarely she) was expected to be accessible, holding regular 'surgeries' at which employees could, at least in principle, bring any problem, even personal ones, to the attention of the director. He was expected to live modestly, in the same conditions as the mass of his workers. The good director was not soft, since the success of the enterprise depended on the discipline of the labour collective, but he was expected to be 'firm but fair'. In many enterprises the director was even known respectfully as 'Papa'.

The concept of the labour collective is central to an understanding of the system of 'authoritarian paternalism' which defined the distinctive forms of Soviet management. Paternalism within the Soviet enterprise was much more than a management practice, a means of intensifying the labour of the working class, as is the case in a capitalist enterprise, but was embedded in a wider paternalistic structure under the domination of the state, just as the labour collective of the enterprise was only a part of the working class in whose name the state ruled. The whole structure of paternalism was subordinated to the priorities of the state. Thus we have to see the content of paternalism not only in the additional benefits selectively provided by the enterprise to its employees, but also in the fundamental guarantees of employment and a minimum subsistence provided by the state to all its citizens, guarantees which were fulfilled through the enterprise. It was this guarantee that appeared to be the basis of the social stability of the Soviet system and, as such, was monitored and administered by state bodies which had a degree of independence from enterprise management, in particular the trade union and Party committees. It was these bodies which ensured that the enterprise management did not take matters into its own hands, laying off unproductive workers and increasing pay differentials in order to increase the surplus retained within the enterprise. The Party was ultimately responsible for regulating the contradiction between the egalitarian principles of social policy and the inegalitarian tendencies of incentive systems of payment and reward.[16]

The differentiation of the labour force

The rhetoric of egalitarianism contributed to the depiction of the labour collective as a homogeneous body, devoid of internal conflict, whose common interest was represented by the troika of enterprise director, Party and Komsomol secretaries, and trade union president. However, in reality the labour collective was by no means a homogeneous body. It was precisely the fact that it was differentiated and divided that enabled management to ensure that its activity was subordinated to the demands of the plan.

In the first place, there was a very sharp division between manual workers and the engineering-technical workers (ITR), who were identified in the workers' eyes as mere agents of the system of exploitation. This identification was perfectly justified. Most ITR were engaged in the activities of drawing up plans, monitoring performance, maintaining records (incompetently and/or fraudulently), calculating wages which were, in the workers' eyes, entirely unproductive. In terms of education, work activity, pay scales and career trajectory the ITR formed a part of the enterprise administration. Moreover, they depended entirely on patronage for their career prospects and, unlike manual workers, did not enjoy any legal protection in the face of discipline or dismissal, and so were very vulnerable to victimisation, making most of them the craven supporters of the enterprise administration.

Workers were far more antagonistic to the ITR than they were to the majority of managers, whom they saw as performing tasks essential to production (securing supplies, co-ordinating production). While workers regarded virtually all ITR as parasites, they would distinguish between good and bad managers, the good manager being someone who understood production and the problems faced by the workers, who negotiated a good plan, and who maintained the flow of supplies. Nevertheless, workers identified the failings of the system as a whole

[16] On enterprise paternalism see Petr Bizyukov, 'The Mechanism of Paternalistic Management of the Enterprise: the Limits of Paternalism' and Samara Research Group, 'Paternalism: Our Understanding', both in Simon Clarke, ed., *Management and Industry in Russia*, op. cit., and Vladimir Ilyin, 'Social Contradictions and Conflicts in Russian State Enterprises in the Transition Period', in Simon Clarke, ed., *Conflict and Change in the Russian Industrial Enterprise,* op. cit.

with the failings of its more senior managers and of the bureaucrats in Moscow. There was therefore a strong tendency for workers' confidence in management to decrease sharply with distance.

The Soviet enterprise relied very heavily to achieve its plan targets on a core of production workers and line managers who were reliable, skilled, enterprising and flexible (the elite of whom would be recruited into the Party), and who formed a kind of 'labour aristocracy' whose efforts kept the whole system going. These people often worked extremely hard, and enjoyed relatively good pay and extensive privileges. The strategic significance of this stratum was not determined simply by its technical role in production, but rather by the fact that production was organised socially around this crucial stratum.

Recruitment into this stratum of the labour force was not just a matter of technical training, the quality of which was, in general, very low, but also of passing through a series of filters in which the workers' 'moral' and 'ideological' qualities would have been evaluated in addition to their technical skills. Once recruited into this stratum a worker was relatively secure, so long as he (or occasionally she) continued to toe the line.

This core stratum of relatively skilled workers formed a bridge between workers and management – they were better paid than all but the most senior managers, in some cases even earning more than the general director, and some could expect to progress into management as shop chief, chief engineer, general director and even higher. They had access through their Party membership and trade union activity to senior management and to the processes of enterprise decision-making. Their position within the hierarchical status and pay structure of the enterprise underpinned their 'activism' and their identification with the productive tasks imposed on them.

There were gradations within this stratum of core production workers, depending primarily on their position within the overall system of exploitation.[17] Thus, the best paid and most privileged workers were those in the core branches of production: heavy industry, energy, the military-industrial sector. Within any particular enterprise the highest status was enjoyed by those workers engaged in making the strategically most important products (for example, military as opposed to consumer production) and those closest to the final product.

17 Irina Kozina and Vadim Borisov, 'The Changing Status of Workers Within the Enterprise', in Simon Clarke, ed., *Conflict and Change in the Russian Industrial Enterprise,* op. cit.

Alongside this stratum of core production workers there was an army of 'auxiliary' workers. Again, the position of these workers was not determined by the technology, but by the social organisation of production. The auxiliary workforce included those responsible for service and maintenance, who might be highly skilled but who would earn significantly less than the core production workers because they did not play the key role of the latter in ensuring plan fulfilment. However, the majority of auxiliary workers were low-paid unskilled, often female, manual workers engaged in very labour-intensive low productivity tasks, particularly involving loading, unloading, handling, transporting and delivering materials, cleaning, guarding etc.[18] There was a similar army of clerical and supervisory workers, who prepared, processed and filed mountains of documents, and who counted, checked and recorded everything that could be counted, checked and recorded.

Many in this subordinate stratum of manual workers worked extremely hard, if irregularly, in appalling conditions, but it was this stratum that comprised the bulk of the notorious labour surplus hoarded by the Soviet enterprise. These workers constituted a labour surplus not so much because they did no work, but because the vast majority of the tasks they performed could easily have been mechanised, or eliminated by a simple rationalisation of production and administration; yet, despite the chronic labour shortage that appeared to characterise the Soviet system, virtually no effort was ever made to do so.

The existence of this labour surplus is conventionally explained by the uneven demands of production in the face of irregular supply. However, 'storming' to meet the plan at the end of the month was not usually based on mobilising this labour surplus, but on the intensification of the labour of the 'core' workers, with production workers being compelled to work double and even treble shifts, illegal overtime, weekend working and so on.

The surplus of unskilled auxiliary labour was by no means supernumerary. It functioned as an 'internal reserve army of labour'. On the

[18] On gender at work see Lena Lapshova and Irina Tartakovskaya, 'The Position of Women in Production', in Simon Clarke, ed., *Management and Industry in Russia*, op. cit., Galina Monousova, 'Gender Differentiation and Industrial Relations', and Elain Bowers, 'Gender Stereotyping and the Gender Division of Labour in Russia', both in Simon Clarke, ed., *Conflict and Change in the Russian Industrial Enterprise*, op. cit. Sarah Ashwin and Elain Bowers, 'Do Russian Women Want to Work?', in Mary Buckley, ed., *Post-Soviet Women*, Cambridge University Press, Cambridge, 1996.

one hand, enterprises were required to provide labour to the municipality, on the demand of the local Party committee, for municipal construction, including the building of housing, roads, municipal offices and cultural facilities, as well as routine maintenance and cleaning. They were also required to provide often large quantities of harvest labour to neighbouring state and collective farms. It was advantageous to the director to maintain a reserve of low-paid unskilled labour to carry out these duties rather than to lose production by allocating core production workers to such extraneous activities. These workers could also be deployed around the enterprise as required, to clean, tidy, load, unload, fetch, carry, paint, build, with a flexibility which could not be demanded of a skilled worker. The director had no incentive to mechanise their tasks to increase labour productivity since, if he did not need them for one job, he would still need them for another. Moreover, with poor motivation and poor labour discipline he would not be inclined to entrust them with expensive machinery.

On the other hand, the surplus of unskilled labour served as a disciplining force against, a reference point for, and a political counterbalance to more privileged workers. It was a heterogeneous stratum, which included older or disabled workers who could no longer work in more productive jobs, young workers on the first rung of the ladder, workers with a poor disciplinary record, particularly for drunkenness, as well as unskilled manual workers.

The existence of a marked status hierarchy dividing one stratum from another implied that there would be only limited mobility between strata. Thus it was only in extreme cases that core workers would be transferred to low-grade jobs as a disciplinary measure, although the possibility was always open to management, and promotion from auxiliary to core production worker was also uncommon. Indeed, the Soviet enterprise was marked by high levels of external labour mobility, as predominantly unskilled and young auxiliary workers moved frequently from job to job, alongside very low levels of internal mobility.

Limited mobility and labour shortages reduced the effectiveness of the 'internal reserve of labour' as a direct disciplinary force. However, there were also hierarchical relations of privilege and authority within each stratum, which were maintained by relatively more subtle and individualised forms of control.

Line managers had an extensive array of levers of influence with which to induce the workers to comply with their demands to achieve their plan tasks. The formal system of control was through the payments system, with most production workers being paid on some form of piece rate. Until the late 1970s individual piece rates, monitored by the foreman, were predominant, but there was then a rapid shift to the brigade system of payment, which was at least nominally based on a collective piece rate, with the allocation of individual payments nominally in the hands of the elected brigadier. Workers and brigades who exceeded their norms received bonuses, and those who fell short were penalised.

The piece-rate system in principle provided an anonymous, formally rational system of inducing workers to meet the production targets, but it was quite inadequate to the purpose of controlling and motivating workers for a number of reasons. The most important reason was that piece rates can only work if the only constraint on output is the diligence of the worker, but in the Soviet system the primary constraint was maintenance and supply. This meant that workers would often lose pay through no fault of their own. In conditions of labour shortage, the best workers would leave if this situation persisted. The foreman and shop chief therefore had to subvert the payment system to ensure that good workers were guaranteed a regular wage more or less regardless of performance. They could achieve this directly, by allocating well-paid work to favoured workers, and indirectly, by redirecting payment through the 'foreman's fund'. The piece-rate system was in practice essentially a discretionary payment system, through which individual workers could be penalised or favoured.[19]

In addition to the allocation of work, line managers had a whole series of other levers through which they could penalise and reward individual workers, particularly in their selective application of the disciplinary code, ignoring or penalising petty violations, and in the selective distribution of the wide variety of non-monetary benefits provided through the enterprise and the trade union. The result is that

[19] This system of control gave rise to a great deal of conflict under the individual piece-rate system, although this conflict tended to be individualised and personal, relating to the allocation of work and to priority in the maintenance and repair of equipment, and the provision of supplies, and so dividing rather than uniting the workers. The brigade system, based on a collective piece rate, introduced on a large scale from the late 1970s, was partly designed to transfer responsibility for labour discipline to the workers' themselves, and it certainly was effective at subjecting individual workers to the collective discipline of the brigade. However, it also meant that when conflict did arise it was much more dangerous because it had a collective character.

within each stratum of the labour force there was a finely graded hierarchy of workers, with privileges and penalties being administered on a personal and individual basis by line managers, which had the effect of atomising workers and undermining the solidarity of the work group by establishing hierarchical relationships among the workers which was the principal barrier to any collective mobilisation of the labour force. Workers could try to escape from their oppression in individual ways, in the form of absenteeism, labour turnover, alcoholism and poor 'discipline' and 'motivation', but they had little possibility of collective resistance.

The social and welfare apparatus of the enterprise

The Soviet enterprise was not just a unit of production, but it also had extensive social and welfare functions in relation to the labour force which underpinned the paternalistic claims of the enterprise. Social and welfare services, including the bulk of social security payments and benefits, were administered through the enterprise, primarily by the trade union. Large enterprises provide kindergartens, nurseries, sporting and cultural facilities, holiday resorts, pioneer camps, medical facilities, housing, education and training.[20] From the late 1970s enterprises increasingly provided subsidised consumer goods, food and clothing, and distributed land for allotments. Thus a large part of the reproduction needs of the worker could not be freely bought with the worker's wage, but could only be secured through the distribution channels of the enterprise. This system of distribution played a very important role in the allocation and regulation of labour within the system of production, allowing the strategically important enterprises to attract and retain scarce skilled labour and providing a powerful lever of managerial influence over the labour force.

The social functions of the enterprise could be represented as one of the most glorious achievements of socialism, and Soviet workers certainly took it for granted that they were entitled to generous welfare provision. On the other hand, enterprise provision also underpinned the dependence of the worker on the enterprise, so that the system of

[20] Once an apartment had been allocated to an employee it became *de facto* the property of that individual, and could be transferred to others by exchange or inheritance, regardless of the place of work. This meant that a growing proportion of enterprise housing was occupied by people who were not employees of that enterprise. Many other enterprise facilities were also available for the use of the local population as a whole.

distribution became an increasingly important way of cutting labour turnover. Moreover, the discriminatory distribution of goods and services provided an extremely powerful means of controlling workers, and was systematically used as such. The administration of these social and welfare benefits, and the distribution of goods and services, was and is the primary function of the trade union.

In theory the Soviet trade union had the 'dual functions' of encouraging the growth of productivity through socialist competition, production conferences and so on, while defending the rights of individual workers. In practice, the main function of the trade union was to maintain labour discipline and motivation, partly through propaganda, but primarily through its supervisory commissions, which were linked to the discriminatory administration of the social and welfare functions of the enterprise. The trade union within the enterprise was effectively a patronage network, integrated into and working alongside the management structure.

Although the overwhelming majority of Soviet workers belonged to the official trade unions in order to secure access to union-administered benefits, the unions were equally overwhelmingly regarded as what they in fact were, 'just the bells of the Party', as they were described to me by the union president in a large enterprise in December 1991.

Although enterprise managers speak as contemptuously of the union as do workers, they have been in no hurry to dispense with the trade unions. Similarly, although the official trade unions are regarded as a bastion of the old order, the Russian government has taken no significant measures to weaken them. The official unions have retained their property, continue to administer state social security benefits (despite a law removing this right from the trade union), have lost few of their legal powers and privileges, and have not been compelled to go through a process of re-registration. This is all powerful testimony to the essential role of the traditional trade unions in stabilising the society by maintaining the dependence of workers on officially administered patronage.

The Fundamental Contradiction of the Soviet System

The left and the right are united in seeing the 'transition to a market economy' as amounting to no less than the full transition to capitalism. However, the development of a market economy in Russia has not been the expression of the emergence of capital or of a capitalist class. In the first instance it expressed the attempt of traditional Soviet enterprises to secure increasing independence within the existing system, an independence which necessarily implied a growing role for market relations. The development of market relations undermined the control of the centre and precipitated the collapse of the administrative-command system, but it did not immediately subsume the enterprise to the accumulation of capital. These developments arose out of the fundamental contradiction of the Soviet system.

The fundamental contradiction of the Soviet system was between the system of production and the system of surplus appropriation. The development of the forces of production was constrained by the exploitative social relations of production, and it was this specific contradiction that underpinned the collapse of the administrative-command system. The centralised control and allocation of the surplus product in the hands of an unproductive ruling stratum meant that the producers had an interest not in maximising but in minimising the surplus that they produced. Since neither the worker, nor the enterprise, nor even the ministry, had any rights to the surplus produced they could only reliably expand the resources at their disposal by inflating their production costs, and could only protect themselves from the exactions of the ruling stratum by concealing their productive potential. Resistance to the demands of the military-state-Party apparatus for an expanding surplus product ran through the system from top to bottom.

This fundamental contradiction defined the specific form in which class conflict was displaced within the system into a conflict over the distribution of resources within a hierarchical framework of patronage and dependence. The interests of workers in the shop were represented within the system primarily by their line managers, and their demands channelled through administrative structures. In this way conflict between workers and management was expressed in the form of conflict within the administration of the enterprise or, if the grievance was taken up by the general director in negotiation with the higher authorities, between the enterprise and higher authorities. The articulation and resolution of conflict between workers and management was therefore intimately connected with conflict within the administration and the administrative-command system. This provided what was essentially an authoritarian bureaucratic-paternalist system of conflict resolution, based on the exclusion of any forms of independent worker representation.

The result was that individual workers and brigades competed for resources within the shop, while uniting behind the shop chief in the competition for resources within the enterprise. Enterprises competed for resources from the ministry, while uniting in the competition for resources with other ministries. The unity of the system as a whole depended on the ability of the centre to retain ultimate control over the distribution of resources, but at the same time it was this centralised control of distribution that was the principal barrier to the expanded reproduction of the system. It was this contradiction that determined that Gorbachev's attempt to reform the system by giving enterprises greater independence inevitably led to its disintegration, as the loss of control of production led to the loss of control of supply on which the system depended, opening up new divisions and unleashing new patterns of conflict.

The stagnation of production eventually undermined the expanded reproduction of the system. The attempts to reform the system from above in order to increase the rate of exploitation only opened up the underlying contradiction between the role of the collective labourer as direct producer, and the role of the collective labourer as object of exploitation. However this contradiction did not appear directly, in the form of class polarisation and self-conscious class struggle, but in the form of the continued disintegration of the system, as subordinate levels sought to harness popular discontent to achieve their own independence from those above. The struggle to secure the independence of the enterprise from its subordination to the ministerial system was represented as a struggle of the labour collective, usually personified by the enterprise Director, to secure to itself the full fruits of its labour. Its result was the collapse of the administrative-command system and the transition to market relations.

FIRST STEPS IN TRANSITION

Bursting the integument

The attempt to replace 'administrative' by 'economic' methods of regulation had lain at the centre of Gorbachev's reform programme. This programme involved the de-centralisation of decision-making within the administrative-command system and an increased reliance on the market regulation of contractual relationships between enterprises. This implied the general application of the principles of self-financing, the juridical autonomy of the enterprise as an accounting unit, and its constitution as a juridical subject able to enter into commercial and financial contracts. However, once the enterprise was constituted as an autonomous unit freely entering contractual relationships with the state and with other economic subjects, the administrative-command system of surplus appropriation was doomed: once enterprises no longer depended on the state to secure supplies, why should they contract for their own exploitation?

The first phase of transition can be dated from the beginnings of the disintegration of the Soviet planning system with the 1987 Law on State Enterprise and the Laws on Co-operatives (1988) and Individual Labour Activity (1987). These laws in principle allowed individual enterprises to escape the straight-jacket of the planning system, particularly in wage-setting and in the sale of above-plan output. They were followed by the Law on Leasehold (1989), the Law on Property (1990) and subsequent Privatisation Law (1991), which in principle allowed enterprises to leave the system altogether on the basis of the leasing, and later purchase, of enterprise assets by the labour collective of the enterprise.[21]

Most western commentators regarded these legal changes as having had little impact, since their implementation was impeded or prevented by ministerial and local political and judicial authorities. While the ministries could control access to supplies of raw materials, means of production and credit they could exert a stranglehold on enterprises under their jurisdiction. However, some enterprises were able to escape. Our two 'pioneers of privatisation' shared what appears to be the typical characteristics of such enterprises: that they were enterprises which had always been a thorn in the appropriate ministry's flesh, primarily because of their systematic failure to fulfil their plans, while being of relatively marginal significance to the ministry's core activity, and so dispensable, while they had relatively dynamic directors who had originally been put in place in an attempt to turn them around. These were, therefore, enterprises which the

21 For a fuller discussion of privatisation see Simon Clarke, 'Privatisation and the Development of Capitalism in Russia', *New Left Review*, 196, November/December, London, 1992, pp. 3–27, and Simon Clarke, et al., *What about the Workers?*, op. cit., Chapter 9.

ministries were not unhappy to release, under enterprising directors who had nothing to lose and everything to gain by freeing themselves from ministerial restraint.

The ideal situation for such enterprises was to leave the state system with regard to the setting of wages and prices and the disposal of enterprise funds, but to retain a core of state orders which gave guaranteed access to supplies at fixed state prices, to state credits and investment funds. Those enterprises which were able to do this were able to make very considerable windfall profits as market prices escalated during 1990 and 1991, which gave them the funds to pay high wages and expand social provision, while leaving enough money to buy the enterprise outright. The impact of these 'pioneers of privatisation' was quite out of proportion to their size or numbers, as their widely publicised (and often grossly exaggerated) success showed the way forward for management as a whole, stimulating the demands for enterprise independence to take advantage of what appeared to be the glowing market opportunities.

Marketisation without money

Price liberalisation at the beginning of 1992 was marked by a price explosion which was fuelled by the monetary overhang built up in the last two years of the Soviet system. The effect of the price explosion was to devalue monetary holdings – not only the savings of the population, but also the limited working capital of enterprises, which found themselves without money to pay for raw materials and intermediate products and, by the summer, even to pay wages. The absence of a banking system with sufficient reserves to provide enterprises with working capital and with sufficient data and expertise to assess the uncertain prospects of prospective clients led to the rapid demonetisation of an already largely non-monetary economic system as commercial transactions were based on the rapid accumulation of inter-enterprise debt. By the summer of 1992 enterprises were falling behind in the payment of wages, which were increasingly supplemented by payment in kind. The immediate crisis was staved off by an effective debt write-off and credit expansion underwritten by the central bank, but this only served to pour fuel on the flames of inflation and lay the basis for a further round of accumulation of indebtedness.

Enterprises responded to the absence of money in two ways. First, by seeking out credit facilities through the emerging banks and financial institutions, many of which were initially set up for that purpose as the 'pocket banks' of large industrial enterprises, others of which developed out of the former state banking system or new commercial structures. At first credit was rationed by access to political power and to financial institutions rather than by price: interest rates generally remained well below the rate of inflation and loans were provided primarily by pocket banks or underwritten by the state. Even new commercial banks were willing to extend credit to state enterprises at negative real interest rates in order to get a foothold in the state sector which gave them some security and where they could make very lucrative side-deals financing commercial transactions and channelling state credits. On the other hand, the pocket banks quite rapidly established some distance, and in some cases considerable independence, from their parent enterprises. The expectation on all sides was that, in the absence of bankruptcy, private credit expansion would be validated subsequently by the monetary authorities. However, although subsidised state credits continued to be granted to favoured enterprises, it was not long before real interest rates became large and positive, so that the huge cost of debt service added to the pressure on enterprise cash flow.

The second tendency was for enterprises to make cash-flow maximisation their immediate strategic priority. In a developed capitalist economy cash-flow maximisation is not necessarily inconsistent with profit maximisation, and the two are often confused. However, in the Soviet system the two were very different because traditionally the only source of cash was sale to final consumers, and the only cash expense was wage payment. Plant and equipment was provided to the enterprise through the ministry, and raw materials and intermediate products were supplied, according to the plan, against earmarked bank funds. The supply of funds was the subject of negotiation between enterprise and Ministry, but within the framework of this bargaining system, although the enterprise could not go bankrupt, it was subject to an extremely hard budget constraint.[22] Despite the collapse of the ministerial superstructure, this system was preserved more or less intact through 1992 – in June 1992 the exchange rate between bank money and cash in some regions approached two to one. The

[22] The contrary view, of a laxity based on the soft budget constraint, derives from Kornai's model of post-reform Hungary. One might debate the extent to which the model applied to the latter case, but it certainly did not apply to the Russian economy.

immediate pressure was relieved by the government's debt write-off and credit expansion, and in the longer-term the rapid growth of the banking sector meant that bank credit became available to supplement inter-enterprise debt, but the crippling cost of credit as interest rates moved ahead of inflation in 1993 meant that enterprises continued to be very short of working capital, the situation being exacerbated by reduced willingness of enterprises to extend credit to one another (apart from energy suppliers, whose attempts to enforce payment by cutting off supply were not very successful), by the sharp reduction in directed state credits from 1994 and by the growing burden of taxation, which had first claim on enterprise funds. Cash shortages and the absence of an effective banking system meant that inter-enterprise transactions have continued to be financed by open credit lines in the expectation of their subsequent validation by economic recovery or debt write-offs and/or take the form of barter, with bank payment playing a secondary role. Through 1994 and 1995 enterprises increasingly responded to the shortage of cash by holding down wages and delaying their payment, so that workers were financing their own employers.[23]

The period following price liberalisation at the beginning of 1992 was marked not only by rapid inflation and cash shortage, but also by extreme instability in relative prices, in the relationship between price and wage growth, and in government policy over the allocation of credit and subsidies. This instability put a high premium on flexible and diversified managerial strategies of adaptation and on political connections as the basis of longer-term stability.

Those enterprises which had been the pioneers of privatisation were initially in a favoured position, since they had already tested the waters of the market economy and had found outlets for cash sale at home and, in some cases, abroad. They were therefore able to continue to pay their suppliers and workers through the summer of 1992. However, these enterprises had, in general, owed their favoured position to the dual economy which had existed until the end of 1991

[23] On 1 November 1994 enterprises owed about 52 trillion roubles to suppliers, 16 trillion in back taxes, 5 trillion in overdue payments to banks and about 4.7 trillion in unpaid wages. Inter-enterprise arrears were about two-thirds of total bank credit, although they subsequently fell back sharply. In October 1994 wage arrears amounted to almost 60 per cent of the monthly wage bill: 18.5 per cent of the working population reported that they received no wages at all, 35.5 per cent incompletely or with delay, and only 39.9 per cent completely and on time (OECD Economic Survey, *The Russian Federation*, OECD, Paris, 1995, pp. 104, 114, 178).

and which enabled them to buy cheap and sell dear. These advantages were rapidly eroded, while inflation and the debt write-off soon removed their advantages in comparison with state enterprises.

The most profitable 'capitalist' activity was to use enterprise assets for commercial and financial speculation, either directly or through financial and commercial subsidiaries and associates. Production for the market could be very profitable,[24] particularly for the sale of processed raw materials and intermediate goods, but market instability also made it risky unless the enterprise enjoyed an effective monopoly or access to foreign markets. While the market provided some with opportunities to make large windfall profits, the key to longer term stability was still political contacts, through which to establish and defend a monopoly position; to acquire export licenses; to secure state orders, subsidies and credit; and to get access to foreign currency and scarce supplies and raw materials.

The unstable market environment meant that it was very risky to undertake investment in new plant and equipment, while productive investment could not compete with the high profits to be earned from commercial and financial speculation. Most large-scale productive investment since 1992 has either been export-related, using export earnings to upgrade equipment in an attempt to meet world quality standards, occasionally on the basis of a joint venture or long-term export contract, or has been for state or military orders, which provided access to foreign currency to secure imported equipment or raw materials. However, Western equipment is seen as the secret of success, as well as being a mark of prestige for the shop or the manager who acquires it and the men (never women) who work on it. Thus many enterprises buy whatever Western equipment they can afford, installing it alongside existing facilities.

In some enterprises new departments were established to work closely with production shops in developing new products for the market, using the existing plant, equipment and labour force. Technological limitations and market instability meant that most such innovations involved custom-building or short production runs, often with inappropriate technology and raw materials. The important point

[24] With high rates of inflation and no form of inflation-accounting it was almost impossible not to make a paper profit: while real interest rates were negative even credit-financed production for stock was profitable. The rising cost of credit put enterprises under more pressure from 1993, but the main threat to solvency came from fiscal liabilities.

about such developments is that they completely belie the popular image of the rigid and conservative Soviet enterprise, showing that the latter can be extremely flexible, innovative and resourceful. However, most such developments were economically extremely wasteful, since the priority was to secure cash flow, without any consideration of economic costs.

Privatisation without capital

I describe the Soviet system of production as non-monetary not because money did not exist, because money clearly did have some functions as means of exchange and as money of account, but because money did not function as a universal equivalent, as a form of value and, above all, money did not exist as capital. The lack of fixed investment, emphasis on cash-flow maximisation and continued reliance on barter and inter-enterprise credit were all symptoms of the attempt to effect a transition to capitalism in the absence of capital. The emergence of new financial and commercial structures indicated the strength and speed of the transformation of money into capital, but this was by no means a sufficient condition for the transformation of the Soviet into a capitalist system of social production, for most of this capital remained confined to commercial, financial and political channels of circulation, with a large proportion flowing abroad.[25] For this transformation to take place the direct producers have to be separated from the means of production and the latter transformed from the means of production of things into the means of production and appropriation of surplus value.

The existence of private property and of a market are necessary but by no means sufficient conditions for the transition to a capitalist system of production. Privatisation in the first instance concerns the constitution of ownership rights and the transfer of title to physical assets to individuals or corporate bodies, not excluding state agencies. Marketisation provides a means by which physical assets, in the first instance goods and services, can be transformed into money. But

25 The bulk of this new capital originally derived from what is politely called 'intermediation' between state and market, i.e. the difference in prices paid to purchase public property and the prices realised in the market and between the (negative) real interest rates paid for state credit and the positive returns realised by their speculative re-investment. Not surprisingly, access to such golden opportunities depended on connections. A large proportion of capital held in Russia is undoubtedly fictitious, created by the recycling of bad debts within the financial system.

neither goods nor money in themselves constitute capital. To be transformed into capital, goods and money have to play their part in the process of the production, appropriation and realisation of surplus value, the process by which a sum of money is laid out in the purchase of labour power and means of production in the expectation of securing an increased sum of money in return. This point is crucial to understanding the process of 'privatisation without capital' – the absence of money capital with which to buy state assets corresponded to the fact that such assets had little or no value as capital.

Within the Soviet system the value of productive assets was determined ideologically and politically in accordance with the use-values which they produced – those assets were most highly valued which produced those use-values appropriated by the state as the physical surplus which was the basis of its own expanded reproduction, above all in the military-industrial sector. The high value placed on these assets was expressed in the higher wages paid to workers in the favoured branches of production; the higher quality of housing, social and welfare provision by those enterprises; the honours and promotion bestowed on the workers and managers of those enterprises; their sheer gargantuan size. The evaluation of the productive contribution of an enterprise and its labour collective bore little relation to the costs incurred in making that contribution. In strictly accounting terms, the value of the fixed assets of the enterprise was accounted on the basis of their depreciated historic cost, the value of its circulating funds being determined by its plan allocations based on the size of its staff list and its authorised levels of wages and social provision.

The valuation of the assets of an enterprise as capital is determined not by their historic costs but by the discounted flow of expected future returns to those assets. Within a capitalist economy such a discounted flow can be based on projections from historic and existing prices and profit levels, but in a state monopoly socialist economy there is no such basis for projecting into a putative capitalist future. Any valuation will be heavily discounted to the extent of the absence of appropriate data, quite apart from the need to discount the risks which arise from uncertainty about the economic and political future. Such discounting will be the least in the case of enterprises dealing with internationally traded commodities which can be valued at world prices and which have a relatively low domestic value-added: those enterprises involved in the extraction, processing and export of fuel and raw materials or those involved in dealing in internationally traded commodities (who are protected from the risk of devaluation of their stocks which confronts those trading in domestic commodities). In the case of Russia, all the evidence from attempts to attract foreign investment indicates that even in such favourable cases the valuation of enterprise assets as capital is extremely low, while the value as capital of the majority of the productive assets which have been built up over seventy years of state socialism is at best zero, and more often negative. The principal barrier to the transformation of Russian productive assets into capital was not the shortage of money with which to purchase such assets, since the world economy is awash with money capital seeking lucrative outlets, but the fact that the vast majority of those productive assets were valueless as capital.

Privatisation can transfer title to assets, but it cannot in itself transform those assets into capital. Thus, in the West it is a precondition of privatisation that enterprises should first be made profitable: the restructuring of unprofitable public corporations is a precondition, not a consequence, of privatisation. Privatisation in Russia involved the constitution of property rights and transfer of title to the physical assets of enterprises, valuation in the first wave of privatisation being based on the book value of assets at historic cost, a sum which, in inflationary circumstances, was derisory. However, this derisory valuation was by no means out of line with the valuation of such assets as capital which, in the first wave of privatisation, would in most cases have been negative since those enterprises which could be considered to have some positive value were deemed to be 'of strategic importance' and were excluded from the first wave of privatisation in order subsequently to be sold by auction.[26] The peculiarly Russian form of 'privatisation to the labour collective' did not represent a victory of conservative, let alone socialist, forces over capital, but

[26] The valuation of these strategic industries was also derisory. Gazprom, the home company of Prime Minister Chernomyrdin, controls 30 per cent of the world's known gas reserves. In the fall of 1994 it was valued at 0.3 cents per barrel of oil equivalent, while British Gas was valued at roughly 10.30 dollars. The valuation per access line of Rostelkom, the telephone monopoly, is one fiftieth of that of Japan's NTT. On the basis of the first round of voucher auctions Boycko, Shleifer and Vishny estimated the value of the whole of Russian industry as amounting to $5 billion, yet at even these prices there were virtually no foreign buyers (OECD, op. cit., 1995, p. 159. The book value of fixed capital assets at 1984 prices was estimated in 1990 as 2,000 billion roubles – 1.2 trillion dollars at the prevailing exchange rate (Philip Hanson, 'Property Rights in the New Phase of Reforms', *Soviet Economy*, 6, 2, 1990)). When the auction of the 'crown jewels' got underway foreign bidders were still scared off by political instability, inadequate legal protection, and direct pressure. The tendency in 1995 was for the shares to be sold to consortia headed by the bank organising the auction.

rather the fact that only the 'labour collectives' could be induced take these liabilities off the hands of the state.

The first wave of privatisation in Russia took place under the 1989 Law on Leasehold and the 1990 Property Law, under which the enterprise could be bought by its labour collective and incorporated as a joint-stock company. In principle such a company was closed, in the sense that shares could only be held by employees, although the law was vague and practice more flexible. In practice privatisation made little difference to the management structure of such enterprises, since the 1987 Law on State Enterprises had already placed state enterprises under the nominal control of the labour collective, represented by the Labour Collective Council (STK). The STK was nominally an elected body, but members of the STK were usually elected at delegate meetings of the labour collective in which the delegates were hand-picked by management, the well-established model for such procedures being the annual meeting of the labour collective to approve the collective agreement and elect trade union officers, with which the meeting to elect the STK was often combined. The annual meeting of the labour collective therefore flowed smoothly into the annual shareholders' meeting, the STK into the Council of Shareholders, both bodies being under firm management control, regardless of shareownership.

Most Russian enterprises privatised under the 1991 Law on Privatisation and the July 1992 Presidential Decree which regulated the implementation of the Law. Under this law the bulk of publicly-owned assets were to be sold off, in the case of small municipal enterprises, or formed into joint-stock companies and privatised within a period of eighteen months from the publication of the decree. The formation of closed joint-stock companies was declared illegal, all companies having to take on the open form in which outsiders were free to acquire shares, with vouchers being distributed to the population to provide them with the means of purchasing shares. These vouchers could be used to buy shares directly, or they could be sold for cash, or they could be invested in voucher investment funds.

The form of privatisation was still subject to the decision of the labour collective, which had privileges in the acquisition of shares.[27]

[27] Exactly who was eligible for such privileges was not defined by the Law. Thus there was considerable discretion in what rights to accord former employees, including pensioners, and those on temporary leave (particularly on maternity leave or military service). There was also discretion in the principles of distribution of privileged shares: whether in accordance with level of salary, with length of service, with the post. These issues were all potent sources of conflict in the privatisation process.

Large enterprises were effectively faced with two alternative routes to privatisation. According to the so-called 'first variant' employees received claims to 25 per cent of the assets of the company free of charge in the form of non-voting shares. They could subscribe to purchase an additional ten per cent of voting shares at a discount of 30 per cent of book value, paid for with vouchers or cash over three years, with a further 5 per cent of the shares being reserved for senior management and an additional ten per cent available for purchase with enterprise funds. The remaining shares were put in the hands of the State Property Committee, which could vest shares and voting rights in other bodies pending the sale of shares at voucher auctions (the second stage of privatisation, at which 29 per cent of shares were to be sold and which got under way at the end of 1992) and cash auctions (the third stage, which got under way in late 1994). The advantage of this form of privatisation for the labour force was that it received its allocation of shares free of charge and for management that these were non-voting shares. The disadvantage for management was that the controlling interest was held outside the enterprise, initially in the hands of the State Property Committee but then, following the auctions, potentially in the hands of outsiders.[28]

The 'second variant' allowed the labour force as a whole to subscribe to purchase claims to 51 per cent of the assets of the enterprise in the form of voting shares at a price of 1.7 times book value, with payment in vouchers or cash, with an additional five per cent being available for purchase with enterprise funds, but no special privileges available for management. The remaining shares were held by the State Property for subsequent sale at voucher and cash auctions. The advantage of this form of privatisation for the labour force was that, although it had to pay for its shares, it received a larger allocation of privileged shares and had voting rights.[29] The advantage for management was that ownership of the controlling interest was vested in

[28] As always in Russia, all is not what it seems. Worker ownership of voting shares was no threat in itself. The key question was into whose hands these shares would fall if and when the workers sold them – the fear of management in potentially profitable enterprises was that workers would sell to outsiders. On the other hand, voucher and cash sales rarely held any terrors for management, since the 'outsiders' usually turned out to be close associates of the 'insiders'. Veronika Kabalina, 'Privatisation and Restructuring of Enterprises: Under Insider or Outsider Control?' in Simon Clarke, ed., *Conflict and Change in the Russian Industrial Enterprise*, op. cit.

[29] The cost of shares was covered by vouchers and, in many enterprises, special accounts set up by the enterprise on behalf of employees. Nevertheless, considerable propaganda was required to induce employees to buy shares, even at knock-down prices.

employees of the company. This also gave management and its associates an advantage in bidding in subsequent auctions, since outsiders were less inclined to bid for shares in companies in which the majority of voting shares was held by insiders.

The choice of privatisation variant had to be approved by at least two-thirds of the labour collective, so that management had to make a significant propaganda effort to ensure that its favoured variant was adopted. In the event over 70 per cent of enterprises chose the second variant. The result of the privatisation exercise was that enterprises employing more than 80 per cent of the industrial labour force had been privatised by the end of 1994, the overwhelming majority being under the control of insiders. Reliable evidence on the identity of purchasers of shares at subsequent voucher and cash auctions is not available, for obvious reasons, but all the signs are that successful bidders have been banks and investment funds which enjoy close links both with existing enterprise management (or one faction of management) and with local, regional or national political authorities or factions. Far from subjecting enterprises to the control of outside owners, share auctions have served to cement relationships between industrial enterprises, financial structures and political bodies.

THE DYNAMIC OF TRANSITION AND THE STRUGGLE FOR CONTROL

Control without ownership

While the majority of Russian state enterprises might be valueless as capital, the enterprise as a corporate entity is a source of a wide range of income flows. Privatised enterprises own buildings (but not the land on which they stand) which can generate rents, and in their trading activities are the conduits for substantial flows of goods and money which can be tapped by the providers of financial and commercial 'services'. Privatised state enterprises continue to have enormous political leverage, not only through historic personal connections but also because of their fiscal, employment and social significance regionally and nationally. They can therefore continue to bargain for privileged access to energy and raw materials, state credit and subsidies, export privileges, monopoly powers and so on. The absence of effective normative, legal, political or competitive mechanisms of corporate governance provides ample opportunity to siphon profit out of unprofitable enterprises through commercial and financial structures.[30] The key is therefore not ownership of the enterprise, which is worthless, but control, which is invaluable. The Russian form of privatisation is one in which capital can enjoy the fruits of control without the burden of ownership.

The enterprise is undoubtedly important as a source of income flows for associated financial and commercial structures which connect the enterprise with the market, the most lucrative being those where state regulation reinforces monopoly profits.[31] However, these flows are as nothing compared to the flows of income which still pass through state structures. Federal government expenditure amounts to around one fifth of GDP, around 60 per cent of which is financed by taxes on enterprises (profits tax, payroll taxes, VAT) which absorb the bulk of the nominal enterprise profits of former state enterprises (new private enterprises largely evade taxation).[32] Moreover, the tax authorities have first claim on the assets of the enterprise, after its payroll, before the claims of its commercial and bank creditors, so that the surplus appropriated by the state is far more secure than that appropriated by the enterprise's capitalist partners. A substantial proportion of government expenditure is channelled back through enterprises and through local and regional authorities, providing further scope for 'intermediation'. Thus the bulk of the surplus in Russia continues to be appropriated through the state, while even the bulk of that appropriated directly through commercial and financial channels derives from state-endorsed privileges. Thus the generation of a surplus in the transitional mode of production continues to depend primarily not on the capitalist production of surplus value but on the fiscal appropriation of revenues by the state, while a portion of these revenues is appropriated by capital as profit in its role as intermediary between enterprises and the state and as state-endorsed intermediary

30 This is by no means a feature of underdeveloped Russian business ethics. Russian businessmen have learned their trade from the multinational corporations with whom they deal, whose motto is 'ask no questions'.

31 Anti-monopoly legislation works by controlling supply prices of monopoly suppliers. No such controls are imposed on the selling prices of those intermediaries who purchase the products, who appropriate the monopoly gains as windfall profits. Trade in most strategic materials is effectively monopolised by private companies linked in to state structures.

32 Most of the rest of state expenditure is in practice financed by credit creation to the benefit of the financial sector and by arrears.

between enterprises and the market. The enterprise is important to its investors and creditors as a source of income, and it is therefore important to them that it remain solvent, but the surplus generated by the enterprise from its productive activity is only a small and often insignificant aspect of its role in the capitalist appropriation of profit. Access to the privileges of state power is at least as important to the new capitalists as it is to the red directors.

Although the labour collective became titular owner of the enterprise which it had built, it was not given the enterprise as capital. The constitution of enterprise assets as capital is taking place not through privatisation, but through the integration of the enterprise with commercial and financial structures which can tap into the income flows which link the enterprise with the market and the state. The dynamic of transition is being played out in this relationship between the labour collective, commercial and financial structures and the state which intersect in their competing claims to the enterprise.

Structural adjustment without mass unemployment

Although there have not been significant changes in the control of Russian enterprises, they have already been through a massive restructuring with a very substantial fall in production, particularly in the military-industrial and light industrial sectors, and significant changes in production profiles, yet these changes have taken place largely within the limits of the traditional social guarantees, without inflicting mass unemployment on the Russia population. What does this phenomenon have to tell us about the dynamics of transition? Is it an indicator of the resistance to reform of conservative enterprise directors, backed up by workers who have been empowered by privatisation, as many neo-liberals presume? Or is it an indicator of an unprecedented triumph of reform, resulting from the great flexibility of the Russian labour market, as other economists argue? Is the Russian working class a solidaristic mass defending its collective class interest, as the first diagnosis implies, or is it a thoroughly atomised and commodified aggregate of labour power, as the second would presume? Let us look more closely at this phenomenon of structural adjustment without mass unemployment.

The absence of mass unemployment is one of the most striking features of the Russian transition, which distinguishes it from the countries of Eastern Europe, with the partial exception of the Czech

Republic. Yet this is by no means a symptom of stagnation, for Russia has seen an extremely rapid restructuring of employment. The average recorded separation rate in industry has been around 30 per cent per annum since 1993 (our own case study research indicates the true figure is substantially higher then even this rate, which is already about three times that typical of a capitalist industrial economy). The majority of separations are officially recorded as voluntary, with fewer than one in five being recorded as compulsory redundancies. Registered unemployment remains very low, with half of those registered finding a job within four months. With such a high separation rate, the rate of hiring has also remained high, amounting to about 21 per cent in 1993 and 14 per cent in 1994.[33] This means that the maintenance of full employment has not been the result of a reluctance of conservative managers to dismiss workers, but of a positive policy of re-hiring to replace a substantial proportion of those who have left.

Some economists hail this as an exemplary case of the labour market flexibility that they have been preaching throughout the capitalist world, with wages adjusting to the marginal productivity of labour and enterprising workers changing jobs in response to higher wages elsewhere, while the less productive have accepted substantial cuts in real wages in order to avoid redundancy. While the labour market certainly has proved extremely flexible, this is hardly a result of the choice of workers as free economic agents.[34]

At first sight this very high degree of employment restructuring would seem to be completely at odds with the supposed reluctance of Russian managers to reduce employment, expressed in the declared ambition of every Russian manager to 'preserve the labour collective'. How can you 'preserve the labour collective' when on average one-third of the labour force leaves every year, so that statistically the entire labour force turned over in the first three years of liberal reform? Yet this ambition was clearly not merely rhetoric: reductions in employment have lagged well behind the fall in production, with workers put on short-time or temporary lay-offs rather than being

33 Construction lived up to its Soviet reputation with a separation rate of 45 per cent and a hiring rate of almost 35 per cent in 1994. Unemployment according to the ILO definition is about three times the registered rate, but is still relatively low (OECD, op. cit., 1995, pp. 108–9).

34 Gimpelson estimated total labour costs as amounting to only 12 per cent of total costs in the Russian economy as a whole in 1992–3 (quoted in OECD, op. cit., 1995, p. 166), so wage reductions will have an insignificant impact on an enterprise's viability. Workers do not choose low wages in order to protect their jobs. Low wages and employment cuts are twin symptoms of crisis, but not a means to its resolution.

made redundant. Enterprises have used all the means available to them to raise cash to pay wages, and initially used their bargaining power to acquire food and consumer goods to be provided to their own workers at subsidised prices. The restructuring of employment has not been in response to the imperatives of production, for a significant proportion of those hired are clearly surplus to any foreseeable requirements.

'Preserving the labour collective' does not mean retaining every member of the collective: the 'labour collective' is a transcendental concept. Thus it is quite in order to follow Soviet tradition and sacrifice individuals for the good of the whole. The idea of 'preserving the labour collective' is not a conservative notion, but one which coexists with the idea of 'renewing' or 'rejuvenating' the labour collective. Managers of those 'pioneers of privatisation' which enjoyed windfall gains in the transition to the market economy were able to pay higher wages than their neighbours and so to attract younger, skilled and diligent workers, while they were also able to impose stricter discipline and force out the unskilled, the old, the indigent – the 'drunkards and absentees' with whom every Soviet enterprise had been burdened. Those enterprises which were less fortunate allowed wages to fall behind inflation; fell into arrears in the payment of wages; assigned workers to maintenance, repair and subsidiary employment; put them on short-time working; or sent them on extended 'administrative vacation'. The effect of such a policy was that the younger and more highly skilled workers left to find work elsewhere, while such enterprises had to hold on to their undesirables and were forced to recruit where they could, even taking newcomers 'from the street'.

Sooner or later such enterprises were forced to confront the issue of reducing the size of their staff, abandoning the strategy of 'preserving the labour collective' in favour of the strategy of 'preserving the skeleton of the labour collective'. In general those who held out the longest were those who faced the largest cuts in production: the former flagships of the Soviet system, the giant military-industrial enterprises, which had the largest reserves of skilled labour, and the light industrial enterprises with a predominantly low-paid female labour force, women being much less likely than men to leave their jobs in response to falling pay, wage arrears and compulsory leave. However, in principle it was open to any enterprise director to choose either option at any time. But practice is never as easy as principle.

The result of such employment strategies was a very high turnover of labour and substantial change in the skill and demographic composition of the labour force of particular enterprises, but the dynamic involved more a reshuffling than a restructuring of employment as younger, more diligent and more highly skilled workers left the giant military-industrial enterprises which had been the flagships of the Soviet system and moved to the new private sector or to those enterprises whose standing had been transformed by the transition to the market.

This reshuffling of employment has been associated with sometimes very considerable reductions in employment, particularly in military-industrial enterprises, hit by the cut in military orders, and light industry, decimated by the fall in consumption and by foreign competition. Employment at Kirovskii zavod in Saint Petersburg fell from 50,000 to 12,000 by the end of 1994, while the textile and light industrial sector as a whole lost 41 per cent of its jobs.[35] Employment in the former state sector as a whole has fallen considerably, although by nowhere near as much as production has fallen. There is a general assumption that those who have left have moved into the new private services sector, but there is no reliable data on private sector employment, a significant proportion of which is subsidiary employment of pensioners and of those formally employed in state enterprises (particularly those working short-time or temporarily laid off).

It is not unreasonable for enterprises to reduce employment by less than what they may still consider to be a temporary fall in production, particularly when we take account of the costs of redundancy against the very low wages and the extent to which the 'non-technological' character of Soviet production implies a high level of firm-specific skills.[36] Nevertheless, the fact remains that some enterprises have cut employment by much more than others, even within the same branch of production. This raises the question of what determines the employment strategy of any particular enterprise.

For those blinded by the neo-classical model the ambition to preserve the labour collective is at best an expression of a misguided sense of social responsibility inherited from the Communist past, and at worst simply a rhetorical device to mask a managerial conservatism which is seeking to resist change at any price, deliberately blocking the necessary restructuring of production. The extent of employment

[35] David Mandel, 'The Russian Working Class and Labour Movement in the Fourth Year of "Shock Therapy"', ms., 1995.

[36] Sergei Alasheev, 'On a Particular Kind of Love and the Specificity of Soviet Production' in Simon Clarke, ed., *Management and Industry in Russia*, op. cit.

reduction is therefore seen as a test of the virility of new entrepreneurship, an indicator of the extent to which management has adapted to the dictates of the market economy. However, the evidence of our case studies is that the extent of employment reduction has little to do with the ambitions or ideology of senior management, but is structurally determined by the character of the post-Soviet enterprise. Thus, almost every enterprise has already tried to implement ambitious employment-reduction plans, but such plans are regularly thwarted.[37]

The positive incentive for senior management to reduce employment is independent of the ideological orientation of management. The red director has as much of an interest as does the capitalist entrepreneur in removing surplus labour in order to upgrade and stabilise the labour force by increasing the wages of those who remain, at the same time enabling him to raise managerial salaries and to siphon off commercial and financial profits. The key question is why neither has a free hand in carrying through such a policy. The liberal economists identify the existing labour force, supposedly empowered by 'privatisation to the labour collective', as the barrier. However, this would be to take collectivism to implausible limits. The labour force does not have a homogeneous interest in avoiding employment reduction – skilled and younger workers have a clear interest in cutting the labour force in order to increase their own wages. Thus the 'pioneers of privatisation', which privatised one hundred per cent to the labour collective as closed joint-stock companies, were also the pioneers of employment reduction, tightening labour discipline and offering generous retirement and redundancy packages in order to boost profits and pay high wages to those who remained. Typically, responsibility for identifying candidates for dismissal in enterprises is passed down to shop, section or even brigade level so that a redundancy programme does not face workers as an anonymous threat but as a means of saving their own jobs. Workers are, perhaps misguidedly, not actively opposed to redundancy. They are actively opposed to low pay, widening pay differentials and the non-payment of their wages.

Opposition to redundancy comes not from workers so much as from line managers, particularly shop and section chiefs. While the Soviet system of central planning may have collapsed, the Soviet system of management has been retained more or less intact inside the enterprise, expressing the persistence of the traditional social relations

37 Surveys, most notoriously those of the ILO, have regularly projected imminent mass unemployment on the basis of the declared intentions of senior management.

within the sphere of production. The shop chief still works to a production plan, with staffing levels and wages fund determined by the size of the staff list. Production at shop level is even more unstable than it was in Soviet times; orders come in sporadically, and then have to be fulfilled in record time to high quality standards, particularly if they are lucrative export orders. To meet these orders the shop chief needs to keep the full range of (often shop or machine-specific) skills of his or her labour force, even if they are only required sporadically. Similarly, the shop chief can use an inflated staff list as a means of attracting additional wage funds to the shop with which to pay discretionary bonuses and incentive payments. Thus it is the shop chiefs who regularly resist and subvert attempts to reduce the staff list by imposing redundancies. This is not because 'red shop chiefs' stand in the way of radical liberal directors, for it is the same shop chiefs who are most active in seeking to upgrade the labour force by tightening discipline and by sacking insubordinate, unskilled and older auxiliary workers in order to retain and strengthen the 'skeleton of the labour collective'. The shop chiefs defend their staffing levels, if not the individuals who comprise their staff, because they retain their traditional orientation to production, putting the needs of the shop as a unit for the production of use-values above the demands of both capital and labour.

The enterprise between capital and labour

Transition is not a dualistic condition in which the new co-exists with and confronts the old, each retaining its purity through their opposition. Transition is a process which expresses the development of a contradictory unity, a development of the contradictions inherent in the Soviet system of production which were themselves already overdetermined by the insertion of the Soviet system into global capitalism.[38] The contradictions that arise out of this encounter permeate the system and underlie the patterns of conflict to which they give rise.

The constitutive contradiction of all class-based forms of social production is the contradiction between the forces and the social relations of production, between the demands of the production of use-values and those of the production and appropriation of a surplus. This

[38] Simon Clarke et al., *What About the Workers,* op. cit., Chapters 1 and 2.

is not a dogmatic slogan but an invaluable heuristic principal, universally recognised as valid for all but the capitalist mode of production – it was Adam Smith who showed that the social relations of feudal production were the decisive barrier to the development of the forces of production, and Friedrich Hayek argued the same for the Soviet system of production on the basis of a direct analogy with feudalism. It is only in the case of the capitalist mode of production that liberals have a blind spot which allows them to see only the positive aspects of capitalist production relations, in encouraging the unlimited development of the forces of production, without recognising the obverse tendency for capital to have to confine the development of the forces of production within the limits of profitability.[39] Yet it is precisely this contradictory dynamic that we see in play in the transition.

The contradiction of the Soviet system of social production was that, like feudalism, it detached the appropriation of a surplus from its production: the Soviet system of planning sought to maximise the development of the forces of production regardless of cost, so that the growing demand for a surplus could only be met at the expense of the living standards and working conditions of the mass of the population. This system was unsustainable, but the issue in the transition is not what will replace it, since its existence cannot be wished away, but into what will it be transformed? What is to be the logic of development of production? Is production to be subordinated to the production and appropriation of surplus value, or to the technological rationality of the production of use-values, or even to the needs of the mass of the population? The first tendency corresponds to the subordination of production to capitalist social relations of production, the last to some (perhaps for now utopian) socialism, the second to an unrestrained technologistic managerialism. These alternative developments are not superimposed on the enterprise from outside, but express different moments of the contradictory unity of the transitional social relations of production which develops through the conflicts to which it gives rise.

The fundamental contradiction is expressed in its sharpest form in the contradiction between the workers, for whom the enterprise provides material subsistence and the social and cultural framework of their lives, and the directorate, as agent of the broader class forces for

[39] Simon Clarke, *Marx's Theory of Crisis*, Macmillan, London and St Martin's, New York, 1993.

which the enterprise is a source of surplus. However, this contradiction is defused by the imperfect subordination of the directorate to such broader forces, whether capital or the state, to the extent that the director can seek the support of the labour collective to establish a degree of independence, in which case the line of division moves outside the enterprise, the director representing himself as defender of the labour collective, expressing its interests in making claims on the state and in resisting external demands. However, while individual directors may be successful in such efforts by virtue of connections or of the size or strategic importance of their enterprise, there are limits to the extent to which the productive sector as a whole can evade the constraints of the finite. Thus the director always has, to a greater or lesser extent, to face both ways at once.

The diffusion of conflict means that the principal line of conflict through which the fundamental contradiction is expressed is not that between the director and the labour collective, but between competing factions of management, typically represented by the new commercial and financial departments, through which the constraints and opportunities of the market economy are transmitted, and the engineering specialisms which have traditionally dominated the Soviet enterprise. The director provides a bridge between these factions, having to balance the claims of each, appealing upwards to the state and downwards to the labour collective.

This conflict is characteristic of all enterprises, expressing the unavoidability of the underlying contradiction. The director of even the most conservative of enterprises has to live within financial constraints, even if these are relieved by subsidies and privileges. Even if the productive enterprise is no more than a power base and a shell for financial and commercial operations, its director has to minimise the drain it imposes on the financial resources at his disposal. Thus every enterprise is marked by internal conflict as financial and commercial departments seek to subject line managers and engineers to the constraints of the market.

The workers play an important role within the conflict, not so much as an independent force but more often as the decisive support for one or the other faction: the workers do not aspire to manage the enterprise, but demand that their managers provide them with an income, with work, with adequate technical resources and satisfactory working conditions. Moreover, however much the state may have abdicated from its traditional responsibilities, the workers remain attached to the values imbued by seventy years of state monopoly socialism, and above all the value of productive labour. Workers do not expect to receive an income regardless of effort, nor do they value work for its own sake. Thus, as far as core production workers were concerned, the main defects of the old system lay in its divorce of effort from reward and in its compelling workers to toil in unsafe and unhealthy conditions with inappropriate machinery and equipment, inadequate maintenance and repair, disrupted supplies and uneven work rhythms. The core production workers looked to change to enable them to work in conditions in which they could earn an adequate income. Their egalitarianism was equally not dogmatic; it was an expression of the primacy of productive labour and the corresponding belief that reward should be correlated with effort. Such workers therefore support increased pay differentials, but such differentials should be justified by results. While they certainly do not believe that managers should be paid more on the grounds of the supposed primacy of mental over manual labour, they do believe that managers who carry out their managerial functions effectively, providing adequate conditions of work, should be appropriately rewarded. Finally, the primacy of the value of productive labour implies that effort should be rewarded not in proportion to the degree of success of the enterprise's marketing department in selling the product, not in proportion to the contingencies of market price and effective demand, but in proportion to the extent to which the workers produce things which meet a social need. For the workers, the enterprise is a unit of production, and their job is to produce. The purpose of sales is not to make a profit, but to secure a just reward for labour and to provide the resources to secure the reproduction of the labour collective as a productive unit.

This ideology of productive labour is the basis on which workers look to their managers for support. It is an ideology which gives workers a clear affinity with the technologistic orientation of their line managers and engineers, which leads them to pin the blame for failure on the enterprise's marketing and supply departments, and makes them receptive to claims that the source of all their problems is the government, whose policies have disrupted established economic relations, destroyed the market by impoverishing the population, and denuded the enterprise of resources by punitive taxation. Nevertheless, if the new market-oriented specialists can promise to mobilise their financial and commercial contacts to improve the situation of the enterprise, they can appeal over the heads of the line managers and engineers for the workers' support. Thus conflict still takes place within the framework of the 'authoritarian paternalism' which was typical of the Soviet system of management, as each faction appeals to the labour force as defender of its interests, with the enterprise director as the paternalistic guardian of his enterprise

Under the Soviet system the power and authority of the director came from above, from the ministry and the Party committee which had appointed him and which alone could dismiss him. With the collapse of the Soviet system, however, enterprise directors lost any such external guarantees of their position. The director became much more vulnerable to attack from an opposition faction of management within the enterprise, particularly if backed by external political and/or financial-commercial interests, and this made it vital for the director to give some substance to the paternalistic rhetoric in order to secure the loyalty of the labour force, which could otherwise be used against him by oppositional forces. By the same token, oppositional forces could best hope to progress by making paternalistic promises to the labour force. Internal conflict, therefore, far from weakening paternalism tends to strengthen it.

As noted above, the structure of senior management was traditionally technologistic and hierarchical, with the core management team being made up of the director, chief engineer and shop chiefs. With the transition to the market economy there has been a tendency for enterprises to establish new departments of marketing, commercial relations, finance, foreign trade and so on. But more generally there has been a change in the balance of power, even where there has been no formal restructuring, in which the senior management team is increasingly defined by its economic functions, rather than its technical role. The chief engineer and the shop chiefs then find themselves in a subordinate position, expected to meet the demands of the marketing department, within the limits of the resources provided by the economists or the finance department. The chief engineer is usually easy to neutralise, since he or she is either awaiting retirement or hoping for promotion, but the shop chiefs cannot evade their responsibilities for meeting the production plans.

In the absence of productive investment the development of new product lines in response to the demands of the market depends very heavily on the initiative and responsibility of the workers. The shop chief is expected to maintain the workers' motivation, to recruit and retain good workers, to meet production targets, to secure necessary supplies, and often even to find contracts and collect debts, while getting progressively less material and moral support from upstairs, and seeing his or her status and relative economic position in relation to senior managers being eroded. The result is growing tension between shop chiefs and senior management, expressed in the conflict between a technologistic logic and an economic logic, as line managers struggle to preserve the paternalistic apparatus of control in the face of growing pressure from above and from below. However, this managerial conflict is only a displaced expression of the emerging proto-class conflict, as shop chiefs find themselves being forced to decide on which side of the line they stand.

The role of the workers in managerial conflict is an expression of their status as the determinant force of social production – the enterprise as a social organism is no more and no less than the social activity of the workers as a labour collective: the struggle between engineers and financiers is the struggle to subject the creative powers of the labour force to an economic or to a technological logic. The ability of the workers to influence management conflict has little if anything to do with their status as shareholders, since management has innumerable ways of controlling the casting of their votes. Thus, for example, the independent influence of workers has probably been the least in those 'pioneers of privatisation' which privatised as closed joint-stock companies, owned one hundred per cent by the labour collective, while their influence has been the greatest in the coal-mining industry, where privatisation has been purely formal, and in the transport sector, which remains wholly state-owned.[40]

Even where the controlling interest falls into the hands of management and its associates, they are only able to exercise their rights of ownership within the enterprise to the extent that the workers recognise the legitimacy of their claims. In our experience, far from legitimating managerial control, private ownership weakens the position of managers who have traditionally legitimated their dominant role through the paternalistic rhetoric of 'social partnership', which is hardly consistent with the assertion of a proprietorial

[40] The real issue underlying the struggles around privatisation is not that of ownership, but that of control. The juridical process of privatisation plays only a superficial role in this struggle, particularly in a society in which the state does not have the power to enforce property rights, because the basis of control is not property but the paternalistic hierarchy of authority. It is for this reason that the privatisation programme has had to bend to the reality of power, and transfer ownership to the labour collective and its management.

authority. Workers have been told for the past seventy years that the enterprise has been built by their labour – indeed in most enterprises the old slogans still adorn the dilapidated buildings – and it is not surprising that they feel cheated when the product of their labour is appropriated as private property by anybody else.[41]

The shop chief and the line manager always played an ambivalent role in the Soviet system of production, representing senior management in the face of the workers, but also representing the workers in the face of senior management. This ambivalent role is one that shop chiefs are finding it increasingly difficult to maintain. While their instincts tend to be authoritarian, and their aspirations are to advance their own careers, they depend on the support of their workers to meet the plan day in and day out. The more paternalism breaks down at enterprise level, the more likely are workers to look to their line managers as their paternalistic defenders, and the more likely are their line managers to respond.

Paternalism was the most effective means of preserving the authority relations of the enterprise intact in the transition to the market economy. However, the ability of the enterprise to pursue an effective paternalistic policy depended on the resources available to it. Within the Soviet system enterprise paternalism was part of a total social system. Its reproduction depended, in particular, on the existence of the redistributive mechanisms that ensured that enterprises had the resources required to meet their paternalistic obligations. The destruction of the administrative-command system removed these redistributive mechanisms and so compromised the reproduction of paternalism as enterprises were subjected to the pressure of the market.

In the last analysis neither line managers nor accountants represent the interests of the workers as social subjects, nor can either faction count on the workers' unquestioning support. Workers are no happier with a line manager who forces them to toil in appalling conditions to make products which nobody wants to buy than they are with a chief accountant who sends them on administrative leave because there is no money to pay them wages. The disintegration of paternalism therefore threatens to unleash industrial conflicts which have an

41 Workers do not in general regard private ownership as being inconsistent with paternalistic care. Indeed, they have been so bombarded with images of caring US capitalists that they believe that a 'real owner' (*khozyain*) is a pure paternalist, who claims no more than a modest profit as reward for his concern.

increasingly marked class character as management ceases to respond to what the workers consider to be their legitimate expectations and aspirations. However, it is precisely this threat of autonomous action on the part of the workers which provokes a counter-reaction, reinforcing the claims of the shop, the management faction and the enterprise for subsidies and support to secure the reproduction of paternalistic structures. In this way, despite the fact that Russian workers do not constitute an autonomous political force, conflicts and even potential conflicts on the shop-floor reverberate through society as a whole and present a barrier to the expanded reproduction of exploitative social relations of production.

The enterprise director is the focus of all these conflicting internal and external pressures. As director of the enterprise he has both to manifest his paternalistic concern for the labour collective and ensure the financial viability of his enterprise. It is often extremely difficult to determine the balance of these interests, and the balance between the director's private interest and his professional duties. This is particularly the case in his relations with financial and commercial structures.

The most profitable activities are financial and commercial speculation with enterprise assets, reinforced by monopoly powers which can be secured by political or criminal means. The traditional supply, sales, financial and economic services of the enterprise were ill-adapted to the new market conditions, and it was almost impossible to attract young specialists to reform such departments. The director therefore has no choice but to seek connections with outside financial and commercial structures, which frequently have their own criminal and political connections. Punitive taxation, anti-monopoly legislation, bankruptcy laws which give the state the first claim on enterprise assets, all conspire to make it desirable for all concerned to channel financial and commercial activities through informal and often illegal structures. This informality and illegality combines with the inadequacy of legal processes to ensure that contracts and agreements can only be enforced by informal means – by force or the threat of force. Thus, even the most honest enterprise director, with the interests of the labour collective at heart, has little choice but to embed himself in networks of financial, commercial, political and criminal interests in order to secure the financial viability of his enterprise. Who is to express surprise if this honest director, aware of the insecurity of his position, limited in the amount he can pay himself as salary, avails himself of the opportunity to tap these sources of income and to accumulate a little nest-egg? Who is to say where altruism ends and corruption begins?

How capitalist is Russian capital?

The neo-liberal model of transition has the structure of a morality tale, as the forces of good and evil fight for the future of humanity. Red directors and red shop chiefs rely on the labour collective to fend off capital, in the form of the capitalist financial and commercial sector and new capitalist 'small and medium enterprises' backed up by the reforming state. The central issue for this model is whether the logic of capital can impose itself on the enterprise. Having achieved its initial aims of marketisation and privatisation to little effect, the state, as architect of reform, now focuses its efforts on the tightening of monetary and exchange-rate policy so that enterprises will be subjected to competitive pressure and hard budget constraints. However, enterprises responded to tightening credit through 1994 and 1995 by cutting production and employment and by deferring payments to suppliers, workers and the tax authorities, while it proved impossible to implement bankruptcy legislation because neither banks, nor local authorities nor tax authorities could bear the financial, material and social costs which mass bankruptcy would impose.

The failure to subordinate the enterprise to the logic of capital by subordinating it to macroeconomic pressures has led the liberal reformers to seek to penetrate 'the hidden abode of production', so that they are now preoccupied with the struggle for control of the enterprise itself, focusing on the issues of 'corporate governance' and seeking to break 'insider control' by imposing outside shareholding. But even this is thwarted, as the outsiders rapidly 'go native' or prove even less 'governable' than the insiders, indicating once again that the dynamics of transition are not determined voluntaristically by the outcome of the battle between good and evil, but are structurally constrained. The growing integration of commercial and financial structures with industrial enterprises does not express the subordination of the latter to the logic of capital, but the reintegration of financial and commercial capital, concerned primarily with the redistribution of the surplus, into the state-enterprise nexus, which remains the primary moment of surplus appropriation.

The liberation of the enterprise from the straightjacket of the ministerial system freed it from its subordination to the Soviet social relations of surplus appropriation. For the directors of many enterprises, particularly those which could sell at inflated market prices at home or abroad, the market initially seemed like a heaven-sent opportunity.[42] The new co-operatives and the pioneers of privatisation had already shown the way forward, their much-proclaimed prosperity fuelling the growing demands for enterprise independence from 1989 through 1992. Far from opposing privatisation, the 'red directors' enthusiastically embraced it, provided only that they could ensure that they remained in control of their enterprises.

Once they had achieved their independence, enterprise directors had new opportunities to secure their own economic well-being and that of their enterprise. As noted above, the enterprise director had no choice but to establish relationships with the financial and commercial intermediaries which had already developed within the pores of the declining Soviet system. The relationship between the state enterprises and the new financial and commercial structures was symbiotic: the latter had a monopoly of new skills and connections, while the former controlled huge material and financial resources and, in many cases, retained close contacts with state structures. The bargain between the two was therefore mutually advantageous.

This symbiotic relationship means that it would be quite wrong to see the new financial and commercial structures as forces of capitalist regeneration confronting conservative state enterprises, just as it would be equally wrong to see the pocket banks and commercial institutions set up by state enterprises as a subversion of the market by red directors. Directors of state enterprises knew full well that they could not do without the market institutions which they embraced with enthusiasm to get access to markets, supplies and financial resources which had formerly (if only formally) been guaranteed by the state. Directors also had a strong personal interest in developing such connections, which could bring them (and their family, friends and associates) considerable financial rewards and security for the future which the Soviet system had never provided.

However, the new commercial and financial structures were by no means autonomous capitalist institutions. They also had deep roots in the established system. The most powerful commercial structures,

42 The fact that transport and energy costs continued to be heavily subsidised, amortisation was based on historic costs, wages were so low, enterprises paid nothing for land, and the extractive industries paid no royalties, meant that it was extremely difficult for enterprises not to make a 'profit' in the new market environment.

many of which are now closely linked to associated banks, initially prospered by using personal connections to secure and exploit state-granted foreign trade privileges in association with their partner state enterprises, particularly in the extractive and raw material processing industries, and have continued to prosper to the extent that they have been able to sustain their monopolistic positions, by fair means or foul. The largest banks had been established on the basis of the state banking system, the numerical majority of banks had been established as pocket banks by state enterprises (although many soon established their independence from their parent enterprise), while the new commercial banks, which dominate the banking system in terms of assets, had been established on the basis of 'redirected' (if not simply misappropriated) public funds, and continue to accumulate their funds on the basis of financial and commercial intermediation with state structures (including short-term credits to privatised enterprises, transmission of state funds, short-term financing of commercial activity and speculation in currency and securities markets). The principal sustainable source of profit for the banking system as a whole has continued to be intermediation between state and former state structures and state-related financial operations (particularly in state debt and foreign currency).[43] Thus state and non-state structures are connected through a web of financial and personal connections.

The developing relationship between industrial enterprises and banks cannot be seen in isolation from the relationship of both parties to the state, which remains at the apex of the triangle. Bank lending to former state enterprises has increased considerably since 1992, which has relieved some of the financial pressure on the latter and is one reason why the 1992 crisis of inter-enterprise debt has not been repeated. However, this lending has not been entirely voluntary on the part of the banks. The initial momentum came with the issue of short-term loans by pocket banks to their parents and lending to enterprises by commercial banks channelling subsidised state credits. When these loans were not repaid the banks rolled them over and supplemented

[43] 'In 1992, as much as 50 per cent of all commercial bank credit took the form of directed credit from the government. In 1994, the bulk of bank lending (short- and long-term) still consisted of on-lending government funds.' (OECD, op. cit., 1995, p. 102.) Although they have a relatively small asset base, the former state banks still dominate the system by on-lending to commercial banks in the interbank market. The state savings bank, Sberbank, is still the only bank with a significant deposit base, with '60 per cent of its assets in the form of loans to other banks'. Commercial banks hold about one-third of their assets in (almost entirely short-term) loans to enterprises, less than they lend to one another (ibid., p. 164).

them to enable the enterprises to continue to service their debts. Banks are positively encouraged to roll-over non-performing loans by the current state of bank regulation, including the failure of the monetary authorities to monitor non-performing loans and positive pressure on the banks not to make provision for losses (which would cut both their dividend pay-outs and their tax liabilities). Banks were also put under more direct political pressure from regional and national authorities to sustain unprofitable enterprises which remained the principal source not only of employment and of social and welfare provision, but also of local and national tax revenues. The banks, dependent on the favour of the state which, directly or indirectly, provided the bulk of their business, had no choice but to comply. At the same time, the absence of effective bankruptcy procedures gives the debtors the whip hand.[44]

The growing indebtedness of an enterprise gives its creditor bank an increasing interest in involving itself in the day-to-day running of the enterprise to try to reduce the drain on its resources. The foundations of such involvement were often already laid with the participation of the bank in the privatisation programme as an associate of senior management, which would give its favoured bank privileged access to the enterprise to allow it to purchase shares at discount prices from workers (and often on its own behalf), and then secure it an insider position in the subsequent share sales. The banks could then exploit the foothold they had gained to move their own nominees into positions of power, particularly in financial and marketing departments of the enterprise, and to nominate members of the board of directors. However, only in very rare cases does such a development represent a take-over of the enterprise by outsiders. In general it is a spontaneous development of the symbiotic relationship between the industrial enterprise and the financial and commercial structures which mediate its external relations, the outsiders being closely linked with the dominant faction within enterprise management – normally that headed by the General Director. Moreover, the close connections between banks, enterprises and political structures means that such initiatives are rarely undertaken without the tacit or

44 Bankruptcy is very beneficial for the bankrupt, the only real victim being the general director, who is required to resign. Creditors, municipal authorities and tax authorities all stand to lose heavily, the banks in particular rarely being in a position to write-off a large debt without facing insolvency themselves. In general a bankruptcy declaration is only politically possible on the basis of a coalition of the latter interests (Pavel Romanov 'The Regional Elite in the Epoch of Bankruptcy', in Simon Clarke, ed., *Conflict and Change in the Russian Industrial Enterprise*, op. cit.).

active involvement of appropriate state bodies, which have an interest in the fiscal appropriation of potential profits of the enterprise and a concern with the social and political impact of enterprise restructuring, while having the power and resources to determine the fate of any particular coalition.

Enterprise indebtedness and outsider shareholding are the levers by which enterprise independence is eroded not to the benefit of the anonymous power of capital but by coalitions of state and financial interests. This is the basis of the reconstitution of redistributive structures based on an integration of capital and the state expressed most fully in the tendency, as yet more an aspiration than a reality, to the formation of 'financial-industrial groups'. The ultimate tendency of such a development could be a system which has existed hitherto only in the textbooks of the Soviet era, the system of State Monopoly Capitalism, in which profit is appropriated through the exercise of state-sanctioned monopoly powers and redistributed through a system of fiscal appropriation, a system marked, as the Soviet textbooks tell us, by the stagnation of the forces of production and by a growing polarisation of class forces. However, that is for the future.

2. Plastmass: Pioneer of Privatisation

Elena Varshavskaya and Inna Donova

Plastmass is a closed joint-stock company which was formed on the basis of a former state research and production association in the region of Kemerovo, Western Siberia, producing a range of chemicals, plastics and plastic products and now employing just over 3,000.

Plastmass was evacuated to Kemerovo from the Moscow region in the autumn of 1941, beginning production of chemicals for military use on February 3, 1942, in a variety of hastily adapted buildings spread around the city. A period of reconstruction after the war, from 1947–57, concentrated all production on a single site, with the main products being a wide-range of plastics for civil and military use. This was followed by a period of rapid expansion and diversification between 1957 and 1966 during which the gross output almost quadrupled, concentrating on the production of phenol-formaldehyde resin and pheno-plastics (bakelite and related plastics). 1966–75 was a period of extensive technical re-equipment and modernisation, with the introduction of a range of new products and production processes, followed from the mid–1970s by a relative stagnation, so that by the mid–1980s its equipment had become old and outdated. In 1977 the factory was linked to the adjoining Scientific Research Institute of the Chemical Industry which had been established in 1962 but, as usual in Russia, there were few substantive connections between the two.

The main products of Plastmass by the 1980s were phenol-formaldehyde and ion-exchange resins, press powders, formalin, textolite and simple plastic goods for industrial and consumer use, but both the product range and the equipment were archaic by Western standards. The priorities for technical development for the 1990s were re-equipment to raise the quality of the leading products and diversification into new areas of production, including acids, extruded plastic film and varnishes for the furniture and cable industries.

Plastmass was a pioneer of perestroika under the leadership of

Vyacheslav Ivanovich Komarov, a Candidate of Chemical Science, whose background was in chemical technology. Komarov had worked at the enterprise since the early 1970s, being appointed General Director in 1984. Komarov is a traditional Soviet autocrat in temperament, style and appearance, but he displayed an early commitment to the radical reform of his enterprise. His motives were not clear, but subsequent events would tend to confirm the supposition that his commitment was not to reform as such, but to the traditional managerial ambition of making his mark by raising the public profile of his enterprise. However, he aligned himself firmly with the forces of democratic reform from the very beginning of perestroika, and became a leader of the democratic block in the *oblast* soviet in the late 1980s, standing unsuccessfully for the chair of the soviet, and later was a member of the executive 'small soviet'. In the December 1993 election Komarov was one of the leading organisers of Russia's Choice. He explained that he had long been committed to the transfer to 'economic methods of management', being a firm believer in 'the idea of developing material incentives on the basis of the ownership of the labourer in the products of his own labour'.

The driving force of the reform was Vladimir Martov, who was brought to the enterprise by Komarov in 1986 as chief economist, at that stage a relatively low status position, heading twelve staff in two departments. The appointment was unusual in that Martov was both very young (only 32) and an academic, a graduate of Aganbegyan's Institute in Novosibirsk. Martov was recruited from the Department of Industrial Planning of Kemerovo State University, where he had been researching and developing programmes of managerial restructuring for which Plastmass was one of the pilot projects. Martov's early work was focused on the theme of parallel managerial structures, which he believed led to over-staffing, duplication of effort and confusion of responsibilities, and this theme remained at the centrepiece of his reform strategy. That strategy was designed to create a streamlined managerial team based on principles of collegiality and devolution of responsibility, a sharp break from the traditional principles of one-man management embodied in the person of General Director Komarov.

Once Martov was in post he began to work patiently to create the conditions for a radical reform of the enterprise, oriented from 1988 to the transition to a market economy. In 1988 he established a fortnightly seminar to discuss the latest legislation and decrees, as well as wider questions of economic reform, with a selected group of managers from the economic and commercial departments. This seminar provided an informal framework within which Martov could identify his own candidates for promotion. Thus he gradually transferred or retired the more conservative members of the administration, and brought in those who shared his point of view. This included recruitment of postgraduate students direct from the university, whom he selected on the basis of invitations to conduct their diploma research in Plastmass, while within the enterprise he recruited primarily from the commercial and economic departments. As a result of this process Martov built his power base, eventually becoming Deputy General Director for Economics with a status equal to that of the Chief Engineer, heading five departments employing about 250 people, with a core of half a dozen highly qualified specialists around him, all of whom knew at least one foreign language, and all of whom had had the opportunity of study abroad.

Having established his core team, Martov's strategy, actively supported by Komarov, was to forestall conservative resistance by introducing a wide range of reforms piece by piece and at short notice, without revealing his strategic designs. The pace and frequency of innovation forestalled any attempt at concerted opposition to what we call his 'administrative innovatory onslaught' on the part of Martov's opponents. During the period of radical reform in the enterprise, between 1990 and 1992, Komarov spent much of his time away on business trips in Russia and abroad, including three months in Britain learning English during 1992. In his absence the chief engineer was formally in control of the execution of policy within the enterprise, but in practice many decisions were made by Martov.

The initial basis of the strategic alliance between Komarov and Martov seems to have been their common desire to free the enterprise from ministerial control, albeit for different reasons. The 1987 Law on State Enterprise (Association) included provision for an enterprise to lease its assets, and many enterprises took advantage of this provision to subcontract part of their work to co-operatives. However, a more radical possibility was the leasing of the entire enterprise from the state, a move backed by Gorbachev at the Party Conference in June 1988, but only given a legal formalisation in the Soviet Law on Arenda (Leasehold) of November 1989, which included the subsequent right of the labour collective to buy the enterprise outright. Martov's study group immediately saw the possibilities of leasing as a route to privatisation, and began to make their plans.

THE PROCESS OF PRIVATISATION

As soon as the Law on Arenda was published, Martov and his team began the process of transfer to a leasehold enterprise and even to plan the subsequent privatisation of the enterprise. In Martov's words:

> The law included the possibility of buying the enterprise, but nobody ever imagined that anybody would actually do it. But we decided that if we had such a right to buy, why shouldn't we exercise it?

The problem with exercising their right was that the law provided no mechanism for actually doing it. Martov went to Moscow to talk to specialists in the Ministry, where there was no opposition to their plans since Plastmass had been a permanent thorn in their flesh, failing to fulfil the plan year after year. However, they got no positive guidance, so in the end they had to find their own way forward through a web of bureaucratic obstruction.

The enterprise was formally transferred to leasehold on 23 November 1990 with a right to buy, a right which the management immediately tried to exercise. The members of the labour collective were given individual named shares in the leasehold company, and the ultimate decision-making body became the Leaseholders' Council, answerable to the annual Leaseholders' Meeting (which in practice was more or less the Labour Collective Council (STK) renamed). The formal position was that the enterprise leased the buildings, plant and equipment from the state, with a right to purchase at a residual valuation (written down book value of assets at historic cost) which amounted to 65 million roubles. Under an agreement signed on 27 June 1991 this could be paid off over ten years, but in fact the management was anxious to secure the buy-out as soon as possible. The buy-out was initially financed by taking credit from a credit bank (Plastmass did not have its own pocket bank), which the management considered a risky course of action in conditions of such uncertainty, but in the event the 1991 profits from the first year as a leasehold enterprise (117 million roubles) were more than enough to buy out the enterprise lock, stock and barrel, with some money left over to distribute to the most profitable shops, the credit being fully paid off on 17 February 1992.

The decision to privatise the enterprise was formally taken at the annual leaseholders' meeting on 6 December 1991, following a period of intensive propaganda within the enterprise through the plant radio and newspaper and shop meetings at which management explained its plans to the workers, a process which had similarly preceded the transfer to leasehold. Bureaucratic obstruction from the local authorities prevented registration of Plastmass until 3 June 1992, and the actual registration of shares until November.[1]

Plastmass was formed as a limited liability joint-stock company of a closed type with an authorised capital of 99 million roubles. The original shares in the leasehold enterprise were converted into shares in the joint-stock company, some additional shares were distributed, and some sold at their nominal price of 1,000 roubles. Although Plastmass is a closed joint-stock company, under its Articles shares can be sold outside the company with the permission of the Board, at a price set by the Board.

The issue of the principles of distribution of shares was a matter of some controversy. There was a strong lobby within Plastmass for an equal distribution, or a distribution in accordance with length of service, and these views tended to predominate in the shop meetings prior to the transfer to *arenda*. However, at the meeting of the labour collective the proposal of the senior management group to distribute shares in accordance with pay was adopted, which implied a very unequal distribution since differentials in favour of ITR and managers had already been significantly increased, and since the latter in general had considerably shorter service than the ordinary workers.[2] It also implied a very small allocation to the pensioners of the enterprise, which was the source of considerable discontent.

Martov's long-term goal was to ensure that 'by fair means or foul the controlling packet of shares, by which we mean 51 per cent, should be held by specialists such as the directorate, shop chiefs and heads of departments', with around 25–35 per cent of the shares in the hands of the senior management team:

1 The regional privatisation commission tried to prove that the purchase of the enterprise's assets had been improper. The city executive committee tried to prevent the *raion* executive from registering the enterprise, an attempt over-ruled by the arbitration court.

2 Everybody who had worked continuously at the enterprise between 8 December 1990 and 17 February 1992 received free of charge four 1,000 rouble shares plus an additional allocation proportional to pay for the period 1 June to 31 December 1991. This penalised not only workers, but also those who had been off sick, on maternity leave, serving in the army and so on. The conversion of shares in the leasehold enterprise into shares in the joint stock company also carried over the differentiation which had marked the distribution of the former.

> The company will be viable under one condition, if ... let us say, 2–3 per cent of the shareholders own 25–35 per cent of the shares ... because these 2–3 per cent will take the real decisions, while the owners of the 75 per cent can control them, so that these 2–3 per cent do not live at the expense of the rest.

Workers could not understand the advantage of share ownership, which was explained to them in terms of nebulous rights to control the enterprise, with little if any mention of dividends, and they approached the whole affair with deep suspicion. In the first distribution of shares around 30 per cent of the employees chose to take cash in lieu of shares, at the nominal valuation of 1,000 roubles, many of those who did buy shares only doing so on the grounds that 'the shop chiefs bought them, and they know what they are doing, so we bought them too'. Those shares undistributed or returned were then held by the Board, and were available for sale at the nominal price, which by the end of 1992 was between one thirtieth and one sixtieth of the claimed asset backing. Not surprisingly the bulk of the available shares were bought up by the senior management group.

Workers had little understanding of privatisation. According to the trade union president in June 1992:

> All this was so new, beyond our experience. The workers asked questions like: Who needs this? Why is this necessary? And they could not work it out. But after they had been given explanations they stopped asking questions, although people did not really know where they were going, they took it on trust and they followed.

Workers were able to cash in their shares for the nominal price at any time, a practice introduced during the cash shortage in the summer of 1992, when many workers did sell their shares in this way. In May 1992 the Board announced an exchange of shares, replacing the 1,000 rouble nominal shares by new shares denominated at 10,000 roubles. Those who did not own a multiple of ten shares had the option of redeeming the odd shares at their nominal price, or making up the difference. In practice the workers tended to do the former, managers the latter, leading to a further considerable concentration of share-ownership. At the end of 1992 Komarov took out a bank loan of seven million roubles with which he purchased a large packet of shares at their nominal price, immediately following the Board's reversal of an earlier decision to raise the nominal price of the shares.

The distribution of shares in Plastmass is not publicly available, but the best estimate is that by the beginning of 1993 the General Director held 10 per cent of the shares, about 60 of his close associates held a further 15 per cent, and around 400 other ITR held about 10 per cent, so that 35 per cent of the shares were in the hands of management, as Martov had planned. The remaining shares were held by about 2600 of the company's 3650 employees, most workers holding between one and four shares. According to the head of the economic planning department, one of those who had worked out the privatisation plan, when asked in December 1992 if there was a process of stratification among the shareholders:

> From the point of view of the number of shares held, there is a process of stratification, but people are not strongly aware of it yet. However, there has already been one shareholders' meeting, at which voting was on the basis of the number of shares held, and the differences were striking – some had one, some 10, some 20 votes. But people will feel it much more acutely at the end of the financial year when we begin to pay dividends. That is when people will sense really keenly that there is differentiation.

Indeed, the employees did soon come to sense that there was differentiation. The comment of an electrical fitter from shop 1 was typical:

> This is not privatisation but *prikhvatisatsia* ['grabbing']. The ITR have privatised it all for themselves. And the workers feel that they have been deceived. And then, when they transferred from arenda, they began to give out shares to the labour collective. They did not explain anything to the workers. The workers all ran around and asked one another: 'Will you buy them?' 'And you?' 'But what are they?' As a result some bought a few, some bought absolutely none. And then the price of the shares doubled and the dividends on them also.

But by then it was too late – the shares had already come to be concentrated in the hands of a restricted circle of people.

The supreme body of Plastmass is formally the Board of 30 people, which was originally elected in December 1991. However, the Board is controlled by the core group of managers around the General Director, who is simultaneously Chairman of the Board. Only three Board members are workers, although all three with a past reputation for independent activism, and two are foremen. However, the Board itself plays a purely passive role, merely ratifying proposals presented to it. Thus, for example, Board members only receive the papers when they arrive at the meeting or, in the best of circumstances, a few hours in advance. Thus, in practice the enterprise continues to be run by the senior management team.

FIRST FRUITS OF PRIVATISATION

At first sight Plastmass is a shining example of the benefits of privatisation. Its 1991 profits of 117 million roubles enabled it to pay off its debt. The profits for 1992 amounted to 2.8 billion roubles, which was barely dented by the payment of a 100 per cent dividend to the shareholders. Even allowing for inflation this was a considerable return, and was more than double the previous year's rate of profit over costs at 115 per cent. In the payments crisis in the summer of 1992, although Plastmass shared in the general shortage of cash and was overdrawn in the bank, it was one of the very few enterprises in the region not to be entered on the card index of technically insolvent enterprises, with outstanding credits of 1.5 billion, far in excess of the outstanding debt of 300 million. This put Plastmass in a very strong market position because it was able to pay for its raw materials, a position reinforced by the privileges enjoyed by private enterprises in the government's mutual debt settlement programme.

This growing profitability was reflected in the valuation of the enterprise, which increased from its original 99 million roubles, at the old state prices, to over 3 billion on the basis of a revaluation of its basic funds and an estimated market value of 6 billion by the end of 1992.

Workers, who were at least nominally the owners of Plastmass, also shared in its initial prosperity. The average wage of the employees of Plastmass in 1991, the year of leasehold, was 1,164 roubles a month, almost twice the average wage in chemical enterprises in the *oblast*. In October 1992 the average wage had reached 26,320 roubles, 2.3 times the industry average of 11,484. In the social sphere Plastmass appeared equally flourishing, with the enterprise expanding its housing construction programme.

The main reason for the initial results, as in most of the other enterprises which were pioneers of privatisation, was the advantage that Plastmass initially enjoyed of being able to escape from the straightjacket of state prices, which was what allowed the high profits of 1991. This good fortune was compounded by the fact that Plastmass enjoyed an effective monopoly in the supply of its main product lines (its only two competitors are situated in European Russia), which became in very short supply with the disintegration of the Soviet Union at the end of 1991. The management decided to take ruthless advantage of the opportunity presented to it, increasing the price of its principal product, press powder, from 400 to 120,000 roubles a ton over 1992. The head of the planning-economic department, commenting on the results for 1992, gave rather a grandiose gloss on this good fortune:

> If one assesses the results of our economic activity as a whole, they have really turned out rather well. We have worked profitably. We have managed to pay a 100 per cent dividend and to begin 1993 with a healthy residue to carry over – 800 million roubles of profits. Some people think that we were able to do this because we hiked up our prices, but we think that it was for another reason, because at the beginning of 1992 we set off in the right direction, taking account of the market situation, taking account of those laws which will govern the development of the economic life of society as a whole, of the whole national economy and using those, so to speak, opportunities which opened up for us and the legislation, and the concrete situation, which developed in the country. By these means we established an adequate safety factor ... In the first half of 1992, well at least in the first quarter, we were able to sell our products without any difficulty, we had lots of customers and were free to set our own prices. To set our prices taking account of the demand for our products. For the first time in the entire history of our enterprise we were able to set the prices of supply and demand for the product and thus to generate sufficient profits for the development of the collective, for technical re-equipment, to resolve our social problems (construction of apartment blocks, support of our social and welfare facilities), as well as for the financial support of our employees.

However, Plastmass management was not just sitting back and enjoying the fruits of prosperity. Martov and his team carried through a series of radical reform measures, particularly in the spheres of management structures, employment and pay.

REORGANISATION AND REFORM

The reorganisation of management structures was carried out in accordance with Martov's ideas about the elimination of parallelism and about collegial forms of management. Administrative departments were merged and re-organised (the planning, wages and norming departments were merged and the chief engineer took over responsibility for science and technology as well), with new departments (trade, marketing) created and some existing departments strengthened (legal, scientific-technical information and management information). Production shops were amalgamated, eliminating duplication of functions, increasing flexibility, facilitating lay-offs, and reducing conflict between shops over such issues as the distribution of scarce raw materials and maintenance and repair work. In effect each of the new enlarged shops was a separate factory, dedicated to a particular product line. Thus shops 1, 6 and 8 were merged to form the new shop 1 devoted to the production of press-powder, while shops 2, 3 and 4 were merged to form the new shop 2, devoted to the manufacture of consumer goods.[3]

The biggest restructuring involved the absorption of the scientific research institute into the main enterprise from February 1993. The institute had worked for the industry as a whole, providing very little input to Plastmass. With its privatisation the management had no intention of providing scientific support for its competitors, and decided to integrate the institute into the enterprise, combining it with the factory's own laboratory to create a slimmed-down scientific-engineering centre supporting product development and diversification, and an information service for senior management. This rationalisation had the additional benefit in Martov's eyes of reducing managerial duplication. Wages of those staff transferred from the institute to Plastmass were substantially increased, since in the past they had earned significantly less than in the industrial enterprise.

There was undoubtedly a fundamental change in the orientation to innovation within the enterprise. Within the administrative-command system there had been little incentive to innovate, but in the new conditions innovation became the order of the day. These innovations involved not only the development of new products but also the design and construction of new equipment, but the chief engineer, speaking in October 1992, acknowledged that this was not so much the result of any structural changes or of privatisation as of the need to survive in the face of the collapse of production, reinforcing the traditional Soviet self-sufficiency:

> We were a scientific-production association, but in reality I do not think that our firm, our production association, was anything of the kind. It was an enterprise which had an institute and an experimental shop. The most radical

[3] The chief of one of the combined shops said: 'Now [after the combination of the shops] I no longer come to work at 7 o'clock in the morning, as I used to do, to be the first to the stores and to grab a wagon-load of raw materials. If I was even a bit late my competitor-colleagues would intercept the tank ... Apart from that, every shop chief had two, or even three, deputies, who were not fully employed but it was not possible to sack them, they were needed. After the integration of the shop it was possible to reduce the number of ITR, including deputy chiefs, and workers too.'

proposal was for the transformation of production through 360 degrees (or 180 degrees if you like) from one thing to another. You know it left us in a condition of stagnation in production which lasted for decades. What does that mean – the period of stagnation of production? Production was directed at the output of certain products and we drifted, we drifted. And it took an enormous amount of effort, huge battles, to try out something new. Well, I experienced this myself. From 1985 I was the deputy director for science, and at that time, for a year or a year and a half, I was simultaneously chief engineer. That is to say, I was responsible both for science and for new technology – and this was a correct decision. Absolutely correct. This was a radical turn of production in a new direction. Thus, in the past, almost any proposal which came from the institute was rejected, was dragged out, on any pretext. Nobody had any desire to do anything new. We fulfilled the plan, our wages arrived – everything was stable, everything went smoothly, everything was good. Or at least it seemed good.

Now the picture is the reverse. Now I think that production cannot have too much science... Now we have come to feel the need to innovate. Then all they said was 'Come on, come on. Give us whatever you can'. This year we have introduced more changes (both experimental and industrial) than in the previous five years put together. The production and the experimental shops have begun to work with a lot of initiative. This is not only in getting their work done, but in designing and constructing new plant and introducing new products. All this is because we want to survive. It is an incredible difference, there is simply such a huge contrast between what was and what is now. And now they cannot give us enough new ideas.

When a shop is working at 50 per cent capacity it is ready to make everything it needs for itself, if only to increase the volume of production, to increase the output which people will buy. That is the most important point. This tendency has already been in place for a year, and this year it has been particularly obvious. And working in this way is much easier, much better. It is not necessary to persuade anybody. Now we work with a common purpose. Even the most conservative shops understand that there is no survival without innovation!

Management was in the hands of a group of nine highly educated specialists, who normally met weekly. The second tier of management comprised the senior specialists and shop chiefs, who also met on a regular basis, and senior specialists frequently visited the shops to consult with shop specialists, and on all accounts day-to-day management was indeed on a collegial and consultative basis, with a well-integrated team of close colleagues, all of whom had been selected by Martov.

In the area of employment, the strategy of management from the start was to reduce overstaffing, and this strategy appeared to be spectacularly successful according to the official figures, with employment being reduced from 4,751 at the end of 1990 to 3,959 at the end of 1991 and 3,539 at the end of 1992, a cut of 25 per cent in two years, the 1992 rate of lay-offs being maintained through 1993 (falling to 3,073, a total cut of 35 per cent), particularly with the liquidation of the research institute. Such a scale of cuts was completely unprecedented in the city, where the majority of enterprises continued to do all they could to hold onto their workers. According to the official figures these cuts were across the board, affecting all categories of employees more or less equally (the number of ITR fell proportionately slightly more in 1992, workers in 1993), but this is certainly not the view of the employees themselves – both workers and ITR believe that they have borne the brunt of the cuts. Thus, according to the chief of shop 2 speaking in December 1992:

> This concerns workers to some degree, although not so much. But the number of ITR was cut in half. I can even give you an example from our shop. When there were four separate shops there were around 13 ITR there, but now only three remain. This affects the press department as much as the casting department. Now 41 ITR work in the combined shop. But if you look at it according to the old system there would have been about 80 people.

Managerial rationalisation and the amalgamation of shops led to a substantial reduction in the number of managerial posts. Those designated for redundancy were offered retraining, particularly in areas such as accountancy which were in high demand in the new co-operative sector, and were placed in jobs in other enterprises in the city, which was still suffering from labour shortages, while potentially redundant staff of the research institute were offered the opportunity of establishing their own small enterprises on the premises of the enterprise, which many took up. There was also a certain amount of redeployment, with some administrative staff being transferred to shops, which gave the workers the impression that there had been no real cuts in administrative and technical staff at all – in the words of an electrical fitter from shop 1:

> They are mainly cutting workers' jobs. But in the office they still sit four aunties to an office. Or they cut ITR in one place, but they appear somewhere else. In our shop they cut the technologist, but now she works in another shop as the 'production training foreman'.

However, another fitter, from shop 2, shared the view of the ITR:

> They cut the structures which worked in parallel, doing exactly the same work. That is what happened to some degree in the reduction of overheads. In place of one person, two or even three worked here.

The first phase of redundancy amongst workers involved the removal of 'dead souls', that is the elimination of vacant posts from the staff list, which primarily affected the establishment of production workers, but did not involve any actual redundancies. Following on from this was a reduction in the number of auxiliary workers, whose complement was normatively defined in relation to the number of production workers. Those made redundant were primarily working pensioners (with an early pension offered to those near pension age), and those with a poor disciplinary record, particularly for drunkenness and absenteeism (although only 30 people were officially dismissed for disciplinary violations in 1991 and 44 in 1992), and later those who could not make the norms. Women disproportionately suffered redundancy among both workers and managerial staff.

The subsequent fall in the number of workers was connected with the fall in production as the economic situation deteriorated, and workers who found themselves reduced to basic fall-back pay left for other jobs (only 10 per cent of the cut in 1991, but 70 per cent of that in 1992, was accounted for by voluntary severance). This led to anomalies, as experienced workers were laid off when production fell, and inexperienced workers had to be drafted in once production resumed, leading to dissatisfaction among the existing workers.

The reduction in the labour force was, according to the senior management, part of a package designed to increase productivity. The policy was explained by the new deputy director for economics in December 1992:

> The growth of the productivity of labour presupposes not only the introduction of more productive equipment and technology, but also a reduction in the number of superfluous people. But superfluous people are all the same our people. Thus this is a painful process, but a necessary one. It has already been going on for one or two years and we must make more reductions, each time selecting the best of the best, to leave only the very best. Because there is no other way.

However, even the radical management of Plastmass did not identify increasing productivity with cutting costs, the prime beneficiaries of the cuts being the workers who remained, the savings remaining within the shop under the principles of financial devolution. This minimised any collective opposition to redundancies, although it gave rise to other grievances as it led to substantial differences in pay between shops. In shop 12, for example, there had already been substantial cuts on the initiative of the shop chief before privatisation, leaving no scope for further cuts, so that wages in shop 12 were the lowest in Plastmass. Redeployment also hit the pockets of some workers hard. For example, in shop 2 press-operators had been used to making good wages by operating two or even three presses at a time, but with the amalgamation with other shops each operator was allocated only one press, while the norms were cranked up, with a significant loss of earnings.

The procedure for identifying workers for redundancy hardly conformed to the supposed principles of retaining only the best workers. The economic-planning department defined the number of workers required in each sub-division in accordance with the planned level of production. The shop chief was then responsible for drawing up a list of those to be laid off on the basis of consultation with section heads, foremen, trade union officials and labour collectives. These decisions were based not only on work qualities (qualifications, productivity, disciplinary record), but also, as was repeatedly stressed in interviews, the social situation of the worker (family circumstances, family income, housing situation) and, not least, loyalty to the administration.

The chief of one of the largest shops described the procedure thus:

> There was only one principle – the collective itself decides. When the shops were combined I said right away that not all the jobs would be preserved ... Where I had to make the decision as chief of shop, I made the decision myself. Where I could, the workers themselves decided in the collective, and those who were nominated were sacked. It is your right. Because those who work together know one another's attitudes to work better than I do.
>
> — And in which areas did you yourself decide who should be sacked?
>
> Basically among the ITR who are directly subordinate to me. I have the most to do with them. Of course I did not decide on my own who was needed, I also consulted and kept those on whom I could always rely. I kept those who could really earn their high wages, so that they, and I on their behalf, would not be shamed in front of our operatives, fitters, electricians, so that the latter could not point the finger at them and say that they have high pay, but they know nothing ... And I got rid of some trouble-makers, those who love to muddy the waters.

Overall the process of employment reduction was achieved without mass conflict. The main reductions were made in a period in which other enterprises were not yet reducing staff, so there were plenty of jobs available elsewhere in the city. The fact that the administration provided retraining and redeployment, and did not simply throw people onto the street, also helped to avert sharp conflicts, although a few people took the company to court since they had been transferred to lower-paid work. Representatives of higher management were constantly visiting the shops to keep the situation under control, 'stopping with the workers from 7 in the morning to 8 at night'.

Nevertheless, conflict situations around redundancy did arise in the shops on three occasions at the time of the transfer to arenda although, according to the chief of the production-technical department, the instigators of these conflicts were not the workers but the shop chiefs, who had their own interests to pursue. The first strike threat came from the shop producing foam rubber, and it was the shop management which negotiated with the factory administration on behalf of the workers. The trade union president, far from representing the workers in these disputes, claimed credit for extinguishing the conflicts which had arisen. There were also several reports of sabotage of equipment.

The Plastmass management retained the traditional rhetorical identification of the enterprise with the interests of its employees, and made high wages the touchstone of its reform policies. The substantial increases in wages made possible by privatisation certainly eased the path of management in carrying through its reform programme. However, the high wage policy was also connected with Martov's determination to dismantle the traditional paternalistic apparatus of the enterprise, to reduce or eliminate the wide range of benefits in kind provided to the workers, and to pay them the wages to enable them to buy whatever they chose.[4] However, the workers regarded the reduction in benefits in an entirely negative light, not regarding higher wages as providing any compensation for what they saw as an expression of a lack of management concern for their basic welfare. Thus the attempt to eliminate the provision of benefits provoked widespread unrest among the workers in the conditions of continued shortages in 1992, exacerbated by the cash crisis, and many facilities were retained.

4 This was a central plank of management's platform: 'The workers should be paid enough to buy everything they need without difficulty outside the enterprise'; 'It is not the business of the enterprise to provide workers with food and consumer goods'; 'Everyone should concentrate on his own business: enterprises on producing goods, shops on selling them'.

Although management claimed in public that it had discontinued the barter and distribution of consumer goods, in fact the distribution of sugar never ceased, and in 1992 barter increased, partly in response to demand from workers, but also in response to the growing problems of cash settlement, both in Russia and in exports to China. Thus the enterprise opened two shops on its own premises, and in the cash crisis in the middle of 1992 provided workers with credit accounts in local shops. Moreover, at the annual shareholders' meeting in February 1993 General Director Komarov reported with pride on the increase in the sale of automobiles through the enterprise, and rebutted claims of profiteering on the sale of barter goods. Although the enterprise continued its house-building programme, workers were not happy to be told that the new apartments released at the end of 1992 would be sold, with discounts according to length of service, but still at prices beyond the reach of the workers, instead of being allocated to those on the housing list.

While many workers resented the dismantling of the paternalistic apparatus as a violation of their traditional rights, higher wages defused opposition. However, the increase in their pay was not sufficient to ameliorate the workers' discontent with what they regarded as a much more serious affront to their status, which was management's policy to open up considerable pay differentials between workers and ITR, which changed from the traditional approximate parity to a ratio of 2.3 to one between 1990 and 1992.[5] This policy was explicitly presented as recognition of the greater value of mental as opposed to manual labour, justified by the need to attract the best specialists to Plastmass. Far from reducing over time, as management had hoped, the workers' grievance at the disparity increased, particularly because with every pay increase the absolute size of the differentials grew. According to local TV, Komarov received 350,000 roubles in December 1992, about ten times the average wage in the factory, with department chiefs earning about four times the average.[6]

5 It is worth noting that, while management was keen to widen differentials between ITR and workers, they were much more cautious in trying to avoid conflict by ensuring that the traditional differentials between different groups of workers, particularly between basic workers (mostly women) and auxiliary workers (mostly men) and between workers of different shops, were maintained.

6 It was claimed at the alternative shareholders' meeting in February 1993 that the total of the directors' earnings was more than 6 million roubles.

The payment system in Plastmass is discussed more fully in Inna Donova, 'Wage Systems in Pioneers of Privatisation', in Simon Clarke, ed., *Labour Relations in Transition*, Edward Elgar, Cheltenham, 1996.

The principle of 'payment for brains' provoked sharply contrasting reactions from different groups of employees. One of the deputy directors said at the end of 1992:

> We face the same conflict as under any socialism: Mister Working Class cannot come to terms with the idea that the ITR should be paid more. Although we consider that the system of payment in the past, under which a foreman received 150 roubles and an operative 300, meant that we lost lots of specialists. We have quite a lot of people with higher education working in workers' jobs.

A chief of one of the shops justified the differentials in terms that we heard more than once:

> Yes, there was a sharp increase and a gap remains. But our decision was as follows: the more the workers receive, the more will the ITR receive, that is we depend directly on the pay of the workers. We have an interest in their pay being higher.

The view of the workers at the same time was rather different. At the end of 1992 shop 1 sent a petition, signed by 70 per cent of the shop, protesting at the size of differentials. Komarov and Martov came to a meeting in the shop, and defended the differentials on the grounds that the low level of technology in the factory meant that the ITR were indispensable, to maintain production and to introduce new methods. Martov told the workers that they were working with spades, when they should be working with computers. The workers replied angrily that they were still working with spades. These are some of the workers' comments:

> In the shop we had a meeting. The deputy general director for economics came to it. We put the question to him: 'Why is there such a difference in pay between ITR and workers?', and he answered that in Japan it was even more, ten to fifteen times ... Why has he only brought us the difference in pay from Japan? What about the equipment, the technology? Have you seen how our loaders work? They carry up to one ton of raw material on a three-wheeled barrow. And they trundle this barrow over a ribbed metal floor. The rubber wheels of the barrow become square as a result of this. That is what passes for technology here! But the differences in pay are completely Japanese.

> Talk about the high earnings at Plastmass is created by the higher levels of ITR and management.

> Yes, at Azot the hard-workers do not earn any less than us!

> People are dissatisfied. There are such differences throughout the factory – how much do ITR and ordinary workers receive? We are not Japanese, certainly, we do not have such high labour productivity that we only have to pull knobs, to work as operators or controllers. More than half our work is very physical. And they receive many times what we get ... The ITR, it seems to me, still do little to earn such pay.

Workers' irritation was also increased because they were stuck on piece rates, while the ITR were protected in earning a salary, losing only the bonus part of their earnings when production is interrupted. The workers explained their grievances as being not so much at the high levels of pay of the ITR as the fact that they do not earn their money. This is particularly the case when production is at a standstill, for which the workers blame the ITR and managers. A machine operator from shop 9 complained:

> The supply of materials is bad: at one time one thing is missing, at another time something else, so we stand idle as a result. I myself went on a business trip in 1991 to Angarsk for stirol – there was no stirol. I think that if they are paid for this, it means that they should also work, so that people are supplied with all that they need.

The last plank in the management platform was a major programme of investment and re-equipment. Allocation to the consumption fund was slashed (from 20 per cent of profits in 1990 to 9 per cent in 1991 and just over 1 per cent in 1992), partially compensated by an increased allocation to the social development fund (12 per cent in 1990 and 9 per cent in 1991, raised to 19 per cent in 1992), with almost half of the post-tax profits being allocated to the fund for the development of production. However, the instability of production, the inability to attract external private or state funding and growing financial difficulties meant that the ambitious investment plans never got off the ground. Workers on the shop floor continued to struggle with antiquated and unreliable equipment, while diversification was largely confined to the adaptation of existing equipment to the manufacture of new products.

FROM PROSPERITY TO CRISIS

The spectacular success of Plastmass was not to last. Despite the apparently very substantial cuts in employment, production fell more rapidly, by 16 per cent in 1991, by 30 per cent in 1992, and by a further 46 per cent in 1993, with the production of press-powder being more than halved. The result was that labour productivity, which fell marginally in 1991, dropped by over 20 per cent in 1992 and by 42 per cent in 1993.

There was a variety of reasons for the fall in production. There had already been some fall in 1990, which was a result of supply difficulties created by a serious fire at the principal supplier of phenol, the main raw material of Plastmass. Supply difficulties increased through 1991 and the first half of 1992, exacerbated by the reduction in military orders and the collapse of the Soviet Union, and then by the debt crisis in the first half of 1992, but the strong financial position of Plastmass enabled it to buy the necessary supplies in the market and to limit the fall in production, assisted by the diversification of production. Shop chiefs, specialists, and even ordinary workers were sent on business trips to prospective supplier enterprises where they had close friends or relatives, and the same system was later used for the collection of debts and in the hunt for sales outlets. Supply problems became more acute from the middle of 1992, but the real problem was not supply but sales.

At the beginning of 1992 Plastmass was in a position to refuse to supply customers except against pre-payment, enabling it to limit the impact of the debt crisis in the middle of the year. However, growing problems of sales meant that this policy could not be sustained, and debts began to mount. Similarly, Plastmass had to reverse its policy of eschewing barter in favour of cash payment, the wide range of goods received through barter being sold through its own shops and commercial department to raise cash to pay wages. Komarov defended the return to barter at the 1994 shareholders' meeting:

> The alternative is this – either we wait until our customers have money, and stop production while we wait, or we work and take commodities from our customers. That is life. Even if it is not normal!

Payments problems, particularly with Ukraine which had formerly been an important market, and the general decline of production in Russia were important factors, but by far the most important was the simple fact that Plastmass had priced itself out of the market. According to Martov, the pricing policy adopted by Plastmass was a simple cost-plus pricing to define the minimum price, with the price then being increased to what the market would bear. This enabled Plastmass to make enormous profits in the first half of 1992, but when demand fell the management did not cut its prices, on the grounds that if it did so in conditions of rapid inflation it would not have the money to buy raw materials. The result was that sales fell sharply. As the deputy director for economics said at the time:

> Now it has become difficult, and you cannot sell, for example, press-powder by the wagon-load as in the past. Customers have begun to count their money, so that they only buy goods, including ours, which they really need.

The possibility of a large order from China, which could take the whole production of press powder, was held out throughout 1992 and 1993. Although exports to China did increase by 32 per cent in 1992 over 1991, transport problems, problems of credit and delays in payment meant that the promise was not realised. In the spring of 1993 Plastmass shipped 7,000 tons of press-powder to China in a barter deal. However, the contract did not stipulate any penalty for late payment, and it was not until the autumn that the barter goods supplied in exchange arrived, their sale taking several more months, so that Plastmass suffered heavy losses on the order. The view in the factory was unanimous: 'The old chief economist would never have allowed it.' Transport costs mean that China is the only export market which can be realistically considered but even with China, despite its proximity, there are considerable difficulties with transportation.

The problem of sales went from bad to worse through 1993 as raw material prices, which comprise 50–70 per cent of costs, escalated. Plastmass to all intents and purposes lost the European market, while the Asian market was too small to absorb Plastmass's basic production – in Eastern Russia there are only two enterprises, in Angarsk and Krasnoyarsk, that buy Plastmass's main products. Although a marketing department was finally established in the spring of 1993, Plastmass was not able to recruit qualified staff, and it was shop chiefs who were primarily responsible for scouring the country for orders, on the grounds that they knew the capabilities of their shop and so could decide what they would be able to produce and at what price.

The engineering centre developed an ambitious programme for the development of new product lines, but Plastmass simply did not have the financial resources to pay for the necessary re-equipment. This meant that diversification took place on an *ad hoc* basis with existing equipment, producing a growing range of consumer goods whenever orders could be found, shop chiefs playing a major role in soliciting such orders.

This policy of diversification was a sharp reversal of the initial strategy, which had been to reduce the product range by cutting out unprofitable product lines (Plastmass had produced 163 different products) and to concentrate on its core activity (which, of course, is what all the managers had been taught to do on their expensive foreign courses), a strategy which proved disastrous when the market for that principal product collapsed. So in 1993 Plastmass found itself reintroducing production of the simple consumer goods which it had cut out the year before.

The priority of management during 1993 was to reduce costs in order to recover its markets. One of the chiefs of the economic service characterised the situation at the time thus:

> We were convinced that if we delivered products without payment in advance, the goods would simply disappear. For months, for three months, for half a year, for more than a year even, there would be no way, legal or illegal, that we would be able to get hold of our money. So it was decided, as a rule with only the rarest of exceptions, that we would deliver goods only against advance payment. And as a result our output has fallen sharply. This was the big problem with which we began to live in 1993. However, the crisis of non-payment, alongside its negative aspect, also has, in our view, its positive aspect, from the point of view of teaching industrial producers about a truly market approach.
>
> Because it became absolutely obvious that we are by no means willing to accept customers for any product at any price. The priority task that follows from this is to reduce production costs. We are now convinced that with such expensive material resources as we have, we really can increase production while reducing production costs, thus creating the conditions for the reduction of prices. Thus we are now taking a most serious approach to the problem of reducing our production costs.

However, the establishment of a special group of leading specialists and the offer of bonuses for cost-cutting suggestions yielded few results, Komarov reporting to the 1994 shareholders' meeting that it had yielded only one significant suggestion.

In the absence of significant investment or reorganisation of production the only way to reduce costs was to cut wages.[7] Although

[7] Wages were determined unilaterally by management on the basis of what the enterprise could afford. Komarov insisted in December 1993 that wages would be determined by the economic possibilities of the firm, refusing to follow the example of many other enterprises by taking bank credit to pay wages.

average pay in Plastmass remained well above that in other chemical enterprises in the city throughout 1992, the latter were steadily catching up as Plastmass management sought to hold off pay increases. Moreover, the large differentials, the withdrawal of other benefits and the insecurity created by waves of redundancy meant that most workers did not feel better off. By April 1993 the relative monetary advantage of Plastmass workers had disappeared, and by November 1993 Plastmass workers were receiving substantially less than those elsewhere, the average wage being 10 per cent below that of comparable enterprises in the city, which provided significantly more non-monetary benefits as well. Profits, meanwhile, also came under pressure, the rate of profit over prime costs falling from 115 per cent in 1992 to 19 per cent in 1993. Moreover, over a third of the 1993 profits came from an arbitration award relating to dollar receipts for exports dating back before privatisation, and a further 10 per cent from commercial and other sources. From November 1993 Plastmass found itself in the position of many other enterprises, of not having the money to pay wages, and delays in the payment of wages of one to two months became frequent thereafter, with workers receiving vouchers which could be exchanged in the company' shops in place of cash.

1993 was, in the estimation of the Director, 'not the most successful for Plastmass'. His deputy for economics was rather more categorical:

> 1993 was a most difficult year for the firm. In 1993 we experienced for ourselves the consequences of inflation, the full weight of non-payment on the part of customers. We began to get to know what market competition and the struggle for customers is all about. Over the past year, we have confronted the problem of the loss of the firm's traditional markets. Finally, we have learned from our own experience what are monopolies, particularly natural ones, and what it is to be dictated to by them.

Along with falling wages and cuts in staff came an intensification of labour, driven by the fear of losing one's job. The comment of a shop chief is typical of many:

> You know, we are all forced to rush around all the time. We have virtually no free time at work, no time to stop for a chat, we are all hard at work. We work. No account is taken of the time. We have practically no dinner. Well, if there is dinner we have it. But we do not simply allow ourselves to get weaker, because the work is always intense.

This fear of the loss of a job meant that the workers became much better disciplined, particularly while wages were high in 1991–2. Thus the number of disciplinary violations officially reported fell from 402 in 1991 to 211 in 1992. Line managers are virtually unanimous that drunkenness at work and absenteeism have become extremely rare, cases of lateness and leaving work early have been significantly reduced, as has the number of thefts from the workplace. The chief accountant noted with some satisfaction in 1992:

> People now work as much as is needed: in the evenings, on Saturdays and on Sundays. One of our collectives is female. All I have to do is to define the task and the time for its completion and if the person feels that it is not finished, she stays behind. Women workers especially come to me and ask, 'Tat'yana Vasil'evna, will we be able to get this or that statistical accounting form ready in time?' This kind of thing never used to happen.
>
> – And why does it happen now?
>
> The first reason is the increased pay, that very material stimulation about which we always spoke, but did practically nothing. The second reason may be, and this is bad, but the fear of losing their jobs. In the past year the small number of bookkeepers has been reduced from 39 to 25 people. And now there may be further cuts – 2 or 3 people.

This situation did not last long – by 1993 the reductions in numbers had reached their limit, and falling wages meant that labour turnover was increasing, with skilled workers in particular leaving for better paid jobs. Labour turnover during 1993 reached 41 per cent for the enterprise as a whole, 54 per cent among workers, with 1,259 people leaving, of whom 1,016 were workers, with dissatisfaction with the level of wages being the main reason for leaving, despite the fact that external labour market conditions were deteriorating as other chemical enterprises in the city began to lay off workers (although shortages of high-skilled workers persisted). During 1991–2 there had been no official recruitment, with most of the posts filled being vacant low-paid unskilled jobs (industrial cleaners, painters and plasterers in construction groups) which were usually filled by workers who had been laid off elsewhere in the enterprise (in fact recruitment never stopped, throwing some doubt on the real scale of the cuts in the labour force). However, in August 1993 Plastmass had to advertise for new workers (machine-operators, smiths, welders, turners, mechanics and others) for the first time for eighteen months, in connection with the commissioning of production of polyethylene film. The situation deteriorated further during 1994, with advertisements for an increasing number of vacancies appearing regularly in the local press, the loss of the skilled workers who were the core of the labour collective disrupting production, with a reduction in quality and increase in the length of the production cycle.

This process of redundancy followed by recruitment also contributed to growing discontent among the labour force. In shop 2, from which 100 people had been sacked out of a total labour force of just over 600 by the spring of 1992, the appearance of a new order later in the year led to the recruitment of workers who had previously been dismissed from other shops. The reasons for this were not explained to the existing workers in the shop, some of whom complained that 'they have sacked our workers and brought strangers into their places'. The trade union organiser saw this as a prime cause of the deteriorating quality of work in the shop:

> We began to work worse only because of the cuts everywhere. Our shop was like a magnet: everyone who was sacked somewhere else was brought to our shop.

Another consequence of falling wages was growing conflict within the enterprise, with a succession of small strikes. However, although these conflicts harnessed the dissatisfaction and declining morale of the workers, the instigators seem in almost every case to have been not workers but line managers, seeking to increase the pay of their workers in order to reduce conflict within the shop and to strengthen the position of the shop or department within the enterprise as a whole. The only effective independent worker activist, who had led a threatened strike in his shop in 1992, was co-opted by being elected to the Board of Plastmass, the result being that his fellow workers soon lost confidence in him.

The response of management to these conflicts was to make piecemeal concessions to the workers, awarding bonus payments or pay increases which were rapidly eroded by inflation. These concessions were sufficient to defuse active protest, although they did little to raise morale or to eliminate the growing sense of 'them and us' which was beginning to prevail on the shop floor. However, workers themselves were increasingly reluctant to risk dismissal by speaking out, and so continued in the traditional way to look to their line managers to represent their interests.

Finally, the long history of Plastmass's battles for independence against the local and regional administration has also left it politically exposed, particularly as the local 'liberal' and 'conservative' political forces had sunk their formerly irreconcilable differences to establish a unified ruling bloc, so the Director could not look there for political or financial support.

The most dramatic impact of the deterioration in the economic position of Plastmass was not on the growing tension between workers and managers, but in opening up conflict within the senior management team, leading to a long drawn-out confrontation between Komarov and Martov which resulted in the reversal of the reform process.

TENSIONS AND CHANGES IN THE SOCIAL STRUCTURE OF THE ENTERPRISE

Martov's management reforms entailed a fundamental change in status relations within the enterprise. In the traditional Soviet enterprise the core management team comprised the line managers (shop chiefs, section chiefs, foremen) under the chief engineer, while the staff specialists (particularly economists, accountants, planners and personnel management but also technologists, norm-setters and so on) performed routine accounting and record-keeping functions. With Martov's reforms the latter specialisms came to the fore and played a leading role in the formation of management policy, their enhanced status being reflected in the expanded size and functions of their departments and in the level of their pay. The line managers were by no means excluded from management, the chiefs of all the production shops having seats on the Board, but they undoubtedly saw a relative decline in their status.[8]

The ideology and practice of the senior management team departed in significant ways from the traditional paternalism of the Soviet era, weakening the feedback which they received, so that they had little

8 In addition to the formal management team, there was a woman whose lowly official position, as a kind of 'engineer for the monitoring of the carrying out of decisions', belied her key role in the administration as the director's right arm and the principal informal channel of communication between the director and other managers. Such 'small but indispensable people' are often to be found in Soviet enterprises and organisations.

idea of the reaction of workers, or even of line managers, to their innovations.[9] In interviews senior managers and specialists showed little interest in the views of workers, being concerned only with their own vision of the reconstruction of production and the optimal organisation of labour and its pay. The chief engineer confessed:

> I mix much less with workers and, on the whole, I cannot speak very confidently about the workers' mood. My sphere of contacts is the ITR, but nevertheless I do things like this: when I make new plans, make some kind of new installation, it is interesting to pose the question, to ask myself: will it be better for the workers, or not? I think that the workers undoubtedly accept this, because everything that we do leads to the reduction of manual labour, the improvement of working conditions, automation, mechanisation of the process, which makes it possible for us to remove the spade and allows us to push buttons. So how could it be perceived otherwise than as positive for this system?

The new deputy general director for economics took a similar position:

> Recently I have rarely associated with them. I hardly mix with workers, only when they come about pay. It is much more difficult for the chiefs of shops to work in this relationship. You see they deal with many questions. An employee is on a completely different level. And then there is a mass of people who do not understand anything.

Asked who is included in the phrase 'We – the firm', a catchphrase of management, she answered:

> Six months ago I would have said that 'we' is some kind of small management team in the factory management. But now this includes the shop chiefs and shop ITR.

Workers were conspicuously absent from the formula, and none of the managers ever mentions the participation of workers in management decisions.

The divisions between line managers and staff specialists were largely hidden during the 'innovatory offensive' of 1990–2, when the atmosphere of constant and rapid change left the majority of the workers with the impression that management was intervening in all aspects of the running of the enterprise and the scale and pace of change left workers feeling that it was impossible to oppose any of the

9 In the past the Party Committee had provided a principal channel for such feedback.

changes. This increase in managerial authority, reinforced by the combination of lay-offs and high wages, reconciled the line managers to the changes taking place within the management body.

The weakening of the economic and financial position of the enterprise from the middle of 1992, and the falling wages and growing shortages of labour through 1993 and 1994 to some extent reversed this trend, with some erosion of managerial authority and the opening of divisions within the management team.

Despite high wages, levels of worker dissatisfaction were high from an early stage in the changes, the main reason for dissatisfaction in 1992 being the loss of a sense of stability in relation to pay, in relation to the security of employment and in relation to the content of their jobs, a feeling of greater dependence on the administration of the enterprise, a feeling of a lack of concern on the part of management for the well-being of the workers and the feeling of a reduction of their status in relation to the administration. However, there was little overt protest since workers had an overwhelming sense of their own powerlessness in the face of the fear of loss of pay, job transfer and redundancy and in the absence of any effective trade union or workers' organisation to protect them.

These factors gradually weakened through 1993 and 1994. From the end of 1992 the focus of the innovatory offensive shifted from the production shops to the scientific-research department so the sense of administrative pressure was eased on the majority of workers. Even during 1992 Plastmass workers did not feel that their earnings were particularly high, insisting in interviews that Plastmass's reputation for paying high wages derived from the level of wages of management and ITR, not those of workers whose wages were already compared unfavourably with wages available elsewhere, while the high differentials aggravated their sense of social injustice. Increasingly through 1993 the fear of workers was transformed from a fear of losing a well-paid job to the fear of losing a job as such, a fear reinforced by the memory of recent reductions. However, even this fear was moderated as redundancies came to an end and Plastmass faced a growing shortage of labour.

The general mood in Plastmass became increasingly pessimistic through 1993 and 1994 as management appeared less and less willing or able to do anything about the deteriorating economic and financial position of the enterprise. From late 1993 Komarov appeared to be more interested in furthering his political career (becoming acting

President of one of the Russian social organisations, seeking nomination to the Federal Duma and establishing a regional organisation for Russia's Choice, whose election candidates were nominated on the basis of the collection of signatures through the Personnel Department of Plastmass) than in the prospects of his own enterprise.

POSITION OF THE TRADE UNION

The trade union in Plastmass does not exist as an effective force, remaining one of the unreformed institutions within Plastmass and having been reduced to a 'pocket' trade union at an early stage in the reforms. During 1991–2 the union abandoned a whole range of its activities and its primary groups withered away. The reforming management had no interest in giving the trade union any effective role within the reform process, but for the trade union officers themselves, as one of the workers put it, 'it is always more comfortable for them to sit in management's pocket, particularly if that is where they are used to sitting'.

Nevertheless, the enterprise trade union committee is still quite active in relation to the functions which remain to it, although figuratively speaking 'the brain still lives, but the extremities are already cold'. The remaining trade union functions are largely formal: participation in the redundancy procedures, involvement in disciplinary procedures (which have become increasingly rare), provision of financial help for those in need, allocation of workers' children to kindergartens. Until 1993 the trade union was also responsible for the allocation of new housing, but this has now been taken over by the enterprise's social development department. The status of the trade union is reflected in the fact that the resources at its disposal are those of the enterprise, while its role is a secondary one of resolving minor problems and distributing an insignificant proportion of social goods.

The structure of the trade union organisation in Plastmass is traditional. There is a trade union committee (profkom) at the level of the enterprise and shop committees in the shops – in the shops there are also profgroups at the level of the brigade. Since 1991 the number of members of the factory profkom has been cut from 28 to 11. The president of the profkom and his deputies are full-time. In the shop the basic work is carried out by the president of the shop committee and his or her deputy. According to the president of the profkom 'they are not full-time, we pay for the amount of time that they are not working, but that is often not large. We pay them a bonus every quarter'. In general these posts are taken by ITR, technologists, foremen and those who work permanently on the day shift. However, in reality the situation is somewhat different. The president of the shop committee of shop 2 said: 'I am in practice a full-time official, although I count as a foreman'. This is a fairly widespread practice in Russian enterprises.

The vertical connections between the various levels of the trade union organisation have weakened and in the majority of situations the functions carried out by a particular trade union body are determined by the personal position of the head of this body. As a rule, when the trade union leaders speak about the trade union, they have in mind only the factory's trade union committee, and do not include in the understanding of the trade union the lower levels, let alone the workers the union is supposed to represent. Thus, the deputy president of the union noted that the trade union is not concerned with questions of distribution, for which the enterprise has created a commercial department, which includes representatives of the shops. However, it turns out that the majority of shop representatives are the leaders of the shop trade union committees, so that the trade union at the level of the shop continues to carry out distributive functions, having been integrated formally into the apparatus of management.

The leaders of the profkom noted that they had a lot of work related to the fact that social insurance had been transferred to the trade union. Apart from this, according to the president of the profkom, the profkom carries out the functions of the defence of the workers' interests. Typically, according to the profkom president, a group of workers will take a grievance to the general director or a senior manager through the trade union committee because in that way it is easier to get access to management. However, in practice it is rare for workers to take grievances through the trade union. It is significant that it is typically a group of workers who do so, rather than an individual.

Apart from this, the leaders of the profkom participate in the preparation of the collective agreement, which was last revised in 1992. The head of the profkom recounted with pride that the collective agreement was prepared very thoroughly, so that the conference of the labour collective called to sign it lasted only two hours, while 'in other enterprises it goes on for two days'. An ordinary fitter commented :

Agreement! You know how they did it? They only gave out the text of the agreement at the conference. To read it – that would have been simply impossible, let alone to put in any amendments. It is still lying around at home somewhere with my comments.

The collective agreement was certainly prepared very competently by the administration of the enterprise and anticipates everything to guarantee uninterrupted production. Management persuaded the profkom to agree to overtime without additional pay, the point being expressed as a right of the workers:

Point 8.1. The workers have the right to work more than 40 hours a week in the following circumstances: working to satisfy the conditions for payment; additional work will not exceed 32 hours per week; to observe the norms and rules of labour safety and technical care. Work beyond the normal hours, but in conformity with the schedule, is not considered overtime. Such additional work forms part of the composition of the schedule of the shift.

The rights of the trade union are described very abstractly in the collective agreement, but there are no guarantees or mechanisms for their fulfilment. Some of these rights would normally be considered the responsibility of the administration, for example the trade union assumes responsibility for finding jobs for redundant workers, for training and re-training and for industrial safety.[10] In point 3.7 it is stated that 'the Profkom is the single juridical organ for the defence of the socio-economic interests and rights of the workers', a clause introduced by the administration to protect itself against the emergence of independent workers' organisations, two small subdivisions having withdrawn from the official trade union at that time, while the members of a workers' committee based in the factory had called a meeting to discuss setting up an independent trade union.

In contrast to the abstract definition of the workers' rights defended by the trade union, the rights of the administration are concrete and are practically nowhere limited by the collective agreement. The administration reserves the right:

[10] Point 3.2: The profkom defends the rights of its members to labour, takes part in the working out of the programme of placing workers, proposes measures for social protection of people freed from the enterprise. Point 3.5: The trade union committee has the right to demand from the administration support for the workers and their aspirations: to increase their professional competence; supply the full realisation of their functional capacities; to provide good conditions for high quality work; to anticipate accidents.

> to manage the operational affairs of the enterprise, labour power, including the right to hire and fire workers on its own initiative, THE RIGHT TO TRANSFER TO OTHER WORK IN CONDITIONS OF ABSENCE OF WORK OR FOR ANY OTHER LEGAL REASON, conforming to the legislation in force ... to abolish or combine departments ... Recognising the need to protect the property of the enterprise and the workers, the Board in the person of the administration has the right to search the personal cupboards, bags and cars of workers having entrance to the territory of the enterprise. The search will take place on entrance to or exit from the enterprise. Any workers refusing to be searched will be subject to disciplinary sanctions.
>
> In the course of the period of application of this agreement the profkom must not declare or approve of a strike, or the management a lockout, in connection with any issues reflected in it.

The profkom defends its concession of the right to declare redundancies to the administration by arguing that 'if we do not have redundancies, the enterprise as a whole will become bankrupt. And if we do not cut now, for example 100 people, then we will have to cut all three and a half thousand'.

Recounting the functions of the profkom, the deputy president of the union also claimed that the profkom had participated in working out the new system of pay in the enterprise. However, the deputy general director for economics could not assess the work of the profkom: 'It is difficult for me to speak about the work of the profkom. I really hardly ever bump into them.'

Many workers turn to the profkom for help in getting housing. At the end of 1992 two apartment blocks were completed and prepared for occupation. However, the administration decided not to give apartments to workers free, as had always been the case in the past, but to sell them to them, with some privileges being given to workers selected by the social development department, in practice for their loyalty to the enterprise. This created a great deal of unrest, but the trade union did nothing to support workers in relation to these two buildings.

Apart from this, the functions of the trade union have been preserved – the traditional distribution of holiday vouchers, sanatorium places, holidays and the distribution of goods. 'We are also concerned with servicing and helping the pensioners. We give them material help, we visit them, we take care of them ' (president of shop committee).

Ordinary workers express regret that the profkom of the enterprise has stopped distributing commodities. The majority of them cannot define concretely what the trade union does do. This question turns out to be the most difficult for everyone to answer. Before muttering something indistinctly, many kept silent, sighed deeply and thought hard, trying to remember something. At the level of the primary group, trade union work has stopped completely. To the question of what she does as the shift trade union organiser one activist said frankly:

> Nothing. You understand, when everything collapsed here – the Party and all the rest, the calm here became terrible, nobody did anything. Even the shop committee did not work.

At the same time she noted the very important help rendered by the representative of the shop committee in conflict situations, although the main advice given by the latter to the workers was to by-pass the union:

> Generally they defend us, the lads. They even teach us. Maybe for that reason we don't fuss them: they suggest things to us illegally. The administration relates to them as a devil may care. Therefore the trade union organisers said to us, it is better for you, workers, to go yourselves.

The covert support of the shop trade union activists for workers against the administration, like the participation of the shop administration in negotiations with the factory administration, is an important feature of the inter-relations between various levels and subdivisions of the organisation. But still most workers say things like: 'We ignore the trade union committee.' 'We don't have anything to do with them.' 'If it vanished tomorrow – we really wouldn't notice.'

The workers were not able to oppose the administration in the period of radical reform because there was no organisation able to express their interests, although there were workers who understood quite well the changes that were taking place, who understood that a few scattered shares which workers buy are not enough for their real participation in management, who realised the need to get the workers together and create some kind of workers' organisation. The number of such workers was small. Many of them, well-known people in Plastmass, had worked at the enterprise for 20–30 years, and may in the past have been Komsomol, trade union and Party grass-roots activists. More recently they had tested their strength as leaders of local (shop) conflicts. They were the ones who were usually elected from the shop to represent the workers in negotiations with the administration. Such workers in interviews expressed a unanimously negative view of the activity of the trade union and argued that it was necessary to create a new independent workers' organisation.

The most active and most respected leader had worked at Plastmass for thirty years, and had been a Party and trade union activist who in the old days was often taken to Moscow as a workers' representative in negotiations over resources. He became active in the democratic movement, and in 1989 joined the City Workers' Committee as an activist in the workers' movement which emerged in the wake of the miners' strike. At this period he was a member of the still-born Union of Kuzbass Workers, sponsoring Komarov as a democratic candidate in the elections to the *oblast* soviet in 1990. However, following privatisation he concentrated his activism within Plastmass. He remained neutral in the conflict between Komarov and Martov, opposing both. He had briefly tried to work through the trade union committee, but had soon become disillusioned:

> Once I also believed that one could change something in the trade union committee, correct something, support something. But the trade union committee ... has never opposed the administration. As a whole I have no hope for the trade union committee because a single trade union cannot defend both the director and the workers. I am all the more inclined to the view that the trade union must be more independent, more independent of the administration.

A small group of these activists tried to create such an independent trade union, but their attempts were unsuccessful, the workers did not come to their meeting, they did not seem ready for such a decisive step. The majority of workers were sceptical of this initiative:

> People already live according to the principle: a boss comes, he pushes us about ... They cannot understand that their own interests are in their hands. And the improvement of their lives, all depends on them.

Finally these initiatives were successfully neutralised by the administration, which arranged the election of the three principal leaders to the Board. Once on the Board these leaders lost authority since, as a small minority, they could have no influence on the Board's decisions, but were nevertheless identified with those decisions in the eyes of the workers. As one of the leaders said, 'you cannot explain to everybody how you voted at Board meetings'. He remained on the Board, but now spends his spare time fishing.

Despite the complete disappointment of workers in the trade union structures, there has been no mass resignation (according to the president of the profkom, in 1992 five people left). This is related to the fact that the workers are alienated and fear the negative consequences for themselves: if workers leave the trade union they lose a whole series of privileges, even the right for their children to receive new year presents.

It is hardly surprising that managers have a condescending attitude to the trade union. But even trade union activists themselves are well aware of their minor role. When disputes arise within the shop even the trade union activists advise their members to take the matter directly to management, so that workers simply ignore the trade union committee, although when workers send a petition to management a copy is still sent, according to tradition, to the trade union committee. Shop trade union activists also play an important role using their informal connections to find jobs elsewhere in the enterprise for workers who are made redundant, but the union itself has no authority in the eyes of workers or of management.

The most significant role remaining to the trade union is that of the defence of workers who are dismissed, but in the redundancy procedures the trade union frequently plays the role of voluntary or involuntary accomplice of the administration. A member of the shop trade union committee of shop 2, speaking in December 1992, explained the role of the trade union in the main wave of redundancies:

> The reduction was carried out like this: the shop chief informs all the heads of the subdivisions of the general number of reductions in the shop and distributes them according to the staff schedule of each subdivision (of which there are fourteen in shop 2). Then the chiefs of each subdivision decide locally precisely whom to sack. The administration decided to share responsibility, so that they can cut anyone. Then the proposal prepared by the head of the subdivision and the trade union organiser was discussed by the trade union group at a 'five-minute' meeting. Further discussion took place with the shop chief in the shop trade union committee. If the shop committee agreed, but the person dismissed did not, he or she could apply to the conflict commission, which has to exist in every shop. In shop 2 this comprises 7 people: the shop chief, three ITR and three workers. As a rule the employees agree to the decision about their dismissal. In the past a case of disagreement went first to the shop conflict commission and then to the factory commission. Now the factory commission does not exist, or at least I have not heard about it. At any rate, now, after the shop conflict commission, it goes to the factory trade union committee. But this has not happened in our shop.

If one of several candidates for dismissal is considered 'necessary' by the administration the latter will suggest to the trade union that it take note of some aspect of that person's difficult material, family, household or personal situation. In such a situation the trade union assumes its protective function, and protests against the dismissal of that person. Such situations, in which the labour collective initially nominates a better worker over a less well-off person for redundancy, only for its priorities to be reversed by the trade union, are fairly frequent.

The workers have no regard for the trade union, but equally the majority have little conception of the need for a trade union, continuing to look to management to resolve their problems.

The deterioration in the position of Plastmass since 1992 has led to a growing mood of pessimism among its employees, and a sense of their inability to exert any control over the course of events. This growing pessimism has led to a marked increase in levels of conflict within the enterprise, but these conflicts were expressed first and most dramatically not in a confrontation between workers and management, but within the management body itself.

CONFLICTS IN PLASTMASS

Despite the rapid changes, levels of conflict in Plastmass over 1990–1 were markedly lower than in other enterprises in the city. There was a number of reasons for the reduction in the level of conflict. The first was the reduction in the level of disciplinary violations. This was partly a result of the relatively higher wages paid at Plastmass, but more a result of the large-scale redundancies, which focused on violators of discipline and on those known as trouble-makers. As a result disciplinary violations, which are often the spark for larger conflicts, became much less common in Plastmass.

The second major source of conflicts in other enterprises in this period was disagreement over the distribution of goods acquired by the enterprise by barter. In most enterprises barter goods were sold to employees at markedly reduced prices on the basis of some kind of rationing or lottery system. Such goods were usually allocated by the administration to the various shops, and then allocated within shops and sections, leading to conflict between shops and subdivisions as well as within the shops. In Plastmass such conflicts were largely avoided both because of the relatively low level of barter sale at this time and because goods acquired by barter were put on free sale in the enterprise's own shops.

The third major source of conflicts in Soviet enterprises was conflict over the allocation of rights, responsibilities and material resources between and within shops as line managers struggled to make the plan in conditions of scarcity. In Plastmass in this period the relative prosperity of the enterprise meant that it did not suffer as seriously from supply shortages as other enterprises, but also the management reorganisation and the reinforcement of the authority of senior management reduced the scope for such conflicts and provided more effective means for their resolution.

The main area of conflict in Soviet enterprises has always, not surprisingly, been that of pay, and Plastmass is no different. Conflicts with management as a result of pay began almost at once after the liberalisation of prices in January 1992. The first dispute was in February, when one shift of women workers in shop 2 stopped work, fed up with their low pay. Various senior managers, including Komarov, went to the shop. Komarov asked the workers to be patient, stressed how difficult the situation was, and that with the forthcoming reconstruction of the shop it would become more difficult still. The workers complained at the size of differentials enjoyed by the ITR, who were now making good money. The workers did not demand parity, but only that the ITR should earn not more than twice the workers' wage. According to the trade union organiser in the shop, Komarov told the workers:

> When the engineering-technical services, and the foreman too, received 120 roubles, they did not make any fuss, you worked on production and received around 300 – not one of you spoke out in their defence, and they have not forgotten the scandals, they suffered. Now I will pay them, they are not idlers, the institute spent money, taught them and, to cut a long story short, they will only receive as much as is necessary, as much as is agreed.

Komarov told the workers to be patient until May, and work resumed. In May Komarov returned to the shop and told the workers that the shop would be closed for reconstruction.

> Naturally we are all women, we all have families, we decided not to stop, we agreed to work. He said to us that our pay would also fall, because the shop will

> be reconstructed, but this will only be for 2–3 months, he said. Nonetheless, a year has gone by, and nothing has got better for us.

The same shift protested again in October, when their pay fell once more:

> Our shift is aggressive. Well it is not so much aggressive, but simply all the people working in the shift are old.

The shift did not strike, but slowed work down for an hour or two:

> Upstairs, they understood and they again sent for Komarov and he said (yes, again he came here) that it had already been decided that this month pay will be increased by 25 per cent, and after the new year there will be a general increase for us. But nevertheless, our workers' pay is less than in any of the other chemical enterprises, although he always says to us: ours is the highest of all.

In shop 1 the workers declared a pre-strike situation over what the workers considered to be low pay, in view of their difficult working conditions. A group of workers called on the General Director, who explained the principles of calculation of pay. However, the workers were not satisfied and announced that they would not leave the pre-strike situation, although they decided not to declare a strike, since the administration read out the law on strikes, declaring that this would be an unlawful strike and warning them of the consequences of breaking the law. A conciliation commission was set up, but the president of the profkom served as a mediator in the negotiations between the workers and the administration, adopting a neutral position rather than joining the conciliation commission as representative of the workers, his place being taken by the president of the shop committee. The profkom president explained such an unusual function for a trade unionist by the fact that literally the day before the strike declaration he had finished a course organised by the American AFL-CIO for trade union leaders and had learnt about negotiations through mediators, which was precisely why he had been selected for the post. Nevertheless, he insisted:

> I would have been on the side of the workers, but as I was a mediator I could not take sides. I have to act only according to the law. ... If they had selected me for the commission, I would certainly have fought for the rights of the workers.

The conflict was resolved by an increase in the pay of the workers of the shop.

The third conflict in this period took place in shop 9, where for some unexplained reason the pay of machine operators was much less than that of machine operators in other shops (in shop 9 they got 5,000 roubles a month, in other shops up to 20,000). The machine operators held a meeting and wrote a letter to the enterprise administration, the ITR who were at the meeting supporting their demands. Two machine operators were elected to attend a meeting of the Board and to find out what the administration had to say in response to their demands. The chief of the shop also went with them, being expected to speak in defence of the interests of the machine operators. However, the General Director was absent from the Board meeting. The shop chief got nowhere in his negotiations, the administration insisting that everything was normal, but that they would 'look into everything'. The matter was only settled when Komarov returned from his business trip.

A further conflict over pay in shop 2 was expressed in a milder form. Since, according to a worker in the shop, people were afraid to speak out openly:

> A piece of paper was passed around the shop saying that if anyone is not satisfied we ask you to sign this sheet. More than enough were found who wanted to sign.

The letter was handed over to the administration, and the workers got a pay increase, but the rise was soon eaten away by inflation.

The division of the enterprise into basic and auxiliary shops led, as in all Soviet enterprises, to high levels of tension and mutual recrimination, but did not lead to open conflict. The president of the profkom explained:

> Managers and workers are still conscious of the difference between basic and non-basic shops, although the basic shops all understand perfectly well that without the auxiliary shops they would not get anything repaired, they would have no electricity supply, there would be nothing in the shop, and they would not be able to work. But they consider themselves the basis, and at the same time in the auxiliary shops they say that without them there would be nothing in the factory. We must receive more. And this is despite the higher pay in our enterprise, this is not a pleasant situation, when one considers that he must receive more, and the other that he must receive more. However, this does not lead to direct conflict.

It should be noted that in many conflicts with the administration it is the old workers who emerge as the most active, those who have worked at Plastmass for many years. Between them and the present chiefs there are informal 'community' relations, formed earlier, when the managers still worked in the shops and did not hold higher posts. As the militant trade union organiser in shop 2 explained:

> Well we converse with them like with our own chiefs. They grew up in front of our eyes, they are younger than us, all the chiefs. Pastukhov was our foreman, directly from the army, the lad was young. We treat them as simple people.

The biggest and most persistent source of tension was the opening of substantial pay differentials between workers, on the one hand, and managers and specialists, on the other. Moreover, although management had hoped that the workers would soon become reconciled to the new situation, in fact their sense of grievance increased. The chief of the economics department explained in March 1993, after two pay increases which had marginally reduced the differential, that the reduction had more of a symbolic than a monetary significance, but that it was crucial at a time at which the issue had led to a virtual breakdown of communication between workers and management. The deterioration in the situation arose because of the continued violation of workers' deeply held feelings of social justice, but also because of their deteriorating real wages.

This problem was the inevitable consequence of the initial philosophy of management, that 'money can resolve many problems'. While Plastmass had money, its problems could be resolved, but once it ran into difficulties these problems mounted, while the means of their resolution were increasingly difficult to find.

The standard means of resolving conflicts in Plastmass, if only temporarily, was handing out 'a bit of money'.[11] When conflicts arose in the shops, the workers involved would be paid off with a small increase in their pay, or with the promise of such an increase in the future. When asked how a particular conflict in shop 1 was resolved, one of its managers replied with a wide grin 'people remember that they have been pretty well-paid for the last couple of months'. However, while such methods could head-off conflicts temporarily, they

[11] One can regard such concessions, eroded by inflation within a month or two, as a feature of a 'market-oriented' management strategy, in contrast to the traditional Soviet response of transferring workers, sacking 'unwelcome workers' and removing the shop or section chief for 'not coping with the responsibilities of his post'.

did nothing to remove the basis of the growing tension in the enterprise. Indeed, many of the workers themselves regarded their pay increases at the end of 1992 and in March 1993 in a negative light, even though they reduced differentials, as 'crumbs from the rich man's table'.

The other traditional method of resolving conflicts in Soviet enterprises, maintained in Plastmass, was for the general director or one of his deputies (in this case usually Martov), to 'go to the people'. When a conflict arises which cannot be resolved within the shop it is normal for either the shop management or representatives of the workers to invite senior representatives of the enterprise management to the shop. The shop managers, in particular, prefer to pass the buck in this way, rather than to negotiate with the workers on their own initiative. The senior manager arrives and calls a meeting in the shop, at which the workers present their grievances or demands, but even if concessions are made the meeting soon turns into a lecture, with the manager on the platform mouthing empty slogans, 'be patient, things will get better', or 'be patient, or things will get worse', or 'it has been done (or decided), and that is how it will be, and good riddance to those who don't like it'. This kind of response is less a way of resolving the situation that has arisen than of exerting moral pressure on the workers, which merely increases the irritation and dissatisfaction of the latter. As a result, even if the workers' immediate demands are satisfied, the grounds are laid for further conflicts which inevitably arise.

Declining real wages, the persistence of high differentials and late payment of wages led to a marked increase in conflict over 1993 and 1994. Typically such conflicts flare up in one shop or another. The conflict will begin with increasingly emotional conversations among the workers, who decide to make a written complaint to management, a representative of which attends a meeting in the shop, makes some concessions, and presses the workers back to work. However, there were also some clear changes in the character of conflicts during 1993, and particularly in 1994.

In the past workers could be mollified by reference to difficult external circumstances – the problems in the country and so on – and exhorted to return to work in the interests of the collective. However, the workers have developed a much sharper conception or, to be more exact, a sharper feeling of their status as wage labourers, and are much less willing to listen to talk about the difficulties faced by the enterprise, instead addressing management as the owners of the enterprise and as employers. Thus, the following statement of a worker in June 1994 is typical:

> Our factory already has an owner, or a few owners, but they do not behave as real owners: they are cutting off the branch on which they sit – the collective is falling apart, the experienced workers are leaving, we are losing our customers. Although it is quite possible that this is where their interest lies. But all these appeals to save everything – water, heat, steam – are hypocritical. This is all theirs [indicating everything around]. If they don't care about me, why should I care about their raw materials.

On the other hand, the management tried to increase even more its demagogic-ideological pressure on the workers. A clear example of this is the appeal to the workers of the General Director published in the factory newspaper in April 1994:

> Recently I have visited a number of shops. The workers demand increased pay ... Their demands are justified. However, people do not think about the fact that losses of water, steam and electric power mean that we have to pay for the resources that we waste and for the fines we incur, and we have to pay for all of this with your money, from our own pockets. And if we do not manage to save on absolutely everything, then we will not be able to live well.
>
> The kind of extravagance that we allow ourselves today is foolhardy – it is like a feast in the middle of a famine. We have to remember that everything has a price – raw materials, water, your working hours, the time that automobiles hang around, the cost of railway transport – everything is paid from your own pocket. There is no money to pay for what we throw around, we break, we lose, we literally run on money.

THE BATTLE FOR POWER: KOMAROV VERSUS MARTOV

During the period of radical reform, Komarov had largely delegated the day-to-day management of Plastmass to Martov and his associates while he was away on extended business trips at home and abroad. While he had never opposed Martov's schemes, he had never shown any great commitment to them either, being happy to give Martov his head while his reforms showed positive results. However, once Plastmass began to run into difficulties relations rapidly soured, and the two became locked in a bitter struggle for control of the enterprise.

The origins of the conflict between the two men are difficult to disentangle, since a clash of ambitions was inextricably bound up with an apparent clash of principle. According to Martov the problems really began in July 1992, during the preparations for the first shareholders' meeting. Martov and his group planned to propose Martov to be President of the Board, on the grounds that Komarov should not combine that post with his responsibilities as General Director of the factory. In the event Martov did not allow his candidacy to go forward because he judged that he lacked sufficient support and Komarov was elected unopposed. On 1 November 1992 Martov resigned his post at Plastmass, while remaining a member of the Board and continuing to discuss a common programme with Komarov.

The fundamental issue of principle was that of the clash between Martov's collegial system of management, and Komarov's commitment to the perpetuation of the authoritarian system of one-man management. According to Martov, there was a secret agreement within the group of senior managers that they would take bank credit through the enterprise to buy 20 million roubles' worth of shares at their nominal value (amounting to 20 per cent of the issued shares). Since they planned to recommend to the annual meeting in February that they should pay a 100 per cent dividend, the loan would be repaid almost immediately. Martov applied to the Board to buy shares to the value of 1.3 million roubles, his allocation under the agreement. However, Komarov returned from a business trip in November and unilaterally took a bank loan of 7 million roubles with which he bought corresponding shares for his personal benefit, without submitting this purchase to the Board for approval.[12] When Martov heard of this on 20 November he took it as a declaration of war, and launched a struggle for control of Plastmass. Martov complained to the Board and confronted Komarov in person, only to be told 'I am the owner of this enterprise and I will do what I want'. Martov then proposed to the Board that Komarov should be removed, but got no support. Instead, his application to buy shares was refused on the grounds that he was no longer an employee of Plastmass. With these rebuffs the struggle moved to the annual shareholders' meeting on 13 February 1993.

In preparation for the shareholders' meeting both Martov and Komarov waged intensive campaigns. Martov, having left Plastmass, now worked through his own company, Trast, which claimed at the

[12] The shareholders' meeting voted to scale down dividend payments *pro rata* to the time the shares had been held, which would have cost Komarov dear. The decision was later reversed by the Board.

time to be the largest securities trading company and financial consultancy in Kuzbass.[13] At his own expense he hired loudspeaker vans and distributed leaflets at the factory gates accusing Komarov of attempting to seize power for his own benefit and by illegal means. He also denounced Komarov from the pages of the local newspaper, charging him with autocratism, of making idiotic decisions, of worsening the financial and economic position of the enterprise, of persecuting highly qualified specialists for disagreeing with him and of acting illegally. Komarov in turn issued rebuttals through the factory newspaper and over the factory radio, and denounced Martov for abusing his position.

Having been isolated from his own supporters in management, Martov formed a strategic alliance with his former opponents, those 'populist levellers' who had favoured an equal distribution of shares and control of the enterprise by the labour collective, establishing a Committee for the Democratic Reform of Plastmass at the end of January 1993, whose programme was published in the local press. However, although the leader of this group, a former chief engineer of Plastmass, was popular among the workers, the combined forces were not able to get the 10 per cent of votes needed to include their proposal to remove Komarov from the Board onto the agenda of the shareholders' meeting.

The shareholders' meeting was to be held in the hall in which meetings of the labour collective had traditionally been held, which had seating for a maximum of 500 people so that meetings could only be held on a delegate basis. Komarov used the traditional method of selecting delegates to persuade worker–shareholders to give their proxies to ITR and senior shop management, many of whom in turn transferred the proxies to Komarov, with the result that, as emerged in the later court proceedings, Komarov held 2,000 proxy votes in addition to those of his associates and his personal holding, whose legality Martov was contesting. The first hour and a half of the meeting was taken up with a series of challenges from Martov: challenging Komarov's right to chair the meeting; accusing him of illegal purchase of shares financed by credit and demanding the annulment of the purchase; charging that Komarov's associates in the meeting had not allowed those shareholders into the hall who had demanded the return

13 Trast offers to help 'the heads of privatising enterprises to manage their enterprises during the privatisation process and with the formation of a controlling block of shares'.

of their proxies once they discovered that the proxies would be assigned to Komarov. After a series of heated exchanges Martov and about half those present walked out of the meeting, announcing that they would hold an alternative shareholders' meeting later in the month. In his absence Martov was denounced by Komarov and dismissed from the Board, on the grounds that he no longer worked at Plastmass. A series of other proposals of the General Director were overwhelmingly endorsed by those remaining, who held proxies for 78 per cent of the voting shares, and the meeting closed following questions from the floor, most of which were complaints from workers regarding their pay.

The situation in the enterprise following the meeting remained very tense. In an attempt to restore his prestige among the workforce Komarov visited all the main shops, talking to the assembled workers for up to two hours, criticising Martov's 'mini-monetarism' and making extravagant promises to settle the workers' principal grievances by increasing wages, distributing shares to pensioners and guaranteeing an apartment to everyone on the waiting list within two years. Komarov also gave a long interview to explain his position on prime-time local TV, rebutting claims that he was over-paid, denying that there had been major redundancies at Plastmass, stressing the high wages of the workers, and particularly the extensive housing programme and the policy of housing sales which benefited not only Plastmass employees but residents of the city as a whole. At the same time, opponents of Komarov were transferred or sent on long business trips, threatened with dismissal and loss of privileges.

In May 1993 Martov's two leading allies in the administration were sacked. The first was the deputy chief engineer, who had a reputation for independence and whom Martov had invited to head the conflict with Komarov. The second was the senior specialist of the engineering centre, a man who had worked at Plastmass for 30 years, including twelve years (1978–90) as chief engineer, who knew the plant like the back of his hand, and who had a very high reputation among the workers. With these two removed, Martov had no open supporters left within the administration.

Martov's alternative shareholders' meeting was a flop. A shareholders' petition circulated among the workforce before the meeting got only a 3 per cent response because it was necessary for people to identify themselves, and the administration threatened to sack anybody who got involved. The 250 people who gathered at the alternative meeting held fewer than 5 per cent of the shares, many of those being held by former employees who now worked for Martov's firm and by pensioners. Following this failure, Martov's alliance with the 'populists' collapsed, the latter now allying with Komarov's political opponents and seeking to have the privatisation of Plastmass declared illegal on the basis of the improper formulation of its founding documents.

As a result of this failure Martov changed tacks. First, he launched unsuccessful proceedings through the courts to declare Komarov's share purchase and the refusal of the Board to sell shares to Martov illegal and to annul the decisions of the shareholders' conference on the grounds that the proxies had not been notarised and Komarov's opponents had been excluded. The court first met on 2 April, but the hearing was postponed since Komarov did not turn up. The same thing happened three more times, until the case was finally resolved in Komarov's favour on 7 May, a decision confirmed on appeal on 13 July. Second, the *oblast* soviet established a commission to investigate the legality of privatisation in the *oblast*, and selected Plastmass as its first case. This was hardly surprising since Komarov was a leader of the opposition democratic block in the soviet, and had stood against the regional political boss, Aman Tuleev, for the position of chairman of the soviet. Martov was invited to join the commission, but this was a little awkward since he had drawn up all the privatisation documents in the first place, so his levelling ally took his place. However, Komarov simply refused to recognise the authority of the commission, which had no clear juridical powers. When the Commission visited Komarov he refused to produce any documents and told them 'fuck off the lot of you'. The chair of the commission produced his accreditation as a people's deputy, so Komarov produced his in return and threw the commission off the premises. However, the case was hardly likely to have succeeded since the documents had all been interrogated minutely throughout the process of privatisation.

Having failed to make progress through democratic and legal channels, Martov began to try to get control by buying up Plastmass shares. Throughout the summer of 1993 there was a war of advertisements in the local press, as Martov's firm Trast and the Plastmass Board offered to buy up shares at steadily increasing prices, with the Board revaluing the shares to a price of 40,000, and Trast offering 65,000, with the Board repeatedly issuing statements that all share purchases through intermediaries, including Trast, were invalid. Meanwhile

Komarov escalated his propaganda campaign against Martov and Trast, and took measures against known Martov supporters at the level of line management, not having any way of knowing how many shares Martov now controlled, or what he intended doing with them. However, Martov withdrew from the battle in the autumn of 1993, declaring that Plastmass no longer interested him, and that he was now concentrating on building up his own firm, which was prospering and diversifying, establishing new subsidiaries, with Martov himself becoming head of the regional branch of a large Russian industrial-investment fund. Trast no longer actively bought up shares, but was willing to buy them if workers came into the office.

Komarov's political opponents continued to take advantage of the conflict in Plastmass. At the end of October 1993 a new conflict erupted with the *oblast* administration. On privatisation Plastmass's housing had been transferred to a commercial enterprise which went bankrupt in the summer, apparently as a result of massive fraud, and so was unable to maintain the housing stock. Kislyuk, the chief of the *oblast* administration, pressed Komarov to support the firm financially to avert a housing crisis. Komarov insisted that this was not his problem, and it should be resolved through the courts. Kislyuk replied that the administration had levers to press the enterprise, and indeed the *oblast* administration sent in waves of experienced investigators to check on violations of tax, accounting, pollution, energy and every other kind of regulation. In the end the dispute was resolved administratively, with the transfer of both the housing and Plastmass's city centre swimming pool to the municipal authorities.

At the end of 1993 Komarov became heavily involved in political activity. In October he was elected acting president of a body representing directors of privatised enterprises, replacing Gaidar, as the basis of a further attempt to make a political career, his previous attempts to advance up both the ministerial and political hierarchies having been thwarted. According to his own associates, Komarov felt that he had long since outgrown the framework of his own firm, which he saw only as a stepping stone to higher things. In the run-up to the December election Komarov tried unsuccessfully to get on to the election list of the Movement for Democratic Reforms. He then transferred his allegiance to the 'government party', Russia's Choice, mobilising the majority of managers to collect signatures on behalf of its candidates, with the result that Gaidar, on his one-day visit to Kemerovo during the election campaign, held his meeting with

Russia's Choice candidates at Plastmass. Although Komarov, against many people's expectations, did not put forward his own name as a candidate to the regional legislative assembly, it was thought that he had not given up his political ambitions.

Many observers expected the stand-off between Martov and Komarov to come to an end with the annual shareholders' meeting on 16 April 1994. However, Martov and most of his supporters stayed away from the meeting, having decided it was pointless to continue the struggle since, in the words of one of his supporters, 'the weakest goes to the wall'. There were also reports that Martov had been offered a deal on the eve of the meeting, that if he did not attend he would be given help in dealing with some of his debtors. Nevertheless, Komarov showed in his behaviour at the meeting that he still regarded Martov as his main enemy and principal problem, his final speech being littered with derogatory comments about Martov, his firm and his associates, for example:

> I could name those who have placed their trust in him [meaning workers who had invested vouchers and money in the firm Trast], but I will not dishonour them. Well, dishonour is too strong a word. I won't name them. But many people would like to do so.

During April and May a series of muck-raking articles on Trast appeared in the factory newspaper.

Meanwhile Komarov reversed most of the managerial reforms which had been introduced by Martov. Although diversification continued, and the research institute was integrated into the main enterprise, Komarov reverted to the traditional style of management, ending the regular consultative meetings, forcing out independently minded managers and bringing in placemen, with loyalty to Komarov being the only criterion of preferment. Martov's replacement as chief economist was another academic brought in from a very radical joint-stock company which repaired shoes, and Komarov himself took over direct responsibility for financial and economic matters, with sometimes disastrous consequences.

The result was a very considerable weakening of the Plastmass management, both in removing competent managers and in undermining the authority of senior management in the eyes of both line managers and workers. The conflict between Martov and Komarov further increased the already substantial distrust of management on the part of the workers. Where workers would say 'they cheat us', they now say 'they cheat us always in every way'. The outcome is not so much an increase in overt conflict, as an increase in the degree of passive resistance to any actions and initiatives of management. Similarly the conflict dispelled any illusions among the workers that their shareownership gave them any effective right to participate in decision-making, and brought home to them their real status as hired labourers.

In an attempt to restore his authority among the workers Komarov reverted to the traditional rhetoric and practices of paternalistic management. Komarov's change of policy was reflected in a sharp reversal of priorities in the use of profits for 1993. While the plan had been to allocate two-thirds of profits directly to the development of production, in fact only one-third of the sharply reduced profits was used for this purpose, with a number of construction projects being frozen. Meanwhile, the allocation to consumption and social development was increased from a planned 17 per cent to an actual 30 per cent, with the plan for 1994 increasing the allocation further to a total of 71 per cent, including a massive increase in housing construction. The result of this reassertion of paternalism was to undermine any tendency for workers to develop their own independent organisations to represent and defend their interests, although they have a strong sense of 'them and us' and insist that the difficulties of the enterprise are not their concern, nor a reason not to pay adequate wages, since it is management's job to manage.

In the wake of the conflict between Komarov and Martov the role of the Board was reduced to virtually zero, not meeting at all for the first three months of 1994. Martov and five of his followers on the Board were dismissed from Plastmass during 1993 which meant, following an illegal decision of the 1993 shareholders' meeting that only employees could be Board members, that they had to leave the Board and were not replaced. With the removal of Martov and the downgrading of the Board the traditional Soviet principles of one-man management and a rigidly hierarchical management structure were restored.

1993 proved the low point of Plastmass's reform experience. 1994 saw a stabilisation of production which, with a continued sharp drop of almost 20 per cent in the size of the labour force (mostly made up of workers, plus a big cut in the employees in kindergartens), was associated with an increase in labour productivity of 17 per cent, although profits remained depressed at only 7.5 per cent of prime costs. The recovery continued through 1995, with employment falling by a further ten per cent, while production increased by ten per cent over the first ten months with the introduction of new kinds of products on the basis of imported equipment to make simple plastic pressings and a new line to process wood pulp. However, these new products were introduced in the traditional way, with little reference to the marketing department and economic service which had lost power and status with Martov's departure. In 1995 Plastmass was the first large enterprise in the region to buy the land on which it stood. Nevertheless, Plastmass was by no means out of the woods. Production was still only one third of its 1990 level, and continued to be very irregular. About two-thirds of sales were by barter, there were still acute shortages of working capital and wages were regularly paid one or two months late.

IMPACT OF THE CHANGES AT SHOP LEVEL: A CASE STUDY

As part of our research we have focused on changes at shop level, in particular in shop 11 which makes phenol-formaldehyde resin, which was itself a pioneer of reform. At the beginning of 1994 the shop employed 150 people, of whom 15 were managers and specialists. The shop works round-the-clock with four brigades working two twelve-hour shifts a day. In addition, on the day shift two brigades of fitters work on equipment repair, there is one brigade of electricians, one brigade of fitters to clean the machines, known as the 'wild brigade', and various auxiliary workers, including laggers and laboratory assistants.

The structure of the shop has been subject to frequent change: following the separation of shops into independent subdivisions from 1992, individual sections were regularly transferred to the neighbouring shop 1, of which shop 11 had previously been a part, and then brought back again. Each of these transfers was dictated by senior management and was associated with a 'restructuring' of personnel and even conflicts. In particular, for two years after the division of the shops (in 1988) a major conflict over pay arose: workers of shop 11 received less than those of shop 1 (with whom all comparisons were made 'according to old memories'), despite their higher labour productivity. The instigator of many of these conflicts with other shops and with the administration was the chief of shop 11: the workers in the shop link almost all the structural and personnel changes in their shop with the personality of their chief. The shop was the first to begin the process of structural change based on the reduction and upgrading of the labour force, without any reference to the ideas of the chief economist, as the shop chief loves to point out.

The shop has sacked between 70 and 80 people for drinking since 1986, cleared out flooded cellars in the raw materials section, broadened the training of machine operators so that now any operator can work on any retort and can even carry out minor repairs. This complete interchangeability of the workers makes for a much more flexible system of planning and management. Since 1990 there has been a steady reduction in the proportion of ITR in the shop, mainly at the expense of shift foremen and section chiefs as the various sections were integrated into the shop. The shop chief also launched his own 'innovatory onslaught' in the technological field.

The working conditions in the shop are dreadful. Most of the equipment is old, with endless leaks and breakages which have to be fixed with whatever parts and materials are to hand. The whole area is covered in dust, littered with debris and permeated by noxious fumes. Pipelines snake around in all directions, with nobody apparently knowing what goes where since they have been modified and patched up so often.

Work has begun to set up an experimental section to develop the continuous production of resin, rather than the previous periodic production method. The shop has developed its own recipes for making new kinds of resins, and the shop is actively working with prospective consumers of these resins in other enterprises. In working out new recipes, and up-dating old ones, the shop technologists are aiming to replace existing expensive resins with other cheaper ones, allowing considerable economies. At the beginning of 1994 the shop began to reduce the phenol content of its finished products with a view to attaining world quality standards.[14]

Although production was only at 20 per cent of capacity over the period 1992–4, the shop managed to keep afloat without the long breaks in production experienced by other shops. However, the scale

[14] This is a classic example of the market reinforcing the traditional Soviet autarchic tendency for every enterprise and every shop to reinvent the wheel.

of redundancy and the uncertain future demoralised the workforce. By the middle of 1993 the shop management felt that the labour force was at its optimum size, but by September, following further job losses, they felt that it had reached the critical point at which the shop would not be able to accommodate even a modest increase in production and at which technical safety was seriously compromised. In November 1993 the shop found itself in the position of having raw materials and orders available, but of being able to work only in batches because of the shortage of operators. The shop chief complained:

> There are not the people to work on all the different kinds of equipment. Here we have tanks with various kinds of raw material, but we only work on one kind, for example only on resol, and then we will work on another.

At the end of 1993 it was particularly the highly qualified auxiliary workers (fitters) who were leaving, but by the beginning of 1994 even the operatives were leaving so that the shop, like others in the factory, was short of workers despite the dramatic fall in production.

The other problems of the shop are principally economic. As in other enterprises, the mechanisms by which the wages fund are determined are completely mysterious. While the formal procedures are quite simple, closer study raises more questions than it provides answers. The ability to 'create wages' for the shop is a test of the professional skill of the shop chief, and a matter of his greatest pride which he prefers to keep to himself. According to the shop chief, the workers in shop 11 feel that their wages are inadequate. Although their wages are on a level with those of other shops, the shop undertakes a lot of activities on its own account, using its own technological and financial resources to develop its production capacity, so there is a feeling that the wages fund received by the shop is inadequate.

In general the wages fund of a particular shop at Plastmass is determined by formula as the product of the volume of gross output in accounting prices, the wage norm and a factor expressing the degree of plan fulfilment, plus a bonus made up of profits from additional activities and the insurance fund. Each item in the formula poses its own problems for the shop chief.

The volume of gross output is based on the following month's deliveries and is in theory limited only by the production capacity of the shop, although in practice it depends on the planned volume of sales, which is not under the control of the shop but depends on the marketing department, market conditions and the solvency of consumers. Thus, in effect, the shop still works to a plan handed down from the administration, although this might fluctuate wildly and might turn out to be far below the shop's production capacity, a source of considerable discontent on the part of the workers who had been promised that under the new system they would be paid according to their work.

The wage norm is different for each shop and here everything depends on the skill and persistence of the shop chief and on the character of his relations with 'the General' (the General Director). As the chief of shop explained:

> Recently I managed to secure a revision of the wage norm for the shop, increasing it by 15–17 per cent, and how much time that took! The chief of shop N reached such an agreement with the General, they do not depend on the results of their work, everybody feeds them. You can't break through anywhere, the approach is abstract, nobody ever explains anything to anybody, there is paper, but there are no discussions!

The scale of the income of the shop from additional activities (that is, from the sale of additional products to other shops or enterprises) is obviously a matter for the shop management. They can always increase this part of the wages fund by manipulating resources, but any gains under this heading tend to be evened out across the firm, because that is where the overall wages fund is determined for the firm as a whole. The result is that, in the opinion of the workers of some of the shops, the situation arises in which one shop 'feeds' the other shops, receiving equal compensation with them. According to the shop economists, in practice wages are 'adjusted' by the administration of the firm according to the staff list of the shop and hardly ever vary by more than 10 per cent one way or another from this. Despite the fact that the wages fund is calculated on the basis of the work done by the shop (the volume of gross output), the administration of the firm has all sorts of levers to manipulate this fund.

For example, the shop is set a fairly high plan target for the month, the percentage of whose fulfilment will affect the wages fund. This would make sense if the fulfilment of the plan depended exclusively on the diligence of the workers of the shop. However, in the face of difficulties with sales and in the absence of any kind of long-term sales contracts, the key point is not planned production but achieved sales. The reactors in the shop are only started up when orders for production arrive, or a supplier arrives personally from another enterprise, and nobody can say how much the following shift will make. It is inevitable that the plan will not be fulfilled. It is at this point that the administration of the firm makes a 'big gesture': an order is issued declaring 'indemnification for non-fulfilment of the plan is issued to shop N to the extent of X per cent of the total non-fulfilment'. The percentage of indemnification is arbitrary, a matter for negotiation between the economic services and the management of the shop, and can vary from 50 per cent up to 90 per cent of the shortfall. Favoured shops have a good chance of getting maximum indemnification for their shortfall, while a disloyal shop chief risks receiving only a pittance. The chief of shop 11 falls into the latter category, so the economic position of the shop cannot be called brilliant, but the wages of the workers are stable and high.

Such sops from above became particularly widespread and acquired a 'baronial' colouring following Martov's departure at the beginning of 1993. Whereas under Martov the shop economists were regularly consulted by the firm's economists and participated in economic decision-making, even if in a subordinate role, with his departure decisions were once more simply handed down from above.

The social insurance fund, which comprises 25 per cent of the profits of the shop, is the shop chief's patrimony. Manipulation of the social insurance fund is his principal lever of influence over his subordinates, so naturally he has an interest in maximising this part of the fund. There are several ways of doing this, one of which is the imposition of punishments. As a foreman explained:

> In the past there was usually only one monetary punishment – payment at the minimum level. Now they use the so-called KTU [coefficient of labour participation – a coefficient applied to determine the individual wage] – for example, to pay only 10–20 per cent of the bonus. And if you take into account the fact that the basic is 5,000, but the bonus 11–15,000, then this is appreciable. But KTU is used only as a fine, it is hardly ever used to increase pay. Apart from that, a certain percentage of the pay is deducted for the social insurance fund – this is a kind of reserve, from which wages can be paid during periods of slack production. Money paid in fines goes into this same fund, so that the shop chief has an interest in imposing fines. And if the reserve is not used for a long time the money accumulated is paid out as compensation.

The shop management uses monetary levers of influence not only to achieve production tasks, but also to secure and demonstrate his status. A foreman, whom the shop chief considered guilty of a minor act of insubordination, explained how the chief got his revenge:

> According to the instructions I should sign in the journal at the end of the shift that the shift has handed over. Usually I always do this, but somehow I had forgotten. The chief saw that nothing had been signed – 'disorder! violation!' – and he punished me by imposing a KTU of 0.2. Formally he has the right to do so, but I know why he did it to me.

The fact that such 'wage payment' episodes always involve the shop chief and not the shop economists is not accidental. Although the role and influence of the economic department at the level of the enterprise was considerably increased by the management changes, at shop level very little changed. The status and authority of middle level specialists remained much lower than that of line managers, although informally they often play the role of 'shadow' of the shop chief.

On the whole, for workers the only real force able to exert a significant influence on the level of their pay is the shop management, with its wide-ranging powers both to impose fines and award bonuses. And these opportunities have considerably expanded recently. At the beginning of 1994, in particular, shop 11 was reorganised into a so-called 'shop-brigade', with all four shift brigades combined into one because of the uneven distribution of work, and so of pay, between the shifts. The shop chief himself served as the brigadier, which considerably increased his leverage. As one of the shift foreman commented:

> All the money is dumped into a common heap, and the chief sets the KTU for everyone, and in general he does whatever he wants. Whereas in the past the brigade set the KTU and the chief only approved it (well, he also corrected it, certainly), now, without even a scrap of paper from the brigades, he just gives to each person however much he wants. A kind of situation can arise with the KTU when, for example, I might have boiled up resol, which is a heavy operation, for which an increased KTU is fixed. But I do not know whether he has taken this into account or not – you do not climb up to the office to check it out every time. Especially because the wages are paid late and you cannot remember what you did when. Of course you can go and look in the logs and see what the situation is, but you don't get around to it.

The line managers themselves create this situation. This provides them with some compensation for the significant reduction in their status in comparison with the factory managers.

In every other respect shop 11 is considered 'difficult', 'inconvenient'. Its management takes a position independent of the administration on many issues, and among the workers there are many competent, energetic and simply 'bright' people. Even in 1992 the shop chief declared himself to be dissatisfied with the work of the

Board, characterising himself and some other members as an 'independent minority'. At the 1993 shareholders' meeting his short statement was presented as 'constructive criticism', but inflicted the most serious damage to the position of the General Director. He was the only shop chief to attend the alternative shareholders' meeting ten days later, and the workers of shop 11 were the most active and well-organised team, appearing on the platform more often than any of the others. The Organising Committee for the Democratic Reform of Plastmass pinned its hopes particularly on the workers of shop 11 as its core support, a pocket of opposition among the industrial collectives. For various reasons these hopes were only partially justified.

The most important reason was the attempt of the shop management to withdraw from the mechanism of intra-enterprise equalisation by creating a small enterprise on the basis of the shop. By the autumn of 1992 the documents had already been authorised and a bank account opened. However, with Martov's departure the General Director at first held up the registration of the enterprise, and then buried the idea completely. The creation of clear and fully documented economic relations between the shop and the firm (even though it would remain in many respects still dependent on the latter) would have meant a fundamental reduction in the levers of manipulation of one of the largest and most profitable divisions of Plastmass, which the present administration of the firm simply could not allow. Thus it may be that the transition of the shop chief to a position of open opposition in February 1993 was the result of his seeing this as the last chance to achieve the economic independence of his shop, gambling on Martov's return to manage the firm. However, the revolution did not take place and the active participants in the February meetings have either been burnt out and resigned themselves to the situation or have been compelled to keep quiet under the strong pressure of the administration. The shop chief himself has been removed from the housing queue on a specious pretext and his wife, who works in the factory administration, was threatened with redundancy. As the chief himself confessed at the end of 1993:

> I could have left ... but I have no moral right to do so, I have retreated into my shell, they have pressed me into the corner ... I did everything so that my people in this shop would not be cattle, and now they think ... the General openly said to me: 'we are not going to work with you'.

In general the mood of workers in shop 11 in 1994, as in the rest of the firm, was completely sceptical and pessimistic. The absence of a programme of work for the future weighs especially heavily. In the words of one shift foreman:

> Now we keep working somehow, on demand. Just as a year ago, sometimes we are stopped, sometimes we are working. It would be better to work full-time for a few weeks and then everybody could be laid off for a month. But at the moment we are neither stopped nor are we working. It is terrible.

The crisis of non-payment led to the introduction of the payment of wages in the form of credit notes exchangeable in the enterprise's own shops, in place of money. This led to a further burst of discontent. However, there is none of the earlier pressure, moreover the workers understand the difficult position of the shop chief, which has been compounded by the personal tragedy of the death of his son in the spring of 1994, and have not taken any serious steps against the administration of the firm because the shop management will be suspected of inciting such action and then the shop would lose its strong chief. The separation of the mass of the workers from the shop specialists has increased somewhat, but the authority of the shop chief remains fairly high.

For all the respect of the workers for the competence and initiative of the shop management, there is no trust or understanding between them. The situation at the top of the enterprise ('there everyone deceives one another, and us too') is reflected in relations within the shop ('they also will not forget about themselves'). Thus workers complain about management's neglect of the equipment:

> The experimental equipment is not everything. We still have German reactors from 1943 in the shop – and it is only our skill that keeps them working! On the second floor there are two reactors, but they only work by a miracle, they won't stand up to the pressure tests. And they only change the pipelines, for the sake of appearances ... the working conditions – only dust.

At the level of the primary work collectives the 'macro-politics' of the firm have had little impact, and even the most energetic external processes are smoothed out in the depths of the enterprise and have little impact on the social processes there. In Plastmass now 'perestroika from above' has come to a stop, while 'perestroika from below' was never carried out.

THE STRUGGLE FOR REFORM

What are the implications of this story for the reform process?

Martov had been the driving force behind the development of Plastmass, given his head by Komarov and building what looked like a strong and cohesive management team. While Martov drove full tilt for reform, Komarov provided a steadying influence. Yet when Komarov withdrew his support, Martov's entire strategy collapsed and he found himself isolated.

Why did Komarov withdraw his support? In part it was undoubtedly because of Martov's impending bid for power, so that Komarov needed to consolidate his own position. However, behind this lay the growing dissatisfaction within Plastmass at Martov's strategy as wages fell behind prices and those of neighbouring enterprises, as sales collapsed, as insecurity of both workers and ITR increased with the threat of redundancy. The rejection of enterprise paternalism and the transition to market methods was all very well when it could guarantee high wages, but as the economic benefits were eroded there was growing pressure to return to the old system of authoritarian paternalism. Thus, when the confrontation came to a head even Martov's close managerial associates and all but one of the shop chiefs unequivocally supported Komarov. Meanwhile, neither Komarov nor Martov enjoyed much support among the ordinary workers.

The conflict both expressed and intensified divisions within the enterprise which had been opened up by Martov's rationalisation programme. A survey which we conducted in the enterprise just before the February 1993 shareholders' meeting showed that over half the workers supported Martov's proposal to submit the Director to re-election, with only ten per cent opposed (the exact reverse of the response of managers), and only one in eight workers would vote for the General Director's re-election, as against three quarters of managers and 40 per cent of ITR who would vote for him. None of the managers questioned admitted to planning to vote for Martov, but almost as many of the workers said that they would vote for him as would vote for the General Director and the same number again would vote for Martov's temporary 'levelling' ally. However, the general mood of the workers on the shop floor was one of distrust and dissatisfaction with management as a whole, with an increasingly explicit mood of 'them and us' separating workers from both managers and from ITR. This appeared in our survey, in which almost three quarters of workers were dissatisfied or completely dissatisfied with the work of the management, with only one in eight satisfied (40 per cent of ITR and almost a quarter of managers were also dissatisfied), and almost half of the workers did not support any of the potential candidates for the post of General Director. 'It makes no difference to me who is going to cheat me, the Director or the Chief Economist' was a typical comment.

While 45 per cent of the managers saw problems connected with sales difficulties as among the most acute facing the enterprise (48 per cent pinpointed the need to change the product range, 31 per cent reduction of the labour force and 29 per cent the cutting of costs), 65 per cent of the workers identified low wages and 75 per cent pointed to pay differentiation as among the most serious problems (40 per cent referred to sales difficulties, but only 2 per cent referred to cost-cutting and 18 per cent to labour force cuts as among the most serious problems).

The sharp division between workers and managers was not simply the result of an inadequate management strategy, of a failure to attend to the concerns of the ordinary employees or to develop an adequate institutional framework for handling industrial relations. The underlying problem was the failure of the enterprise to establish the conditions for long-term survival in a market environment. This was not for want of managerial initiative and determination, nor a result of the undoubted failure to transform production relations, since production relations could not be transformed without a fundamental upgrading of production technology which would make possible a more rational organisation of labour. In the last analysis the failure of reform at Plastmass has to come down to the failure to put in place the missing link of the reform process, the massive investment programme for which the firm was never able to find the resources. But finally we have to ask whether this was not always a pipe-dream? What prospect could there ever be for profitable investment in a chemical enterprise in the middle of Siberia, with archaic technology, outdated skills, no local sources of raw materials and limited local markets for its products?

THE LEGACY OF REFORM

Martov's departure and the re-establishment of the system of one-man management made it clear that his reforms had been as superficial as Plastmass's prosperity had been short lived. Although there had been some managerial rationalisation, the further down the enterprise one went the less change there had been. At shop level there had been no significant changes in the forms of management or the organisation of production, and the ordinary workers were treated with even more contempt by the reformers than they had been by the traditional management. The brief success of Plastmass was purely and simply the result of its ability to exploit the privileges of a non-state enterprise in 1991 and its monopoly position in 1992.

The once much-trumpeted cuts in the labour force turned out on closer inspection to be less dramatic, although they hit some categories, such as pensioners and women workers disproportionately hard. The first round of cuts was largely accounted for by the fact that Plastmass only took over a part of its predecessor's activity, an affiliate in Novosibirsk and part of the social and welfare apparatus being separated from Plastmass. The second round of cuts was primarily a paper cut in the staff list, removing 'dead souls'. The third round of cuts involved primarily voluntary severance as skilled workers moved to better-paid jobs elsewhere and as employees of the research institute formed nominally independent small enterprises on the territory of the plant.

The financial results were not as good as they looked at first sight either, and those of 1993 were disastrous, because they were not based on inflation accounting. Although there were large provisions out of profits for the development of production, amortisation provision was minimal. Amortisation for 1992, for example, was only 77 million on sales of 6.7 billion roubles.

The reforms to the pay system, with sharply increasing differentials, produced no observable positive results in the commitment or work practices of ITR, while generating considerable resentment on the side of the workers. Similarly, the threat of redundancy bred divisions within the workforce, acrimony and suspicion, and a decline in morale, while the pay increases provided as compensation were rapidly eroded by inflation.

Through 1993 Komarov tried to consolidate his position by moving back to more traditional bureaucratic managerial methods, at least to the extent of reviving authoritarian-paternalism and raising the status of shop chiefs in relation to specialists (although Martov's replacement was another academic). The Director's first measure following the February shareholder's meeting was to declare a pay increase from 1 March which marginally reduced the differentials (workers received 20 per cent, ITR and employees only 15 per cent), a policy which was sustained throughout the year so that the relation between pay of ITR and workers fell from 2.35 in 1992 to 1.96 in 1993 and that between the pay of chiefs and workers from 3.13 to 2.35. Moreover, he followed a traditional policy of maintaining employment in the face of the fall in production at the expense of wages, which by June 1993 had fallen behind those in comparable enterprises in the city. As a result of low wages and the distrust and disillusionment that pervaded the enterprise Plastmass rapidly lost its skilled and experienced workers, to the extent that it had to resume recruitment in August 1993 for the first time in eighteen months. Moreover, it was also losing its most independent and enterprising employees as the Director put a premium on loyalty and passivity.

At one level the change of direction at Plastmass appears to be the result of a conflict of temperament and ambition. But underlying this conflict are more fundamental issues of management style and priorities. For Martov the rationalisation of the management structure was a means to the creation of a modern capitalist enterprise, the culmination of a long-term plan which he had worked on with his associates over almost a decade. For Komarov, however, it was only the means to the traditional end of building up the prestige of his enterprise and of his position as director. The two ambitions came into conflict with one another as tension mounted within the enterprise and as its economic position deteriorated. The competition to secure support at shop level then led both contending parties to undermine the possibilities of a radical restructuring by appealing to the traditional values of paternalism and egalitarianism.

This conflict equally indicates the limitations of Martov's plans. Martov was forced out just at the point at which economic pressures brought forward the need to undertake a more fundamental rationalisation of management, which would reach down to the shop floor level and perhaps enable Plastmass to compete in a market environment. However, for Martov the limit of such reforms was to integrate the research centre as the basis for the development of new products. This market-led managerialism did not address the more fundamental issue of the transformation of the social relations on which production was based.

Martov's managerial reorganisation was concerned strictly with the rationalisation of administrative structures, the structure and functions of management in relation to production remaining unchanged, so that Martov did not challenge the underlying social relations of production on the shop floor. However, his managerialist reforms created growing social tension by challenging workers' egalitarian expectations, and opened a gap between shop chiefs and senior management which eroded the loyalty of the former to the latter. The attempt to dismantle the authoritarian–paternalist structures of control removed the traditional means of handling such tension, and threatened to lead to increasingly overt social conflict. It was in this context that the confrontation between Martov and Komarov acquired a more fundamental strategic significance.

The net result of the reforms in Plastmass turned out to be surprisingly small and had very little to do with increasing productivity or orienting to a market economy. The main result was that managers enriched themselves by widening pay differentials and concentrating share-ownership, while attempting to keep the lid on workers' unrest with the carrot of piecemeal pay rises and the increasingly large stick of the threat of redundancy. We went in to Plastmass because we wanted to study a pioneer of capitalism in Russia. But what has actually emerged is strikingly similar to what is happening in state enterprises of every kind all over Russia.

CONCLUSION

The history of reform in Plastmass anticipates in microcosm the fate of the reform initiative in Russia as a whole. But it cannot be seen simply as a struggle between conservatives and reformers, any more than can the political drama in Moscow. Komarov is a leading member of the democratic block on the *oblast* soviet, and a vociferous opponent of its leader Aman Tuleev, who has built huge support in the *oblast* as a populist opponent of reform, rejoining the Communist Party in 1995 and leading it to over 50 per cent of the vote in the *oblast* in the December 1995 *duma* election. Komarov identifies himself unequivocally with the rhetoric of reform, of the transition to a capitalist system, and has done very well out of it himself. He insists that the enterprise should not be controlled by the labour collective, but that its director should be elected by the owners, with the trade union (which at Plastmass, as elsewhere, is a pocket union) representing the interests of the workers.

If Komarov was as committed as Martov to reform, why did the reform initiative fail? It was not for a lack of knowledge of capitalist systems of management, finance and accounting, because Plastmass had some of the best educated specialists in the *oblast*, and even in Russia, who really knew and understood their job. They followed, as best they could, the prescriptions of Western advisors. They restructured the management system, putting economists and financiers in power over engineers and technical specialists, with economics, finance and marketing dominating the management structure and strategic planning of the enterprise. They largely separated the welfare apparatus from the enterprise, massively cut the system of paternalistic distribution and ended the system of free allocation of housing, in favour of higher wages which would leave the workers free to choose how to spend their money. They increased differentials in favour of managers and technical staff to provide an appropriate system of incentives. They slimmed down the labour force by a nominal 35 per cent between 1990 and 1993 (over 50 per cent by the end of 1995). They retained the vast bulk of profits for the development of production. They contracted the range of products to specialise on their core activities. It is difficult to see what more they could have done to satisfy a Western consultant, within the limits of their objective circumstances.

Was it those objective circumstances that explained Plastmass's failure? Certainly economic and financial instability, the general collapse of production, the cutting of traditional economic links, inflation and the debt crisis explain the collapse of production. But at the same time the reform strategy itself exacerbated the problems faced by Plastmass in a number of ways. The most important external failure was that in abandoning its traditional economic and political commitments to municipal, regional and branch authorities and to supplier and customer enterprises, in favour of a purely market orientation, it left itself without a lifeline when the market collapsed. More conservative enterprises which maintain their traditional links find it much easier to call in obligations when difficulty strikes, to elicit subsidies and state contracts, to maintain supplies on credit, and to dispose of the product, whereas Plastmass was not only on its own, but had left a widespread legacy of antagonism.

Perhaps the more fundamental failure of the reform strategy was the antagonism that it provoked on the shop floor, which left a sullen and discontented, if silent, workforce which had lost any commitment it might have had to making a success of the enterprise, and whose traditional identification with the enterprise had been broken. This is not just a matter of bad personnel management, because a Soviet enterprise depends crucially for its success on the commitment and motivation of at least a core of workers who can keep production going, and this is particularly the case in an enterprise such as Plastmass with antiquated equipment and complex and diverse production processes. This workers' opposition did not find any direct expression, but it lay behind the growing disillusionment of middle management with the reform strategy, and so laid the grounds for the return to an authoritarian–paternalist populism on the part of Komarov.

There remains the question of whether a more radical restructuring of Plastmass might have proved more successful. After all, capitalism is meant to be about investing for the future, not maintaining the past. Perhaps if Plastmass had had the financial resources it could have invested in modern equipment to re-establish its competitive position in the European and even in export markets. But this then raises the question of how, faced with escalating transport costs, any enterprise in Western Siberia in any branch of production can be competitive in outside markets. Does Siberia have any place in a market economy at all?

3. Lenkon: Capitalism and Scientology

Veronika Kabalina, Galina Monousova and Valentina Vedeneeva

Lenkon was the first enterprise with which our research group made contact, so to speak, 'from the street'. At the end of the 1980s we still got research access to enterprises through the Party or trade union committee. This meant that research was limited to particular themes (for example, conflicts around production, workers' attitudes to change and so on). The criteria for the selection of enterprises were also traditional: branch of production, number of employees. We learned of the existence of Lenkon initially through its television advertising – it was probably the first industrial enterprise in Russia to advertise on television, something that is still rare. We saw the opportunity to research a dynamic new type of enterprise, so we telephoned and arranged a meeting with one of the senior managers. This initial openness of the enterprise and amenability of management to outside contacts was sustained throughout the period of our research, giving us unrestricted access to observe and to engage in dialogue with managers and workers at all levels.

The research continued with varying degrees of intensity from March 1991 to June 1995.[1] Over this period approximately 250 interviews were conducted with managers of various levels, specialists, workers, men and women, old and new employees, veteran and young workers, as well as several group discussions with workers and a survey on aspects of social tension. We spent many hours simply observing the life of production units, or following a foreman or section chief for the day, and participating in meetings as observers. We read through hundreds of pages of documentary materials to which we had access.

1 The first fifteen interviews were carried out with workers in March 1991 by Alla Nazimova and Galina Monousova.

In laying out the results of our research we have tried to follow the chronology of events and the logic of changes in the enterprise. We have devoted the first pages to the story of privatisation since, on the one hand, the changes in the enterprise began with the change in the form of ownership. On the other hand, privatisation was a necessary condition for management to acquire the freedom to carry through the transformation of the enterprise. However, the direction of reorganisation of the enterprise and the limits of the freedom of management in the period during which we carried out our research, in our opinion, were defined primarily by external factors.

Structuring the material for publication, we have tried to reflect the sequence of changes 'from top to bottom', beginning with changes in the relations of the enterprise with external agents, then in functions connected with responses to the developing market situation (sales, supply, finance), and only then changes in production and employment. Alongside this we have focused on those processes which were typical of precisely this enterprise (in some cases unique). Lenkon carried out many experiments with organisational restructuring and frequently altered the payment system, so we have described the changes in these areas in some detail.

Recognising the dominant influence of external factors on the reorganisation of the company, we consider the process of adaptation of the enterprise to new challenges as a result of the interaction of the principal characters – the heads of the company, managers and workers – which most often appear in the form of conflict. We pay a lot of attention to the role of particular individuals, and especially to the personality of the president of the company, the initiator of all the changes until his tragic death early in 1995; to conflicts within the management team which accompanied management reorganisation, but also to those changes which occurred under pressure from the workers.

The small size of the enterprise has not only allowed us to study labour relations in all the main industrial subdivisions of the enterprise in some depth, but also to show the variety of their models within the framework of one enterprise. We have tried to show that this variety is determined by the technology, the composition of the labour force, the management style of its chief, as well as by the compromise concerning its status reached between higher and line management.

Finally, we have described on the basis of our observations how institutional and organisational changes affect the position and identification of ordinary workers, their attitudes to management, the possibilities of conflict and the mechanisms of its institutionalisation.

GENERAL FEATURES OF THE ENTERPRISE

Lenkon was one of the first state enterprises in Russia to go down the road of privatisation. The company was based on a light engineering plant which was established in Moscow for the production of industrial ventilators at the beginning of the 1940s through the amalgamation of a group of craft workshops which had been set up on the site in 1938. The basic structure of the enterprise was laid down at that time, with a press-stamp section (21 people), a mechanical section (21 people), a tool-making section (28 people) a section assembling medium fans (52 people), a small-batch section (36 people) and a repair section (24 people). The factory was incorporated into an association of related enterprises producing equipment mainly for the construction industry based in Khar'kov. For this reason it came under the jurisdiction of the USSR Ministry of Road-Building Machinery, although the enterprise has never had anything to do with roads or road-building.

The principal raw materials used by the enterprise are sheet metal, used for making the fans and casings of ventilators, and electric motors, which make up the bulk of the cost of the ventilators. The enterprise received supplies of metal mainly from Armenia and Azerbaidzhan, and motors from Yaroslavl', Vladimir, Omsk, Kemerovo and from enterprises in Ukraine, with which there were close industrial links. The enterprise did not experience any difficulties with the supply of raw materials and intermediate products.

In the middle of the 1980s the enterprise went through a difficult period: the plan was not fulfilled for several years in succession, and managers were frequently changed. The factory was not large, the number of employees never exceeding 500. The factory's products were technologically unsophisticated, and their production did not require skilled workers, so that it tended to recruit workers who could not find jobs anywhere else. The factory had a reputation as, in the words of its personnel director, 'a cesspit, employing every drunk and layabout in the district', characterised by very high labour turnover. The equipment was hardly ever updated, the proportion of manual labour was high, workers, in their words, 'basically worked like donkeys [*kuvaldoi*]'.

In 1987 an energetic new director arrived, a 39-year-old instructor from the industrial department of the *raion* committee of the CPSU, Aleksandr Minenko. His appearance at the factory marked the beginning of a new era. He began by asking all the line managers, down to the level of foremen, to recruit new workers by contacting 'all those people who can be useful to the factory, who do not work here any more'. Several specialists who had worked at the factory in the past responded to the call, and the new director created conditions in which they were able to work independently and creatively. Young engineers were recruited to head the production sections and were given the opportunity to display some initiative in the organisation of production. An experimental design bureau was established which, together with a newly formed brigade for new technology, began to design and produce experimental kinds of products. The initiative of the new chief was noted 'above', in the ministry: the department which was concerned with new technology gave the factory a subsidy to develop new models of machines for the whole branch.

However, the most dramatic initiative of the young director, which had the most radical influence on the fate of the enterprise, was the change in the form of property. The enterprise was one of the first in the Soviet Union to go through the process of privatisation, its president being acclaimed by no less an authority than *The Economist* as one of the 'ambitious class nimbly skipping from a career in communism to the pioneering of Soviet capitalism' (18 May, 1991, p. 102). Initially the labour collective bought out the enterprise, but then this common ownership was transformed into private property with the creation of the joint-stock company Lenkon.

Our research focused on four sections which form part of a single technological cycle. The design service draws up plans for the toolmaking section (IU) which prepares the tools needed to work on a particular model of fan. The press-stamp section (PShU) prepares the parts of the future fans for assembly (body, mounting, frame and so on). The assembly section for medium fans (USSV) and the small-batch section (UMS) assemble the finished products. The technical preparation department (OTPP) prepares the whole technological process.

THE STORY OF PRIVATISATION

The story of privatisation began with the transformation of the state enterprise into a co-operative. On 1 July 1989 the factory left the structure of the USSR Ministry of Road-Building Machinery and leased the property with a right to subsequent purchase. How was the factory converted into a co-operative? An agreement was made with the ministry to buy the factory by instalments. Although the factory's employees had in practice become leaseholders, juridically they avoided the status of a leased state enterprise, preferring to operate under the cover of the Law on Co-operatives. This appealed to the management because it gave them greater freedom from the conservative constraints of the Labour Code. They also expected, as a newly formed co-operative, to receive tax privileges, but in fact they never got them. The enterprise had to pay 25 per cent of its entire income in taxation which, eating up almost all of the profits, quickly led the co-operative to the brink of financial collapse.

There were other reasons for the enterprise's initial difficulties. Above all, the factory inherited from the state enterprise extortionate payments for its fixed capital assets (which was now called rent). The management came to the conclusion that the only way out was to break the leasehold relation with the state by buying all the property ahead of schedule. This was what they did, and in May 1990 the co-operative became free.

The Finance Ministry offered the company a loan to buy the fixed and circulating capital (at residual value), but only on the most exorbitant terms. However, since the products made by the factory were in short supply the enterprise's traditional customers were willing to help out, lending a total of seven million roubles. In particular, one large Leningrad industrial association provided an interest-free credit of three million roubles over ten years, in exchange for which it was guaranteed a stable supply of the factory's products. Thus it was the factory's monopoly position that secured it the preferential interest-free credit.

Was this credit really free of charge? We should remember that, at the time when the factory made this bargain, it sold its products at prices fixed by the state. But the buyers of scarce products always had to make some kind of additional payment to get hold of them: either to give the supplier some equally scarce product in return, or spend time waiting in a queue, or pay money to move up the queue and so on. In this case the additional payment took the form of the provision of interest-free credit, which secured future deliveries of the factory's products.

Having successfully coped with the financial aspects of the transformation of the enterprise, the initiators of privatisation ran into internal difficulties, connected with the passive opposition of the employees.

Initially an initiative group of 30 people was established representing all the factory services and it was around this group, under pressure from below, that a co-operative was formed. However, when the share subscriptions were gathered, only 87 of the 475 people working in the enterprise became members of the co-operative. The remainder said that they did not object to becoming members of the co-operative, but they did not have the money to pay for their shares. Thus it was decided to create the co-operative on the basis of the most complicated section, the press-stamp section which made the parts, whose work affected the work of the whole factory. To do this they had to replace the section chief, who was opposed to the co-operative, and they raised the salaries of the workers in that section.

Everybody who wanted to become a member of the co-operative had to pay 350 roubles, of which 50 roubles was the initial fee to join the co-operative and 300 roubles was the initial shareholding, the basis on which future dividends would be paid. This might seem a surprisingly low sum, but this share had no particular economic substance. The initiators admitted that their aim was not to use this money to constitute any kind of founding capital of the co-operative. The main thing that they sought to achieve was to give people an interest in the success of their undertaking, having tied themselves to the enterprise with a 'monetary bond'. This 300 rouble share in fact fulfilled the role of a monetary pledge. The dividends declared on the basis of the results of the first quarter amounted to 60 roubles (80 per cent per annum), which had nothing to do with any real growth of the income of the enterprise but was simply a reward for the trust in management shown by those brave enough to have taken the plunge and food for thought for the less resolute. However, when these 87 people, having paid out for their shares, received their 20 per cent return for the first quarter, that is to say an additional 60 roubles on their pay for having invested 300, other people were attracted to the co-operative and came to hand over their money. The fact that wages in the press-stamp section, which was the basis of the co-operative, were almost twice as high as the average for the factory, also played its part.

In the end 200 people volunteered to join the co-operative. The remaining people preferred to continue to work as hired labour, not any more for the state, but for their own comrades. There is no evidence that any of those who did not join the co-operative experienced any material discrimination.

The co-operative had been created on the basis of a disorganised state enterprise, which in previous years had regularly received grants from the ministry. In its first year working as a co-operative the factory not only paid off its debts, but accumulated surplus funds in its account. As a co-operative the factory made profits of 13 million roubles, while the largest profit it had ever made as a state enterprise had been 3,000 roubles (at comparable prices). The volume of production increased by 25 per cent. Pay increased significantly – in the first half of 1990 the average monthly pay amounted to 407 roubles. The co-operative began to sell its products on Western markets and in the first year received 300,000 dollars in export earnings.

At this time the co-operative had a board of management and a Labour Collective Council (STK) at the same time. However, despite the fact that the management encouraged the workers to think of themselves as the owners of the enterprise, the workers were interested above all else in the level of their wages. It was precisely when the enterprise became a co-operative that it experienced one of its first overt collective conflicts. The majority of workers in the section which assembled medium fans signed a collective petition demanding an increase in their pay. This petition was handed to the president of the co-operative at a meeting, and he promised that this petition would be considered in the immediate future by the STK. But in fact the president himself took the documentation to the accountant and resolved the question together with the section chief. At the same time he talked to the brigadiers and the workers.

Establishment of the joint-stock company

After a year the management decided that it was not satisfied with being in the position of 'industrial *kolkhozniki*', formal owners of an indivisible property, and on the initiative of the director of the factory transformed the co-operative into the closed joint-stock company Lenkon. The founding meeting was held on 6 September 1990, the founders being those employed in the enterprise (at that time amounting to 513 people). The joint-stock company also included a factory at Kryukovskii, a village outside Moscow, producing similar products, which joined the company in 1991, and a number of 'small enterprises' (in 1992 there were seven).

It was decided to issue shares to the full value of the fixed and circulating capital, amounting to 6.5 million roubles (at the official exchange rate at the end of 1990 this amounted to 3.6 million dollars) and to sell them to the employees of the enterprise.

Distribution of shares

It was planned to sell shares by a method similar to that used by American ESOPs to sell shares in the enterprise to its employees, which avoided the difficulties raised by the fact that the workers did not have the money to pay for them in full. This mechanism in the first instance gave all the employees an equal chance to buy shares. The senior managers placed particular emphasis on this aspect:

> Our privatisation was more honourable than what they do now. Everyone had an equal opportunity to buy shares. Everybody used their privileges equally. The council of the shareholding company, half of whose 15 members were workers, was selected to take account of the fears of the workers.

In order to make share purchase accessible to ordinary workers credit was granted on favourable terms to all those who wanted it. Initially the credit was granted at a rate of interest of 12 per cent, later increased to 25–40 per cent. The dividends paid out on these same shares were used to repay the credit. But these soft loans were only granted to those who invested some of their own money in cash, the credit being only to make up the difference. The shares were issued at a nominal 1,000 roubles, of which 200 roubles had to be paid immediately in cash, the remainder being covered by the loan. Alongside this, one restriction was added: no employee could invest more than 10,000 roubles in cash, which thereby restricted the purchase of any one person to a maximum of 50 of the 6,500 shares. On average the employees invested 4,000 roubles, and in less than a month 360 of the 490 people (73 per cent) then working in the enterprise had invested over one million roubles in cash, the remainder not wanting to become shareholders.

Following the initial distribution of shares among the employees of the enterprise only 600 shares, worth a nominal 600,000 roubles (10 per cent) remained for new recruits to the factory and for business partners.

Forms of participation of employees in the profits of the enterprise

By contrast to some privatised companies in which the shares were distributed in proportion to earnings, Lenkon took another route. The management considered that, with the existing payment system, wages did not reflect the workers' contribution to the general outcome. The management considered that the distribution of a part of the company's income to shares would make it possible to take account of the contribution of capital, since those who buy shares thereby limit their consumption, and they believed that this also had to be encouraged.

However, problems arose subsequently when workers whose wages had been held down in the interests of the company were confronted with the appearance of new employees at the factory who had the money to buy a larger number of shares than they, the old-timers, had. Many people expressed their dissatisfaction with the principle of distribution:

> Those people who have worked here all their lives, who, one can say, have given their lives to the factory, have few shares, because they have no money to buy shares – pay was low.

This feeling of insult cannot be reduced to the economic loss suffered from owning a smaller number of shares. As one of the section chiefs noted:

> It is only those workers who have worked here for 30 years and more who have the feeling that they participate in what happens in the enterprise, so these pensioners consider that the factory is theirs, that they created it. But the young people, who came after privatisation, although they also have shares, they just think 'well, if things get bad I will clear off'.

Despite its apparent benefits for the employees, privatisation proceeded with difficulty. The workers, with little understanding of the essence of the changes, were afraid that they were being cheated and so they had to be persuaded to buy shares.

What did the shares mean to the workers?

In the first place, the ownership of shares strengthened the workers' feeling of security. As an assembly fitter put it:

> Shares are a desire to make yourself secure. If you invest your money you can be more confident that they will not sack you.

But shares were seen by workers predominantly as a means of increasing their well-being by receiving dividends, and this perception became the basis for the manipulation of the workers as shareholders by management. Thus, in the founding agreement of the company it was laid down that if a person leaves the enterprise he cannot take his shares with him until he has paid off the credit which he had received to buy the shares. Only that amount of cash could be taken out which had already been invested. In other words, the shares remained with the company, but the worker received as 'compensation' that amount of money which he had originally invested in buying the shares. It hardly needs to be said that this money depreciated rapidly in the face of inflation.

Three ways of using their dividends were open to the workers. A significant number of workers 'capitalised' their dividends, using them to buy new shares in the company. On the one hand, one can consider such behaviour as mature and intelligent, as the worker-shareholders did not 'eat up' their dividends, but invested them in buying their firm's shares, thereby allowing it to increase its capital. On the other hand, conversations with workers showed other motives for such behaviour:

> At every meeting they explain the same thing to us: we must re-invest this money in shares, so as to avoid taxation.

The workers accumulated their dividends and converted them into shares over several quarters. The workers were angry that on one occasion the management did this automatically, without even asking the workers to sign an application, as had been the case in the past.

Participation of management in surplus profits

On the basis of the argument that the company has to break with the principle of levelling in pay and incentives for the key people in the company whose labour has the biggest influence on its general success, the charter of the company lays down the participation in extra profits for those people holding the ten most senior posts. Once the dividends have been calculated on the shares as a whole, 15 per cent of the remaining profits earmarked for distribution was allocated to these ten people, including 3 per cent for the President himself.

However, although the factory employees had approved this system of management participation in extra profits at the general shareholders' meeting, within a year they were regretting having supported this proposal of the president:

> People were inexperienced, how could we know how much profit the factory would make ... We never imagined that they would be pouring out in millions of roubles. (Section chief)

> They proposed it to us, and we blindly voted for it. They, the managers, know how to manipulate. But the workers themselves did not listen to those who spoke against it at the time. (Worker)

A section technologist had spoken against the proposal. As he recalled:

> When the President asked for 1,500 roubles pay for himself, plus 3 per cent of the residual profits, everybody put up their hands in favour. I said, 'lads, what are you doing? In the bad times, when we did not make the plan for a couple of years, we still made profits of around two million roubles. Just think how much three per cent of two million will be. And now it will certainly be more.' But everyone threw up their hands and said, 'yes, OK...'.

Redistribution of shares

Despite the initially egalitarian distribution of shares, workers were soon induced to sell their shares back to the company, which could then resell them at low prices set by the board. The concentration of shares in the hands of the president of the company and his deputies proceeded very rapidly. What mechanisms were used?

Workers sold their shares to the board of the company to pay off debts which the workers had incurred to buy shares, to buy garden plots and *dachas*, to buy consumer durables which were sold through the factory, and because of their inadequate wages. The workers claim that management deliberately held down wages in the spring of 1992 in the face of massive price increases in order to persuade workers to sell their shares. More positive incentives were provided by the arrival of a large delivery of consumer goods at the same time, which workers were encouraged to buy with shares if they lacked the cash.

They also used other covert methods to induce workers to part with their shares. Thus, at one shareholders' meeting it was decided not to pay the dividends with which the workers had hoped to repay the loans which they had taken out to buy shares. At the same time the purchase price of shares was increased from 1,000 to 1,400 roubles. And then production began to fall and rumours spread through the factory about the sorry condition of the company so that some workers, believing the rumours, left and sold their shares.

The concentration of shareownership was considerably reinforced by the subsequent issue of new shares, the initial issue of 6.5 million being increased to 100 million in 1993. Existing shareholders were allocated one nominal 8,000 rouble share in the second issue for every 16 shares held, with a cash handout of 500 roubles per share for shares not counting towards the rights issue. This meant that most worker-shareholders received a small cash bonus, but no additional shares, while the rights issue and the purchase of additional shares was monopolised by management and the company's associates. A further share issue took the authorised capital of the company up to a nominal 500 million roubles in 1994.

Within two years of the creation of the company 20 per cent of the shareholders among the company's employees commanded 80 per cent of the votes. The largest shareholder was the president of the company, who held 8.4 per cent, and two vice-presidents who held 3.1 and 3.3 per cent respectively. Thus these three alone held almost 15 per cent of the shares. We got this information initially from estimates of specialists, but later it was confirmed in interviews with senior managers of the company. However, this information was not available to ordinary shareholders. Nevertheless, the latter got a direct impression of the distribution of shares among the employees at the shareholders' meetings, where votes were counted not according to the method which most suited them, by a show of hands, but according to the number of shares held.

> Here it is absolutely secret who owns how many shares, the directors do not advertise it. But at the last shareholders' meeting ... then I could see who beat the votes of the workers. Many cards were held up in favour of paying a

dividend, while those for not paying were few, but the result was a decision not to pay (a worker).

Participation of other enterprises in the founding capital of Lenkon

Although Lenkon was a closed joint-stock company, some of its shares were sold to more than ten enterprises with which it had an established relationship, so as to increase their interest in the company's results. Thus, in order to receive electric motors without interruption shares were offered to a Belarussian enterprise. Lenkon also exchanged shares with the Yaroslavl' electro-mechanical factory, its main supplier of electric motors. Financial privileges in the distribution of the secondary issue of shares were also offered to enterprises which collaborated with Lenkon.

Participation in the capital of other enterprises

In its turn Lenkon invested money in buying the shares of those enterprises with which it sought a closer relationship, including both suppliers and, particularly, the distributors of its products. This strategy was conducted particularly actively in 1993–4, when Lenkon adopted an expansionist strategy. The production of new items required a large number of rigs and special tools, so Lenkon bought at auction a controlling interest in a tool-making factory, where special equipment will be made and the production of industrial fans has been organised.

The strategy of widening the company and conquering new market segments informed other actions of the management, including plans to create a subsidiary company on the base of one of the workshops of a Murmansk shipyard which would produce marine ventilators.

Widening of the company

The unification of the Moscow factory with that at Kryukovskii in 1991 could be seen at the time as a successful step and the beginning of the expansion of the young company. The Kryukovskii factory had a large area at its disposal and mass-produced fans, although their quality was lower than that of the Moscow plant. To improve the situation at Kryukovskii, and to improve the quality of its product, the

Moscow factory shared its experience of management and production organisation with the Kryukovskii factory, to which it transferred some of its mass-production equipment and some of its orders. The latter sacrifice was particularly significant, if one takes into account the subsequent substantial fall in production on the Moscow site.

It was the workers of the Moscow factory who paid the price for this sacrifice. They connected the subsequent move of their factory on to a four-day week, with its consequent loss of earnings and substantial redundancies, directly to this transfer of part of their production to Kryukovskii.

Despite the difficulties, the collaboration of the two factories working under the wing of Lenkon bore fruit, particularly for Kryukovskii, where production grew month by month, and the workers' earnings grew more rapidly than in Moscow. The Kryukovskii factory also bought two blocks of apartments with the company's money.

However, collaboration turned out to be fragile: in the summer of 1993 there was an explosion in the company, the basis of which was a conflict within management, which set the two factories against one another. Kryukovskii separated from the company, with all sides incurring substantial losses. The Moscow factory had to resume the production of those items which had previously been transferred to Kryukovskii and find new production capacity for its own development. Experienced managers left the company, taking with them not only their knowledge, but also their connections, depriving the Moscow factory of some of its key customers and suppliers.

But Kryukovskii also lost some of its orders and lost the help and support of specialists from the joint-stock company, seeing its production fall by half within three months of its separation and having to incur considerable expense opening two commercial offices in Moscow. All the evidence indicates that the two factories, which complemented each other well, would go on suffering losses from their separation. In Moscow there is a developed communications network, a scientific-technical centre, skilled workers and an industrial base for marketing and for the mastery of new specialised and technically complex products. Kryukovskii has a large production area and the labour force for series and mass-production of these products. Lenkon continued to insist that it was always ready to welcome Kryukovskii back into the fold, but as a daughter company, not as a partner.

Opening of the company

In March 1993 the company was transformed into an open joint-stock company with an authorised capital of 500 million roubles, with the sale of 400 million roubles' worth of shares following the earlier issue of new shares which had increased the authorised capital to 100 million roubles. According to the management this was motivated by the state's taxation policy, as a means of avoiding taxation on profits. The share issue was handled by the up-market firm Financial Consulting, whose chief became a member of the council of the company. It was decided to sell nominal 1,000 rouble shares for 8,000 roubles on the securities market, and to allocate a significant proportion of the second issue to the shareholder-workers of the enterprise (approximately 250 shares per person, a quarter at subsidised prices). As a result 27,530 shares were distributed among employees at a nominal cost of 1,000 roubles (in essence, at a subsidised price) in proportion to their average earnings, which by now, following reform of the payment system, were supposedly an indicator of their investment of labour in the company. Some of the shares were distributed among shareholders on the basis of one share from the second emission for every sixteen shares (valued at 8,000 roubles each) owned by the shareholder, the cost of which was met from the dividends.

The search for external investors

The opening of the company was connected with the ultimately abortive negotiations which the management of the company conducted through 1992 and 1993 with one of the largest engineering concerns in Europe with a view to establishing a joint venture. The management was willing to give up a substantial part of its rights and freedom – a controlling interest – in exchange for the prospect of creating an effective firm. They expected that the future partner-owners would

> for their part bring equipment, technology transfer, training of staff, transfer of experience or new products. Of course, it is not obligatory to bring dollars and marks, we need to receive those things that we need to produce things. (Chief engineer–technical director)

Following the breakdown of these negotiations, in 1994 the

scientific-technical centre and the economic-juridical department worked out a business plan, since the management of the company intended to widen the search for western business partners. This time they were ready to offer an investor 10 per cent of the voting shares for $500,000, based on a 'market' price of $10 per share. They needed the money to develop seven new kinds of special products. The programme envisaged carrying out research, preparing special technological tools and equipment, the acquisition of universal equipment and the reconstruction of the production sections over the period 1994–5. However, these initiatives led to nothing and there were no further contacts with potential large investors.

Relations with the state and commercial organisations

As for many enterprises which were pioneers of privatisation, the change in the form of ownership of the company signified a weakening of its connections with the state. However, by contrast to those enterprises which achieved their freedom through conflict with the ministry and subsequently faced isolation and limited access to state resources, the management of Lenkon proceeded more cautiously.

> At the very beginning we wanted to reject everything which connected us with the ministry. But one cannot say that we do not now maintain relations with state bodies, we do, but only with those which have real resources – with the Economics Ministry, the Finance Ministry and so on. Many relations are based on old personal contacts. (Vice president for economics)

The original success of the company, up to the end of 1991, derived from the fact that it still had a large state order through which it was able to secure the supply of parts, and particularly the electric motors that made up about two-thirds of the cost of the product, at low state prices. Thus the company depended for its prosperity in the first phase of its existence precisely on its position as a pioneer which was able to straddle the two systems. However, the enterprise has not received subsidised state credits.

During the 1980s and 1990s the enterprise held money in the West and lent it out through a pocket bank, in which it held 80 per cent of the shares. The vice-president spoke of the company's relationships with the bank in 1992:

> The bank helps to resolve questions concerning cash and resolves them

> effectively. They can do everything on the phone: I phone and they pay. It is simpler like that, less formalism, they don't need any certificates. If we need to get credit, they find it. In the bank they do what we ask the way we ask. One has to say that we need them more than they need us. They are accountable to us, we talk to them, we try not cheat one another. But there are people there whom we trust, not casual acquaintances: I have known the chief accountant of the bank for thirty years, others I know through various other channels. We have a definite degree of trust.

For Lenkon, according to its management, it was not necessary to join any association of enterprises, since its position on the market was perfectly satisfactory. There was one attempt to create an association under the aegis of Lenkon, but it did not get support and the management was not worried because at that time they were not experiencing any competitive pressure.

PRODUCTION AND STRATEGIES OF ECONOMIC DEVELOPMENT

In 1991 enterprise management's principal headache was securing supplies for the production of state orders, since only half the supplies were guaranteed, the remaining materials and parts being bought partly on the Moscow commodity exchanges and partly through barter deals.

For that reason the management put its main emphasis on work with suppliers, concluding long-term agreements with them and tying them to the company through its shares. Although the management of the company claimed that there were no problems with the supply of raw materials, parts and assemblies, our own observation in the factory during 1991–2 showed that the situation was not quite so rosy. One quite often found production subdivisions at fever-pitch because of the failure of supplies of metal or assemblies to arrive in time. Incomplete machines were piled up in the stores as a result of delays in the supply of electric motors from Yaroslavl'. Indirect confirmation of the unsatisfactory situation with supplies was provided by the criticisms of the supply service expressed by several members of management in confidential conversations with us. The workers were much more frank: 'the fish rots from the head'.

After its initial economic success the company was hit very hard by the general collapse of production in 1992 following the liberalisation of prices and disruption of economic links in the former Soviet Union. Sales collapsed in the spring of 1992, and the problem was compounded when the supply of electric motors dried up because supplies of copper had been diverted to export. Everybody was mobilised to look for orders, with management promising to pay a commission on all pre-paid orders.

In April 1992 the factory was at a standstill and the workers were sent on vacation – initially paid, and then administrative. Production resumed in the summer, but in August 1992 production again came to a complete standstill as Lenkon tried to clear its stocks, production resuming at only 10 per cent of capacity working. In the autumn of 1992 increasingly insistent rumours circulated that management was planning to sell the plant and lease its buildings to a foreign company to provide warehousing and office facilities, which would be perfectly consistent with the actions of management at that time. This would explain why the top management had shown no interest in the development of production, transferring machinery and the simpler mass production out of the city to the low-wage Kryukovskii plant, concentrating the remaining production on a small part of the site (the other building was claimed to be for the development of new production, later it turned out that it had been intended for Lenkon's prospective European partner: when the deal fell through the medium fans section moved back into the building), holding down wages and running down the workforce. However, if there were such plans, they came to nothing, and it may be that the management's story was genuine, that its strategy was to raise the technological level of its product, to fill a niche in the market for custom products, exploiting the skills and experience of the core of its labour force.

Wages lagged behind inflation as the economic position deteriorated, and the enterprise went onto a four-day working week. As wages fell below the city average the more active and more highly skilled workers began to leave. Management decided to cut the labour force by 30 per cent, with most of the cut falling in the second half of 1992, in order to be able to keep up the wages of those who remained. However, low wages meant that many workers left voluntarily, while there was no resistance from those dismissed.

Despite the massive fall in production, the enterprise was still not in a bad position. There was a number of mitigating factors. First, the enterprise had substantial reserves of money and materials. Second, its products are investment goods with a short production cycle which meant that funds turned over fairly fast. Third, the factory had a certain degree of monopoly in the market. Finally, the decision to stop production and lay off workers when orders dried up eased the financial pressures, at a time when hardly anybody else took such a bold step. The management was equally bold in its plans for marketing and product development.

In an attempt to deal with the problem of sales the company established a marketing department in 1992 which gathered information from various sources, including business and financial publications, although the main source of information was work with traditional customers. At the same time, a long-term strategy document was adopted, laying out the development strategy for the following three years. This was an internal document which defined the strategic directions of production, the search for markets and the development and reorganisation of production. Management decided not to reorient the factory to the production of consumer goods, as was the fashion at the time, but to try to extend the market for its basic products by widening the range. The essence of this strategy, as it was described by the vice president for economics, was 'to become leaders in a narrow area, where we can become better than others', working to order for specific customers, which really meant to become a monopolist in a specific area. This entailed the development of new kinds of ventilator and the modernisation of 'know-how' and equipment so as to compete in the home market and increase output for export. A subdivision was created within the marketing service, the market promotion service, to advertise the new kinds of products and work with potential customers.

Up to 1992 the factory had produced only two types of radial fans, but its catalogue for 1993 included a wide choice of special types of machine, to be used in various conditions for various purposes including roof fans, dust-extracting fans, high pressure fans, axial fans, fans with heaters, marine fans and so on, all produced with the same outdated tools and machinery, relying on the skills of the existing labour force.

The development of production was guided by the market research carried out by the marketing department. For example, market research revealed that the main producers of a particular kind of cooling equipment in the former USSR now lay outside the borders of Russia, so that only 20–30 per cent of the domestic demand was satisfied by expensive imported equipment and by the production of domestic unspecialised producers. On the basis of demand projections for this equipment an investment plan was worked out to develop its production.

Similarly, the factory developed the production of small air-conditioning equipment for cottages built by individuals, farmers and peasants and has established connections with large agricultural enterprises. It also developed the production of electric heating fans to be used in small garages, industrial buildings and shops.

Market research also suggested a new sphere of activity. The most long-lasting part of the product is the electric motor, whose cost amounts to about 70 per cent of the cost of the final product, so that it is more profitable for customers to repair their existing equipment than to buy new. It was decided to establish a special service and repair section to meet this demand. The service section was partly staffed by personnel transferred from basic production. Now Lenkon not only produces equipment, but also offers a comprehensive installation, maintenance and repair service for cooling systems in the Moscow region. To tie in new customers, Lenkon signs a guaranteed service agreement with the purchaser of the equipment.

After the sharp fall in the summer of 1992 and the first half of 1993, production was somewhat stabilised in the summer of 1993, although the factory was still working at only 30–35 per cent capacity and was keeping going by taking orders for anything it could produce. For example, in the spring of 1993 the press-stamp section was sustained by an order from the Netherlands for simple metal cabinets. However, management's development strategy was sharply dented by the internal conflict which led to the separation of the Kryukovskii factory in the autumn of 1993. Although production and sales from the Moscow factory increased three times, most of this was at the expense of Kryukovskii, which had accounted for over half the company's output and whose own sales were halved on separation, the total sales of the two plants being less than their combined sales had been previous to separation. Nevertheless, such an increase was the basis for the restoration of the five-day working week in the summer of 1993, the move away from time-wages, which had been adopted in the face of the earlier fall in production, and the adoption of a fairly optimistic plan for the Moscow factory for 1994. Mass production, which had previously been transferred to Kryukovskii, was resumed. The installation of the new lines began in the autumn of 1993, with mass-produced machines being expected to account for half the volume of production in future. As a short term reaction to sales difficulties from the end of 1993 the company had to abandon its strategy of insisting on pre-payment of orders and began to supply on credit, for a 50 per cent down-payment.

The strategy of the firm for 1994 anticipated a doubling of production, to sell 76,380 units, spread over the quarters as follows:

First quarter	15%
Second quarter	30%
Third quarter	40%
Fourth quarter	15%

However, in January and February the plan was only 50% fulfilled. The main reason for the failure to meet the plan, according to the manager for economics, was a legacy of the separation of the Kryukovskii factory in the summer of 1993.

> They returned some of the equipment which we had earlier transferred to them, but you should have seen the state of it – it was just scrap metal.

However, there were other reasons for the fall in production. First, the insolvency of many of Lenkon's customers, the production plan relating only to paid orders. Second, some of the former customers were taken with them by the two members of the board who left to join the Kryukovskii factory. Nevertheless, the enterprise managed to reduce the price of its fans below those of Kryukovskii, despite the much lower wages paid by the latter, by reducing its production costs, and so managed to increase production by 5 per cent over March and April 1994. One reason for its ability to undercut its former partner was that some of the ventilators are bought from Tula, where they are made by the forced labour of prisoners, for 180 million roubles, only being finished off in Moscow before being sold for 210 million, so making 30 million roubles on each ventilator sold. However, according to one of the foremen, these fans are very poor quality,

> recently we received a complaint that our fans were only 5 per cent efficient, because of failures due to breakdowns. I said to management that this will do us no good.

Despite the resumption of mass production, management still pinned its hopes for the future on 'niche marketing'. In 1994 between

50 and 70 different articles were produced in any month, and the range was altered practically every month. The increase in production planned for 1995 was based on the introduction of further new types of product which were much more complicated than the products traditionally produced by the factory. The enterprise developed the new products using its own resources, having created a Scientific-Technical Centre (NTTs) to which specialists were recruited from one of the leading scientific research institutes in the industry. The Centre maintains links with other research institutes which enables it to acquire the latest technology.

Although the priority of management was to secure its position on the domestic market, Lenkon gradually tried to open up the western market, access to which depends on guaranteed quality and delivery. The company claims that its own foreign trade department has representatives in all the CIS countries, as well as Belgium, Germany, Holland, Ireland, Vietnam and Cuba. In its advertising, in addition to the sale, servicing and repair of various kinds of ventilators, it offers 'intermediary services in foreign economic activity' (*Kontakt*, 3 December 1993). Nevertheless, the main market remains the countries of the former Soviet Union.

In 1993 the company had planned to expand the geographical distribution of its sales, overcoming the problems of distance by increasing the product quality, fulfilling orders more rapidly, selling kits and setting up daughter companies to produce in more distant regions. The core of the marketing strategy was to decentralise sales from Moscow to the regions by setting up a dealership network so as to establish closer supply and service relationships with customers. However, the economic situation in the country as a whole, including escalating transport costs, led to a modification of this strategy and forced the company to place less emphasis on distant companies in favour of an attempt to consolidate its position in Moscow and the Moscow region, although by 1995 dealerships had been established in Nizhni Novogorod and a number of cities in the Urals.

The company introduced a number of other modifications to its production strategy at the end of 1993 as the anticipated recovery in the national economy failed to materialise, with the further decline in industrial production, the crisis of non-payment and the continuing high level of inflation which precipitated a financial crisis in the enterprise, although it remained solvent with its working capital still exceeding its short-term debts by 20 per cent. Nevertheless, all subdivisions of the factory were required to restrict their payments for services from outside organisations and to maximise the use of their own personnel and resources. As a result of the shortage of working capital, purchases of machines from Tula to be finished off were also curtailed. The ambitious plans to expand by buying up the shares of other companies, through which it had been hoped that Lenkon would become a conglomerate by the year 2000, had to be frozen.

Management decided to concentrate its sales efforts on those enterprises which were scheduled to receive investment funds through state and other investment programmes, and also to widen the range of dual-use (industrial and domestic) ventilation products and marine ventilators to be produced by its daughter plant in Murmansk. Great hopes were placed in the growing demand from small entrepreneurs trading from kiosks, for whom the company planned to produce small heating fans. It was also decided to compensate for the continuing fall in production by increasing the volume of repair and service work.

In the middle of 1994 the company held 22 per cent of the market in Russia, its share of the CIS market having been 13.8 per cent at the end of 1992 and around 15 per cent in 1993. Its prices were broadly similar to those of other Russian producers, and amounted to about 70–80 per cent of the price of Western products on sale in Russia.

Most of the company's efforts, and its limited investment funds, went into sales and marketing and into product development. Neither increasing the productivity of labour nor improving the quality of the product was considered a priority. In such declarative statements as the business plan, whose function is to show the company in the best light, it is recognised that technological backwardness and low labour productivity are barriers to the deeper penetration of the market. It is recognised that the basic method of resolving such problems is the technical re-equipment and modernisation of production. One of the last meetings of the Council of Directors of the company that we attended was devoted to precisely this problem. The discussion showed that for now technical re-equipment remains a matter of wishful thinking and long-term plans, and in reality all that is considered is the modernisation of the most antiquated of the existing equipment.

The need to work on ageing and deteriorating equipment annoys the workers and gives rise to growing unrest within the labour collective. In the workers' words, they are constantly having to work 'on our knees, manually', without the kinds of equipment they need.

According to the chief of the small-batch section 'half the equipment needs replacing'. It is remarkable that we have heard the workers say time and again that they would agree to the dividends being reduced in order to pay for the purchase of new equipment, and they have even raised this question at the shareholders' meeting.

The overall results of Lenkon in the period of our research are summed up in the following table:

Financial Results (thousands of US dollars)

	1990	1991	1992	1993	1994
Net sales	19244	34999	5426	6011	13930
Cost of goods sold	9334	13300	2285	3031	9751
Gross profits	9910	21699	3141	2980	4179
Other expenses	337	4296	65	97	196
Other income	1191	457	237	564	216
Net income	10765	17860	3328	3447	4199
Income after tax	8101	9802	2260	2296	2797

These results are calculated on the basis of the official dollar exchange rate of $1 to 1.67 R for 1990 and 1991, and subsequently at the weighted average market rate of $1 to 262.5R in 1992, $1 to 808 R in 1993 and $1 to 1200R in 1994.

The 'indicator of maximum potential income' (ratio of net profits to founding capital) in 1990 was 2.06; in 1991 it was 0.92; in 1992 it was 7.86 and for the first nine months of 1993 it was 13.2. Thus net profits per share of nominal value of 1000 roubles amounted to 13,200 roubles at the end of 1993.

ORGANISATIONAL STRUCTURE AND MANAGEMENT

Frequent changes in the organisational and management structure have become one of the most noteworthy features of the development of Lenkon. Various processes are hidden behind these changes: on the one hand, structural reorganisation crystallised changes in the distribution of forces within the company; on the other hand, the president of the company attributed an independent role to organisational change in the transformation of the company and the enterprise.

Apart from these internal processes, organisational restructuring also reflected wider tendencies in the development of the company – firstly, the aspiration of the company to widening and expanding its activity; secondly, a move towards a decentralisation of decision-making and responsibility, which gave way to a reverse tendency to the centralisation of power at the top of the company. These tendencies were primarily influenced by external demands of adaptation to the current market situation and the strengthening of the position of the young company.

Corporate structure

The joint-stock company, Lenkon, should be clearly distinguished from the Moscow factory, which had its own separate management. At first Lenkon comprised just one enterprise, the Moscow factory. The initial distribution of shares to a series of enterprises, Lenkon's suppliers and customers, widened the circle of shareholders. However, the appearance of external shareholders, who together owned about 10 per cent of the shares, was not reflected in the composition of the management bodies of the company.

Following its unification in October 1991 with the Kryukovskii factory, one could no longer say that Lenkon and the Moscow factory were one and the same thing. From this moment the general shareholders' meeting began to take the form of a conference of shareholders involving elected delegates on a quota basis. Representatives of the Kryukovskii factory joined the management bodies of Lenkon.

Management bodies of the company

From the moment of the creation of the company in the autumn of 1990 until the moment of completing the research in the middle of 1995, the management bodies of Lenkon underwent an evolution which was reflected in two stages in the development of the company.

The two bodies which were initially created to manage the company between shareholders' meetings, the board and the shareholders' council of the company, were merely the renamed administration and STK (Labour Collective Council) of the enterprise. And despite the fact that in the statutes of the company the shareholders' meeting and shareholders' council have the decisive significance, the real weight and corresponding power concentrated in these bodies was traditional:

> Really there is only the board. The general meeting and shareholders' council are the audience (from a group discussion with workers).

The chiefs of the industrial subdivisions were members of the board, and they put their conflicts over production questions to the board ('everyone pulled the blanket over to himself'), just as they always had in the administration. The president alone represented the general interests of the development of the company, which otherwise receded into the background.

The shareholders' council, half of whose members were workers, was a decorative body whose main function was to confirm the decisions of the board. One of the members of the board characterised it as 'a shock-absorber and on the whole fairly passive body for communicating between management and employees'. It is understandable that many workers associated it with the STK. The fate of this council, seen by management as a body transitional between the STK and the directors' council, was predetermined by the redistribution of shares among the employees to the advantage of senior management and the appearance of enterprise-shareholders and external shareholders which reduced the weight of the worker-shareholders. The most powerful factor affecting the function and the composition of the management bodies was the struggles and conflicts within the management team.

Management team and conflicts

During the first stage of development of the company, which lasted until the summer of 1993, the management team comprised the president; his four vice-presidents (the technical director, commercial manager for marketing and co-operation, the 'control' director (up to spring 1993 called the director for economics and forecasting) and the director for foreign economic relations); the chief accountant; the director of the Moscow factory; the director of the Kryukovskii factory and the chief of the personnel department.

All the directors of the company were between 35 and 45 years old, with an average of 15 years managerial experience. All, without exception, had higher technical education, with three, including the president, also having higher economic education.

Despite the outwardly democratic appearance of the president, from the very beginning he demonstrated an authoritarian inclination in the management of the factory and the company, an aspiration to concentrate all power in his hands. Having come to the factory as director, he simultaneously headed the Labour Collective Council, then combined the posts of president of the co-operative and director of the factory, and subsequently president of the shareholding company and president of the board. But in contrast to the position of the director of a state enterprise, who was nominated in the past by the minister with confirmation by the Party bodies, Minenko went through a process of election, so that his legitimacy rested on a much broader base, although his position turned out to be vulnerable in conflict situations.

His weakness, which was the other side of his authoritarianism, was that he paid insufficient attention to the creation of a cohesive management team. In the end, the appearance of contradictory interests within the board led to open conflict whose consequence was the destruction of the original company. Some of our key informants, close to Minenko, link the conflict to mistakes in his selection of his senior managers and consider that he is primarily responsible for the collapse of the company:

> Although I am Minenko's person, I consider that Minenko must draw the conclusions from this conflict. He selected the people, and we have all had to pay for his mistakes in selection.

The superficial reason for the conflict was an argument among the senior managers over the size of the dividend. The president proposed that the dividend should be cut in order to increase wages. This was opposed by some of his colleagues who held large packets of shares and stood to lose millions of roubles of additional income from such a decision. These two fractions saw the long-term development of the company differently and adhered to different strategies. One of them cared more about their own personal profit than the future of the factory. This fraction was headed by the vice-president for foreign economic relations, about whom they said:

> He does not give a damn about the factory, the most important thing for him is his pocket. He is involved in various machinations: under the wing of the factory, since it has an export license, he resells parts abroad, but he puts the money into his own pocket.

The second member of this faction was the director of the Moscow factory. At one stage a specialist was employed to work out precisely how many workers of what specialisms were required, and how much of the profit needed to be invested in the development of the factory. When he presented his report, the director of the Moscow factory simply said, 'Why so much detail? We need something broader, something general.' 'And, really, what did he need it for', commented the specialist. 'They want to do everything secretly, so as to make their own profits.'

The third member of this fraction, the vice-president for economics, controlled all of the financial activity of the company, with the accountant, financial department and computer service subordinate to him, but with no control over his own activity. 'There are no plans (control figures)', said one of his subordinates, 'everything is paid out *ad hoc* and in comparison to the corresponding period the previous year'. And this was the person who had previously been the brains behind all the transformations in the company.

In August 1993 at the general shareholders' meeting a new board and shareholders' council were elected. The chief accountant and the vice president for economics were removed from the board, the latter resigning his post which was filled by the chief of the labour and wages department. The council was cut to seven members from eleven, only one of whom was a worker, and the representatives of the Kryukovskii factory left, as they had declared their intention of separating from the company. Legally Kryukovskii had a right to split away if two-thirds of its workers voted in favour at a general meeting. However, the final separation was legally complicated because Lenkon owned all the shares in the Kryukovskii factory, but in practice the company Lenkon and the Moscow factory became once more one and the same, with a single bank account.

From the autumn of 1993 Lenkon began the structural reorganisation of management and production 'according to Hubbard' (see below). It was carried out under the slogan of increasing the quality of the management of the company. It was recognised that the existing management bodies, the council and the board, needed a more professional approach, particularly the council which, by contrast to the board, works on a voluntary basis, but which has greater authority than the board. The council of the company was abolished, and replaced by the directors' council as the supreme management body between shareholders' meetings. Members of the council can only be shareholders or those nominated by shareholders with a minimum of 10 per cent of voting shares, and can only be removed by a minimum of 10 per cent of the shareholders' votes. Its president formerly worked in the Kryukovskii factory and now works in the scientific-technical centre, which is headed by another member, who is a Candidate of Technical Science, and who formerly worked as a designer in the prestigious Zhukovskii Cosmic and Aviation Research Institute (TsAGI). Other members of the council are the president of the company, the chief consultant of the firm Financial Consulting (the only outsider on the council), the former director of the Kryukovskii factory (as one of our informants said, 'he is near retirement, I have no idea why he is on our council'), and one worker representative, as required by the charter, an assembly fitter and brigadier in the medium ventilator section, although he is no longer really a worker representative since in 1994 he became the head of the new service and guarantee department.

The executive body remains the board, which has the 'right of legislative initiative in all questions within the competence of the general meeting or the directors' council'. Initially the board members were the president, the first vice-president (former director of the Moscow factory), and the managers for foreign economic activity, for personnel and for sales, but soon the board was widened to bring in the other senior managers. The board normally meets on the 20th of each month.

According to the statutes, the highest management body is the general meeting of shareholders, and there is also a revision commission. The general meeting of shareholders and the directors' council are legislative bodies which work out strategy. The directors' council meets fairly regularly once a week, although in practice it is the president who decides all the strategic questions. As one board member explained 'Minenko is the main person in the directors' council and on the board. And all the big wigs flock around Minenko.'

The conflict in the summer of 1993 marked the watershed between the phases of decentralisation and re-centralisation of management.

The fate of small enterprises: is it terrible to divide power?

Almost simultaneously with the conversion of the co-operative into a joint-stock company small enterprises appeared on the territory of the factory on the basis of contractual relations with the company: they paid rent for the buildings, for electricity and so on and shared part of their profits with the company.

Some of these small enterprises were involved in activities which had nothing to do with the profile of the enterprise (for example, manufacturing furniture), but were in fact using not only equipment, but also the raw materials coming into the factory. Other small enterprises met the needs of the factory by transporting products (the small enterprise 'Trans – motor transport' and a railway branch-line).

We did not even try to discover whether these small enterprises provided an additional source of income for the bosses of the company, although there were clearly close connections and there was indirect evidence from the struggles between the senior management of the company and the heads of the small enterprises. One can surmise that initially, as elsewhere, co-operatives and small enterprises provided the bosses with opportunities for semi-legal commercial activity. At the beginning of 1992, one of the senior managers of the company, explaining the attitude of management to the existence of small enterprises on the territory of the factory, said:

> We are not afraid to give up our power of command, because we have had a taste of economic methods of interaction with these collectives. We give them maximum responsibility for the results of their work, but they use their rights on a mutually beneficial basis.

But two years later, when all the small enterprises were liquidated with the end of self-financing, a senior manager gave a very different evaluation:

> The small enterprises give Lenkon nothing, on the contrary, they live at its expense, we decided to close them down: some of them merged with Lenkon, others ceased to exist on the territory of the factory.

STRUCTURE OF PRODUCTION MANAGEMENT

Until the autumn of 1993 the immediate management of the factory was in the hands of its director and his three deputies (technical questions, production questions and operations). The production sections were responsible through their chiefs to the deputy director for production. The section chiefs had acquired substantially more authority and independence than in the past, partly as a result of the separation of the enterprise from the vertical ministerial structures, but also as a result of the strategy of Lenkon's management to try to 'straighten out' the managerial chain. In practice the 'owner' in the section had become not the foreman but the section chief. It was he or she who took decisions about recruitment and dismissal, he or she, alone or in conjunction with brigadiers and foremen, who determined the level of bonuses. The results of the labour of the section depended above all on the chief, particularly in conditions of a sharp decline of orders, when the section depended on him or her going out and finding work.

The post of chief engineer had been abolished at the beginning of 1993, when the chief engineer resigned following a clash with the new chief technologist. However, the former chief engineer was then appointed to the post of deputy president for technical questions, to which the functions of chief engineer were transferred. However, this then led to conflict as a result of the considerable duplication of functions between the deputies for technical and production questions, as the former recognised himself, referring to:

> a lack of co-ordination in our work. For example when I, unknowingly, follow in the footsteps of the deputy for production and give people the same tasks, or vice versa.

This tension between the two deputies leads in turn to tension between the deputies and the heads of subdivisions subordinate to them.

Internal self-financing

Even before the beginning of the Gaidar reforms the directors of Lenkon had been forced to transfer some of their control over the organisation of production to their subordinate subdivisions not under the influence of external pressures but as a result of a compromise between higher administration and two enterprising middle managers who were seeking more independence on the basis of self-financed accounting. These two managers headed the two most important technical services of the enterprise – the department of the chief designer, which included a new technology brigade, and the department of the chief technologist, which included the tool-making section.

The first collective to be transferred to internal self-financing was that of the designers and workers from the new technology brigade. The final product of this subdivision was not drawings, but prototype machines made in metal. This collective became the 'pioneering group' for the whole enterprise, since it was the first to use the new form of activity. It was given the right to conclude contracts, to carry them out and to sell its products independently. The designers and workers from the new technology brigade were the first in the factory to work with individual customers and the acquisition of orders became one of the basic concerns of the chiefs of this subdivision. How did they do this? When the factory put advertisements in the press, the management of the department asked that the telephone number of the design department should be included in the list of telephone numbers to contact. Thanks to this customers began to make direct contact with the department. This led to reprimands from the recently established marketing department, which saw the self-financing design department as a competitor.

The department had its own self-financing account within the factory and all the money received from its contracts went into this account. The lion's share of this income was paid over to the company for the use of administrative and industrial premises, payment for electricity, water supply and so on, which were defined in a contract with the company. Apart from these payments, the contract also laid down that it would pay a proportion of its profits to the company. The department had the right to dispose of the remaining money independently (distribution of pay, hire of temporary workers for concrete orders and so on).

One of the chiefs of the design department explained in an interview:

> We do all our own accounting and distribution of money to the extent that we do not use the services of our accounts department. Our accountant does only one thing for us – she confirms the receipt of money in our account. The accountant's department tells me the total amount of money in the subdivision, and I myself allocate the money to everybody. Nobody from the factory management has any right to amend the amount of pay which I assign, for example, to Ivanov.

However, in practice, conflicts often arose between the heads of self-financing subdivisions and the factory management, and in particular between the head of the design section and the deputy for technical questions who supervised this section. One of the lines of conflict centred on the distribution of power between managers of various levels, the basis of which was the unwillingness of the senior management to give up their levers of control over the corresponding services, in particular through their control over pay. At that time, although the deputy for technical questions did not interfere in decisions taken about the number of personnel employed or the level of individual pay of the self-financing subdivision, he reserved his right to control the total size of the wages fund. Tension arose between the deputy for technical questions and the head of the design section when the latter prevented the former from revising the pay of the workers in the department, which he considered to be too high.

This line of conflict was only a particular manifestation of the more general conflict between the interests of the factory, represented in this case by the deputy director for technical questions, and the interests of the self-financing section, defended by its chief. In the words of the deputy director:

> A self-financing subdivision has every right to take work on the side to provide itself with earnings, so long as this does not conflict either with our basic direction or, most important, the fulfilment of the plan to supply finished products.

The attempt of the deputy director to review wages in the department reflected his attempt to control the fulfilment of the factory plan and to impose the priority of the interests of the factory over those of the self-financing section.

One year after the appearance of self-financing subdivisions the wave of managerial decentralisation rolled over the other production sections. However, in this case the devolution of power to the level of the section was a response of higher management to the unstable situation, fall in production, and shortage of working capital in the wake of the 1992 reforms. Things reached such a point that management even asked individual employees to look for orders, promising to pay them a commission. Mobile groups were formed from junior section managers whose function was to 'beat out' money from customers who had not paid for the goods delivered to them, with management promising to pay a commission of 1.5 per cent of the money received. This continued until the enterprise moved to a system of pre-payment.

The management of the company expected the section chiefs to become more independent figures, giving them the right to seek additional orders and secure income for their sections independently. In the view of one of the board members, the section chiefs gained from this for a while:

> He goes to look for orders. He has a foreman who can keep the production process going. The section chief must have a direct interest in finding orders for the section, since this provides additional income for his employees. After all the expenses have been covered, and he has deducted amortisation which is paid to the factory from the profits, all the rest he takes himself. Nobody stops him doing this. But the section chiefs are not very quick, they prefer to sit in the section.

The increased power and responsibility of the section chiefs was also a result of the management policy of trying to 'straighten out' the management chain and to reduce the status of the foreman. The head of the personnel department defined the approach of management to the foremen:

> The foreman is just a worker who has a certain power which he must use for the benefit of the work. His basic function is to supply people in the section with work.

In the past the foremen were 'rulers of the section': they took workers into the section, distributed the work amongst them, but most important of all, they distributed the money: under the system of piece-rates the foreman controlled the wages fund. Then, while keeping the function of distributing work in the section, the foreman lost the right to recruit workers (the labour contract was signed by the section chief). With the introduction of time-wages the foreman lost control of the wages fund, but retained control of the 30 per cent of the expenditure which went to the bonus fund.

In our view the restructuring of the hierarchy of production management in the Moscow factory, manifested in the changed status of the foreman, was not the result of a thought-out strategy but the outcome of a developing situation. The foremen were made the scapegoats for an over-expenditure on pay which inflated production costs in 1992. They were accused of stealing money by inflating the staff list, signing up 'dead souls', although, in the opinion of a number of specialists, the over-expenditure on wages arose as a result of the transition to time-wages (see below) and the absence of any objective job-evaluation to serve as a basis for the calculation of wages. When the factory was transformed into a joint-stock company the planning department of five people, which dealt with questions of norming and wages, had been abolished as part of a reduction in the managerial staff. The vice-president for economics of Lenkon took over responsibility for wage issues, but he only considered these questions at a strategic level. Thus the effective calculation of norms and of corresponding rates of pay was neglected.

The foremen were also victims of the struggle for power within the management team. The new head of the personnel department was seeking to increasing his status by centralising the functions of personnel management (in particular, recruitment) and undermining the power of the foremen.

Divisions

In 1992–3 the formation of a new structure of production in the enterprise began, the aim of which was to create, following the experience of western firms, divisions – independent subdivisions within the framework of the Moscow factory. The president decided that he wanted to implement the idea of divisions after a number of German students came to study the Moscow factory as an example of a Russian enterprise, defending their diplomas and writing their recommendations. One of these recommendations was to form divisions.

The proposal was to create three divisions. The design division had already been established in 1991 to prepare drawings and specifications for the new custom-produced fans. The department for the technological preparation of production (OTPP) was created in 1992 on the basis of the merging of the department of the chief designer and the tool-making section, to design technical processes and prepare tools for the production sections. However, neither of these divisions was fully established, with no clear definition of the authority of their heads in relation to the deputy directors supposedly supervising them or in relation to the chiefs of the existing sections and services, so that the old management structure based on section chiefs and senior specialists has largely been maintained, partly on an informal basis, alongside the formally new responsibilities. The third division, combining the four production sections (press-stamp, small-batch section, section for assembly of medium fans, repair-mechanical section), was formally established in the management reorganisation in October

1993, which also abolished the OTPP, but on a very different basis from that initially envisaged.

At the beginning of 1993 the first signs of the tendency to the re-centralisation of power in the company appeared. The marketing and foreign economic relations departments were combined under a vice-president of the company. In the summer of 1993 a new personnel management and communications department was created on the basis of the old personnel department, headed by the former chief of the latter, comprising three departments: in addition to personnel were the departments of communications (supplying internal information) and inspection and statistical surveys, headed by the former head of the social-psychological service, who was at the same time a consultant to the president of the company.

The tendency to centralisation of power took on its final form after the conflict over the summer of 1993 with the reorganisation of the management of the company according to the prescriptions of the late L. Ron Hubbard, the founder ideologist of Scientology.

THE REORGANISATION OF THE STRUCTURE OF MANAGEMENT 'ACCORDING TO HUBBARD'

The initiator of the restructuring of Lenkon according to Hubbard was the company's president, a man fascinated by and enthusiastic for innovation, who had discovered the scientologists by chance when he attended a seminar in 1992. But why did the choice fall on Hubbard? Was it merely a chance confluence of circumstances? Was it that the managerial philosophy which underlay the techniques adopted corresponded to the internal demands of the head of the company for authoritarian management? Or were the techniques offered by Hubbard already implicit in the objective tendency to the centralisation of management which received an additional impulse following the conflict within senior management? These are issues which we still discuss, and on which we are not agreed.

It seems that one of the lessons of the conflict within the management team for the president was an understanding of the importance of a common philosophy and aims for a team of like-minded people. It was precisely the divergence in the various senior managers' orientations to life that led to the conflict and collapse of the company. The inculcation of a purely managerial technology which was nevertheless based on a definite philosophical foundation could perhaps play an instrumental role in creating a team of like-minded people by creating a common philosophy in the firm.

Corporate philosophy

The management techniques of Hubbard appear to have attracted the attention of the president of the company and those closest to him because they contained an ideology. In their very first interviews management representatives had stressed the great importance they attached to the philosophy of the firm, its dynamism and its orientation to the market – 'a restructuring of the consciousness of the shareholders', which included above all the creation of a sense of devotion to the firm. The president, Minenko, stressed the restructuring of the consciousness of the shareholders in all his public speeches. This is only one example:

> The most important thing for the success of the firm is the presence within it of an internal philosophy, ethic and culture, perceived by employees and shareholders as their own convictions. For this we have to educate and train people.

However, there was a recognition that to change consciousness one needs not so much words as a concrete company policy. One of the deputy directors of the factory had this to say:

> The restructuring of consciousness – that is what our leadership was doing when the transformation from a co-operative to a joint-stock company began. It was necessary to get people to feel that they could influence their own pay by their own efforts. They were interested in participating in the income of the company, and they felt this, because the percentage paid in dividends here is quite high. Of course there are other manifestations as well, for example a sense of patriotism towards the factory. We have people who have worked in this enterprise for twenty or thirty years. Of course, not everyone is devoted to the factory, different people feel it to different degrees or it is only superficial. But when it is confirmed materially, when a person has no problems with child care, when problems of vacations are resolved, when a person does not have to stand in a queue, but can get some goods here at fairly low prices (without a commercial mark-up), all that is also significant and attracts people.

Subsequently, to encourage those who demonstrate their devotion to the company, the system of *klassnost'* was introduced as a basic form of payment (for details see below).

The Hubbard management technique

This is not the place to expound the theory of management systematised by L. Ron Hubbard, although it would certainly be useful to compare this theory with its practical embodiment which we observed in Lenkon. However, a more difficult task for the researcher was to distinguish the ideological packaging of the innovation from the real content and immediate results of the restructuring of management according to Hubbard.

We were struck by the amount of attention that was paid to the ideological accompaniment of reform in the company. Sometimes it reminded us of our time in the Pioneers as children. A logo was adopted by the company which contained the company's new slogan, 'we prepare air for Russia and an atmosphere of happiness for people', and also the general principle of the company, 'in the organisational structure there must not be simply employees. We must all learn to be managers, able to evaluate and take decisions.' In many documents issued by the company at that time, as well as in the public speeches of the president, the accent was put on the role of personality and consciousness in the development of the company.

Explaining to the general shareholders' meeting the principles of the main changes in the structure of the company, Minenko declared:

> We have chosen, come to know and to appreciate the Hubbard philosophy of organisational structure. The principal feature of this philosophy is the reference to the person as the centre and basis of the activity of the organisational structure, which is treated as a living organism, making it possible to perceive and react to changes, and not as a mechanism in which people fill the role of cogs and which fails in the face of the smallest changes in the external conditions.

The implementation of the Hubbard philosophy focused on increasing people's flexibility and their knowledge of their own and others' responsibilities. This implied a considerable increase in the information flow and levels of technical and managerial training within the enterprise.

However, behind all these attractive and vague phrases stood a hierarchy personally regulated and controlled by the president. The factor increasing the efficiency of the organisational structure of the company was a person who reacts consciously, but nevertheless knows his place. In the new organisational structure goals were established, responsibilities of posts defined ('hats' in the terminology of the Hubbard philosophy), 'valuable final products', a statistic for each specialist, department, management and the company as a whole were laid down. Great importance was attached in the adoption of the Hubbard philosophy to the training of staff, and especially of management staff.

Management Training

In 1992 the top managers began periodically to attend short courses at the company's expense, and a psychologist was brought in to carry out employee testing. Training for middle managers was arranged through the Hubbard 'Academy of Management', which also sent personnel management students on placement, one of whom was appointed to the marketing department of the Moscow factory.

In 1993 it was realised that the new stage of reform demanded a large expenditure of time, effort and money on training, not only for senior management, but also for middle managers, in order to 'stand up to the rising competitors'. The president spoke most persistently of all about the need for retraining:

> I consider that the main task of this coming stage is the priority investment in training, in retraining personnel. In new conditions one can only work successfully with new knowledge.

He ordered the assembly of a library of management literature so that every member of the management team could acquaint himself or herself with the relevant literature. Every manager was given a reader's card and the president himself monitored the diligence with which the members of the management team improved their qualifications. It was announced that the performance of senior and middle managers in self-education would be taken into account in their testimonials. In 1993 expenditure for the training and improvement of personnel amounted to 5–6 per cent of profits.

The Scientology connection was one of the reasons for the breakdown of negotiations with the European multinational, and also for the departure of the Kryukovskii factory, since Lenkon proposed to send 20 specialists from the two factories to the Scientologists' college in Sweden for one month at a cost of 100 million roubles. In fact the whole 30 strong management team of Lenkon and the Moscow factory followed courses over the summer and autumn of 1993 to learn the Scientologists' management methods, some in Moscow and some in Stockholm. In order to extend its training the company purchased a license from the Scientologists and on 5 October 1993 a contract was signed to open the 'Hubbard Academy' within the framework of the company, to train carefully selected employees, primarily specialists and line managers, whose increased qualifications would serve as a basis for their promotion up the career ladder. The plan was to spend five per cent of the company's profits on providing training in the Hubbard philosophy for all the company's employees within a year or a year and a half. However, one immediate result of the training was that managers were even more distanced from workers, conversing in the Hubbard language which was understood only within a narrow circle. The workers, meanwhile, took little interest in training or in the Hubbard methods, although one young worker from the small-batch section passed through the courses.

From 1 October 1993, with the separation of the Kryukovskii plant, Lenkon functioned as a single body. Formally the Moscow factory ceased to exist as a separate entity, and the post of director was abolished. The company had eight large subdivisions (economic-juridical; personnel and communications; progress towards the market; foreign economic relations; finance; production; technology centre; sales).

In the view of the president's assistant for management questions, the new structure 'in essence formalised what already existed in the company', but through this it became clearer 'where there was a surplus and where there were inadequacies, the tasks of each subdivision stood out more clearly'.

Our observation showed that people did not react to these changes in organisational structure unequivocally. The workers tend to see any changes in management as an inflation of the staff, and in general take little interest in changes in management, above all because they realise full well that they cannot have any influence on these questions. In the view of the workers the administration was indeed merely inflating the staff, taking on surplus people, building smart offices for themselves instead of putting the money into the technical re-equipment of the production areas. The declaration of one worker was typical:

> I went to the shareholders' meeting when the changes in the management structure were discussed. It was not interesting. The president decides everything. He kicks out people he does not like.

At the same time the initiators of the managerial restructuring did not manage to explain the essence of the changes to the ordinary workers:

> I have the feeling that the sense of all the changes in management has not got through to the workers. The worker himself cannot get through to the top, and we, sitting at the top, cannot reach down to the worker. On the one hand, the minimum of information gets through to him, on the other hand, we do not succeed in following up how the changes are experienced below. (A board member).

The introduction of the new methods had more dramatic consequences at the level of management. 'Restructuring according to Hubbard' split the management team into two groups from the beginning: on the one side, the president and his team, those who actively instilled the Hubbard ideology, on the other side, those who for one reason or another opposed it. Over time the balance shifted in favour of the latter faction, which included both young technocrats who wanted a high degree of independence in their work, and those managers for whom any change means the disruption of a comfortable state of affairs. 'They are quite happy to have nothing to do, to have nothing said to them, so that one would hardly expect an enthusiastic response from them to the reorganisation of management', as the president's assistant for management questions put it.

A little later the attitude of the second group to the Hubbard methods changed from being restrained to being sharply critical, as did the form of its expression, from speaking in private conversations to sabotage and departure from the company.

It would be a gross over-simplification to reduce the opposition to the management restructuring to a psychological aversion to innovation. It is quite obvious that the organisational restructuring violated the established balance of interests between various groups of managers and gave rise to new conflicts of interest.

Many of the opponents of the Hubbard management methods told us that these methods were completely inapplicable to Lenkon, or were no more than 10–20 per cent applicable, since a cumbersome management structure was being introduced in a relatively small enterprise, which leads to the breaking up and even atomisation of the interests of managers within a vertical hierarchy. For example, the production manager has five deputies who in turn have five subordinates, the department heads.

However the main focus of criticism was the 'hats', the complex of duties attached to a post, including a number of indicators, usually three or four, and the indicators of the 'personal statistic', according to which the work of every manager was evaluated and their pay and bonuses calculated. People called these indicators 'forced' and 'contradictory'. According to the chief accountant, who later left the company, 'this outrage', as he called it, leads to constant conflict within the management team and makes the work of the accountant much more difficult ('it messes up the work'). For example, according to the Hubbard philosophy the task of the personnel department is to expand the staff of the enterprise. But the task of the economic service is to reduce expenditure, the main means of doing which is to cut the personnel. The absurd situation therefore arises in which the head of personnel gets a bonus for increasing the number of employees, while the economic service has to resort to forgery to avoid paying the super tax on the excessive expenditure on wages. In general, in the view of the chief accountant, the personal statistics have not been thought out, but the Hubbard methods have just been slavishly copied. The chief technologist also left the company in the autumn of 1994, since he felt unable to work in a situation of permanent organisational change and conflict with the director of the scientific-technical centre. His view was that the generally low cultural level of the specialists led them either to fail to understand the Hubbard philosophy, or to a primitive and rigid interpretation of its postulates.

The management of the company was not entirely deaf to these criticisms. In May 1994 the various statistical indicators (personal, managerial, departmental) were reviewed to co-ordinate them with one another. Nevertheless there was still an objective basis for the negative evaluation by the managers since the introduction of personal statistics and the hat signifies strict control over their activity, above all by the president.

Centralisation of management of production

As part of the general process of restructuring according to Hubbard, the changes affected the production sections and the power of their managers. The idea of this restructuring was supposed to be

> an increase in the responsibility of each section for its own work and, correspondingly, an increase in the responsibility of its management. Now managers

> of the sections do not need to waste time looking for orders or metal. This will be done by the appropriate factory service. Thus planning, accounting and supply will all be centralised (from 20 January 1994). The section chiefs will retain only one area of independence – making decisions about the pay of the workers in their subdivision (economics manager).

However, the Hubbard rationalisation was not the only reason for the attack on the independence of the section chiefs. With the departure of the Kryukovskii factory it became more urgent to increase production in the Moscow factory, leading to growing contradictions between the chiefs of the company and line managers of the sections who were not able to fulfil the plans. The reason for the failure was identified as being the excessive independence of the section chiefs:

> We were concerned at the growing authoritarianism of the section chiefs. Maybe we had given them more independence than necessary, they allowed things to slide and lost control of them and they abuse this position. (Board member)

As in the case of the foremen, who had been the focus of the previous attack, the redistribution of power in favour of the higher levels of management was chosen as the way of resolving the particular contradictions that had arisen between various levels of management. This had the biggest impact on the self-financing subdivisions, which were liquidated, which implied a reduction in status for their managers. For example, the chief technologist, head of the OTPP, who had been brought in to the post with a great fanfare at the beginning of 1993, lost his managerial status when the OTPP was abolished with the transfer of technical services to the new technology centre. A new post of 'assistant to the head of production' was created for him, but he resigned in the autumn of 1994. The whole design service similarly had to put up with subordination to the management of the technology centre.

In the opinion of the former chief technologist, the liquidation of the self-financing sub-divisions, the OTPP and design service, was 'voluntaristic and irrational'. In his view the reason for this was the competition between these services and the new technology centre, which was headed by the former chief engineer, who had resigned his post following an earlier clash with the chief technologist only to be appointed vice-president, and the change certainly looked like the revenge of the former chief engineer. In the past the self-financing

OTPP had brought a substantial income into the company, fulfilling outside contracts as well as work for the other sections, with a balance on its own sub-account of 4 million roubles at the time of its liquidation ('that is enough money to pay all the workers of those subdivisions for two months'), while the technology centre was expected to cost the company more than one billion roubles a year.

The chief accountant gave an equally negative evaluation of the decision to liquidate the self-accounting subdivisions, considering that this would have a negative impact on the company finances and would lead to a fall in the productivity of labour in the former self-financing subdivisions, which had now been transferred to time-wages.

Formation of production divisions

In parallel with the reorganisation of the management structures was a restructuring of the organisation of production. One element of this was the creation of divisions, but on a different basis from that originally worked out and partially realised with the creation of the OTPP and design services. The new reorganisation was directed at the formation of subdivisions each based on a complete production cycle, so that each section would produce a particular kind of final product, a particular type of ventilator.

> Our aim is that each section should work on its own cycle, ... to create closed cycles producing a final product. The result must be a growth in the responsibility of the section for its own work, and a corresponding growth in the responsibility of its managers. (Economics manager)

On the basis of this conception they began to break up the press-stamp section and to 'shove it' into the assembly sections; what remained of the mechanical section was turned into a section for the production of large fans, after parts of it were transferred to the small-batch and medium fan assembly sections.

The then chief technologist, in April 1994, believed that this reorganisation had not only not improved the situation within and between divisions, but had resulted in a serious slump. Thus, for example, 'despite what one can politely call lenient plans, the small-batch section has not managed to maintain the production plan'. There were several reasons for this: the building has no facilities for the storage of even enough metal for one week's work; the equipment transferred from the mechanical section does not have sufficient capacity to make the number of parts required; the assemblers are not used to doing the work of stamping and mechanical work, and so on. The result is that the chief of the small-batch section still has to turn to the press-stamp section, which in practice has to continue to do what it did before, although in much more difficult circumstances than previously.

Of course the management considers that there are completely different explanations for the failures in the production sections, and particularly the small-batch section: they have bred democrats, they organised an STK, they have plenty of time for meetings and discussions, but they never have time to work, and so on.

The chief of the small-batch section himself had at first responded positively to the idea of establishing a closed production cycle on the basis of his section, apparently because he was attracted by the idea of having some independence in decision-making:

> It is a good idea. … In the past I was dependent on the press-stamp section, on the mechanical section. And now I will depend only on myself. I will decide what to do first, I will make a scale of all the work that has to be done … I will sort it all out myself.

However, he soon decided that the idea of divisions and independence was unrealistic:

> But it did not turn out like that. To do all this you need the right equipment, I was supposed to take it from another section, and then I could work only for myself. But the other section would come to a standstill without this equipment. To scatter the equipment around, which they are doing now, is a nonsense. People went back to the mechanical section again, but the machines were spread around three sections … I try to transfer the work which the other sections do to my equipment, so that I can meet my plan. But I often have to do their work at my expense and I cannot avoid it. That is the situation.

The tendency to the centralisation of the decision-making process in management as a whole is obvious. The previous independence of section chiefs, particularly in the self-financing subdivisions where the section independently secured its own orders, has been liquidated. In 1992, when production collapsed, the management of the company was only too happy to get rid of its headache and transfer responsibility to the section chiefs. As the situation stabilised and production increased the independence of line managers, particularly in the self-financing subdivisions, became a hindrance. Once production begins to recover they move to the centralisation of management. In the words of one of the members of the administration, the self-accounting subdivisions began 'to work more on the side than for their own enterprise, in order to earn more'. Thus the management decided to 'take them in hand', depriving them of their independence, and also to 'shorten the lead' of the rest of the line managers.

Towards the end of 1994 there was a marked increase in dissatisfaction within the management of the company, an increase in the distance between the higher and middle levels of management. One of the section chiefs confessed:

> In general it has become very hard to work, very difficult. Everyone is afraid. If you say something critical of the president or of the board you are sacked ... There, at the top, there is constant bickering. The workers see this.

Not surprisingly, the section chiefs responded negatively to the erosion of their independence implied by the Hubbard re-organisation. Like the workers, they saw the change as inflating the management staff: 'They need to be cut in half.' 'They equip their offices, spend millions of dollars on Hubbard College, it would be better to pay the workers properly and buy equipment', said one.

LABOUR RELATIONS

Employment

In the area of labour relations the administration has pursued a strategy of individualising relations with employees, and of excluding the trade union from participation in the resolution of employment issues. With the reconstitution of the enterprise as a joint-stock company some of these issues came to be regulated by the charter of the company. Thus, in the charter it is stated that the dismissal of a shareholder-worker is subject to the agreement not of the trade union, but of the shareholders' meeting. Subsequently a contract system to determine conditions of employment replaced the collective agreement. These changes took place before corresponding changes and additions were made to the Labour Code of the Russian Federation (25 September, 1992).

Since March 1992 all the heads of subdivisions and the majority of workers have been transferred to fixed-term labour contracts, while indefinite contracts were concluded with some workers. This latter category comprised, in the words of the factory's director:

> The best, in whom we have confidence, whose work suits us ... who do not violate discipline, have good attitudes to their work, a long period of service, that is, who are qualified.

Contracts shorter than one year are concluded with some workers, depending on the type of work and on their attitude to work. This is how the director described the purpose of fixed-term contracts with the workers:

> If one has a person who does not work as one would like, you conclude a contract for a shorter period, so that he already feels that he is not so necessary to production, to the enterprise. And this may in some way urge him on psychologically to work better.

We know of at least one case in which a worker who had earlier been dismissed has been re-employed. They took him, as one of the foremen said, 'for purely humanitarian reasons', although as a result he had lost his rights to vacation and his seniority, which could have a subsequent impact on the size of his pension.

Workers did not feel that their position was under threat as a result of the move to individual contracts. On the contrary, in conversations they expressed the judgement that 'the contract guarantees my position, it stipulates the grounds on which it can be terminated, and the grounds on which it cannot'.

In resolving questions of employment the role of the section chief was increased: he or she was given the right to select workers and conclude contracts with them, although it is true that these had to be endorsed with the signature of the director. In the past it had been the foreman who had selected workers for the section, now they have moved back to the second rank, although they are not completely excluded from the process.

Redundancies

Before the transformation of Lenkon into a joint-stock company there was a directive that not one person would be dismissed, but that labour should be redeployed within the enterprise.

However, during the sharp fall in production in the summer of 1992 there was a significant reduction of personnel, by 30 per cent. The policy of reduction in relation to the Moscow and Kryukovskii factories was different. A member of the board described the priorities underlying this differentiated approach.

> The problems of reductions at the two factories are different. The factory outside Moscow is the only enterprise in the village and it is dangerous to throw people out on to the street, they will be hooliganised and it will do more harm than keeping him at work. Our task is to find people other jobs. This is a big problem, we realise this ... We want to organise homeworking, but the problem is that people are passive.

There were no redundancies at the Kryukovskii factory, which employed 1500, but wages were held down instead. The attempts of management to keep up the earnings of the Moscow workers, by contrast, led to a reduction in personnel in the summer of 1992 of 30 per cent.

At the Moscow factory the first people to be sacked were engineering and technical workers (ITR), women, pensioners, unskilled and low-skilled workers, and 'absentees and drunkards'. Under the pretext of punishment for violations of labour discipline the factory management also got rid of 'trouble-makers', the most active critics of the administration. The selective approach to the laying-off of ITR and workers was also related to hidden, unarticulated criteria, and more particularly to the presence of labour dynasties, above all among line managers, junior office workers, and auxiliary workers (storekeepers, controllers) who were not affected by redundancy.

With the reduction of personnel in the summer of 1992 the following mechanisms were used for taking the decision. The overall number of employees to be made redundant, in the enterprise as a whole and in each of its subdivisions, was defined by the management of the joint-stock company, while the 'tactical' decisions were taken independently by the line managers, usually by section chiefs themselves, although in one section lists of employees of the section were handed out to the workers and they were told to strike out the surnames of those who, in their view, should be dismissed. After this the results were compared and it turned out that the view of all the workers with regard to seven of the candidates for redundancy coincided, so that the decision to sack them was taken by the workers themselves. The trade union endorsed the dismissals without question.

In self-financing subdivisions there were no reductions as such: less skilled workers were dismissed, but in their place young skilled workers were recruited. As the chief of the tool-making section put it, 'it was even necessary to take people back, to manage to fulfil the volume of orders'.

It is remarkable that the declaration of redundancies was unexpected by the factory's employees, people finding out about it on their return from vacation. The absence of information about the redundancies led to an increase in tension within Lenkon whose echo was felt several months later. In the factory rumours circulated that the factory would soon be closed, and the land and building rented to a foreign firm. People only calmed down at the beginning of the following year, 1993, when they were convinced that their fears were groundless.

At the beginning of 1993, 310 employees remained at Lenkon, of whom 60 (19 per cent) were ITR and 226 (73 per cent) workers.

After the redundancies the skill and age composition of the labour force 'improved'. And although a fairly large number of workers of pension and pre-pension age remained in the factory (around 28 per cent between 50 and 70 years old), the majority of workers were now men between 30 and 50 years old (67 per cent), of whom around 43 per cent were between 30 and 45. Young workers, up to 30 years old, made up a little more than 14 per cent of the workers. The overwhelming majority of workers in the factory were men (around 90 per cent). The average skill grade was 4.5, on an internal five grade scale. As concerns the educational level, more than 60 per cent of the workers had either general or specialist secondary education.

As a result of the redundancies in the factory the 'skeleton of cadres' was preserved. One of the foremen defined these people as 'those people who have worked at the factory for decades, who love their factory, and have real experience'. In the view of another foreman, 'age and seniority are not important, the main thing is that a person should be disciplined and should know how to do 100 per cent of the operations on the conveyor'.

Nevertheless, despite the reduction of staff, in the view of the vice-president for economics the factory still had too many employees and in the summer of 1993 a further round of reductions was planned, to cut the labour force by a further 30 per cent. However, with the departure of the Kryukovskii factory from the joint-stock company, the production situation changed and the question of recruitment of personnel came to the fore.

Recruitment policy

In 1994 the management of Lenkon completely rejected a policy of redundancy. By this time it had been carried away by the philosophy of Scientology and by the restructuring of the enterprise 'according to Hubbard'. According to Hubbard a successfully operating firm should be constantly expanding, so the main principle of employment policy in Lenkon became EXPANSION.

The essence of the policy of recruitment of new workers was to attract young specialists and high-skilled workers to the factory. With regard to the specialists, the principle, particularly in the new departments such as the marketing service, was that they should ideally be not older than 30–35. There was a definite policy with regard to workers as well: they basically recruited high-school graduates who had spent six months doing their industrial placements at Lenkon. The less well qualified and older workers were transferred to other, lower paid, work. Informal connections played an important role in recruitment – acquaintances, recommendations – while they tried not to take people 'from the street'.

In the opinion of one member of the board, the optimal situation is one in which there is a constant inflow and outflow of people, so that around 10 per cent of the employees are renewed every year. This would lead to a situation in which 'the best are left'. The chief of the department for personnel management and communications considers that 'there must be a constant growth of the company', the previous redundancies 'did not justify themselves'.

One should note that there is another view of this question, expressed by the former chief of the department of wages and norms, who became vice-president for economics following the split in 1993. He considers that there is no objective foundation for an expansionist strategy, since the company is experiencing difficulties related to the fall in the volume of production, the insolvency of many customers, the loss of markets and so on. He considers that the position of the head of personnel management is determined by the fact that his 'personal statistics' are primarily determined by the recruitment of skilled workers: the more of them he recruits, the better will his personal statistics look. In 1994 new workers were not needed for production. Indeed, in the opinion of the vice-president for economics, a new wave of redundancies was needed.

In 1994, according to his information, 520 people worked at

Lenkon, an increase of 200 people over the previous year.[2] According to the personnel management department, 50 per cent of the new workers in the company were skilled workers (there are about 30 to 40 of them), and the remainder were ITR: designers, technologists and so on. The new Hubbard management strategy defined a particular proportion between the number of workers and the number of specialists, including ITR, based on the 'trinomial principle' of organisation of production and of the enterprise as a whole: the executors (in this case the worker), the manager, that is the person who provides the worker with his or her orders (work), requisite materials and tools, and also a third person, carrying out the function of monitoring the execution and organisation. Following on from this conception the senior management of the company intended significantly to increase the number of ITR and specialists. At the beginning of 1995 it proposed to recruit 20 people. It should be noted that the growth in the number of employees in the offices, or the 'White House' as the workers call the administration building, gives rise to discontent and irritation among the workers.

In April 1994 a programme of selection of specialists for Lenkon was adopted. Testing was established as the basis for making decisions about every single candidate. Moreover, the results of the test, independently of whether or not the candidate is offered a job in the company, were to be entered on a special card index of potential employees, classified according to their specialisms. If the candidate achieves satisfactory results in the test, he or she has an interview with the head of the personnel department or head of personnel management. The final decision should be taken by the president of the

2 Different documents issued by the company give different figures for the numbers employed. If one trusts the business plan for 1994–5, the company employs 1200 people (and the president of the company gave this same figure in an interview), of whom 35 per cent are ITR and management personnel. The section chiefs said that they had taken on new workers in the course of the year, but this amounted to no more than 4–6 people in each section. In the autumn of 1993, when the business plan was developed, Lenkon consisted of little more than the factory. How is one to interpret such divergences in the figures for the number of employees? One of the senior managers of the company helped: the enterprise has artificially exaggerated the number on paper, that is the formal number of employees, in order to avoid the tax on excessive wages, which has to be paid on all wage payments above the average of six times the minimum wage. The best estimate of the number is that there remain fewer than five hundred workers, even taking into account the recruitment of new workers and specialists. According to the figures of January 1994 there were 40 members of the management team, 40 line managers and specialists and 350 workers, making a total of 430 people.

company. The recruitment of workers remains within the competence of the chiefs of sections and subdivisions.

The president takes personal responsibility for the selection of managerial staff, which gives rise to clear discontent on the part of the production director. In his view, it would be much more rational for business if he selected his own deputies and closest subordinates himself: 'I have to work with them'.

The company still uses the contract system of hiring for work, although today, in the words of the personnel manager, 'the contract system has lost its sense', since the recommendations of the Ministry of Labour (introduced in 1994) forbid the inclusion of the conditions for dismissal in the contract of employment. And the Labour Code in force, which applies equally to private companies, does not allow the dismissal of workers for turning up drunk for work without a medical examination. The head of the personnel service considers that their hands are tied, and thinks that it is not right that the same labour law should apply to state and private enterprises. The management cannot adopt a new form of contract, above all with ITR and specialists, because there is still no law on commercial secrets. And the question of the preservation of commercial secrets acquires considerable significance here. For example, several categories of specialist, who have access to commercial secrets and who influence the development of the firm, will be paid more highly, alongside which their duties will be laid down in more detail.

Another problem has arisen in recent months – child labour. Lenkon is keen to recruit school and college graduates, since the management believes that it must itself train its own skilled labour force. Moreover, 'young workers can be trained to be what we need'. But at the same time this violated several legal formalities: the young workers worked a full working day, which was a clear infringement of the Labour Code. A recent inspection revealed this violation and the company was strictly forbidden to violate the law in future. The reaction of the management of the company was to decide not to recruit under-age workers at all, since it was unprofitable to obey the letter of the law (for example, the factory is not in a position to provide, as the Labour Code decrees, a foreman-instructor for each under-age worker).

PAY

One can define the pay policy of the Lenkon management as a policy of trial and error, with no clear strategy or, more charitably, a 'policy of flexible reaction'.[3] Changes in the organisation of the payment system have been exclusively a reaction to changes in the situation in the enterprise: few orders and a fall in production led to a transfer to time-wages; an increasing number of orders and growth in production led to the introduction of elements of piece-work and attempts to reintroduce elements of the KTU (coefficient of labour participation) system; a further fall in production led to a rejection of the KTU and payment of scale wages. Experiments with pay began in the spring of 1992 with the introduction of a special kind of payment for *klassnost'*.

Klassnost' as an indicator of loyalty to the firm

Klassnost' was an indicator of loyalty to the firm, 'it should show who has contributed most to the firm'. In fact *klassnost'* was a moral evaluation of the worker and not compensation for work done, and was defined by the enterprise as 'an additional reward as a means of evaluating the activity and present and future services of the worker to the shareholding company'. The most important of the criteria for awarding *klassnost'* is that of 'loyalty as the embodiment of all aspects of attitudes – both to work and to property'.

First class, which paid 3,000 roubles a month and could go to not more than 20 per cent of specialists in a subdivision with a minimum of five years service, required a high skill and ability to work in various trades and specialisms; high discipline; a conscientious attitude to work, i.e. systematic display of initiative in carrying out work, independently taking decisions to improve the organisation of work and removal of barriers to the carrying out of tasks.

Second class paid 1,500 roubles per month and could go to not more than 30 per cent of specialists with two years service, high skill, high discipline, and a conscientious attitude to work and the property of the company.

Officially *klassnost'* was 'awarded by the director of the factory on

[3] For a more detailed examination of the payment system in Lenkon up to 1993 see Valentina Vedeneeva, 'Payment Systems and the Restructuring of Production Relations in Russia', in Simon Clarke, ed., *Management and Industry in Russia: Formal and Informal Relations in the Period of Transition*, Edward Elgar, Cheltenham, 1995.

the recommendation of the chief of the subdivision on the basis of the views of the labour collective'. The award was not once and for all, a worker could be reduced a class or deprived of it altogether for disciplinary violation or an unconscientious attitude to work. Around half the workers in the factory were awarded *klassnost'*, most of whom were middle-aged and older workers, frequently referred to in interviews as the 'skeleton' of the factory. It was understood that it was much more difficult for young workers to achieve *klassnost'* because of their lack of experience and qualifications. And, as one of the foremen noted, young workers 'participate less morally in the life of the factory'.

The workers reacted negatively to the introduction of *klassnost'*, whether or not they had it themselves, seeing it as a violation of social justice, since payment was not immediately related to the results of their labour. They repeatedly asked the section chiefs to change *klassnost'* and divide the money between all the workers in the section.

One reason for dissatisfaction was the absence of clear criteria for its award and the artificial categorisation into first and second class. Even more, *klassnost'* was introduced on the eve of the first wave of redundancies and its introduction served one further purpose: to rank the workers to facilitate the taking of decisions about redundancy. The administration did not conceal the fact that those without *klassnost'* would be first in line for the sack if cuts were necessary. As the vice-president for economics put it, those without *klassnost'* were 'those workers whom we would give up first in a crisis situation'.

The line managers were also not so keen on the system, partly because they bore the brunt of the workers' grievances, and partly because its award from above was an erosion of their own authority, since the additional payments for *klassnost'* came not from the foreman's fund, but from the company's funds. However, in practice they managed to subvert the system. In principle workers were only eligible for the award of *klassnost'* after a particular length of service, but in fact it was possible for it to be awarded early. As the head of the personnel department explained:

> A high-class specialist can receive *klassnost'* inside the fixed term formally laid down in the rules for *klassnost'*, even within a month. For this the section chief has to petition management.

Usually the section chief would do this not on his own initiative, but at the request of the foreman. Thus this provided a lever for the foreman over the workers: the workers insisted that the advanced award of *klassnost'* was only possible for those 'with protection', with a particular relation to the section chief and/or foreman.

However, the management of the company attached great significance to the system. In the words of the head of the personnel department, those with *klassnost'* were those who

> without a word, without pressure and without extra pay agree to stay on after the shift and to come in on their days off ... the introduction of *klassnost'* has proved itself.

However, *klassnost'* was eventually abandoned. When asked why, the deputy for economics replied:

> We recognised that we had to pay for work, that is earnings had to become the basic incentive: the better you work, the more you will earn, and the division into classes was not very objective and largely artificial – the workers did not understand it.

However, it also seems likely that higher management saw *klassnost'* as a system which in practice strengthened the position of line managers, and so abolished it as part of the centralisation of power. As one of the line managers said,

> The allocation to classes was not very objective and to a significant extent it was artificial. The workers did not understand this.

Transition to time-wages

In the autumn of 1992 it was decided to abandon the previous piece-rate system of payment, and in the main production sections time-wages were introduced from 1 October. In management's words, this step was forced on them, because it was necessary to hold on to the skeleton of the labour collective, to keep the skilled workers in the factory in conditions of a sharp decline in the volume of production. Keeping to the piece-rate system with the fall in production would have meant a corresponding fall in earnings. The transition to a four-day week and even reductions in the number of employees turned out not to be enough. Moreover, the management was re-orienting its policy from an emphasis on quantity to an emphasis on quality, so it had to organise a new payment system.

In the Moscow factory a mixed system of payment was introduced, with piece bonuses and time bonuses for the workers. ITR and the administration were put on fixed salaries, with additional percentage bonuses dependent on the results of their work. In the self-financing section the workers' pay depended directly on the results of their work, on the speed and quality with which they fulfilled their orders. The size of the bonuses was determined by the section chief, depending on the profits received.

In establishing the minimum hourly rates the administration was guided by the Soviet Uniform Skill-Tariff Handbook (EKTS), although it turned out that the requirements laid down there were too high for the Lenkon workers. It was therefore decided to introduce their own internal grading system. The base level for the determination of the internal five-grade pay scale was the profession of assembly fitter, to which other wages were connected by a coefficient. The minimum tariff coefficient (from 0.6 to 1.08) was applied to the auxiliary workers, the maximum (1.93) to the fifth grade tool-making fitters. The new grades which were given to the workers were not written in their labour books because the process of grading was not a completely formal process. This made it possible to overcome various formal barriers, for example to 'leapfrog' grades, so a grade 2 worker could immediately get a 4th or 5th grade, which is officially forbidden.

Up to December 1993 the wages fund was made up of two parts: from one part wages according to grade were paid (70 per cent), while the other part (30 per cent) was the bonus fund. The director of the factory, together with the deputy for production, determined the scale of the bonuses for each section, using the following indicators:

- the term of plan fulfilment, observation of schedule (12.5 per cent)
- quality of production, defined by the section quality controller (12.5 per cent)
- 'culture of production' (keeping the premises and machines clean and tidy) (5 per cent)

Within the section, money from the bonus fund was distributed by the section chief, sometimes with the collaboration of the foreman and brigadier. According to one of the workers, this division of the wages fund into two parts, basic and bonus, allows the administration 'to put them on a lead', more effectively controlling their work. In the opinion of the small-batch section chief the management uses the bonus as a stick more than a carrot, deliberately putting them in a position of dependence since the section chief has the right to reduce the bonus.

In addition to this the workers could receive payments from the so-called 'foreman's fund', which was made up of the following funds:

- 50 per cent of the payment by the enterprise for employees of the section on sick leave
- 50 per cent of the money paid by the enterprise to cover employees on vacation
- money for vacant posts in the section (on the basis of average monthly earnings)

The foreman usually used this fund to provide incentives for the most enterprising workers. In the words of one section chief:

> If a person works with spirit and initiative, concerned not to waste time but with the results of his work, then he will receive additional payment from the foreman's fund.

This fund also serves to provide incentives for those workers 'who do not refuse, when it is necessary, to work on into the evening after their shift, or to come in on a Saturday', overtime being paid from this fund rather than from the basic or bonus funds, there being no right to overtime pay. While it is only the section chief who can set the level of salary (by assigning the worker to a particular wage category), the distribution of the bonus and of money from the foreman's fund is in the hands of the section chief together with the foreman and brigadier.

Among the workers payment from the foreman's fund is taken for granted – not as an encouragement or stimulus but as an obligatorily established part of their monthly pay. This is why they often protest against black Saturdays or work on Thursday which is paid out of the foreman's fund ('we would have distributed this money amongst ourselves in any case') and demand additional payment from the funds of the enterprise.

The basic rate of pay was supposed to be reviewed periodically by the board to take account of inflation. But in fact the level of scale pay was increased in proportion to the growth in commodity output or sales. For this they used an index of the rate of growth of commodity output calculated as a relation of the volume of production at current prices for the relevant month to the volume of production at current prices for the base month. Workers also had a guaranteed minimum pay no less than the legally established minimum pay of workers in budget organisations.

Conflict

The transition to time-wages was a fairly conflictual process. The reason for the most dramatic conflict was the dissatisfaction of the workers in the small-batch section with the minimum hourly rate (35 roubles). In their view, supported by the accounts, to maintain the level of earnings that they had had previously on the piece-rate system, their hourly rate would have had to be set at 70 roubles. This is what one of the workers in the section said about it:

> They told us that we would go on time-wages, but they did not tell us the rate. Then somewhere around the twelfth they told us about the hourly rate and it seemed very low to us. They explained that it started at 35 roubles an hour for the first grade, and then how much someone got depended on the grade, the coefficient. The average pay, including the assemblers, came out at 10,000 roubles across the factory. But we got more than that on piece-rates. If they paid us at 35 roubles an hour we would have lost pay, we were earning about 12,000 … but the other sections would either be getting a pay rise or earning the same. And we lost out, our section.

The conflict came to a head at the end of October 1992. The workers did not resort to strike action, because they understood that if they went on strike they would be in violation of the charter of the company, which included an article forbidding strikes on pain of dismissal. As a result the workers wrote their demands for an increase of their hourly rate from 35 to 70 roubles, with monthly indexation, and submitted them to the trade union committee and to the administration. After a week they had received absolutely no response. Then from the board of the company came a refusal to meet any of their demands. A week later the administration of the factory came to the section and a discussion of the situation took place after work, during which a temporary compromise was reached – to set the hourly rate at 40 roubles.

The willingness of the workers to agree to a compromise was determined not least by the fact that many workers at that time felt themselves to be shareholders. Recounting the motives of their comrades' behaviour, one of the assembly fitters expressed the widespread mood:

> We could have put pressure on if we had been simply employees of the factory, but since we now also receive dividends, how can I press when this pressure is simply on my other pocket, into which the dividends go. If we pushed it to the finish, we would have to forget about dividends, break and destroy everything. We did talk among ourselves about the possibility of stopping work, of going on strike. But the majority was against violating the charter of the company. I myself voted for this charter, so how can I go against it?

Apart from the point about pay, there was also a point in the workers' demands about increasing the subsidy for lunch from 15 to 35 roubles. This was a demand addressed to the trade union committee since this subsidy was set by the trade union, although the money for this purpose was allocated to the trade union committee out of the profits of the company. This demand was also partially fulfilled – the payment for lunch was increased to 25 roubles a day. In general, representatives of the trade union committee did not take an active part in this conflict and in fact took the side of the administration. The other sections did not support these workers in their conflict over the introduction of time-wages.

More detailed interviews with other, direct and indirect, participants in the conflict reveal a more complicated picture. The workers in this section came out with their demands not only because they lost more than others in the transfer to time-wages, but also because the workers in this section had been told about this measure in advance by their section chief. The latter had worked out and told the workers how much each one would receive. Taking these calculations as a basis, the workers had calculated the hypothetical hourly rate corresponding to the volume of work which they had done when they were on piece-rates. However, as the section chief explained:

> Then our orders fell, and we should have cut the number of personnel by 60 per cent, but what happened in the end was that we cut by 30 per cent, and the remaining people transferred to time-wages.

The workers in the other sections had kept quiet because they did not know anything about the introduction of time-wages, since the chiefs of these sections had not told their workers anything.

At the end of April 1993 a further conflict arose in relation to the failure of the management to fulfil the promise made in February to increase the minimum hourly rate from 75 to 150 roubles an hour. In March pay was increased by only 40 per cent, management promising to pay the remaining 60 per cent in April, but on 30 April, pay day, the workers only received the same as they had received in March and they stopped work. In their opinion the money had gone to pay the dividend. The chief of the section and the foreman formally adopted a neutral position and remained in the background in this dispute, although their sympathy lay with the workers.

On 28 May the situation was repeated and again pay was not increased. The workers of the small-batch section (UMS) held a stormy meeting, and turned for support to the workers of the neighbouring medium fans section (USSV). These two sections had worked together in one room since November 1992. Initially there had been some tension between the workers of the two sections because of the cramped space and the deterioration in their working conditions, as well as differences in wages and the pace of work in the two sections, but gradually everything settled down and completely good-natured, business-like relations were established between the sections.

> How could there be conflict between workers? On the contrary, we have always supported them when they have spoken out, and we will continue to support them. Their section is better organised than ours

was the answer of one of the UMS assembly fitters to a question about conflict with the workers in the neighbouring section as a result of differences in pay. The UMS workers wrote their demand for an 80 per cent increase in pay in a letter which they prepared themselves and planned to put forward to the administration, which they asked everyone to sign. According to the workers of the USSV, practically all the workers in their section signed the letter. One of the four foremen refused to sign the letter, defending his behaviour by arguing that 'this is the workers' business, it is not ours'. The workers responded very critically to their foremen, saying that they run around for their chief, butter him up and are afraid of him.

According to the workers, the bosses had found out a day or two before the workers handed over their letter to the administration that they were preparing such a letter. The workers assumed that it was the foremen who had informed top management about it, so that the latter was already prepared in advance for discussions with the workers.

On the Friday, 28 May, the workers of the two sections held a meeting during their lunch break which was attended, at the workers' request, by the deputy director for production and the chief of the personnel department, who was at the same time the president of the shareholders' council. The workers particularly noted that nobody was there from the trade union. Since the management had been forewarned about the content of the workers' demands, they were able to inform the workers at this meeting that management had decided to increase the wages of the workers, but by different amounts in different sections: the demands of the workers of the UMS would be met in full, with an 80 per cent increase in pay, but the pay of the workers in the USSV would only be increased by 40 per cent. They explained these differences in the extent to which they were willing to meet the workers' demands by arguing that the labour input in production in UMS was higher than in USSV ('they evaluated our production as being cheaper').

One foreman of the USSV asserted that the increase in pay in their section had been achieved basically at the expense of the foreman's fund, that is to say they had not increased the tariff part of the pay, but only the bonus part, and only 15 per cent of the 40 per cent was taken from the factory funds, with 25 per cent being taken out of the foreman's fund. If there had been no conflict then he, the foreman, would have had to distribute additional pay non-uniformly from his fund, depending on how people had worked, but as a result of the conflict he had to hand out the money to virtually everybody, excepting only a few individuals, 'loafers' in the expression of the foreman.

The workers remained unhappy with the behaviour of the management representatives at the meeting. According to the workers, the managers responded to all the workers' questions with reproaches for bad work, although the workers insist that it is the management that pushes them to do bad work. For example, they impose a tight plan, and then do not provide the means to fulfil it: the parts arrive only at the end of the month:

> The foreman whips on the plan, and the deputy director comes along and says: 'that is badly painted – repaint it'. And in general they catch us for everything they can.

The partial satisfaction of the workers' immediate demands did not resolve the issue, and the factory remained in a ferment through June. However, the president of the company suddenly came forward with a programme to resolve the conflict:

> The way to reduce contradictions between labour and capital in AO LENKON:
>
> - Transfer the centre of gravity in income from dividends to earnings.
> - Exclude from the contracts of members of the Board additional compensation in the form of dividends.
> - Implement the free sale and quotation of shares

responding to demands which had already been made by the workers, but hitherto rejected by management.

Pay and dividends – antagonists

The sudden change of policy on the part of the president of the company was noteworthy because the hitherto hidden contradiction between the two parts of the income of the majority of the workers, wages and dividends, came to the surface in the course of the conflict, which was yet another factor in the split which appeared in the company through 1993. From the inauguration of the joint-stock company the management had pursued a policy of increasing dividends. The percentage return on the shares grew steadily each quarter:

Year	I	II	III	IV
1990	86			
1991	12.5	17	25	55
1992	300			
1993	250	250		

Over this two and a half years the workers' perception of the dividend had changed. Initially the workers looked forward to the shareholders' meeting and the distribution of profits as dividends, which they perceived as a means of improving their material well-being. But over this period most workers had sold most of their shares, which they increasingly came to see as a fraud:

> the workers have few shares, while the administration have many, so they are increasing their income at the expense of the workers.

The high level of dividends began to arouse increasing discontent on the part of the growing number of the workers who did not hold a large number of shares – in general they had a few dozen shares, while only a handful of people held several hundred. They clearly understood that the large shareholdings were held by the senior managers of the factory and the company. Signs of this growing discontent could be observed over a long period of time, and erupted into the open conflict over pay between the workers in the UMS, supported by the workers in the USSV, and the management of the factory and of the company in the spring of 1993 described above.

At the shareholders' meeting in February 1993 the workers, supported by several managers (in particular the chief of the UMS), had proposed that the part of the profits going to dividends should be paid out monthly, not at the end of the year, and in the form of wages.

> I think that the main part [of profit] should go to pay, and less to dividends. But at the moment it is the other way around. Of course if I invested money I could receive a part of the profits, but if someone works well, he should not receive less than me. (UMS worker)

> Profit will go into a general fund of pay, for everyone, from this pay will be increased for everyone, then there will be no difference between shareholders and non-shareholders ... well, if the workers are on the same grade, a single skill, then pay will be increased for all of them. (Chief of UMS)

The management of the company came out strongly against this proposal, but at the meeting at the end of May 1993 the workers raised the issue again: 'We invest, but they [meaning the owners of large holdings of shares, the members of the board] just turn up and receive money'. Discontent was also expressed at the fact that the heads of the company themselves arbitrarily set the sale price of Lenkon shares. There were calls for a strike, with the demand to change the proportion in which income was divided between wages and dividends to the benefit of wages.

Those with the strongest interest in a positive response to this demand were those workers who did not own any shares, since in this case their pay would be increased, and the differentiation of income between worker-shareholders and workers who did not own shares would be reduced. This was the common interest, in essence, of hired workers.

Thus, what appeared to be a conflict over pay also became an expression and crystallisation of the conflict of interests of hired employees who had in fact become small shareholders, and employers, owners of the bulk of the shares in the persons of the managers of the company and the enterprise.

This conflict coincided with an aggravation of the relationship within the management of the company between the president and one of his deputies, about which more will be said below. To strengthen his position in this conflict the president decided to fulfil the workers' demands and declared his intention to change the policy on the payment of labour, transferring the stress from the payment of dividends on shares to wages and removing the payment of additional compensation in the form of dividends from the contracts of members of the board. At the summer shareholders' meeting (July 1993) these decisions were approved, with the guiding principle being that 40 per cent of profits would be paid out for wages. The free quotation and sale of shares was also promised. Apart from this, it was proposed that henceforth all expenses of members of the board, including payment of expenses for foreign trips, would be reported to the shareholders. The council of the company resolved to inform the company's workers of the contents of an agreement between Lenkon and a European company, and to reveal to them the text of documents concerning foreign partners.

Not only workers but also line managers responded positively to the changes in the pay policy of the company for pragmatic reasons. First, since most of the shareholders work in the enterprise it is to their advantage in conditions of rapid inflation to receive increases in their income every month, rather than waiting for quarterly dividends. Second, the higher level of pay makes it much easier to attract high-class specialists, which at that time was a concern of both the enterprise and the section chiefs. It is remarkable that some members of the management even cited ethical motives in their evaluation of the outcome of this conflict:

> We found ourselves in an abnormal situation, when some people received several millions a quarter in the form of dividends alone, while others – primarily the overwhelming majority of workers – received only their pay, which was barely enough to live on. That was unethical.

Subsequently the share of net profits paid out in dividends was reduced from 40 to 27 per cent and dividends were paid at a lower percentage rate:

Year	I	II	III	IV
1993			100	50
1994	50	50	100	100

The indirect result of the conflict was the establishment of a scale of pay differentials between different categories of labour, beginning with the president of the society, with a coefficient of 23, and finishing with unskilled labour with a coefficient of one. Two-thirds of the labour force were workers on skill grades 3–6, with coefficients of 3 or 4. Thus in October 1993 the average monthly wage amounted to 180,000 roubles, ranging from 48,000 roubles for unskilled workers up to 400,000 for senior managers and 890,000 for the president.

Innovation

The transfer to time-wages in the face of a decline in production was not only essential from the point of view of the preservation of a certain level of wages and the maintenance of the skeleton of the labour collective. It was also a compromise between the interests of higher management and the interests of the line managers. Higher managers, immersed at that time in the commercial business of the company and cool to production problems, could not provide the personnel with the necessary volume of work. Moreover, before the introduction of time-wages the department of labour and wages had been liquidated, in other words the enterprise had in fact rejected the previous norms and forms of accounting of labour-time. In these conditions it was assumed that the main burden of responsibility for the provision of work and earnings for the production workers rested on the shoulders of the section chiefs. However, not all the section chiefs justified the hopes of senior management, appearing ham-fisted. Time-wages provided a convenient way out of the situation.

However, the negative effects of this payment system soon began to appear. The system kept up wages in the face of the collapse of production, especially with the introduction of a four-day week, but management of the company was then faced with over spending on wages. Line managers experienced the negative effects of time-wages to the highest degree, pointing to the reduction of the workers' commitment to working hard, especially sensitive in a critical situation.

One of the section chiefs complained:

> They [the workers] have got used to working calmly so that when there is a rush job and we have to work intensively, one has to drive them on, which never used to happen.

Many workers felt, 'now we have time-wages, what's the hurry?' The reduction in the commitment of the workers and in the incentives available to management led to the more frequent disruption of the production process as deliveries from one section to another were delayed, leading to friction between the section chiefs, while workers increasingly frequently expressed their dissatisfaction at the irregular pace of work. The section chiefs considered that the workers' complaints about the organisation of production were justified and tried to shift responsibility to the factory-wide level. In the middle of 1993 the factory management estimated that labour productivity had fallen to around one-third of its former level, with the quality of the product being the same as in the past.

The workers themselves considered their pay levels to be pretty low, despite the fact that they were still higher than in many neighbouring enterprises, but they compared their pay with the cost of living, and with the price of their own product, as well as with the administration: 'In the White House [administration building] they are raking in money, but they don't pay any more to the workers'.

In these conditions the management of the company decided that the period of uncertainty should come to an end, and it decided to modify the payment system to take some account of the productivity and norming of labour. During the early summer there was an attempt to establish new norms, organised by a young specialist brought in for the purpose. Every worker filled in job sheets for every task, countersigned by foremen and/or section chiefs, for a period of two months, the sheets which piled up in the office of the personnel supposedly providing a scientific basis for determining the new pay norms. It was then decided to undertake a further round of re-grading.

At the beginning of the autumn preparatory work for re-grading was carried out, returning to the six grade tariff scale in place of the five grade scale. The idea was to connect the rate of pay to the quality and volume of work carried out. The commission for re-grading comprised the section chief, the deputy chief engineer, the engineer for safety and the chief mechanic, but in fact all the decisions were made by the section chief, since it was considered that he or she knew his or her workers better than did the others. Thus, once again it was not objective criteria, which were the responsibility of the engineers, which played the main role, but subjective considerations. As a result of the re-grading 20 workers had their grades increased. However, the increase in grade did not so much reflect the workers' control of production (we should note that there were no representatives of the workers on the re-grading commission), as the fairly strong position of the line managers, who managed to get higher pay for their workers by overestimating their labour input.

The workers in some sections were not even informed about the changes in grading, and the transition to the new system of pay was made secretly. Only a few workers were interested in the innovations made by their immediate superiors, most of the workers declaring that it was all the same to them, as long as they were paid a decent wage. Only the women workers in the PShU section openly expressed dissatisfaction with the level of their pay, which they compared to the pay of the men in their section, the conflict being resolved by the intervention of representatives of the administration.[4]

From December 1993 the production sections which had been on time-wages were transferred to so-called 'payment by final result' (a time system of payment with the use of normalised tasks). The innovation consisted of the introduction of a pay norm which was calculated on the basis of the estimation of the amount of work required for each separate type of ventilator, supposedly based on the job evaluation exercise carried out earlier in the year. Thus the wage norm was included in the production cost of the fan, comprising about 50 per cent of the total cost. On the basis of the actual output of fans the sum of the normative costs was calculated and this formed the unified wages fund of the section. This fund was made up of the following parts:

- Tariff (normative) wages fund of the workers.
- Additional wages fund of the workers.
- Wages fund for managers and specialists, in accordance with the staff list (salaries).
- Incentive fund for the payment of the collective of the section

4 On the gender dimension of this conflict see Galina Monousova, 'Gender Differentiation and Industrial Relations' in Simon Clarke, ed., *Conflict and Change in the Russian Industrial Enterprise*, Edward Elgar, Cheltenham, 1996.

(the maximum bonus was set at 60 per cent of the tariff part of the wage or salary).

This payment system was adopted in the UMS, USSV, PShU, RMU, UKV and the service section. In practice the pay of the workers in these sections was calculated on the basis of the normative expenditure of labour corresponding to the volume of output produced.

The system was different in the tool-making section, which had previously been self-financing. From 1 January 1994, in connection with the liquidation of the system of internal self-financing within the company, the piece-rate system of pay which had been retained in this section was replaced by a new system of time-wages. The unified wages fund in this section was made up of :

- Planned wages fund of the workers (based on hourly tariffs).
- Wages fund for managers and specialists.
- Additional wages fund (representing the difference between the actual expenditure of labour, that is the norm-hours, and the wages fund corresponding to the staff list).
- Incentive fund (bonuses).

A system of time-wages was also adopted by the auxiliary industrial sections. Here the unified wages fund was as in the tool-making section, but without an 'additional wages fund'.

The size of the incentive fund for each section was defined every month by the so-called 'balance commission', although in practice such a commission does not exist as an independent body. The board of the company determines the size of the incentive fund at its monthly meetings, when a decision is taken about the percentage bonus to be paid to each subdivision for the month, based on the fulfilment of the monthly production programme, or, in the language of the Hubbard management methods, 'the value of the final product' of the subdivision. The workers receive the bonus for the prompt production of quality products, while the criteria for the award of bonuses to managers, ITR and specialists are their personal statistics.

The percentage bonus depends on the dynamics of the statistics: ten per cent (of tariff wage or salary) if each of the indicators is positive. If the 'hat' (the complex of indicators either of personal statistics or statistics of the subdivision, including the section) has four indicators, then two of them are evaluated at 10 per cent, and the two others at 5 per cent, so that the maximum total bonus is 30 per cent. There is also an indicator of a 'condition of abundance', which signifies a rapid growth of the indicators over several months. In this case a 20 per cent bonus can be paid for one indicator.

Thus the incentive fund of a section, division or department is determined by multiplying the wages fund by the percentage bonus. Each section receives a different amount, whose distribution is under the control of the section chief (the internal criteria for the determination of the bonus will be discussed below). For specialists and managers the process of determining the bonus is somewhat different. A manager cannot receive a bonus higher than the general level for his or her subdivision, so that if the department has a bonus of 30 per cent, that is the maximum bonus that its managers can receive. At the same time his or her subordinates may receive either more (to a maximum of 60 per cent) or less.

This is the general rule, but the determination of the policy for the distribution of pay within the subdivision is a matter for its management. The position of the heads of the company is that the chief of any industrial section or other subdivision has the right to make any changes in the distribution of pay between employees in that subdivision. The only condition is that the production plan should be strictly fulfilled or that the manager should have positive personal statistics, everything else is up to his or her personal discretion. As a result virtually all the industrial sections differ from one another in the ways in which the payment system is organised. For example, in UMS, where payment is according to the final result, the pay of each worker is calculated on the basis of the establishment of a labour participation coefficient (KTU); workers in PShU fill in index cards, prepared by the former economics manager, where the actual expenditure of labour is recorded; in USSV wages are calculated according to the scale.

Despite the nuances in the determination of the workers' pay in the various sections, they all have a guaranteed minimum wage, which is that laid down by the tariff scale. This is not very convenient for the section chiefs, who cannot punish a guilty worker if they need to, or at least cannot pay below the tariff wage. As one section chief complained:

> We have to calculate the tariff wage every month. The president once promised the workers that they would not be paid less than the tariff. There are people who earn less, but I have to pay them according to the scale.

Despite the fact that the workers' pay depends on their grade and tariff, the pay levels of skilled workers on exactly the same grade vary depending on their ability to work on several machines rather than on just one. They can earn much more if they have been able to work on additional machines that month. This arrangement was established in particular sections at the end of 1992. At that time many workers were unhappy about it, and it gave rise to a few small local conflicts. Now everybody has got used to it and such differentiation does not create any problems.

The section chief also distributes (alone or together with the foreman and brigadier) bonuses from the incentive fund. The internal criteria for the award of bonuses, according to one of the section chiefs, are the following indicators:

- Observation of labour, industrial and technological discipline
- The culture of production

In the past there were formal criteria and definite limits to the bonus (for example, for observing the 'culture of production' the worker could receive a 5 per cent bonus payment), today everything depends on the good (or ill) will of the section chief, and also of the brigadier and foreman whom he or she consults.

> All our workers are under observation, we see for ourselves who is working how, so we decide for ourselves to whom we should give how much bonus.

Such a method of distribution of bonuses, without any clear criteria, is usually accompanied by conflict between the section chief and the workers (if the section chief takes the decision on his or her own). Workers accuse the section chief of encouraging only his 'favourites'. These conflicts are generally resolved at the level of the subdivision.

In one of the sections the labour collective council (STK) was revived, whose basic function was the distribution of bonuses, although this did not lead to any reduction in the level of conflict around questions of pay (the STK will be discussed further below).

The application of the system of payment by final results, in which a planned wages fund calculated on the basis of tariff scales was incorporated, also turned out to have negative consequences. The section chiefs significantly exaggerated the estimated labour inputs in order to increase the earnings of their workers. As a result there was a systematic failure to achieve the planned tasks. In order to focus the section on the fulfilment of the plan, the company management worked out the idea of linking the tariff to the amount of work done by the section. For example, if the production plan was only 80 per cent fulfilled, the workers would only be paid 80 per cent. However, the section chiefs found another way of resolving the problem of plan fulfilment, but at the expense of an increase in the number of workers.

In the middle of 1994 practically all the production subdivisions were once again moved onto time-wages, and it was decided to index pay to inflation monthly (February 1.5, July 1.8, August 2.16, October 3.11, November 3.73, December 4.48). The nominal level of workers' pay in Lenkon in June 1994 (excluding bonuses), amounted to an average 300,000 roubles; ITR received a little more than 400,000. This was 85 per cent higher than the average industrial wage at that time.

Wages of ITR and specialists

The basis of the pay of ITR and specialists, as in the past, is determined by the salary attached to their post defined in their job specification. However, a new element entered into the organisation of the pay of line managers. In particular, from January 1994 the pay of section chiefs has been strictly related to the pay of the workers in their section. In addition to their official salary and bonus, the shop chief has the right to draw an additional income from the section funds, so long as his pay does not exceed double the average monthly pay of the workers in his section. In this way he has a direct interest in increasing the pay of his workers (in fact none of the section chiefs has done this so far, for 'ethical reasons': 'it is not opportune to pay oneself more than one's immediate superior'). For ITR the same coefficient is 1.5. One should note that this linking of the pay of managers and specialists to the pay of their workers gives them a very strong incentive to exaggerate the workers' labour input. There is good evidence that particular section chiefs commit this sin.

There is a continuing tendency to 'pay for brains', which can be observed in many other enterprises as well, although it is true that the rate of growth of earnings of ITR and specialists lagged behind that of workers in the first half of 1994. From the outside this looked like a temporary disciplinary measure through which the management of the company tried to encourage the ITR and specialists to speed up the development of their personal 'hats', the indicators of their personal performance. Representatives of the ITR see things differently: 'Now the attitude to the ITR in the factory reflects the fact that they are considered to be useless'.

At the end of 1994 a new system for working out the salaries of ITR and specialists was adopted, which connected their pay closely to their personal performance indicators. If these indicators were positive for a period of six months, their salary would be increased. The underlying ideas in these changes in the pay of specialists and ITR were, on the one hand, to link their pay to the results of their work and, on the other hand, to establish a hierarchy of employees according to their place in the firm, the level of their responsibility, their access to secret information and so on. Thus a similar approach which had previously been taken to the workers with regard to the award of *klassnost'* was now being taken to the ITR and specialists. However, by contrast to the workers, all these criteria are supposed to be taken into account in drawing up individual contracts.

The workers respond calmly to the differentiation in pay between workers and specialists, but only to the extent that they are satisfied with the level of their own pay. Recently, when the rate of growth of their pay has lagged far behind the growth in the cost of living, the workers have much more frequently expressed their dissatisfaction with the level of their pay. However, by contrast to 1993, when this dissatisfaction was openly expressed and the workers went for short work stoppages, today the situation is different. They are afraid to speak out openly because they are afraid of losing their jobs. The differences in income between ordinary workers and their bosses, which the workers remark on very emotionally ('this is not a difference, it is not even a gap, it is an abyss'), arouses them less than the gap between their growing demand for things to buy ('there is so much of everything in the shops') and their ability to pay. In group discussions with us the workers stated their position more than once: 'It is OK for the chiefs to get a lot, but let them also pay us a bit more.'

Social sphere

For all its commercial orientation, Lenkon management has not abandoned its paternalistic obligations. Apart from direct payments in the form of wages and dividends, the workers also have subsidised catering, for which the enterprise pays out of its profits. The amount of subsidy is regularly increased and amounts to about half the monthly cost of food in the factory canteen. Some years ago, at the beginning of the 1990s, when barter was widespread, the factory supplied its workers with scarce durable goods (refrigerators, washing machines, TV sets, video and audio equipment and so on) and clothes at less than market prices. All the goods were distributed through vertical channels, from top to bottom: managers were supplied first, then, through the trade union, goods were distributed around the sections in proportion to the number of applications received, and those for whom there were not enough goods waited their turn with the next distribution. The result was that virtually everybody eventually got what they wanted. More recently barter supplies have ceased, but there is still a social-consumption department of the administration, located in the trade union offices, which regularly organises the sale of consumer goods. Moreover, thanks to an agreement with a collective farm in the Moscow region, the workers are supplied with fresh dairy products at prices a bit below those in the shops.

The factory never possessed its own social infrastructure, because it had too few workers to justify supporting a rest centre or pioneer camp. This problem was resolved in other ways: the factory shared with another enterprise in supporting a pioneer camp, providing access to all those who wanted it; on the basis of a contract with a sanatorium in the Moscow region they bought places for their workers, and obtained places in tourist centres for vacations in the same way. According to the president of the trade union committee, 'there is and never has been any problem with vacations'. The factory had, and still has, its own kindergarten, which is sufficient for the needs of all the employees of the enterprise. Since 1993 part of the kindergarten has been rented out to a commercial firm, but there is still not enough money to pay for the support of the kindergarten and to increase the wages of its employees: there are few young workers at Lenkon and the kindergarten is almost empty. The management is planning to close down its own kindergarten and pay parents who work in the factory a grant to pay for places in municipal kindergartens. However, the delay in taking a final decision is connected to deliberations about the methods of attracting skilled young workers to the enterprise.

Housing policy has become an element of the social policy of Lenkon. In the past the enterprise participated in the construction of apartments, which it provided for its workers free of charge, but now the situation has changed: worker-shareholders can receive credit for the purchase of an apartment from the company at a fixed rate of interest over 15 years, the size of the interest payment depending on the length of service of the worker at the enterprise – the longer the service, the lower the rate of interest. According to one member of the board:

> Such a policy is by no means simple, it is really a form of redistribution. If in the past profits were redistributed through apartments, now they are redistributed through shares. It turns out that I, as a shareholder owning a large number of shares, have the right to buy an apartment every year, but others do not. So all of this is not simple.

Apart from this, the company pays additional money for those who have to support children and the disabled. In order to encourage people to upgrade their qualifications privileges are also granted to those who study.

In 1993 Lenkon concluded a medical insurance agreement for all its workers who were members of the company, all the fees being paid by the company. If a worker did not visit the doctor or take a day off sick during the year, he or she received 25 per cent of the annual premium.

The trade union was given organisational responsibility for the distribution of subsidies on food, trips to rest homes and pioneer camps. Thus the trade union apparatus was all the more transformed into a part of the managerial apparatus, and the trade union bosses became the part of the administration responsible for the social sphere.

Labour discipline and punishment

During the 1970s and 1980s the enterprise was noted for its low level of labour discipline and high labour turnover. More recently the position in this sphere has changed. There are several reasons for this. Above all it has been the workers' fear of losing their jobs that has strengthened labour discipline, particularly after the wave of redundancies in the summer of 1992. The workers are expecting unemployment to appear in the future, judging by the information provided by the mass media, so that the majority of them hang on to their jobs since they have heard that, in comparison with many other Moscow enterprises, the situation in Lenkon is more stable and reliable. Moreover, despite the fact that the workers themselves consider their pay to be inadequate, they recognise that pay levels at Lenkon are still high in comparison with other enterprises.

Nevertheless, violations of discipline (lateness, absenteeism, drunkenness at work, refusal to carry out the orders of the foreman or brigadier) still occur. There are formal methods of punishing disciplinary violations, following the charter of the company and the Russian Labour Code. These include warnings, fines, deprivation of bonus, reduction or removal of *klassnost'*, threats of dismissal or dismissal itself. It is usually the foreman who monitors discipline. As one of them said in an interview, 'If a worker will not do the work that I give him, I will not pay him this 30 per cent [his bonus]'. However, in practice people are very rarely punished, since the main thing for the foreman is to get the work done. Dismissal as an extreme form of punishment is employed only rarely, the most common form of punishment being reduction or deprivation of bonus.

In cases in which the informal 'rules of the game' are violated, that is to say when the worker formally has the right, for example, to refuse to work on a Saturday, informal methods of punishment can be employed. The foreman might deprive the worker of incentive payments from the foreman's fund, or put him or her on a low-paying job. The workers are irritated by such punishments, but they have no right to protest, since the distribution of money from the foreman's fund is not covered by any rules, and is not governed by any clear criteria.

The trade union as a rule does not interfere in such conflicts, although formally there is a special commission for labour disputes attached to the trade union committee. Discipline in the factory is a matter between workers, on the one hand, and the foreman or section chief, on the other. The section chief has a fairly broad authority and, as one of them recognised:

> As a section chief I can do whatever I like with a person: revoke his contract, dismiss him ... of course, within the framework of the law.

THE PRESS-STAMP SECTION

The press-stamp section carries out the preliminary assembly with which the technological process of production of the fans begins. Here the parts and assemblies are produced, which are then passed on to other sections for final assembly.

The technological process

The production process begins with the receipt of the month's production tasks. The section chief and technologist, on the basis of these tasks, determine the quantity of different types of metal that will be needed, and draw up their requisition for metal. This requisition is sent to the tally clerk, who orders the metal from the store. She is also responsible for reporting on the use of metal.

Composition of the labour force:

Occupation	Number of people	Grade
cutters	4	4 and 5
stamp operators	6	4
grinder	1	4
adjusters	2	3 and 4
electricians	2	4 and 5
electric welder	1	5
repair fitters	2	5
fitter tin-smith	1	6
turners	5	3 and 4
ancillary workers	2	
apprentice	1	

The technological process begins with the cutting of the metal which has been delivered from the factory stores. Then the cut metal is put through the stamping machine, and some of the parts go directly for assembly. The dies for the stamping equipment have to be prepared for each new part by the (male) adjuster. He makes the first part, and adjusts and modifies the die if he notices any faults. Then the (female) stamp-operator takes over the production work. A quality controller from the department of technical control, who is responsible for checking the quality of selected parts, works alongside the stamp operators. A grinder is responsible for the repair of the dies. After stamping, some of the parts are transferred for mechanical processing, some for electric welding. The production of the press-stamp section goes to two other sections, where the small and medium fans are assembled.

At the beginning of 1994 the section employed 29 people: the chief of section, foreman, technologist and 26 workers.

At the beginning of 1993 a labour specialist analysed the level of pay and qualifications of the workers of the press-stamp section, on the basis of technological plans, and came to the following conclusion: The basic forms of work carried out by the vast majority of the workers in the section should be graded one or two. At one time, when there had been expensive orders, the norms had been increased so as to 'justify' the costs. Now these norms do not correspond to the work carried out in the section, which is basically unskilled. In the view of the labour specialist the section does not need as many workers as it has at the moment, it would be enough to keep only one third, 'the skeleton, who could if necessary quickly teach new recruits'.

Organisation of labour and pay

The section chief, a young woman (the only female section chief) came to the factory in 1990 from a reinforced concrete factory, where she had worked as a section chief since 1985. Her arrival coincided with the reorganisation of the section: the section had just been reunited with the enterprise after a year in which it had been working as an independent co-operative. The new section chief replaced virtually the whole of the labour collective, including the technologist. Following the redundancies over the summer of 1992 only four people remained from the previous workforce. Some of the new workers, particularly the stamp operators, the new chief brought with her, and others she recruited from outside. The section chief acknowledges her role in the creation of the collective:

> When I arrived there was no collective. People came and went. I created the section and its collective.

After the wave of redundancies there were 22 people working in the section, including the chief, foreman, technologist and 19 workers. The numbers were increased following the organisational changes in the enterprise through the transfer of the turners from the mechanical section. Workers are not tied to their jobs.

> We are already putting the women on other operations, but almost all the men work at various specialisms.

In this small section, in which an STK had existed until 1991, the principle of one-man (woman) management has been established. This is recognised not only by the chief herself ('I alone decide everything and I am responsible for everything here'), but also by her subordinates:

> The section chief is a great administrator. Everything depends on her. She decides the pay, allocates the workers. She writes the daily orders for the foreman.

The section chief draws up a monthly plan for the production of the separate parts in each operation. And the workers know their tasks for the month, since the chief of the section holds an operational meeting in the section at the beginning of the month to tell the workers the production plan and at the end of the month to report on its fulfilment.

Every day the section chief holds an operational meeting – a 'five-minute' – before the beginning of the shift, attended by all the workers in the section. At these 'five-minutes' the tasks for the day are distributed, the volume of production is specified, the amount of work in hand and the situation with regard to metal and equipment is explained, conflicts are looked in to, and questions about various kinds of violations are put.

The section chief insists on strict discipline. The distribution of earnings is the main economic lever for the management of the workers. If in the past the accounts of the amount of metal used, orders completed, and accounts of pay were kept by the norm-setter, now the section chief makes all the decisions about the distribution of the wages and bonus funds on her own, and reports on it to the workers of her subdivision.

The foreman is the connecting link between the workers and the section chief. The daily tasks defined by the section chief are reported to the workers by the foreman: each worker is given a sheet on which to record his or her working time, which is filled in and handed to the foreman at the end of the day. Many of the workers are irritated by this system:

> We don't understand what the point of it is. Initially they said that they were introducing this system to work out the norms, but it takes time to fill it all in.

One can define the status of the foreman as that of the 'senior worker'. The foreman is always to be found among the workers in the section, sorting out production problems. During the lunch break he sits with the male workers in the smoking area, or plays dominoes with them. According to his functions the foreman is better seen as the technical co-ordinator of operational matters than as a manager. He has in his hands no levers of control over the workers and has no influence over their pay. His own pay is determined by the factory administration and modified by the balance commission. Apart from this, the foreman and section chief's pay is affected by plan fulfilment, the quality of production and technical safety. If a faulty part is sent to another section through an error of the stamp-operator, it is not only the worker who made the error who is answerable, but also the foreman and chief of the press-stamp section.

Influence of gender on labour relations

Extended observation of the dynamics of labour relations in this section has included the observation of two cases of social tension in the development of which the influence of gender differences and stereotypical conceptions of their role in production has been noteworthy.

The first was related to the relationship between the male workers and the female section chief. The workers' image of a section chief includes among its most important features a knowledge of production and technology. But they could not recognise their section chief as a specialist, just because she was a woman. In group discussion they openly said that their section chief did not understand anything about production, and emphasised that she was a woman and that a woman could not manage machine operators. They complained that there were no specialists in the section, apart from the technologist. And they even hinted that her nomination to the post of section chief and her being sent to Hubbard College in Sweden to increase her qualifications had nothing to do with her professional qualities. The workers were also unhappy about what they considered to be her 'dictatorial' management style.

The second case of tension was connected with the relationships between workers performing different operations. One feature of the labour collective of this section is a very strict gender division of labour in the various occupations. Work on the stamping machines is traditionally considered to be for women because of its monotony, and is paid on a medium grade. The remaining operations in the section can be graded at higher levels. This leads to high levels of discontent on the part of the women in the collective. The stamp operators frequently complain about the low quality of the work of the cutters who provide them with blanks, not always with justification. In order to smooth over the situation the woman section chief, who had brought the women stamp operators with her when she came to the factory and felt responsible for them, gave them additional bonuses. This action on her part aroused discontent on the part of the men, although this discontent was less obvious and was not openly expressed, unlike that of the women, who had demanded that the administration of the enterprise should review their grades, creating a situation of open conflict in the section.[5]

Subsequently the section chief decided to change her approach to the management of the collective. Above all she decided to review her relationship with the foreman, giving him more rights to participate in the management of the collective. On her own account, earlier she had been afraid to give the male foreman more independence, seeing him as a competitor for her job. Now she has given the foreman responsibility for managing the stamping machine operators, in that way also freeing herself from their influence. She also decided to impose strict control over the mechanical operations herself, so that she will get to know the work better, and in that way try to increase her authority as a specialist among the men.

TOOL-MAKING SECTION

General characteristics

The tool-making section is central to the factory as a whole as it makes tools and non-standard equipment needed by the other sections to produce the various products of the factory. The basic workers in this section have two main professions – machine operators (mechanical production) and fitters (manual production), and there are also various auxiliary and ancillary workers, a total of 26 workers, organised into three brigades: the repair brigade with four people, the fitters with five and the machine operators with 11. Most of these

[5] On this conflict see Galina Monousova, 'Gender Differentiation and Industrial Relations' in Simon Clarke, ed., *Conflict and Change in the Russian Industrial Enterprise*, Edward Elgar, Cheltenham, 1996.

workers are over forty years old, around a quarter of them are over 45, and there are few young workers. The skill level of the workers is higher than in other sections, so that the workers in this section receive the highest pay of any workers in the factory. Moreover, the work in this section is more intensive than elsewhere since from July 1990 the section was self-financing, and apart from the work necessary for the factory it also makes tools for outside customers.

This status of the section was achieved thanks to the efforts of two young engineers in their early thirties who came to the factory in 1990 from a giant Moscow engineering enterprise, as chief and deputy chief of the section. After privatisation, there was a proposal to create a small enterprise on the basis of the tool-making section, as had been done for other small subdivisions such as the transport section. According to the former chief of the section the bosses of the company were interested in this since:

> All the small enterprises created within the framework of Lenkon had limited profitability, somewhere around 25 per cent, but our profitability was enormous, so it would be profitable to create small enterprises on the basis of the section so as to increase the cost price of services and equipment and increase the profit on the final product, the fan. But such an enterprise would only have been independent on paper, and we did not do it because it was proposed that 100 per cent of the founding capital would be invested by Lenkon. I and the section chief would have been appointed directors of the small enterprise, but our rights would not have been much wider than they are now … it had nothing to offer us: profits would be limited to 20 per cent and so on. But on the other hand, to be fair one has to recognise that they did not demand that we pay expenses, amortisation, pay for resources, and so on. But we decided not to do it since it meant that management would be entirely in the hands of Lenkon.

In August 1992 a new self-accounting structural unit, the department for the technological preparation of production (OTPP), was formed out of the tool-making section and the chief technologist's department, headed by the chief of the tool-making section. In January 1993 this man was appointed acting chief technologist of the whole factory, and his former deputy took over as section chief. However, the OTPP never really got off the ground, and was abolished in October 1993. Nevertheless, with the merger the department was given the right to look for outside orders if the factory did not give it enough work. As the chief of the section explained:

> We get an order, and take responsibility for signing it and fulfilling it. Formally

> it is the factory that signs the agreement – we are not a juridical subject – but it is done on our recommendation. We have the right to keep part of the profits for ourselves. We agreed on 50 per cent of the profit after expenses … But we do not pay any leasehold payments, i.e. a half-hearted decision was taken.

The creation of OTPP, according to its chief, should have reduced the conflict common to many enterprises between the production and design-technology subdivisions. The production departments felt that the designers and technologists 'do everything to make the life of production more difficult'. In their turn, in the words of the chief of the tool-making section:

> Designers and technologists believe that the only reason that no innovations are made in production is because the production subdivisions impede their introduction in every way possible … We hoped that we would work exclusively for the clients, for the needs of production. We should do something not on the order of the chief engineer, who might be rather – well, frankly, he might not be concerned with the needs of production, but work exclusively for the clients, and our clients would be the production sections. The plan was like this: the production plan is set up, there is a deputy director for production and he has in front of him the plan for the next two or three months, he gets the section technologists together, shows them the drawings, shows them the long term plan and says this and that, comrades (or citizens as we say now) tell us what you need to produce these items cheaply, quickly and to a high quality: we need such and such tools and equipment to make such and such a quantity and quality of fans. Having defined the job we in the OTPP would get down to work. We would do the whole thing, in collaboration with the section technologists if there was something else to be sorted out. We can give them some things that we have worked out, which they don't know about, and as a result we give birth to a technological process which we work out and we fit it out and sell it to the production section, we get our money and the production section, on our equipment on our technological process, will earn their money.

That is how the chief of the department saw the technological process. But in practice things turned out rather differently. The problem in the view of the chief was that the tool-making section was a self-financing subdivision and

> Whether you want to or not, you rush around and find how people will earn money. But at the beginning the basic production sections were on piece-rates, then on time-wages. Earlier they had some kind of interest, they pushed us to give them the equipment more quickly, they asked us to make more productive equipment. This may be a primitive method, but all the same … But now that they are on hourly pay they just can't be bothered. Well, what's the point? Only under the stick.

The production process

The design service produces drawings which the tool-making section works out technologically, calculating the cost of materials and labour and estimating its technical characteristics: can the section do this job, should it be done more simply and so on. They also determine the level of production capacity demanded of the plant and equipment. Then they produce the production plan for each section, the 'section account'.

Tool-making production can be broken down into five steps:

1. A fitter marks and drills the part.
2. The machine operator carries out the mechanical operations to create the preliminary shape of the part.
3. The thermist (blacksmith) tempers and cleans up the part.
4. The part is set up on a machine on which it is precisely machined.
5. The assembly fitter puts the parts together.

Two other sections work in the same place: new technology and repair-energy-mechanical. This was a source of some dissatisfaction because the latter were on time-wages and worked much less intensively, but did not earn much less. The chief of the tool-making section spoke for his workers:

> When I see a machine standing idle all day and the worker is nattering away somewhere neither I nor my workers can understand why money should be paid for this. The workers are always asking me about this.

The workers do not express their dissatisfaction openly:

> When I see a worker from the other section come up to one of mine and start to chat, if this goes on for two or three minutes I can understand it, but if it goes on for ten or fifteen minutes I reprimand my worker. And if it happens again I will dock my worker's pay. When he comes up to me at the end of the month and asks why he has been paid so little I explain to him that if he came here to work he has to work. If you work here for an hour or two I do not object, have a rest, have a sit, go and chat to someone – that's your affair, but above all work.

Workers complain constantly about the crush which makes their working conditions much worse. It is difficult to work when the neighbouring new technology section begins to paint a fan. This leads to clashes between workers, but does not go as far as open conflict. 'They swear at each other, and in five minutes everything is back to normal'.

Production is primarily in response to orders from the other sections or from outside customers, and this is the main source of unevenness in the rhythm of production, so that production is determined by demand, not by capacity. Supplies have never been a particular problem, although workers sometimes have to come in on their day off to unload deliveries of parts and materials.

The section chief undertakes the distribution of work himself:

> The distribution of work must be separated from the workers. The brigadier cannot and should not do it because he is one of the workers, and the distribution of work is connected with money, and he does not deal with this.

The section chief controls recruitment, and it is he who regulates the pace of work, to which he takes a very flexible attitude:

> If I have got nothing to do, I have no work, I simply say: lads, let's take a week off, maybe you can earn something on the side, it's up to you, have a rest or earn a bit extra. Our work is really intensive, so we simply have to take a break. And then, when necessary, if there is work, they come in and do it.

There is a lot of manual labour so it is difficult to calculate all the costs in advance. So the chief can only effectively control those workers who make a final product, such as assembly fitters, who must produce a die in a definite period of time. It is more difficult to control the machinists:

> You can see they are standing at their machines working, but the intensity of their labour might nevertheless be low.

True, as the chief says, intensity is not the only indicator:

> We had one worker who grabbed at everything, he tried so hard … he did everything so quickly. But I say: it would be better if he had done nothing, because everything had to be done again. He worked badly, poor quality.

Labour relations

The model of labour relations in this section is different from that to be found in any of the other sections of the factory. One could call this model 'authoritarianism on the basis of self-financing'. Two factors have had the most significance in the formation of this model: first, the self-financing status of the section and, second, the personal characteristics of its two young chiefs.

The section began to work on a self-financing basis at the time at which the situation in the factory began to deteriorate and the volume of production, which implied also the level of workers' pay, began to fall. Remembering that time, the first of the two chiefs of the section recalled:

> I ran around and hunted for work for my workers in other sections and outside and managed to provide them with a sufficient level of pay that they did not leave … for better or worse I don't know, maybe the bosses considered that it was their job not mine, but I think that it was my job to find work … for people. I provided people with an acceptable level of pay. And people worked for me and will work.

Such activism on the part of the section chief gradually led to a situation in which now, as he put it, 'the workers understand that I am a chief for them'. Thus, the legitimacy of the leader of this section is based not only on his industrial competence, but also on his entrepreneurial activity.

Gradually the chief of the section concentrated all the functions of production management in his own hands. There is neither a technologist nor a foreman in this section and the duties of the brigadiers are strictly limited to production tasks: they do not distribute work or participate in decisions about pay. This is a matter of principle for the chief, who sees the brigadier just as a 'better worker'.

Pay

The self-financing activity of the section has also entailed changes in such important areas of labour relations as the distribution of wages and the regulation of employment. There is neither an STK nor any trade union organisation in the section. In the past wages were distributed by the STK, which was then disbanded, and now it is done by the section chief.

> Earlier, when there was an STK, questions of the distribution of pay were resolved with shouts and scandals, and the biggest pay went, in my view, not to

> those who carried the heaviest burden in carrying out the tasks. But after we transferred to self-financing everything was different: if I have the right to look for work and am responsible for it, then I have the right to decide whom to pay how much for it ... I watch how everyone works. When I worked at ZiL we reckoned – the norm-setter, accountant – how much was produced here and there ... Here we don't do that, I know myself who does what. And our workers do not object to such a system ... The workers trust me, if any problems arise they come to me and we sort it out together ... I for my part try to explain to people why they have received just this much and what for.

However, it is interesting to ask what criteria the section chief uses if there is no norm-setter or tally-clerk in the section. His answer was simple: 'It is simply that I myself know who works how', but the chief tries to ensure that the pay of specialists is higher than that of workers ('the head must cost good money').

His attitude to pay is pretty flexible and informal. His criterion is that 'there must be an accurate and just appraisal of labour'. In his view:

> The main thing is not to upset the person, to give him a sense of what he can do, even support him. ... If, for example, someone comes to me I might pay him more at first than he had been earning to give him an incentive, so he will keep trying. I have to see that he tries to master the work, enter into the collective – a lot also depends on that. And if one presses a new person straight away, he simply may not join us. He must enter into a psychological atmosphere that is new to him.

Workers only get their pay after carrying out their orders. As the chief says:

> We decided for ourselves: if the work is not done it is not paid since people's psychology is such: once the money has been paid there is no need to do any more work.

The workers do not object to this system, they keep quiet because, the section chief believes, their pay is higher than in the other sections thanks to their additional orders.

Informal relations

The self-financing status of the section has led to contradictory tendencies in the relationship between the section chief and the workers. On the one hand, the appearance of free money in the hands of the section chief has facilitated the 'monetarisation' of labour relations.

> All our relations are built on the basis of money: If I give someone a job, then I do it taking into account the possible pay for the job, and if I need someone to stay behind in the evening I take that into account in working out his pay.

On the other hand, monetarisation penetrates and strengthens the informal relations which, in the view of the line managers, maintain production. They believe that 'labour relations will not be formalised on all levels', that is to say the manager will not simply play by the rules of a formal game, informal relations will be maintained.

According to the chief, collaboration among workers can only be on the basis of informal agreements.

> Everything is guided by informal relations – from the bottom to the top. For example, the deputy director for production will tell me to clear up a puddle in front of my section. I go up to a worker and ask him to do it. I promise a bottle or some money, 'to show my gratitude'. He does it for me, on what one can call an informal basis. But if one only based oneself on formal demands, then in reply to my request he would say: 'Show me where it says I must do that in my contract?' Let us say it is a fifth grade fitter. 'Why should I clean up the area? I am not paid for that.' And he would be right. ... Yes, there is a cleaner, but she is over fifty, she is ill and it is cold on the street, it is raining. I cannot make her do this work! Labour relations cannot be formalised at all levels, because management simply will not play by the rules, informal relations will be preserved.

There are other noticeable consequences of the monetarisation of relations in production between groups of workers within the section and between sections. Since all the workers in the self-financing section work for a final result, they have an interest in fulfilling the outside orders to a high quality and in good time, so that the workers themselves regulate their inter-relationships within the technological chain, not tolerating any delay in the supply of parts. In their turn, the section managers, linked to the workers by their common interest in fulfilling the orders, try to remove kinks in the technological chain so that no tensions arise in the course of production. The common interest of workers and managers in the self-financing section reduces the feeling of solidarity with other sections ('If a problem arises here, then it is our problem, and they have their problems. Everybody must resolve his own questions himself.').

This increased level of self-motivation is not true of the repair brigade. The repair brigade 'only works under the stick, they never show any initiative' (chief of section), they only work if asked by a worker or the chief. The only way to urge them on is money, their pay depending entirely on the section chief. They hardly ever look after the machines:

> If you force them they will go and grease and clean a machine, but they are not in the habit of looking after them.

There is still a problem with looking after machinery, materials and so on, which is unresolved. According to the chief:

> Its essence lies in different attitudes to property: if you are a hired worker then you will never relate to it as yours. In a better situation (in Germany, for example) workers do everything according to instructions, let us say they grease the machine three times a shift, in a worse situation (as here) in general they do not grease it and do not switch off.

Conflict

The authoritarian orientation of the chief of the tool-making section extends to his attitude to industrial conflicts and the means of their prevention and resolution:

> Everything depends on the manager, on his ability to extinguish conflict. What is important? To get the work done, and the less conflict the better the work goes. That is what managers are for, simply not to allow conflict. I think that everything depends on the manager, on his ability to extinguish conflict. There was a conflict here not long ago: the chief technologist's department had to transfer to our building, and they moved into the former cloakroom. Repairs were carried out there and our workers transferred to another cloakroom. My workers dug their heels in, I don't know why – they thought it would be no good there, crowded. This all depended on psychology. If you give a worker a new machine, much better than his old one, he will still dig his heels in at first and work on his own familiar machine, because he is used to it. So this kind of question has to be resolved in the form of an order. There has not been any open conflict of that kind. I said to the workers that everything would be all right, we must do it so that they – the technical department – would be on good terms with us. If I, as chief, sit in my office, put my feet on the table and do nothing, then conflict would not be avoided ... One can work, but not resolve any of the problems, one can take a strong-willed decision to force people to work and not take account of their needs, to demand more from them than they can do. And you must try to select the collective so that there is as little friction as possible, that is to say you need an appropriate employment policy. If the workers disagree with my behaviour they can turn to the president or the director.

There is a very low level of conflict in this section. Conflicts as a rule are resolved as they arise, the managers of the section try not to allow conflict situations to develop and the chief has unchallenged authority. The workers trust him and if there is a problem they go to him and talk it through. This was confirmed by a survey that we carried out in June 1993 in the section. Eighty per cent said they would turn first to the chief if they had a problem. He says:

> Amongst themselves of course they talk about me, but they rarely make demands to my face, they try not to bring problems to me, they sort everything out amongst themselves.

Most conflict situations within the section arise when workers refuse to carry out the chief's orders. These are easily resolved, he does the work, but the worker 'loses a lot'.

> For example, he may say that he cannot do it or that he has a bad leg or hand. I check up on him and during the week repeat the order and see how he responds. Then I can draw my conclusion.

If a worker refuses to do overtime the chief takes note of it:

> Let us say that I need a worker to work on his day off, and he for some reason cannot, I let him off, I do some work myself, there will be no problem. But if he refuses on some pretext a second time, I will make a note of it.

SMALL-BATCH SECTION

General characteristics

The small-batch section (UMS) produces short runs of fans to order, by 1994 offering 180 types of fan, normally produced in runs of 150. The production process comprises three stages. Parts (the body, mounting, frame) are delivered from the press-stamp section, small parts come from the mechanical section, motors come through the supply department, and tools from the tool-making section. The first stage comprises preparatory work – welding, cleaning up, priming. Then the fans are assembled, and finally they are painted.

Thirty-six people work in the section: the section chief, foreman, technologist and 33 workers, including three women. The majority of workers are in the age range 30–45, although 7 are over 45. The majority have general secondary education. Thirteen of the workers are assembly fitters, 10 electric welders, the rest are auxiliary workers (painter, maintenance and repair, a cleaner, one quality controller and so on).

Traditionally this section had higher pay than the medium fan assembly section because the rate was higher. In the summer of 1992 the numbers in the section were cut as part of the factory-wide redundancy campaign and about 30 per cent of the workers were sacked. In the words of the section chief, they got rid of practically all the pensioners and drunks. The section chief decided whom to get rid of:

> If it was left to the workers to decide the question of redundancy for themselves, they would just quarrel about it. They transferred several particularly highly skilled pensioners, those who could work well, from one section to the other.

The section chief said that the announcement of redundancy was completely unexpected by many. The workers and even the section chief only found out about it when they returned from administrative vacation. 'The bosses did not give us any information at all', said the section chief. According to him the cuts went quietly but he thought that 'the cuts were morally difficult for those who remained, people think: what is waiting for me in a month, in a year…' But he noted that the redundancies had been inevitable:

> If we had not carried out redundancies it would have been the best workers who left first, because they can get a job anywhere, and we would be left with only the drunks and rowdies.

The workers accepted the cuts fairly placidly:

> Many could have been got rid of earlier, without waiting for this redundancy. Many thought that if this is a shareholding company they would rake in the money without having to work for it. (A worker)

Organisation of work

The section works as a unified team. Before the redundancies it had a brigade system, but now there are no brigades in the strict sense, although the name and the post of brigadier remain out of inertia. This is not a purely nominal position, the brigadier participates with the foreman in distributing work and he mediates between workers and the section chief if any problems arise for the workers in connection with their work, although the workers will also turn to the section chief or foreman on their own initiative if necessary. The section chief approves of such initiatives. An example: A worker came into the section chief's office to clarify precisely how to machine a part because the PShU had not supplied enough of the necessary components. Section chief:

> There you see, he came along as a conscientious worker, the man came and asked 'There aren't any of these small angles, what shall I do? How are we going to sort this one out?' Another might not be like that, may not feel that it concerns him, he never comes along and he never asks, and we have to sort it all out as usual. You begin to think maybe we can make it out of another angle, because if we refer it to the design bureau they might take three days to sort it out, and that time is lost, nobody will reduce our plan to take account of it.

The foreman's job is to ensure that the workers are supplied with work, and to monitor technical safety. The foreman, section chief and brigadier remain at work for several hours after the end of the shift every day. At the end of the shift the foreman checks that the day's jobs have been carried out, and then draws up the list of tasks for the following day. The foreman and brigadier enter the tasks for each worker in a special notebook, and these tasks are then checked by the section chief. The foreman places orders with the press-stamp section to secure the supply of parts. The following morning the foreman checks that the parts have arrived for that day, and allocates work to the workers at the five-minute meeting before the shift. During the day he helps sort out production and supply problems, for example helping the workers to interpret the technical drawings, particularly in the case of a new model. The foreman feels there is mutual understanding between himself and the workers: 'You must show respect for one another, then people will listen to you'.

The workers work in groups of five or six people preparing each machine. The organisation of labour is based on mutual dependence, since one person cannot put together a whole machine. Depending on the work there will be two or three teams with 5–6 people in each. People call these teams brigades out of habit. All the workers are linked together by the production process.

> We have always worked in conditions in which we all depend on one another ... Work is work, you see? In the section a collective has formed in which everyone has such a view. It is linked together like this: if I begin to put on the brakes myself then everything slows down for the other lads, and they will immediately let me know about it. In the brigade everything is interrelated, everything is immediately obvious. If someone puts on the brakes, it is felt immediately.

Each worker is permanently assigned to a particular workplace, which he or she has to keep in order: clean it, keep the equipment maintained and in good repair and so on, the so-called 'culture of production'. The work (both 'profitable' and 'unprofitable') is regularly distributed between the workers by the foreman and brigadier, for which they receive additional payment. As the foreman put it:

> We know who can do what, we take this into account when we allocate the tasks among the shift, because workers are varied – some are stronger some are weaker.

On the whole the section works fairly regularly. The reason for interruptions is as a rule breaks in supply – either as a result of failures in the work of the factory as a whole or in the press-stamp section. These failures often lead to tension within the section, between workers and managers, and between section chiefs. In the spring of 1993 failure to make the plan and earn the section's bonus as a result of repeated breaks in work led to open conflict between workers of the UMS and management of the factory. The section struck several times in May, practically every Friday: they demanded an increase in pay rates and additional pay for overtime which they had to work to make up for the failure of materials to be delivered in time.

As the end of the month approached it was obvious that they would not make the plan, and then two days before the end of the month they were given an order for 15 fans which had been transferred from the medium fan section. The administration tried to deal with this situation with the customary informal methods, but the workers demanded double pay for working on Friday and Saturday, which were not working days since the factory was on a four-day week. The administration refused, since they claimed that the situation had arisen because the workers had been working at lower intensity earlier in the month, but offered to pay them one day's wages from the foreman's fund, that is from the money which the workers were accustomed to consider theirs. Apart from this, the workers were unhappy that time-wages do not take account of the intensity of their labour or of the high proportion of manual labour.

> We have already struck three times. Last Friday we refused to work, it turned out only 6–8 people. Management (the deputy director for production) swore at them. And today – we have again not fulfilled our plan, it means that we are 30 per cent short of these 15 fans. Last Friday they promised to sack everybody who struck and they do not have any right to do this, well Friday and Saturday are not working days. They do not pay us for these days, they simply add them to our holidays. (Brigadier)

Working conditions are quite difficult: the equipment is old, the ventilation works badly. The workers themselves, judging by the results of a survey, consider the conditions in the section bad.

> Nothing changes, the gear was and remains the kind of stuff used by clumsy old women, and that is how we work. (Brigadier)

> They violate the Labour Code, but there is no control over them, it's all the same, you don't get justice, there is no one to complain to. The work is hard and the pay is low. (Quality controller)

Since the factory now works to customers' orders, rather than to a fixed plan, the production plans change several times a month, and this is difficult for the workers to get to grips with, particularly if it requires them to make alterations, or to 'perfect' a machine. They are very hostile to requests to make such alterations which 'they see as an insult to their work'. The increased flexibility of production, which requires new modifications to be made every month, has been achieved thus far at the expense of the workers. The main resource is the skills of the workers. There is no new equipment – many of the machines are thirty or more years old, and the workers have to make spare parts themselves. The workers feel that the work has become more difficult because the machines require constant readjustment. Now the workers have to interpret technical drawings, work out how to do the job better, in short, in the view of the section chief, do many of the things that in the past were done by technologists. This increased flexibility has also increased the workload of the technologist and responsibilities of the section chief.

The section chief has much more scope for showing initiative in production questions than he had in the past: for example, in looking for customers, supplying the section with parts and components and accordingly with work, which is very important in a situation in which the volume of production has fallen sharply:

> Now we work for the consumer, more flexibly ... the amount of responsibility has increased, but the problem is the same – to keep to time and not to reduce the quality.

The chief has to resolve a whole mass of problems on his own, only turning to senior management when necessary, and then only with a prepared decision. It is up to him how much he involves the foreman in decision-making. In the small-batch section the chief works closely with the foreman.

The personal character of the section chief plays a big role in present conditions, in particular his or her energy, initiative and willingness to stand up for the interests of the section in the face of management. The chief of the small-batch section is very different from the chiefs of the tool-making section, lacking the independence and initiative of the latter, and blaming his problems on the macro-economic situation in the country and the incompetence of the management of the factory and the company. In answer to the question what kinds of changes have taken place in relations between workers and administration in Lenkon he answered:

> What can one say? Well, first, in relation to the economic situation naturally everybody is embittered. One can see it in the queues, on the buses, in the shops... All the difficulties come from the government, and not from our bosses. The workers ask the bosses to increase pay, but this is not really right, they should not put pressure on the managers of the factory, but on the government, because the head has to think! ... it is not us in the factory who should change our policy, but the government.

Another feature of the head of the small-batch section, typical of his type of manager, is his conception of his own insignificance, his strict observance of hierarchy in the relation chief-subordinates: 'We are all subordinates to the management. The workers to me, me to my manager, my manager to the top.' While the more enterprising type of chief feels himself to be a manager, the second type feels closer to the workers – the senior managers for him are 'them'.

Most of the workers think he is 'a good man but too soft', he 'rushes about' between workers and management when he should be 'forceful', more demanding and firmer with the workers 'so that they will respect him' (interview with a worker). Personal characteristics can be decisive to the success of the section, especially his willingness and ability to get additional orders, including within the factory, to supply the section with work and so with pay. This was critical in the summer of 1992 when there was a sharp fall in the volume of production, there was no work in the section, and the most highly skilled workers left. The supply of parts and materials, the timely repair of equipment and everything that keeps production going smoothly all depends on the chief.

He also has to monitor the fulfilment of the plan. Given the disruptions in work this means that workers have to work overtime or on their days off to make the plan. Since he has no right to demand that they do so, and there is no system of overtime payment, he has to use informal methods to persuade them to work.

> I see each worker personally, I explain why it is necessary. Some people are understanding and some say that they cannot do it – for good reason, there is nobody to baby-sit or something like that, then I have a look to see who I can swap them with. I try to do it like that so that nobody gets unhappy.

Those who do the extra work when needed usually get some compensation from the foreman's fund, the decision being taken by the section chief.

Disciplinary violations are reported by the foreman who decides the level of punishment.

> Questions of drinking I resolve one to one, if that doesn't work, at the five minute meeting [before the shift], and then at a general meeting.

On the whole the workers have much more freedom than in the past. As the foreman put it:

> The workers behave fairly freely, they do not violate basic discipline and we try not to nag them much, especially if they work well.

The foreman tells the workers if there is a delivery of groceries or consumer goods, and they can go over to the administration building during the 'smoking break', although in practice they may often leave their workplace, for example to go out shopping, at any time.

Theoretically smoking breaks are regulated, just as lateness for work and leaving early are forbidden:

> The foreman always threatens violators of discipline, talks to them about it, but in practice they do not punish anybody, the important thing is that the work should be done on time and to a good quality.

But the section chief records all these little violations of discipline, as it seems to us, to use people's slips in case he needs to put some pressure on them. Thus, for example, a conflict arose because workers did not want to work on their days off in order to meet the plan (at the end of April 1993, at the height of the work on their garden plots). The chief remarked of one of the workers who 'was the most indignant of all':

> He is five minutes late for work every day and leaves ten minutes before the end of the shift, but he yells most of all to tell me how hard he works when I remind him of it.

Although many of the functions of the brigadier and foreman have formally been transferred to the section chief, in practice in this section they continue to play an important role in the organisation of production and the running of the section.

Re-grading and the distribution of wages and bonuses

The best indication of the character of labour relations in this section is provided by the conflict over the transition to time-wages which took place in October 1992, discussed above. This was preceded by a re-grading of the workers. The re-grading, which was introduced on the orders of the factory management, was carried out by the section chief, foreman, brigadier and trade union representative.

> Someone who worked well but was on a low grade we up-graded. Those who were on a high grade but worked badly we down-graded.

The section chief described the procedure:

> After work a 'small collective' got together which assessed every worker in the section. They went over each case several times, trying to take into account every factor, even his family situation. They thoroughly evaluated the professional qualities of each person. They cut the grade of those who drank or only had a few months before they drew their pension – I explained personally to

each of the latter that if we did not cut their grade then a young worker with many years to work would suffer. Discipline violators in general did not raise any objection. Since the administration set limits to the number of people in each grade they had to look for non-trivial solutions. For example, two repair fitters were put on the fourth grade, although they were doing fifth graded work, because the quota on the fifth grade was already full. I spoke to them personally about my responsibility. I promised that I would top up their pay every month to that of the fifth grade out of the foreman's fund. I have never deceived them, they trusted me.

According to the section chief the whole thing went on without conflicts: 'Frankly, I was amazed. I had expected that there would be arguments and outcry but everything went smoothly.' He thought this was because 'we tried to assess the person objectively. A person needs not a grade but pay.' Moreover there was no issue for argument, because the grade scale with pay rates was handed down by the administration.

The workers were never reconciled to the system of time-wages, despite the attempts of the section chief to explain the need for it: 'I explain the essence of time pay once a week, that we need not quantity but quality, the orders have fallen, we are doing custom work'. It was the workers of this section who led the factory into the conflict over wages and dividends at the beginning of 1993, discussed above, which led to fundamental changes in company policy.

When the small-batch section was transferred from time-wages to the system of so-called 'payment by final result' in March 1994 the section decided to resurrect the traditional mechanism of distributing pay and bonuses among the workers by the STK (labour collective council) using the KTU (coefficient of labour participation), the only section in the factory to use this system. This was a response to the workers' irritation at their removal from participation in decisions regarding pay, and their grievances at what they considered to be unjust decisions on the part of the section chief, whom they felt paid more to his favourites.

The new system involves both brigadier and STK, which is made up of four people elected by their fellow workers. At the end of each day the brigadier posts the KTU of each worker on the section notice board, with the average KTU being about one. At the end of each month the whole sum of money received by the section for the work done is distributed between the workers, with the decisions being taken by the STK on the basis of the daily KTU recorded by the brigadier and the observations of the section chief, who presents his own records in which he notes violations of labour discipline and the attitude to work of each worker. Then the list of those deprived of bonus as a punishment is consulted, and the incentive fund is divided up among the workers of the section.[6] Although the workers think that this system is much fairer, it has actually led to an increase in conflict, so that 'there are many more rows in the section', but the section chief does not intend to change it because he also sees it as just.

In the opinion of the workers it was necessary to create an organ representative of the workers: 'we need an STK, defending the interests of the workers'. To the question 'from whom?', they answered 'from the administration, to control the administration'.

> They [management] violate the labour laws, there is no control over them at all. I have worked here for three years, but there has never once been any kind of trade union meeting, no kind of election, in place of a trade union we have one Sazonov [president of the trade union committee]. We have never discussed the collective agreement, they simply sign it and that is that (brigadier).

Although formally there is a trade union group in the section in fact the trade union plays no role at all, it does not interfere with anything and is in solidarity with the administration. A year earlier the workers had still felt some illusions towards the shareholders' council, considering it an organ which had replaced the STK. One worker said:

> In place of the STK the shareholders' council was created, the president of it is from our section. There they discuss all problems ... I trust our president and in general I know a bit about the people there.

When asked which side the president would be on in the event of serious conflict between the workers and the administration in the autumn of 1992 he said without hesitation: 'I think on the side of the workers. I am sure of it.' In the spring of 1993 the workers no longer counted on support for their demands in the shareholders' council, and many of them in conversation said that they needed an organ that would represent their interests as workers.

6 This system was suspended between May and July 1994 as a result of the decline in orders, but it was planned to reintroduce it when production picked up again in August.

MEDIUM FAN ASSEMBLY SECTION

The skill level of the workers in this section is similar to that in the neighbouring small-batch section. However, it employs more people (55) since it is engaged in the mass production of machines, with runs of around 2,500 units. Most of the workers are in the age range 30–45, with about 5 per cent being under 30 and five per cent over 50.

There had been more young workers in the past, but with the development of co-operatives and other new forms of economic activity they left the factory for 'commerce'. Then the redundancies in 1992 fell most heavily on this age group since, as the section foreman explained, 'they had lower skills and morally they participated less in the life of the factory'. More recently a number of young workers have joined the section, but turnover remains very high among the young. For this reason management is not keen on young workers. As the section foreman said:

> A young person comes, but he soon leaves. They get into the habit of it you see: if they don't like something, they leave at once, well, they go from one place to another and then they come back. But those young people who stay, they gradually get used to it and work normally. But all the same young and old are different: the old are more diligent, you can rely on them, they see things through, whatever you ask, but the young work without making any effort, and yet they swagger around.

During our research in this section we observed two interesting processes – the destruction of the brigade organisation of labour, and an increase in the distance between the workers and the foremen.

Erosion of the brigade organisation of labour

Brigades had already been established in the factory in the 1970s, but at the beginning of the 1990s the management declared its intention of destroying the brigade system, in favour of individual payment. The brigades were not abolished, and the section at present has six of them. For example, 9 people work in the assembly brigade, mostly between 30 and 40 years old, with an average grade of 5. However, the brigades now exist only nominally, since the brigades have lost all the rights they had in the past. As an assembly fitter says:

> In our brigade there are eight people: assembly fitters, welders and a balancer.

> In the past we ourselves distributed the pay in the brigade. Each person wrote separately on a sheet how much he had done and worked out himself how much he had earned. The section chief gave the money to the brigade, and within the brigade we ourselves knew how much each had worked and in general there were no disputes when somebody earned less, because that person knew perfectly well that we do not reduce pay for no particular reason, but for what he has done, for some deficiency in his work. We also punished people for drunkenness, the brigade did it ourselves. It was better before: if somebody was absent for a valid reason, his money remained within the brigade, and those who were left could do the work for the absentee and the brigade itself divided up this money. Now I work for two people, but get paid for only one, and nobody knows where and to whom the money goes.

Foremen and workers

The distribution of pay was transferred to the foreman, and the workers responded negatively to this strengthening of the foreman's role:

> And he is a dark horse. By what principles does he distribute it? The foreman has his favourites, 'who do not drink and do not smoke', and he pays more to those he likes, not to those who work the best.

One welder said that the foreman once asked him to come to work on a Saturday but he refused. The foreman then said, 'I will remind you about it' and cut his bonus.

The distribution of work within the brigade has also become a function of the foreman. With time-wages the workers were not tied to a particular job and sometimes had to work at something else (for example, cleaning up the premises or loading). If anybody refused to do this kind of work, the foreman punished him by cutting his bonus.

The foreman had a certain amount of money under his control, the 'foreman's fund', which gave him more independence not only in relation to the workers but also in relation to senior management. And we observed how the foremen, brigadiers and chief of this section were able to use this lever to resist or 'correct' the decisions of the management of the company.

For example, in awarding *klassnost'* the line managers had an interest in ensuring that as many workers in the section as possible were awarded extra pay at the expense of the factory and the company. However, the management of the company restricted the proportion of workers in each section who could be awarded first and second class. As a result, in this section ten workers were awarded class one and twenty people class two, the remaining 25 people not being awarded *klassnost'*. However, as the foreman acknowledged, the management of the section tried to ensure that the latter did not lose out, topping up their pay from the foreman's fund.

Several actions of the management of the section revealed the divergence of interests between line managers and senior management of the company: while the latter wanted to deepen the differentiation among the workers, the former were inclined to smooth it over on the principle of 'levelling'.

Once the section management deprived a good worker of his first class 'for discipline' (he took one day off, and turned up drunk the next day). Then, as the foreman described it:

> We split this 3,000 in half and gave it to two other comrades, and now they have second class and get 1,500. We still have candidates for the award of *klassnost'*, but they will not give us any more. But we do not let them lose out, we have a fund in the section, we twist and turn, what we do exactly – that is a commercial secret.

This fund strengthens the position of line management in the section, and above all the foreman as the person most actively engaged in informal relations, particularly in storming situations, which are not uncommon. In answer to the question how workers are persuaded to work overtime the foreman answered:

> We ask them, we pay. They take it in turns, of course. Then we give them extra time off, we pay extra, we talk it through with them, we come to an agreement. If somebody then asks to be let off, that is he wants to have the day free, I am reluctant to allow it, but I will do it. We understand that people are people, one has to have pity for people.

Nevertheless there is less and less room for feelings of pity as a motive for behaviour. When at the end of 1993 the section was put in the difficult position of a sharp increase in the volume of production, the section foremen thought up the idea of 'the replacement of people'. One of them explained the essence of the plan:

> We have just suggested to the chief the idea that we will not cut people, but we will replace them. There are people who are not much use to us, who are slipshod workers, and nobody needs these people now, now people look to production. So we will change those people whose discipline, whose work, is no good to us.

> How will you change them?
>
> We conclude labour contracts with the workers for six months or a year. In March the term of our contracts expires. The new agreements that we conclude with those who do not suit us will be for two months and that is all. We will give them two months notice of termination of the contract, as the law decrees – although we are a joint-stock company we are still subject to this law – and we will replace them. There are good people at the labour exchange who have been made redundant. And we may be able to recruit some very good staff.

Such behaviour on the part of the foremen testifies to the increased distance between them and the workers. And the workers have begun to feel this. One of the workers in the section told us that there are now 'deliberate violations, for example, when somebody does poor quality work to harm the foreman'. And at the same time other workers, seeing that their neighbour is doing hack-work, do not complain to the foreman. Criticisms of the foreman by the workers have become stronger.

> Our foremen are the kind of people who give important orders, but then just go off somewhere else. Or, for example, he himself has to fetch materials, but he tells a worker to do it, although the worker clearly does not know what is needed. Or he does not understand anything about the technology, he is really dumb, but he can slander the worker if he gets something not quite right. And in general for some reason they punish us more than they encourage us. But the workers need a kind word as well.

Collective authoritarianism

The mechanisms regulating pay and employment are different in this section from the others. Many decisions regarding labour relations are taken by the 'holy trinity': section chief–foreman–brigadier. The prevalence of a collegial over an authoritarian model is not the result of a compromise between workers and the section management, as it is in the UMS. The workers are excluded from the decision-making process (although the 'trade union representative' figures among those making the decisions – it turned out that he was a foreman). The workers in the section recognise their alienation.

The fairly traditional model of regulating labour relations in the section is a reflection of the current balance of forces within the management of the section. In particular, the position of the section chief is fairly weak because he does not have any special education, he is afraid for his job, while the status of an energetic foreman is reinforced by the support he gets from senior management. The distancing of section management from the workers is a result of this. The following monologue of a worker testifies to the fact that the workers have become aware of these diverging interests:

> It is very rare for the section chief or the foreman to stand up for the interests of the workers. If there is any kind of complaint, there is only one answer, 'if you don't like it – go'. I do not see any kindness from them. Why have they become like this? Maybe the bosses are getting at the chiefs too. They also have to hang on to their jobs now. And there is a feeling that we each have our own concerns, they have theirs and we have ours. The section chief meets with the foremen, but we do not know what they talk about, they hardly ever give us any information. Five-minute meetings are rare. They only tell us about punishments or investigate accidents. We have no idea what is going on in the factory. Why do they not tell us? It is interesting for me. But they are not interested in us. They only know how to frighten people. But what is the point of frightening us, we are already frightened. A human approach – that is not enough here. But there is nobody for the worker to take his unhappiness to, the position of the administration is 'we do not interfere in the business of the section, this does not concern us, sort it out for yourself'.

RELATIONS BETWEEN SECTIONS

The factory contains three sections (PShU, USSV and UMS) which are interrelated. And conflicts which arise between them are most frequently related to mistakes which were and are committed by the factory administration in the organisation of production. Thus, at one point they abolished the department of the chief technologist, which is the service which monitors the whole technological process from above and lays down uniform standards.

Now there are no strict standards applied in the press-stamp work, the standard has a large tolerance. As a result, even if the final product conforms to the internal standard, it may not be the right size for the subsequent operations to be undertaken in the other sections, so creating problems for the workers in these sections. We asked:

> What do you do if you receive a poor quality part from another section, which threatens the quality of your own work?
>
> Yes, we often get low quality products from the press-stamp section. If we send it back to them for re-working that takes time. We have to choose: either wait and stop work ourselves, or re-work it ourselves.

> Who decides what to do?
>
> We decide ourselves if there is not much re-working, or the section chief may discuss it with us 'well lads, what shall we do?'

Often the workers themselves make the necessary tools instead of turning to the tool-making section:

> because if you give it to the design department they may take three days to sort it out. And we lose time, but nobody is going to reduce the plan for us.

The same workers from the assembly sections make their own rigs instead of ordering them from the tool-making section 'because it is very expensive to make a rig for each separate model of fan, when it may not be needed again'.

Conflicts between sections also arise as a result of 'the poor organisation of work in relation to the failure to supply parts or the slipshod work of supply'. These horizontal conflicts between sections are resolved between the section chiefs. Usually they forewarn one another about those failures of co-ordination in their sections which may affect the work of other sections, especially the USSV and UMS which produce finished products. It is the chiefs of these two sections who have to disentangle the failures. It is remarkable that they do not blame their colleagues, the chiefs of the other sections who, in their turn, have their own difficulties caused by the poor work of the factory services.

> We try to get ourselves out of it somehow, we keep people on for the second shift and we combine them: somebody comes to the first shift, somebody to the second, sometimes they also have to come in to work on a Saturday ... the workers, naturally, do not like to work on their day off.

The section managers unequivocally attribute the large number of horizontal conflicts to the deficiencies of management at the level of the factory and the joint-stock company:

> All this is screwed up beginning from the top, and it reaches the workers, these difficulties naturally give rise to discontent on the part of the workers and the reverse movement begins: discontent goes from the bottom to the top.

In this process the section chiefs play an important role:

> Sorting it all out happens here, at the bottom. I try to do it so that discontent does not develop.

Sometimes the conflicts which arise between section chiefs, which they resolve informally, all the same filter down.

> Over a day or two the workers see that there is little work and they ask why there are no parts. I explain to them. They begin to curse the other section, they have not done their work, and we are the scapegoats, because of them we have got to work on our day off, stay behind in the evenings. The situation is explosive.

But as a rule discontent does not get beyond talk.

INTERNAL DIVISIONS AND GROUPINGS OF STAFF OF LENKON

In this section we would like to consider the differentiation of staff of the company and of the Moscow factory on a different basis. The composition of the groupings in this case has only changed slightly over the period of our research, with the main changes being quantitative rather than qualitative, and we will concentrate on the position at the beginning of 1994. The qualitative changes concern, first, the emergence of a new basis of differentiation within the labour collective and, second, the conscious strategy of management directed at the restructuring of the labour force of the enterprise.

The first division, which is by and large traditional and persisted throughout the period of our research, is that between management (about 80 people) and workers (about 350 people). Management, in turn, is divided into two groups. The first group comprises the president, first vice-president for production, director of the technology centre, board members and their deputies, the president's adviser, heads of departments and services, comprising about 40 people, although after the reconstruction according to Hubbard a definite stratum of top management appeared, comprising the chairman of the directors' council, the president and the economic-juridical department subordinate to him.

Line management (section chiefs and foremen), chiefs of

laboratories and specialists make up the second group in the management apparatus, also about 40 strong. Sixty-five per cent of the ITR have higher education, one is a Doctor and one a Candidate of Technical Science. The status of the ITR has become more clearly defined than it was in the past. In the past the ITR held an intermediate position, but now the ITR and specialists are divided into two groups. One group is functionally closer to senior management, the other group (for example, technologists and mechanics working in the sections) is included in the group of line managers.

The division between core and auxiliary workers persists, as do the categories of ancillary and so-called 'simple' workers (cleaners and so on), whose maximum grade is two. The latter amount to about 60 people.

Up to the end of 1993 management tried to work out an internal classification of the workers' occupations, divided into six categories according to the complexity of their work, each of which included six grades with different hourly pay-rates. Core production workers filled the top three categories, and the remaining three comprised the auxiliary, ancillary and unskilled workers. We did not observe any special tension between these various categories. The introduction of payment for *klassnost'* further divided the workers into two approximately equal groups, those with and those without *klassnost'*.

We have to consider the extent to which this differentiation can be related to the distinction in Western sociology between 'core' and 'peripheral' workers. Such a distinction existed under state socialism, when the 'advanced workers' (those who pushed production forward) were considered the core workers.[7] The criteria for differentiation did not simply refer to their role in the production process, but also to their social role. Today in Lenkon we can see the former division filled with new content, as the introduction of *klassnost'* officially recognised a division between core and peripheral workers as a division between loyal workers and the rest. The status of peripheral workers, those not recognised as loyal, becomes clear when the threat or the reality of dismissal for disciplinary offences looms, although it should be acknowledged that this role is still not fully developed.

7 For further discussion of this issue see Irina Kozina and Vadim Borisov, 'The Changing Status of Workers in the enterprise' in Simon Clarke, ed., *Conflict and Change in the Russian Industrial Enterprise*, Edward Elgar, Cheltenham, 1996.

The division into classes partly corresponded to the division between core and peripheral workers, although it would be more accurate to see this as a division within the core workers. The workers themselves were unhappy with such a division, considering it to be groundless and unjust. However this discontent was expressed against management, rather than between the workers themselves.

There was little change in the age and gender structure of the labour force, with male workers predominating, except among the stamp-operators, some of whom were women, and there are quite a lot of women auxiliary and ancillary workers, so that in general the women working in Lenkon are on lower grades and lower pay than the men. Where the distinction between 'men's' and 'women's' work was fixed in their corresponding rates of pay local conflicts would arise. At the same time tension did not arise between young and old workers, there being only between 5 and 10 per cent in each category.

Privatisation resulted in completely new divisions within the labour collective. Since about 80 per cent of the workers own shares, and those with no shares retain the right to acquire five shares, the division between workers who own and those who do not own shares is not significant. The division between small and large shareholders is much more significant, although we were not able to detect any differences in behaviour among workers according to the size of their shareholdings. However, there is a nucleus of shareholders, consisting of the members of the board and of the factory administration, some section chiefs and foremen, and even some workers who bought a large number of shares on credit in the early days, which they have subsequently held on to. Not all the core workers entered the nucleus of shareholders. For example, older workers were more cautious, and some people did not have enough money to buy shares. Those who bought shares tended to be those who were better informed, that is to say those who were closest to section management (for example, former leading workers or members of the trade union committee). This nucleus of shareholders has contracted as shareownership has become more concentrated, so that the main line of division runs within the middle and lower managerial strata, providing a basis for a degree of unity between those of the latter who have few shares and the workers in general.

WORKERS

Identification and Organisation

For many analysts of the transition period it is a mystery why the workers, on whose shoulders the main burden of the transition crisis falls, remain quiet and patient and do not create organisations or use the trade unions to defend their interests. Our ethnographic research into labour relations in the workplace has shown the decisive role of informal relationships in reducing tension in labour relations, and the pervasiveness of the strategy of authoritarian paternalism to which management has resorted and to which it resorts in this period of transition. Certainly the ground for authoritarian paternalism is preserved where there is a low level of worker activity, where the workers willingly cede decision-making in relation to wages and so on to management. However, there are many myths and a lack of concrete analysis to be found in explanations for the passivity of Russian workers.

A lot is said in very general terms about the existence of a transitional consciousness, and mass surveys are conducted which indicate the demoralising impact of the crisis. But is this demoralisation a temporary phenomenon, connected to the crisis? Our meetings with workers, interviews and group discussions over three years of research have allowed us to sense the fluctuation of the moods of ordinary workers and to identify the dominant ones, not based on our own representations and interpretations, but on those which are really significant for the workers themselves. Indeed, in conversations with us workers themselves touched on the issues which really disturbed them, and sometimes saw in us, the sociologists, the only people who were interested, to whom they could speak with confidence that they would be listened to.

These key issues were the collapse of the collective, the increase in distance between members of the board and workers, the sense of their own uselessness and of their lack of rights.

The theme of the growing cost of living and of wages falling behind prices was constantly present in conversations with workers. However, it did not push into the background their experiences connected with changes in the labour collective, and first of all the sense of its destruction.

> We have begun to receive more money. But it seems to me that money is not everything. We have lost the collective as a collective of like-minded people. It is my deeply personal opinion, but it seems to me that everyone feels this in the depth of their soul. We used to have a collective of like-minded people: we came to work. First, there was discipline here, some kind of order. Second, there were various common interests, and they were public interests. We had a very good artistic programme, there was a concert every holiday. When we came in to work on Saturdays we knew that this was our place and that we should clean it up. (A woman worker with 30 years service)

Workers noted other indicators of this process of destruction of the collective – the growing atomisation and increasing distance between chiefs and ordinary workers:

> Now the collective has fallen apart, everybody watches out for themselves. The chiefs for themselves, and the workers for themselves. (Painter)

The most obvious sign of the separation of the chiefs of the company for the workers is the termination of the practice of 'going to the people' and direct dialogue with ordinary workers:

> In the past they were more affable. Now the president does not come to the factory.

> When Minenko had to, he went to the factory, talked with workers. But for the past year we haven't even set eyes on him. Even though he used to appear in the sections once a month, took an interest in what we were doing. But now they do not even want to talk to us and they do not understand that in this way they demean themselves. They only think of themselves and of how to enrich themselves. People should be polite to one another. They are no different from us.

In this statement, with the contemptuous phrase, 'they are no different from us', one can see the latent democratic beliefs of the workers ('we have exactly the same rights as the chiefs'). But one can also see a refusal on the part of the workers to recognise the right of management to manage, a refusal which has to be set in the context of a 'people's privatisation' – the workers do not regard it as just to be a manager on the basis of property rights.

> It is obvious to everyone that if they [the owners of the bulk of the shares] had come and invested their own money into the factory and become millionaires, that is one thing. But when they pile up capital for themselves at the workers' expense, I consider that that is dirty. In essence, they have created capital by dirty methods. I think that they have cheated the people again. (Section chief)

Similarly this 'original sin' of the new owner-employers can become an obstacle to the legitimation of the chiefs as partners in labour relations. In this situation it will be very difficult to establish trust in the new bosses.

From what elements and under the influence of what factors do the managers establish an authority which is recognised and accepted by the workers in this transition period?

Our observations convince us that the various elements of the behaviour of management give rise to different responses. There is no doubt that approval or condemnation of any particular action depends on the extent to which it corresponds, on the one hand, to current expectations and, on the other hand, to the prevalent norms. Illegal acts of senior management, even if they are presented as being 'for the good of the labour collective' do not by any means increase the trust of their subordinates.

> The higher is a person, the higher his post, the more rights he has, the more opportunity he has to use these rights for his own advantage and to the detriment of others.

It is most likely, therefore, that the commercial activity of management, which is often associated with their personal enrichment, at present does more to undermine their authority than to form the basis of their recognition as businessmen.

The workers in the company were ready to recognise a 'producer' as a good manager, but not a good organiser. In the view of the workers someone who is a skilful speaker is sometimes perceived as a good manipulator.

> Minenko often beautifully describes how things are going, but this does not correspond to reality. I remember once when Minenko was still director, some workers went to him and asked him to increase their grade, but he did not do it. And then he spoke on television and said that his workers in the factory were completely satisfied and demanded nothing.

The divergence of words from deeds among managers in former times was a widespread feature of management culture. It is striking that this feature of Soviet-type managers is today seized on by the workers. On the other hand, they are not satisfied with a chief who only takes an interest in production questions. Thus, workers are critical of the present director, who goes around the sections for his own purposes, takes an interest in production, but talks only with section chiefs, foremen and brigadiers:

> He has remained as he was when he was production manager, he is more interested in things than in relations with people.

It is remarkable that workers should have such an attitude, since he greets workers in the sections, sometimes listens to their observations, but in the view of the workers he does not really take any notice of them. Thus, for the workers it is not enough to show superficial interest, they have an implicit desire to take part in making decisions concerning those production questions which fall within their competence.

Information

The feeling that senior management is distancing itself more and more from the workers is also indicated by the concealment of information.

On the one hand, the concealment of information, in particular about the use of the factory's resources, gives rise to various kinds of suspicion on the part of the workers. When the workers in the press-stamp section were making machines for a Dutch firm, we often heard them say:

> We are making machines for hard currency, but we do not see this money. They ought to post up on the board how much foreign currency the factory receives, and what it is spent on.

On the other hand, the workers need the information not only from simple curiosity, but also so that they can correctly understand the decisions themselves.

> We would like to have a bit more information to be able to look ahead, so that people know where they are investing their money, what they can expect to get from it.

> The management itself has the information and so it knows what to do. But it keeps us in ignorance. There are no meetings, no information, nobody knows what they are going to do.

The previous system of distributing information in the enterprise has broken down. It was part of the Party's ideological work, and was more or less regular, taking predominantly mass forms (political information, meetings). At the critical moment of transition, when the enterprise was changing its legal status, management had an interest in ensuring that all the workers supported the initiators of the transformation. Many of those we talked to remembered that under the co-operative and during the transition to a joint-stock company the president (at first he was director of the factory, and then president) went to the sections every day and anybody could go up to him with simple questions. With more difficult questions workers could go to see him in his office. Information about decisions of the board of the co-operative, the balance commission and other bodies was regularly posted on the announcement board. Now there are even more technical opportunities to distribute information (the company has photocopiers, printing equipment, radio), a communications sector was created as part of the Hubbard reorganisation, but, in the view of many ordinary workers, the collective does not receive enough information.

As has already been noted above, direct contacts of the chiefs of the company with workers were reduced. During the period in which the company comprised two enterprises the shareholders' meeting was turned into a conference, whose delegates did not always find the time to distribute information among their colleagues. Moreover, as one woman worker observed, 'before the information reaches the lowest levels, it gets lost, it is distorted'.

It is remarkable that even the members of the brigade whose brigadier was a member of the directors' council complained at the small amount of information reaching them, although their brigadier knew about the decisions taken above first hand and told his brigade about them.

The main channel of information for the workers is still the section chief, and here much depends on his or her personal position. In one section the chief considers that 'we have to work, it is not our concern what goes on up there'. Another section chief shares information received from higher management with his subordinates. However, he thinks that his openness harms him and his collective (as in the case above, where the possession of information pushed the workers of his section into a conflict over wages).

Some of the most advanced workers have already realised that the possession of information is an important resource in the control of the activity of the chiefs and the fight for their interests, while the absence of information and economic knowledge weakens their position.

> The trouble is that workers do not understand this kind of thing, that is why nobody presses the administration.

The technologist explained the absence of organised conflicts in the factory by the fact that 'people are in the dark here, because they do not know what economics is'.

However, workers still do not have any idea of how to get more information. Some are under the illusion that management has an obligation to distribute information voluntarily:

> These comrades who are on the board are more competent in these matters and they have to give their knowledge to the workers. (Inspector of the trade union committee)

Others are more active and raise the question at shareholders' meetings. After the October 1993 shareholders' meeting, minutes of the board and directors' council began to appear regularly on a stand. According to the workers, this happened because the management of the company was 'simply driven into a corner'. The question had been raised from the floor of the meeting, but in the end the management 'made it appear that' the wider distribution of information to members of the company was its own initiative. In fact, the workers recognise that the bosses have no desire to share information. As one of the workers said, 'you simply don't ask them about anything, they will tell you nothing'.

Self-identification of workers

The absence of a uniform reaction on the part of the ordinary employees to the processes of the destruction of the collective and the separation of a management group from it is completely obvious. Some workers feel the increased distance between them and management as really unnecessary. The sociologists often heard this kind of remark (most often from women workers):

> Now they relate badly to the workers, they do not bother that we feel that they do not need us. To our requests they reply: 'if you don't like it, you can leave'.

We would certainly not interpret such a reaction as merely a reflection of the workers' paternalistic expectations. Such feelings express the confusion of people for whom self-realisation in the collective and through collective labour has been an important value.

Under the influence of the difficulties of everyday life and the atmosphere in the labour collective the workers have become more reserved. This is expressed in their behaviour at work primarily in individual strategies of adaptation to the situation. And although relations within brigades have not become more conflictual, there is a distinct orientation to individual efforts, as one of the workers said: 'I do not ask for help, I get by by my own efforts'.

We think that another factor underlying the deepening sense of individualisation and disintegration (the seeds of which were already sown in the previous system of labour relations) is the erosion of the old collective identity, the most important element of which was stability and predictability.

In this area there have been complex processes, in which the influences of economic crisis and the situation of instability are mixed up, such as the institutional changes related to privatisation and the changing status of the enterprise.

In our view, new moments have appeared in the identification of the workers with the enterprise: first, the workers experience their relations with the factory through an understanding of the dependence of their personal position on the financial situation in the enterprise. Second, undefined and unpredictable factors enter into this interrelationship. Some of the workers relate this indeterminacy with the fact that the enterprise has become a joint-stock company and can count only on itself. It is noticeable that the dual status of worker-shareholders potentially allowed the possibility of the strengthening of a sense of participation in the enterprise and sharing in responsibility for its success and thereby the formation of a new identity on a different basis, as much as of its erosion.

The foreman in one of the sections saw the dividends as one of the incentives to work: 'If there were not people with shares in the factory, who would be willing to work well for pay alone?' And one worker we talked to admitted: 'I have an interest in the profits being larger ... There is no need to regret the development of production. It is our future'. Certainly the mass of workers do not aspire to participate in management and perceive their position as shareholders and shareowners more as a right to vote and a right to be heard.

Even at the time at which half the members of the council of the company were workers, the most intelligent and advanced workers complained that the council took decisions behind closed doors.

> I think that it must work more openly. Although I am not a member of the council, I should have the right to go and listen to its discussions. There should not be any secrets, we are all together. I do not have the right to a decisive vote, but I have a right to speak, to put forward my proposals.

However, events in Lenkon, as in so many other companies, developed in such a direction that these possibilities of forming a collective identity on the basis of the inclusion of ordinary workers in the decision-making process was not realised. The situation developed in the direction of a stratification of the shareholders into large and small, the result of which was the practically complete exclusion of ordinary workers from the decision-making process.

The division into large and small shareholders appeared most distinctly in the period in which the process of redistribution of shares and their concentration in the hands of the top managers took place. The conflict of interest between large and small shareholders appeared at the shareholders' meeting at which the results of the first quarter of 1992 were declared, when the question of the distribution of profits was decided. Fifty-two per cent voted in favour of allocating profits to the development of production, 36 per cent for their allocation to dividends. This division did not correspond precisely to the division between workers and managers, although there was a tendency in this direction.

One could interpret the interest of worker-shareholders in receiving dividends as an expression of their desire to increase their consumption. But the reality was that the workers had to pay a large sum as interest on the credit with which they had bought the shares, and had no money but their dividend income to pay this interest. At this meeting one of the workers said to the president:

> You are a large shareholder and are trying to press me, to buy my shares. But we, conversely, have to concentrate our efforts and act against you, against the big shareholders.

However, this same worker recognised in an interview that 'at the moment there is no unity among us, the workers do not yet feel that they have to oppose the big capitalists'. The management has many ways of putting pressure on the workers. At this same meeting the president warned the participants that if they voted to pay out dividends, they would be the first to be made redundant. The voting was by name, so that it was easy to find out how each person voted.

Now the workers are under no illusions about who is the owner of the factory. It is interesting that in a survey of the workers which we carried out in June 1993 it was noticeable that there had been a change in the addressees of the workers' demands, in comparison with those that we have heard in other enterprises which have set off on the path of changing ownership more recently. The workers in the Moscow factory considered that the resolution of problems in the factory did not depend on the administration of the factory, but on the management of the joint-stock company, on those who held the controlling interest in the company.

However, while the workers answered quite confidently that they did not feel like owners, they would not say with equal confidence that they were hired labourers. This indeterminacy in their identity is one of the serious barriers to the formation of independent organisations representing the interests of the hired workers. Many formal bodies of workers' representation in post-Soviet enterprises retain dualistic features and turn out to be under management control.

We have already referred above to the trade union committee in the factory, 'tame' as the management calls it, which has effectively turned into a branch of the administration. The president and deputy president of the union committee work as the chief and deputy of the social supply department, mainly concerned with securing consumer goods and groceries to sell to the workers. The main activity of the trade union, in the words of its president, is 'to find from whom one can buy things and organise their regular sale at the factory so that there will not be any bad feeling'. Nevertheless, the trade union still belongs to the higher trade union organisation, the city trade union of workers in heavy mechanical engineering, to which it sends 20 per cent of the trade union dues. Representatives of the trade union committee participate purely formally in the resolution of conflicts arising within the factory, always taking the side of management in such cases.

The workers consider that effectively there is no trade union in the factory ('the trade union committee is now an empty place', 'it is separated from the workers', 'I have no experience of it … it will not provide any support'), but at the same time they do not express any desire to change any of the trade union functions and to find an appropriate role for it. Altogether only four people have resigned from the trade union.

Despite the fact that half the members of the shareholders' council established at the end of 1991 were workers, the workers did not see it as a body which represented their interests. One of the members of the council, a worker, asserted in an interview that the council defended the interests of shareholders and not of all the employees of the enterprise. The workers recognised the council as a decorative body which was under the control of senior management, and above all of the president:

> They have already bought them all [the workers who are members of the council]: they have given an automobile to one, an apartment to another, they have promoted a third, and paid off another. The president of the council, who was an assembly fitter, became head of the personnel department.

In its composition and in its functions the council was a transitional body from the STK to the directors' council, the transition being achieved following the concentration of shares in the hands of management, so that those at the top of the company strengthened their monopoly of management in the reconstitution of the governing bodies of the company.

Attitudes of management to bodies of worker representation

When the company was created the senior management of the company and of the factory left the trade union. And although there were no deliberate acts on the part of management aimed at the abolition of the trade union organisation, we know that in private meetings several managers of the company convinced members of the trade union committee that trade unions were not necessary and appealed to them to break their connections with the branch trade union. Subsequently, despite the fact that the top leaders of the company observed various norms guaranteeing the representation of a certain number of workers in establishing the composition of company bodies, the administration's policy has been aimed at minimising the participation of workers in the management of production. Although there is no single articulated position, there is a widespread belief among managers that:

> There is no possibility of workers participating in the management of production here, because the workers do not have enough skill and experience.

And if at the beginning of the research we found that managers avoided or were indifferent to the question of worker representation in the resolution of problems which affected the interests of ordinary workers, the appearance of the STK in the small-batch section forced some of them to define their position more precisely:

> It dissolved into chaos there with this STK, constant squabbles, disputes. I proposed that we break this section up completely and take on new workers. Where from? From the streets, there are fully qualified workers who are only waiting to be asked. I could resolve this problem in a week. But management has not decided to take such a radical step.

But who is ready for such a step? The head of the personnel department, not long before a worker and president of the company council, was rapidly promoted up the administrative ladder. It is most likely that it will be precisely such chiefs – 'neophytes', not connected by social obligations, who will be the 'managers' of unemployment in the near future. Among them are many people who think that

> All this democracy gets seriously in the way of work: if they have time to have STK meetings, to have planning meetings, discussions and consultations it means that that they never work.

And they are ready to throw out from their ranks those managers who 'allow' this kind of activity on the part of the workers. Such people, in the opinion of the head of the personnel department, are not suitable as managers.

The workers are conscious of their separation from participation in management, bitterly assert that nothing depends on them, that everything is decided at the top.

Particular workers, the most highly skilled with close informal relations to management, say that personally they do not need anybody to represent the workers' interests, since they can go personally to the president to resolve any problem.

In the small-batch section a local strike became the mechanism of increasing pay. But the workers are to some degree alienated from one another. The low level of worker solidarity was confirmed by a survey of 72 workers in the three main sections. The majority of those questioned asserted that they were only ready to support workers of their own subdivision in actions in defence of their rights and interests. The workers of the self-financing tool-making section were particularly categorical in this, considering that nothing that happened outside the limits of their small section was anything to do with them. An important reason for this lack of solidarity is the considerable differences in the character of labour relations in each section, as we have seen above. The low level of conflict is also to be explained by the pervasive role of informal relations within and between the sections, by the workers' fear of losing their jobs, and by their dependence on maintaining good relations with line managers for their bonuses and so on.

No informal workers' leaders have emerged at the factory level. Those who could in our view have carried out this role (basically young high-skilled workers) left for more attractive jobs when production fell. Management policy of removing 'troublemakers' from the factory has also played a role.

The workers recognise that in a situation in which the threat of unemployment hangs over them they have no levers of influence over the administration.

> Every one of us now is afraid, afraid to say a superfluous word – you can be thrown out of the gates for what you say.
>
> Now skilled workers have been pushed into the far corner. Those who keep quiet win. They say to us, 'if you don't like it, you can get out'.
>
> There is nobody to turn to. This is a joint-stock company: we are worms and there are owners, they pay what they want, and not what you have earned. If you speak out, it will be your only speech – they can terminate your labour contract at any moment. Such a situation has already arisen in the small-batch section, when the production manager yelled at the whole factory: 'I will remove the ring-leaders'.
>
> They will sack agitators, but people will not intervene. We are all picked off one by one.

This is how one of the section chiefs envisaged the resolution of a possible incident of mass labour conflict in the factory:

> If strikes arise as a result of low pay (and unrest has begun to develop already over this issue), management will try to settle this question. How? Those who appear to be the ring-leaders will be sacked: 'You do not want to work – goodbye, I am cancelling your labour contract', and the person will do nothing. And they will take another in his place. There is no problem in finding people for our enterprise. I am not saying that we have particularly high pay, but people come to us from enterprises where they earn less. That is how one can eliminate conflict. Sack a few people, and the others will keep quiet for a bit.

POSTSCRIPT

In February 1995 a man entered Minenko's office as he was about to leave for a business trip and shot him three times in the head. This was the tragic finale to the struggle for control of the company. Those managers close to Minenko said that they assumed that he had been killed by criminal structures for refusing to launder money through Lenkon. However, there were clear signs of tension within the highest levels of management and of a shakiness in the position of Minenko.

The most important factor in weakening the position of Minenko was his authoritarian strategy and continuous changes in the administrative structure. There had been two major structural reorganisations in 1994 alone, which undermined the activity of management by increasing instability and indeterminacy. These structural reorganisations were accompanied by stricter control of the managers themselves. One of the main problems in the second half of 1994, which the president tried to resolve with his closest associates (his assistant for management and the chief economist), was that of bringing some order to the production subdivisions which were not managing to fulfil their orders and maintain the scheduled growth of production. Measures to enforce stricter control over the line managers were adopted: the foremen were deprived of their funds, so that workers received money only from the cash office.

These measures had been introduced on the recommendation of a new group of management consultants brought in by Minenko. This group was headed by a graduate of Hubbard College who had experience of management and managerial reorganisation in the textile industry and who recommended a new system of reporting by the chiefs of the production departments, who had to fill in a form which included about 30 indicators of the work of the subdivision and its management. The line managers perceived this innovation as a manifestation of distrust on the part of the president and as an infringement of their independence. In the second half of 1994 several specialists and senior managers left. In particular, the two most energetic young managers, the chief of the department for the technological preparation of production and the chief of the tool-making section, left, as did the chief of the small batch section. By the end of the year only two members of the original board remained at Lenkon. In November 1994 one of the leading Moscow newspapers published a full-page article with the expressive headline, 'Stop Minenko'. It is not known who had sponsored this article – it could have been a former manager, but the greatest threat came from those who remained in Lenkon and continued covertly to struggle against Minenko.

The president understood the situation and looked for ways of strengthening his position. The annual shareholders' meeting was due to take place on 10 March 1995. In January Minenko commissioned a group of sociologists (not us, of course) to conduct a survey of attitudes to the management bodies (the directors' council and the board) and the senior managers (the president and his deputies) of the company. He asked them to conduct not a sample but a full survey of the employees, the overwhelming majority of whom were shareholders.

At the beginning of 1995 Lenkon had 1,100 shareholders (individual and corporate), of whom about 500 were employed by the company. About 10 per cent of these were former employees, about half of the remainder had worked at Lenkon for a long time, and the other half were relative newcomers who had bought or acquired shares from the second issue. Financial Consulting had handled the sale of these shares, and also maintained the shareholders' register but, by the beginning of 1995, 140,000 shares remained unissued, although the shares were relatively liquid: the purchase price was 8,000 roubles, the sale price 7,500. External shareholders by this time held 31 per cent of the shares (the largest being the voucher investment fund Eurasia, which held 16 per cent). Minenko was the largest inside shareholder, with 10 per cent of the shares. Thus the majority of shares were still in the hands of employees of the enterprise, which is why it was so important for the president to know their opinions on the eve of the shareholders' meeting.

The president had no objective reasons to be anxious about the attitude to him of the overwhelming majority of ordinary employees since business was not going too badly, the company was profitable and stable, there were no redundancies and wages and dividends (between 50 and 100 per cent each quarter) were paid regularly. At the annual shareholders' meeting on 10 March it was proposed to announce a dividend of 100 per cent for the fourth quarter of 1994, making a total of 300 per cent for the year as a whole.

The company could also look to the future with some confidence and optimism, with orders flowing in for 1995. Indeed, even with a planned expansion of production the company was receiving more orders than it could meet and claimed that it was having to turn potential customers away. The expansion of production promised increasing wages. In December 1994 the average monthly wage in the enterprise was 500,000 roubles, which was above the average for engineering and for industry as a whole. In January 1995 pay was increased to 600,000 roubles, increasing to 850,000 at the end of March. By the middle of 1995 it had reached 900,000, and skilled workers were sometimes earning more than section chiefs.

The enterprise was still short of good specialists and was ready to take on skilled workers. As in the past, production did not require many highly graded workers (grades 5 and 6), but the growing range of products (80 different kinds of fan by the middle of 1995) and frequent changes in production increased the demand for skilled workers who could work flexibly. To meet this demand the enterprise upgraded its workers, sending them for retraining to an outside training establishment with which the company signed an agreement. All workers on grades 2 and 3 were required to undergo training. Moreover, the personnel management department used the database of the local office of the Federal Employment Service, with which good contacts had been established, and selected the workers required, people living near the factory.

The factory also used other methods of renewing its labour force. A mechanism was established to recruit students from the PTU (technical school) to join the factory for their practical placements, working as full-time members of the brigade alongside the permanent workers (instead of the three-hour maximum permitted by law for under-age pupils) and earning full wages. Sections and brigades also participated in the search for new workers.

New workers were employed for a probationary period of three months, after the successful completion of which they were given the same contracts as the other permanent workers. From March 1995 all employees of the company were transferred to annual labour contracts. Each contract detailed all the responsibilities of the individual employee, replacing the former regulations which specified the duties attached to the post.

It appeared that little had changed in the company after the tragic death of its president. In reality this event had little impact on the sphere of production and employment. More notable and significant changes took place in the structure of management.

The Hubbard Academy was closed immediately after the death of Minenko. Fifteen Hubbardists were dismissed at once, among whom were many energetic people, including key specialists who had identified closely with the enterprise (chief economist, president's assistant, young specialists in the marketing department). The organisational structure of Lenkon was simplified and subordinated to the new head of the enterprise, the former vice president, who had previously been chief of the Moscow factory, before that production manager and originally chief of the small batch section. The posts of president and vice president were abolished and the chief came to be referred to by the traditional term 'General Director'. Five departments were subordinate to him: staff, finance, sales, production and the technology centre. At the same time all functions not concerned with production and supply were placed under the personnel department, including not only the usual personnel services, but also administrative services, the transport department, security service, capital construction, social and welfare services, telephone exchange and so on (altogether comprising 140 of the 500 people working in the enterprise). In parallel to this the personnel manager concentrated all information in his hands. He controlled a database which contained all the information about the company and every manager was obliged to pass information to him. If necessary chiefs or their deputies have access to this information, but only in relation to their own department. There are only three general documents accessible to all managers: the strategic development plan to the year 2005 and the current investment and work plans.

This history of the restructuring of this enterprise and of the conflicts within the management team has confirmed the well-known truth: the person who has all the information controls the enterprise. At the first stage of its restructuring the nerve centre was the chief economist, who managed to concentrate in his hands information about the financial, economic and industrial activity of the company and limit the access of other managers, including the company president, Minenko, to this information. The conflict between the president and the chief economist, with the departure of the latter, followed from this. Then Minenko succeeded in establishing his control over the information. One of the real reasons for the organisational restructuring and conflicts within management was precisely the authoritarian aspiration of the president to concentrate all information in his hands. Now it is the personnel manager who aspires to this role of the chief authority in the enterprise.

4. Two Military-Industrial Giants

Samara Research Group

MANAGEMENT STRATEGY IN MILITARY-INDUSTRIAL GIANTS

Kol'tso and Prokat are two giant enterprises in the city of Samara (formerly Kuibyshev) on the banks of the Volga. Both enterprises were part of the military-industrial complex, the former producing bearings, the latter processing aluminium. Both enterprises were among the leaders in their industry, prosperous, well connected, with ample funds both for investment and for building up an impressive social and welfare apparatus. The fate of the two enterprises in the transition to a market economy was typical of many other such jewels in the crown of the Soviet industrial system.[1]

We can identify three stages in the development of management strategy in response to the crisis into which the enterprises were suddenly plunged, a strategy which we characterise as one of 'balancing conservatism', in that its overall aim was, as far as possible, to maintain stability by balancing the various internal and external interests involved in the fate of the enterprise.

The first stage was largely passive. Economic difficulties had begun to develop even before 1989, but it was only with the liberalisation of prices and the collapse of the Soviet Union at the end of 1991 that modest decline turned into incipient collapse. The problems faced by all enterprises in the military-industrial complex at this time were multiple. The collapse of economic links with the former Republics of the Soviet Union disrupted supplies and sales. The collapse in state finances led to a massive cut in demand for the products of the military-industrial complex, with military procurements slashed by

[1] The Samara Research Group comprises the following members of the Samara branch of the Institute for Comparative Labour Relations Research (ISITO): Irina Kozina (Director), Pavel Romanov, Tanya Metalina, Marina Korelina (Prokat), Irina Tartakovskaya, Sergei Alasheev and Lena Lapshova (Kol'tso).

two-thirds almost overnight. Restrictive monetary policies imposed on a primitive banking system deprived enterprises of even the minimum requirements for working capital, leading to a virtual de-monetisation of what was already only a partially monetised economy. In such a framework the use of normal financial indicators as the basis of an orientation to profit was completely meaningless. The priority of management was to secure supplies and orders to maintain production and employment by any possible means, and to worry later about payment and profitability. The general belief within management circles was that the crisis was short-term, that there would soon be a political stabilisation based on the re-assertion of the existing power structures, so that the priority was as far as possible to retain the enterprise and its labour force intact.

The second stage in the evolution of a new management strategy came with the opportunity for privatisation following Yeltsin's privatisation decree of July 1992. Outside observers had believed that industrial managers, particularly in the giants of the military-industrial complex, would be the most die-hard opponents of privatisation. In fact, they seized their opportunities with alacrity. Far from trying to avoid privatisation, chiefs of many enterprises which were initially excluded because of their military significance even tried to reclassify their enterprises to take advantage of the opportunities opened up by privatisation. Lying behind this enthusiasm was the fact that, with the collapse of the Soviet system, industrial managers had gained their independence from the ministerial bodies which had formerly held them in their grip, but had at the same time lost the security which had been provided by that system. Over 1991–2 the senior managers became in practice the owners of the enterprises, even though they had no property rights in them. Up to 1991, in alliance with the labour collective, they struggled for the economic independence of the enterprise. From 1992 the struggle of senior management to become owners of the enterprise began, and in this struggle the interests of management and the labour collective began to diverge.

Privatisation provided a means by which senior managers could consolidate their positions, transforming themselves from state appointees who could be dismissed on the whim of an official to the appointees of the owners of the enterprise. The key consideration of senior management through the privatisation process was to ensure that they themselves controlled the majority shareholding. This they achieved by choosing to privatise by the second variant provided for under the law, according to which the majority of shares were to be allocated to the labour collective on privileged terms, by ensuring that they controlled the voting rights of the employee-shareowners, and by establishing their own financial subsidiaries and partners which could buy up the shares allocated to the workers, and then purchase additional shares at auction.

The continued strategy of 'balancing conservatism' of senior management in this phase was determined by their attempt to preserve their power and social status through the transition in property form. The smooth transfer of ownership depended on the passivity of the mass of the workforce, thus alongside the transfer of ownership almost no changes took place inside the factory: the usual hierarchies remained in place. Correspondingly, the new employee 'proprietors' did not show any increased identification with the enterprise: there was no slowing of the rapid labour turnover nor was there any increase in the interest of workers in the management of the enterprise. The economic position of the enterprise continued to deteriorate independent of all these processes.

Since most enterprises chose to privatise according to the second variant, senior management had to pay some attention to the interest of the employees to whom they were entrusting the ownership of the company. This dictated a continuation of the 'authoritarian paternalist' management traditions which were embodied in the widespread social guarantees provided by the enterprise: guarantees of employment, of a minimum level of subsistence, of housing and of a wide range of social and welfare facilities. This concern underlay the continued commitment to the strategy of 'balancing conservatism', the management trying, within the limits of the resources available, to maintain wages, employment and social and welfare facilities and being reluctant to tamper with the internal structures of production management. At the same time, this conservative policy, together with the privatisation variant chosen (which deprived the enterprise of external investment funds), meant that these enterprises had very limited resources available for any new investment in conversion, while continuing economic instability meant that there was little prospect of attracting outside funding for productive investment. Their survival strategy had, therefore, to be based on the existing human and productive resources at the disposal of the enterprise. The priorities were marketing and financial and commercial activities, rather than any attempts to develop production or to reduce its costs. Marketing departments and financial and commercial subsidiaries were set up to try to improve the cash-flow of the enterprise (and of its senior managers). Shop chiefs were sent out to scour the country for supplies and for orders, if necessary adapting their existing facilities to make new products. Some attempts were made to increase the production of consumer goods, which had always comprised a part of the production of military-industrial enterprises, but in the event consumer markets proved to be even harder hit than those for producer goods and attempts to develop new product lines proved unsuccessful. The result was a continued reliance on traditional customers and traditional suppliers.

With the domestic economy continuing its precipitate decline management faced in two directions at once in its attempt to limit the damage caused by the crisis. On the one hand, management sought to mobilise its old contacts to enlist the support and co-operation of traditional customers and suppliers and, more in hope than in great expectation, to lobby its contacts in the region and in Moscow to secure state-funding, either in the form of investment funds or privileged access to credit. On the other hand, management looked for their salvation to the glittering possibilities of exporting. Exporting provided a secure market in which they could not only sell their products, but even receive payment for them. Moreover, by opening up export markets they could hope to make contact with prospective foreign investment partners who would transform the prospects of the enterprise with their largesse. However, both our case-study enterprises faced serious barriers in implementing both sides of this dualistic strategy. On the one hand, they had lost their political position which had formerly provided them with privileged access to state funds. On the other hand, they faced serious problems of meeting the quality and delivery requirements of foreign customers. During 1993 and 1994 extremely low wage levels and the fact that amortisation barely featured in production costs meant that the enterprises could compete internationally on price, but continuing inflation and the strengthening of the rouble rapidly eroded competitiveness from late 1994.

Management pursued an equally dualistic strategy within the enterprise. On the one hand, the growing commercial and financial orientation of senior management led to quite extensive restructuring of the senior management apparatus, with financial and commercial specialisms displacing the formerly supreme engineers, and new agreements being established with external banks and commercial organisations, with which very close ties were frequently sealed. On the other hand, concern for maintaining stability, and the orientation to survival by expanding sales and raising prices rather than restructuring production and reducing costs, meant that there was very little change in the productive sphere. This dualism was expressed in the separation of production management from commercial and financial management, the latter being concentrated in the joint-stock company, the former in the factory administration. This was often institutionalised in the form of a 'divisionalisation' of the enterprise, with production units being turned into semi-autonomous production divisions. However, this was motivated not so much by an attempt to liberate the innovatory potential of middle management, as to free senior management from its former concern with matters of production.

The separation of senior management from the workforce as a whole was a feature of all aspects of the reform process, institutionalised in reforms of managerial structures, in the concentration of shareownership in the hands of senior management, in growing income differentials, and expressed in the gradual abandonment of traditional managerial practices such as 'going to the people', in which senior managers would periodically tour the shops, and in growing resentment and spontaneous conflict on the shop floor. In such a situation the position of middle management could prove decisive: if middle management retained its loyalty to senior management shop-floor conflict would remain fragmented and could easily be contained. But if middle managers identified with their own employees they could easily focus and consolidate unrest and present a serious challenge to senior management. In response to such pressures, more spontaneously than systematically, the privileges which senior managers had awarded themselves were filtered down to the middle managers, who saw their pay increasing relative to the workers. Increasing the pay of middle managers also made it possible for senior management to pursue a more active personnel policy in filling posts which had in the past been among the least attractive, now selecting middle managers primarily on the basis of their loyalty, and only secondarily on the basis of their technical competence.

As the enterprises came under progressively greater financial pressure it became impossible for them to meet all their commitments: they could no longer simultaneously guarantee employment, satisfactory wages and extensive social and welfare provision. Nevertheless, senior management could not simply renege on its commitments, which were the basis of the internal 'social contract' according to which the workers conceded to management its right to manage. Workers retained their traditional egalitarian and paternalistic values of 'social justice', despite the pressure which social differentiation was putting on those values. The 'manageability' of the labour collective depended on management maintaining the passive loyalty of its workers, which depended in turn on maintaining the illusion, if not the reality, of a concern for the workers' well-being. This meant that management responses to financial pressures were constrained by the need to represent its decisions as unfortunate necessities imposed by external circumstances, rather than being depicted as deliberate strategies imposed by a management now oriented to the single-minded pursuit of profit. At the same time, the ham-fisted policies of central government meant that it was not difficult for management to maintain this illusion, convincing workers that it was the government that was responsible for the non-payment of miserable wages, the lack of investment funds, the collapse of the market and the reduction in the social and welfare apparatus, even while senior management was diverting large sums of money to its pocket commercial and financial companies, whether for their own good or for the greater good of their enterprise. Thus it was possible for senior management to persist with the traditional practices and ideology of 'authoritarian paternalism', behind the traditional cynicism of diverting responsibility for their failures to external forces.

In general the first response of senior management to the tightening financial noose remained passive. The predominance of piece-rate systems and the widespread practice of linking pay scales to enterprise 'profits' rather than to consumer prices provided an automatic mechanism that tied wages and salaries to the declining resources of the enterprise. Government legislation forced the divestiture of part of the housing, social and welfare facilities of the enterprise and reductions in their financing. A passive strategy therefore led automatically to falling real wages, reductions in the availability of housing and declining social and welfare provision. This led in turn to a substantial increase in labour turnover, as those (especially younger, skilled, male) workers with a chance of earning more elsewhere left the enterprise. The result of such a passive policy was a significant change in the skill, age and demographic profile of the labour force.

This kind of passive managerial strategy could not be sustained as the enterprise lost the core of its labour force, leaving many shop chiefs facing shortages of skilled labour despite the collapse of production. It became increasingly clear that the future of the enterprise depended on being able to maintain the pay and benefits of the core workers, and that this could only be achieved by the enforced redundancy of the lower skilled workers and technical white-collar employees who had been reluctant to leave voluntarily because of their weak labour market position. There was a subtle shift in the rhetoric of management, from the priority of 'preserving the labour collective' to the priority of 'preserving the skeleton of the labour collective'.

This shift in managerial strategy was gradual and initially it tended to be spontaneous. Faced with a loss of skilled labour and growing discontent on the part of those who remained, line managers had an arsenal of means with which to induce the less desirable workers to leave voluntarily so that the wage fund could be spread over the smaller number of workers who remained. Unskilled auxiliary workers, violators of discipline – 'drunkards and absentees' – and 'troublemakers' were the first to be sent on part-paid or unpaid administrative leave, while skilled workers were kept on or transferred to other work.[2] The threat of dismissal on some pretext was usually sufficient to induce voluntary resignation, since a dismissal would be entered in the worker's labour book, depriving him or her of any chance of employment elsewhere. Such means of reducing the labour force continued to acknowledge the social responsibilities of the enterprise, being represented as sacrifices necessary to preserve the collective, with the workers' personal and social circumstances being taken into account in their selection for dismissal, so that working pensioners and married women without dependants tended to be first in line.[3] Shop chiefs and foremen also had considerable discretion in the allocation

2 For many workers administrative leave provided an opportunity to increase their earnings on the side. Thus, selection for administrative leave was not necessarily an inducement to resign – indeed it could be a sought-after privilege.

3 While men have tended to change jobs voluntarily, women have almost certainly borne the brunt of enforced redundancy, although this does not show up in the statistics since the overwhelming majority of redundancies are recorded as voluntary severances and enforced redundancy, at least to the end of 1995, was still not widespread. Women are more vulnerable than men on almost every count: they predominate in unskilled auxiliary and lower white-collar occupations; the fact that women live much longer and retire earlier than men means that they constitute the majority of working pensioners; men are protected by the assumption that the man is the main breadwinner in the family (although women's maternity rights are still legally protected and social considerations give protection to single mothers); women's ability to work is hardest hit by the cuts in welfare facilities, especially kindergartens.

of the wages fund, which was increased by the growing proportion of wages paid as bonuses, and the enabled them to alter wage differentials to the advantage of those they wished to retain.[4]

This kind of informal strategy of enforced redundancy provides a solution to the problem of the loss of skilled labour faced by the shop chief, but it does not provide any solution to the financial problems faced by senior management because the savings achieved remain within the shop, the purpose being precisely to redistribute existing resources. Moreover, informal redundancies have an impact primarily on workers rather than on technical and clerical staff, who are much more reluctant to leave voluntarily and whose pay is not at the disposal of line management. Thus, eventually financial pressure means that senior management has to take the initiative and pursue a more active strategy of enforced redundancy, based not merely on removing people, but on cutting the staff list and so the funds available to various departments and subdivisions to pay wages and salaries. Such an initiative, hardly surprisingly, provokes strong opposition from chiefs of departments and subdivisions, although this takes the form of informal resistance and covert subversion as each tries to shift the burden onto others, rather than declared opposition to a strategy whose necessity for the survival of the enterprise is generally accepted by management as a whole. Such a strategy also divides the labour force, with the responsibility of identifying workers for redundancy typically passed down to the level of the shop, the section and even the brigade. The extent to which senior management is able to push through such a programme depends primarily on the extent to which it is able to exploit the divisions within management and the labour force to overcome the various forms of subversion and resistance presented to its plans.

The move from a strategy of preserving employment at any price in the expectation of imminent recovery, to one of maintaining wages was a fairly decisive one in determining the fate of an enterprise because those enterprises which pursued a high-wage strategy were able to attract the most desirable workers, while those whose wages

[4] Formal changes in the wages system tend to provoke serious conflict while failing to achieve the desired results because they deprive line managers of the discretion which is essential to the use of informal levers of influence (Valentina Vedeneeva, 'Payment Systems and the Restructuring of Production Relations in Russia', in Simon Clarke, ed., *Management and Industry in Russia: Formal and Informal Relations in the Period of Transition*, op. cit., and Inna Donova, 'Wage systems in pioneers of privatisation', in Simon Clarke, ed., *Labour in Transition*, op. cit.).

fell relative to others in the city lost the skilled core of their labour force: in circumstances of an ageing capital stock and inappropriate raw materials, machinery and equipment, it is the skills and enterprise of the labour force alone that gives the enterprise the flexibility to maintain production and to modify its profile. In general the move was made earliest by those enterprises, such as Lenkon and Plastmass, which had been relatively unsuccessful within the Soviet system but which were able to exploit the transition to a market economy to amass the resources which made a high-wage strategy and an 'upgrading' of the labour force possible, the payment of high wages removing resistance to redundancy on the part of both workers and managers. Other enterprises were in a less fortunate position, in having to make redundancies as a condition for maintaining wages (rather than the other way around), but had a strong management which was able to exploit divisions within the enterprise to push through a programme of redundancy and labour force restructuring at a relatively early stage in the crisis.

Our case study enterprises are typical of the more conservative pattern which is characteristic of the former giants of Soviet industry, the ambition of whose management was to preserve their privileged position rather than to seize the new opportunities of the market economy to enhance a formerly inferior one. Within this pattern there are some differences in response. Although both enterprises faced a collapse of production and growing financial pressure, Prokat was more successful at maintaining wages, at first by large-scale borrowing. Kol'tso was already in a weaker position than Prokat and was unable to maintain its already relatively low wages, losing workers by natural wastage as its wages fell to the lowest in the city. These differences were reflected in the different directions of development of the skill and demographic profiles of the two enterprises. But in the longer term neither variant of the conservative strategy was adequate to the deteriorating economic and financial situation. By early 1994 it looked as though the burden of accumulated debt would drag Prokat down, when a sudden fortuitous upsurge in exports relieved the situation. However, relief was short-lived as exports collapsed from the spring of 1995, following changes in foreign trade regulations and the freezing of the rouble, pushing Prokat back into crisis. Kol'tso was similarly sustained by export sales and then hit by the freezing of the dollar exchange rate through 1995, so that by the end of 1995 both enterprises were on the brink of collapse once more.

The strategy of 'balancing conservatism' was dictated not only by the external circumstances and the internal social structure of the enterprise, but also by the ideological orientation and corresponding psychological characteristics of senior managers, people for whom a profit orientation was completely unfamiliar (although this was their declared aim and in Kol'tso was even included as the first point in the appropriate section of the collective agreement for 1993). These people, by their age and experience, were formed in the Soviet administrative tradition of 'red directors', feeling responsible for every aspect of the life of the collective entrusted to them. They are not fundamentally opposed to commercial activity or to making profits, although they do little in practice to look for new orders or to draw up business plans, but they are absolutely not prepared to take any kind of risky or unpopular steps, above all to sack surplus labour. This unwillingness is sustained by their hope that they will get through the difficult times and restore production to its former volume, as well as a vague fear of likely social shocks and unpleasantness.

Such characteristics were not inappropriate for the first stage of transition, the passive adaptation to a massively de-stabilising crisis, but such managers could not be expected to take the lead in adopting more positive steps to sustain the enterprise. A change in enterprise strategy was therefore associated with the appointment to senior management positions of people of a quite different generational, educational and occupational background.

Both our case-study enterprises are typical in that such people came into senior management positions in the enterprise from financial and commercial structures with which intimate connections had been established in the course of privatisation. Within senior management these people represent new directions of radical change, based on the imposition of strictly economic and financial decision-making criteria. Their rise to power is therefore closely connected with the emergence of new lines of division and conflict within the enterprise, and between the enterprise and its associated commercial and financial structures. At the end of 1995 such divisions and conflicts were only beginning to solidify and their outcome remains to be seen. However, it is clear from all those enterprises with which we are familiar that the pattern of the 'pioneers of privatisation' is already being repeated, with the radical ambition of new managers being severely constrained by the density of the social structures which they are seeking to transform, embodied in the pivotal position of line managers and shop chiefs, represented by the continued presence of more conservative managers in senior positions. Even an apparently very radical change in management personnel therefore leads to no more than a change in the balance of forces within the framework of 'balancing conservatism'.[5]

HISTORY OF THE ENTERPRISES

Prokat

The decision to build a giant factory on the banks of the Volga to prepare rolled aluminium was made in 1950. There were several reasons for building it in Kuibyshev, including its location within the system of rail and river transport, the availability of energy resources (oil and gas), which were substantially increased with the construction of the Kuibyshev hydroelectric station, and the geographical proximity of aircraft factories, the main users of rolled aluminium. Until 1992 the factory came under the control of the Ministry of Aeronautical Engineering, and the construction of the plant and its productive activity was carried out in conditions of strict secrecy. It was only in 1992 that the factory left the control of the aviation industry and transferred to the department of metallurgy, the trade union simultaneously transferring its affiliation to the metallurgists' union.

The Nameless (*Bezymyanki*) factory began to be built on the outskirts of Kuibyshev in the spring of 1951. The construction of the *raion* of Prokat, in which the workers and builders of the factory were settled, began at the same time.

The factory was designed to be the largest and most advanced in Europe, to meet the needs of military construction. Since much of the technology was new it was necessary to resolve problems of equipment and of training of skilled workers. The equipment was on the whole non-standard, prepared in the factory itself, and cadres had to be trained in its use. Existing plants in Stupino, Verkhnei Salda and Kamensk-Ural'sk could only spare a small number of specialists, so the majority of workers had to be trained locally. Those who showed

[5] See, for example, Pavel Romanov 'The Regional Elite in the Epoch of Bankruptcy', and Veronika Kabalina, 'Privatisation and Restructuring of Enterprises: Under Insider or Outsider Control?', both in Simon Clarke, ed., *Conflict and Change in the Russian Industrial Enterprise*, op. cit.

the most potential in training were selected as potential foremen and were sent in large groups to gain experience working in other plants.

The first aluminium ingot was produced for the 38th anniversary of the October Revolution in 1955, although the equipment was still not fully installed. The foundry only came into operation a year and a half later, and even then the work was carried out in extremely difficult conditions. One of the foundry foremen remembers:

> We had to do everything by hand. Take the loading of the furnace. It had to be loaded using shovels with seven metre handles. Each ingot weighed a pood (12 kg), and we loaded them in pairs. Each charge took a thousand shovels, making 16 tons, and each time you had to run 14 metres to the furnace and back ... There were hardly any instruments. Everything had to be done by eye.

Another veteran of the factory recalled:

> In the winter we had to wear *valenki* [felt boots] working on the mixer. It was freezing in the shop, but around us was water for cooling the ingots. The *valenki* would swell up and we could hardly get to the cloakroom in them. When the water was heated to 60 degrees Celsius it was transferred across ice at thirty below from one container to another, we couldn't see each other for the thick steam, and the ingots were covered with frost.

Khrushchev visited the factory as part of the celebrations for the opening of the Lenin hydroelectric station in 1958. According to eyewitnesses, the city at that time was on the brink of famine, and it is said that Khrushchev's attempt to make a speech about the building of Bezymyanki was met with indignant shouts of protest as the delegation was pelted with rotten vegetables and forced to leave the city hurriedly and secretly. We do not know if this was followed by any repression, but supplies for construction and the city significantly improved.

On 5 July 1960 the enterprise was officially commissioned by a government delegation. Two months later it was given Lenin's name as an indication of its paramount importance to the state, and in October a decree of the Presidium of the Supreme Soviet of the USSR announced the award of 596 orders and medals, including four of the highest honour, Hero of Socialist Labour, to workers of the factory.

The official history of Prokat, as we will call the enterprise, asserts that the enterprise was already profitable in 1961, that it made a greater number of items and was awarded more prizes and awards at international exhibitions than the largest firms in the capitalist countries. In 1962 Prokat began to export its products to Western European markets.

Since it had taken ten years to build the factory and to bring it into production, some of the equipment was already worn out or out of date by the time the factory opened, so that its technical reconstruction began almost immediately. As the largest enterprise in the industry Prokat continued to get the full attention of the Party and the government, its fixed capital assets increasing from 1.263 million roubles in 1965 to 7.188 million in 1970. The social and welfare infrastructure was considerably expanded, with the building of kindergartens, apartment blocks, a large swimming pool, a park with a boating lake, a children's polyclinic, a tourist base and many other facilities. The enterprise was showered with honours and awards at the end of every five-year plan as its production and profits inexorably increased, a total of 2,075 workers receiving such awards, including 22 Orders of Lenin.

The founding director retired in 1979, to be replaced by the chief of the sheet-rolling shop, who spent six years as director before being promoted to the post of Second Secretary of the Kuibyshev Regional Committee of the CPSU in 1984. His replacement was the chief engineer of a large metallurgical plant at Krasnoyarsk. In 1988 the factory was transformed into an industrial association (apart from the metallurgical factory the association included a sulphuric acid plant, located in the suburbs of the city, which produced resins).

For a long time Prokat was an exemplary model and hosted many Soviet and foreign visitors as a sort of demonstrative example. A favoured child is always indulged more than the others, and Moscow was not grudging in providing funds for the expansion of the social sphere and house building.

Prokat certainly fully justified its existence as a productive enterprise oriented primarily to expanding its gross output and to meeting industrial and technological needs, including those of the military sector. By the end of the 1980s the enterprise produced a range of basic products: sheets, strips, panels, plates, varnished strips, extrusions, rods, tubes and forgings, 60 per cent of which was sheet and strip from the sheet-rolling shop, in some of which it had a monopoly in Russia. It supplied 90,000 items to 7,000 customers in the Soviet Union and 25 foreign countries. Customers were glad to get hold of its products and were not too bothered about their appearance. The Soviet Union set the tone for the structure of industry of the socialist camp, defining the quality, range and grades of metal going into the manufacture of aluminium rollings. As a whole, foreign trade did not exceed 10 per cent of sales, with the Soviet market absorbing almost all of the factory's output.

Kol'tso

The ball bearing factory Kol'tso is one of the largest enterprises in Samara. In 1991 the factory produced about 200 million bearings, around 20 per cent of the entire production of the Soviet Union, and 80 per cent of all bearings for military use. Thus the factory was a core part of the military-industrial complex. The factory produced a very wide range of bearings, from one millimetre miniature bearings weighing only a tenth of a gram, to giant bearings three metres in diameter, weighing up to 100 kilos. The factory's products were exported to forty different countries.

The factory was originally based in Moscow, but the entire factory was evacuated to Samara in 1941: tools, equipment, one third of the workers, and even semi-finished products. The first consignment of 3,000 bearings, assembled from transferred parts, was produced in November 1941. By December the factory was already producing 60,000 bearings. In January 1943 the factory was awarded the Order of Lenin for heroism in re-establishing production.

In the Soviet period the factory was always in the forefront of new initiatives, one of the most notorious of which was the transfer of the workers to 'self-checking', without any technical quality surveillance of production. The attempt to introduce this initiative into other factories ('the dissemination of advanced experience') led to a catastrophic increase in defective production. In 1958 the factory was visited by Leonid Brezhnev, who was nominated as a candidate for election to the Supreme Soviet of the USSR from the Kirov electoral district of Samara.

During the 1960s and 1970s there was a significant expansion of production, including various kinds of auxiliary production – abrasives, machinery, tools, semi-finished products and consumer goods such as children's toys, washing machines and so on. Almost half the stock of machines used in Kol'tso was built in the factory. The factory constantly and steadily expanded its industrial base and its social infrastructure thanks, above all, to the importance of its role in the country's militarised economy. Thus, for example, a railway repair factory became a subsidiary of Kol'tso for some years, only to separate off again into an independent enterprise. The enterprise still has a second ball-bearing factory, a small bearing repair plant and a large engineering plant as subsidiaries. During the 1960s and 1970s the factory also undertook a major programme of housing construction. Over the years, tens of thousands of workers have won various state awards – orders, medals, commendations – including awards for agricultural work ('for active participation in bringing in the harvest'). In practice Kol'tso has always functioned as a highly diversified enterprise. Its transport shop has railway wagons, buses, trucks, automobiles – altogether more than 500 vehicles of one kind or another. The enterprise also has a large cultural and welfare apparatus, including a 'palace of culture', profilaktory, a health centre, kindergartens, and subsidiary agricultural enterprises spread around the region. The factory and its subsidiaries cover an area of more than 100 hectares.

In 1971 the factory was awarded a second Order of Lenin. By this time the factory had developed a substantial machine-building capacity, producing machines for other ball-bearing factories around the country, and was producing a wide range of precision bearings. The factory had retained its pre-eminent position in the production of precision bearings for military and industrial uses ever since the war.

In April 1985, before the introduction of the law on labour collectives, the factory was one of the first in the industry to create a Labour Collective Council (STK), headed by a brigadier. The STK did not have any real power and was used by the administration as a consultative body and as a means of pressuring Moscow (thus the STK played a direct role in 'beating out' hard currency allocations for the reconstruction of production distributed by the Soviet ministry in 1990, when the economic crisis was already becoming acute).

Thus, at the beginning of the period of market reform Kol'tso could quite reasonably be seen as a 'prosperous Soviet enterprise', an industrial giant which, by the beginning of the 1990s, employed 30,000 people. Despite a growing crisis Kol'tso still employed 25,937 in April 1993. The enterprise was in every respect 'in good standing', both according to production indicators and in the social benefits provided for its employees. Its location in the centre of the city also meant that it played an active role in every aspect of the life of the city.

THE ECONOMIC IMPACT OF REFORM

Prokat

The aluminium industry was one of the hardest hit by the collapse of the Soviet Union, the bulk of its product being destined for military use. Domestic consumption of refined aluminium fell from 2.3 million tonnes in 1991 to just over half a million tonnes in 1995, the latter including a significant proportion destined for exports of semi-processed aluminium products. The aluminium refining industry turned to export markets, the industry being second only to oil and gas in the opportunities offered for private profit and soon becoming a principal target of organised crime (*Business Week*, 3433, 14 August 1995, pp. 56–7).

The aluminium processing industry was concentrated in Siberia, where its profitability depended on access to cheap power. In order to meet the quality demands of the world market the industry had increasingly to turn to imported alumina, its principal raw material, much of which had in the past been derived from Ukrainian bauxite. Aluminium was exported through 'tolling' arrangements, according to which the multinational companies which dominated the industry supplied the alumina and exported the product, paying the processor a tolling fee. Russian exports of aluminium increased from 250,000 tonnes in 1989 to 2.2 million tonnes in 1994, almost fifteen per cent of world consumption, with an estimated half the output being smelted under tolling arrangements with imported aluminium. This upsurge of exports enabled the smelting industry to continue to work at 90 per cent capacity.

The dumping of Russian aluminium on world markets had a catastrophic impact on the world aluminium market, which was already weak as a result of excess capacity, the price falling by over 50 per cent in 1993. The European Union invoked anti-dumping restrictions in August 1993, and Russia agreed to participate in a substantial output restriction programme in January 1994, although the Russian cuts did not last long. However, this was sufficient for the aluminium price to bounce back to its former levels.

The export of Russian aluminium was dominated by one company, Trans-CIS Commodities (TCC), a joint venture established by a London-based metals trader who had been buying aluminium from the

Soviet trade monopoly for twenty years, and a Soviet citizen from Tashkent, who had good informal contacts in the industry. In the middle of 1992, TCC established a tolling arrangement with the world's largest aluminium smelter in Krasnoyarsk, followed by arrangements with the two other major smelters at Bratsk and Sayansk, which together have a capacity of over two million tonnes. TCC also bought shares in these plants so that by mid-1994 TCC was estimated to control 20 per cent of Krasnoyarsk, around 50 per cent of Bratsk and 68 per cent of Sayansk. Through shareownership and tolling TCC, a company based, according to its head, on trust not written agreements, was estimated to control two-thirds of Russia's aluminium producing capacity – around ten per cent of world production (on TCC's activities see the *Economist*, 21 January 1995).

All did not run smoothly for TCC. The collapse of the world aluminium price in 1993 discouraged potential competitors, but it meant that TCC was probably losing money. However, once the price recovered in 1994 it was estimated that TCC made over one billion dollars in profit over the year. Such a windfall could not fail to attract the attention of competitors, and a struggle for control of the Krasnoyarsk smelter ensued, in which five people died violent deaths in 1994. In October 1993 the general director was beaten up and replaced in April 1994 by the plant's commercial director, the man responsible for export sales, whom the general director accused of being behind the assault and of having stolen 14 million dollars from the plant. Initial good relations between TCC and the new general director soured as it became clear how much money TCC was making from the relationship. In October 1994 Krasnoyarsk stopped delivering aluminium to TCC, and in November crossed TCC off its shareholders' register, a move that was supported by the new privatisation minister, who had just replaced Anatolii Chubais in the post.

The recovery in the world aluminium price continued through 1995 as world demand caught up with supply, and expectations were that the recovery would be sustained. However, the profitability of tolling was rapidly squeezed as the rouble hardened against the dollar, falling from an estimated $520 per tonne in December 1994 to only $70 per tonne by May 1995. Moreover, there were new fears that shortages of alumina, exacerbated by growing Russian imports, would put pressure on the profitability of the refining industry from below (*Financial Times*, 23 July, 25 July, 13 September 1995).

The stable and prosperous situation of Prokat was shattered in

1992, although negative tendencies had already begun to appear in 1989 with the breaking of trade links with the former socialist countries of Eastern Europe, which had formerly provided Prokat with a protected market.[6] On the one hand, it shared fully in the fate of the military-industrial complex with the collapse of military demand for aluminium. On the other hand, its difficulties were compounded by the shortage and rising cost of raw materials as refined aluminium was diverted to export.

The precipitous decline in the market following the break up of the Soviet Union, the collapse of military orders, shortages of raw materials, the crisis of the financial system and the collapse of its main customer, the Samara Aircraft Factory, led Prokat to establish a department of foreign economic relations, which made sales to Western markets its main priority. However, Prokat's technology was outdated and it had difficulty meeting the quality standards demanded by Western consumers. The foreign orders were slow to come, amounting to only 3 per cent of the sharply reduced output in 1992 and virtually all its home and foreign orders in 1993 still came from established customers. This preference for maintaining or restoring established links was not an ideological legacy but a commercial decision, a result of the excessively high prices charged by the commercial intermediaries to which enterprises had had to resort in the period of acute shortage in 1991, the recurrent crises of non-payment and shortages of raw aluminium from 1992.

In the West the principal uses of aluminium sheet and strip are for packaging and for construction, while in the Soviet Union the principal uses were for the military and engineering industries. In principle conversion should have been relatively straightforward for Prokat, since its output is semi-finished products which can easily be adapted to a wide range of needs. Unlike most enterprises within the military-industrial sector, conversion does not require major investment in new plant and equipment, or even a significant re-tooling, although it does imply some change in the balance between its various products. However, the collapse of production in the wake of the disintegration of the Soviet Union hit not only military customers but also the

6 Armenia had been one of Prokat's most profitable markets, but was now blockaded so that aluminium had to be transported by air, which obviously imposed enormous transport costs. Because of payments difficulties Prokat only accepted orders from Moldova against cash pre-payment, brought to Prokat by Moldovan representatives in person. Of the CIS countries, Ukraine took 80 per cent of the orders, but Prokat had hopes of selling to the Asian Republics.

production of consumer goods, so that demand from the latter sector was also in decline, exacerbated by the problem of payments.

The sharp reduction in the demand for its traditional products led the management to seek to diversify the production of the consumer goods which had always made up a small part of its output. The main items produced were cooking utensils and containers of various kinds, but in 1993 production of window frames (initially for glass-houses), and roof-racks, aerials, and hub caps for automobiles produced at the nearby VAZ plant was developed. Nevertheless, consumer goods only amounted to about 8 per cent of the much reduced output.

On the other hand, Prokat was very dependent on its suppliers of raw aluminium, the cost of which makes up more than two-thirds of the price of the product. As Russian producers looked to the world market, the supply of raw aluminium dried up, although Prokat managed to reach an agreement with the suppliers, with the support of government structures, that it would be guaranteed supplies provided that it could pay, which depended in turn on Prokat finding reliable customers. However, while the world market price fell through 1993 with Russian dumping, the price that Prokat had to pay was increasing as domestic prices moved to world levels. Even with the depressed price of aluminium, the rate of profit for 1993 was expected to be only 16 per cent, the lowest in the industry, with the price of the product held down in the face of competition. In 1994 the problem of supply had been resolved but, as the price of aluminium rose, the problem was now to secure supplies at a favourable price.

The situation was somewhat improved by a visit of the general director and a group of specialists to the main raw material producing regions in Siberia, Krasnoyarskii Krai and Khakasiya at the end of 1993, which led to a series of agreements to stabilise the supply of raw aluminium and establish easier terms for payment. The key element in this success was the personal connections of the administration of Prokat with the key leaders of the supplier regions. Judging by the level of those involved in the discussion of the cost of aluminium (the chiefs of Krasenergo and Khakasenergo, first deputy president of the council of ministers of Khakasia and president of the committee for industry) the problem was resolved by reducing the cost of electricity for the Siberian aluminium producers, which had a major impact on the cost of aluminium, since refining is extremely energy intensive.

This problem could not have been solved without the involvement of the Siberian local authorities, since they are almost the only such powers in Russia able to hold out for regional control over the large producers of electric power supplied to the region (Krasnoyarsk, Bratsk, Sayano-Shushenskii hydroelectric complexes) and so to influence the process of price formation in this area. Their support contrasted markedly with the failure of the Samara regional authorities to support Prokat, as one of the region's largest producers. In particular, the factory management was angry that the local authorities had handed ownership of the huge Volga hydroelectric power station, located in the *oblast*, to federal authorities. This avoided conflict with the federal government but the resulting high prices for energy, beyond the control of the regional authorities, make production much more expensive.

The collapse of demand, sharp increases in the price of raw materials and energy costs and the problems of non-payment by customers led to a fall in output of over 50 per cent by 1992, compared to the peak production level of 1989, with a further fall of almost a quarter in 1993, affecting tube production much more seriously than that of the rolling shop, with the output of shop 4 falling by 75 per cent and shop 55 by over 60 per cent in 1993 over 1992, although the production of aluminium sheet only fell by 15 per cent, and the repair, tool and equipment-making shops, which were able to continue repair and maintenance work, maintained their full level of production, with shop 12 even increasing its workload by 20 per cent.

The depth of the crisis is indicated by the production figures:

	Thousand tonnes	Percent of 1989
1989	658	
1990	628	95
1991	513	78
1992	293	45
1993	149	23

By the beginning of 1994 Prokat was in a very difficult situation. The increasing cost of aluminium rollings intensified the collapse in demand as aluminium was replaced by its main competitor, steel. In 1989 aluminium was 1.8 times the price of steel, but by 1994 it was 6–7 times the price, making its use unprofitable in many industries, with a big reduction in demand from the motor industry and with aluminium being replaced by glass, other metals and even wooden barrels in making various kinds of containers, while the main customer, the aircraft industry, was close to catastrophe in 1993. After the crash in Irkutsk of an almost new TU-154, built in Samara, demand for this plane collapsed. By the spring of 1994 the aircraft factory had 11 completed but unsold planes and could not pay Prokat.

In the debt crisis of mid-1992 Prokat accumulated an indebtedness of 3 billion roubles, being entered on the 'card index' of chronic debtors, although it was owed 4 billion for products already delivered. The government's debt-offset package was of little help to Prokat, which continued to have difficulty collecting money owed to it for delivered products, having to send managers to its debtor enterprises and often to settle for payment in kind. Prokat attempted to overcome this problem by insisting on pre-payment from its customers during 1993, although it did not apply this to its long-established customers in the aircraft industry. However, difficulties with securing such pre-payment and unbroken inflation in the costs of energy and raw materials led to a continuing sharp fall in the number of orders and customers. Its debt continued to accumulate so that by the middle of July 1993 Prokat's debts amounted to 12 billion roubles, while it was owed 14.5 billion roubles. In the face of the fall in production Prokat had done all it could to maintain wages and employment, borrowing money on a large scale to keep up its payments. As a result, with rising interest rates, the debt burden became crippling, so that by 1994 debt interest payments exceeded the company's total wage bill.

In an attempt to reduce its debts the management took a whole series of minor measures. For example, it issued an order to review the norms governing the cost of materials used for operational-repair and technical purposes. But it still saw the main problem as lying beyond its control, in the inadequacies of the financial system:

> The problem of non-payment derived from the global inability of the banking system to cope with work in new conditions. We often heard such comments as this from the producers: 'It is not us or our clients who are responsible for the absence of money in our accounts … Our clients phone us – the money was sent a long time ago. Speed up the deliveries, the debts will accumulate!' And we say, 'we cannot, your money has still not reached our account'. We cannot pay for our raw materials, our debts are accumulating, and they have stopped their production in turn, their debts are accumulating – everything is getting bogged down on the way, in the banks. (Shop chief)

The production plan for 1994 was for 150–190 thousand tons, but the first part of the year brought no significant relief, with production falling a further 30 per cent in the first four month, Prokat standing in third place among the hardest hit enterprises in the *oblast*, which had the highest proportion of unprofitable enterprises in the country.

To achieve the production plan for 1994 Prokat needed to buy between 15 and 24 thousand tons of raw aluminium a month, which at the then current prices (from 1.959 to 2.912 million roubles a ton) required 35–40 billion roubles of working capital. However, at such prices the cost of rolled aluminium was far too high not only for domestic consumers, but also for profitable export.

Despite all these difficulties, Prokat remained the largest supplier of rolled aluminium in Russia, its market share in 1994 amounting to 49.1 per cent, with 68 per cent of Russian exports, and remained one of the most prosperous enterprises in its region, continuing to maintain a large social and welfare apparatus, and its wages were still second only to those of VAZ among industrial enterprises in the region.

Kol'tso

When we began our research Kol'tso, like many other engineering enterprises, was already facing serious economic difficulties. In the first instance this was connected with the sharp reduction in military orders for precision bearings. The enterprise was also hard hit by the breakdown of its connections with old customers and suppliers of raw materials (many of whom were located in Ukraine, trading with which became very difficult because of the breakdown of the bank clearing system), the introduction of the system of pre-payment, and increasing energy prices. The factory had 500 million roubles frozen in the bank, and also had 400,000 US dollars frozen in its account with the state international trade bank, Vneshekonombank. The stocks of metal in 1992 fell to 35 per cent of the 1991 level, and stocks of auxiliary materials fell by even more.

Even in 1991 the factory had made the plan by 80.5 per cent, producing over 200 million bearings, but in 1992 production fell by almost a quarter. During 1992–3 the factory was repeatedly on the brink of closure. From July to September 1992 it worked a reduced working week, with four six-hour days, while some sections worked only three shortened days. Workers were also sent on compulsory paid vacation. On any particular day during this period up to 1,000 people would be on compulsory leave, a figure which reached 2,269 people in December 1992.

Although consumers still needed bearings, the factory faced serious difficulties in selling them. Thus, on 1 December 1992 the value of the stocks of unsold finished products amounted to almost one billion roubles, despite the precipitous fall in production. This was partly a result of the 40 per cent fall in production in the engineering industry as a whole, but also of the crisis of non-payment. In 1992, 923 million roubles' worth of products were delivered to customers, but only 418 million roubles was received for them.

The first measure taken in response to the economic crisis, in accordance with the strategy of 'balancing conservatism' described above, was not to try to cut costs but was to raise prices of ball bearings. Although this meant that Kolt'so's prices were very high compared to those of comparable Russian producers, prices were initially still lower than those on world markets which allowed the factory to increase its export sales.

The main domestic purchasers at this stage were the factory's traditional customers. Sales were achieved by direct agreements. There was a small number of new customers, but these were mostly small short-term orders, only amounting to a small proportion of production. It became increasingly common for customers' representatives to arrive, pay for bearings from stock, and take the products away with them immediately.

Since the main problem remained that of sales, the factory administration was anxious to conquer new markets. In place of the sale of bearings to the Urals military factories the administration tried to provide work for the precision bearings shop by selling to the nearby automobile factory. Apart from this the factory undertook no real efforts at conversion, the administration still having serious hopes in the formulation of a 'new defence doctrine of the government (first deputy general director). Until the summer of 1993, when a marketing department was at last established, sales were handled by the department of sales planning, which had no experience of work in market conditions and whose efforts were widely criticised. In an attempt to solve the problem of sales the administration delegated authority to the level of the shop and newly created production divisions, to which 1.5–2 per cent of the profits were allocated to finance the search for orders. However, sales and production fell even more catastrophically, production falling from 150 million bearings in 1992 to 92 million in 1993.

In this period great hopes were pinned on opening up foreign markets. In 1991 10 million bearings were sold for export, 5 per cent of total production. In 1992 export sales increased to 15 million units, a doubling to ten per cent as a proportion of production. In 1993 the factory achieved its plan of selling 35 million units for export which, with the sharp fall in domestic sales, meant that over a third of its output was being exported. The management tried to build up foreign sales directly, without going through intermediaries. In 1993 the general director announced that they would seek international quality certification. There was talk of creating a German–Russian joint enterprise for the sale and perhaps even production of bearings. They even began to reorganise a newly constructed building which had been intended for consumer goods production for this work, but these initiatives came to nothing.

Formally, according to the factory's statistics, it was still profitable. However, the factory did not have any real money in its accounts: like many other large factories it was placed on the card index of debtors. It borrowed money, even to pay wages, usually from commercial banks at very high rates of interest. Kol'tso was not able to get any preferential credit either from the government or through the regional authorities. The factory's debts grew, the workers' pay remained one of the lowest in the city, and strikes broke out in several shops.

The period of winter to spring 1993–4 in the factory was marked by a further deepening of the crisis. The decisive factor was that the factory finally ran out of its stocks of metal in March 1994. These stocks for the previous two years had been the only thing which had allowed the factory to continue in production, even though it appeared to have no working capital. Once the stocks were exhausted, and the financial position of the factory had not improved, the enterprise found itself on the brink of complete closure.

During the first ten days of March 1994 the factory did not work at all, then only those subdivisions which had contracts returned to work (this was in fact only the third and fourth units – instrument bearings and ball bearings, and two shops in the special bearings unit which were working on an export order). The remaining employees were sent on compulsory leave with the payment of an allowance of 25,000 roubles for the month (in February the payment had amounted to 14,620 roubles). In March and April metal was supplied virtually only for export orders, and thereafter was only supplied for production for domestic sales once the needs of exports had been met.

In fact, according to the deputy general director for production, 'in terms of the volume of output we have fallen back to the level of 1965, and in terms of the range, to the level of the 1950s'.

Kol'tso has shared the fate of many engineering enterprises in Russia – the incessant intensification of the crisis has not been interrupted by periods of even a temporary, relative stabilisation. Every new development at the macro-economic level had an immediate and devastating impact at the level of the enterprise. However, it would be wrong to explain all the difficulties experienced by Kol'tso only as a consequence of the deteriorating economic situation of the country as a whole. To understand the deeper reasons for this phenomenon it is necessary to consider the processes unfolding inside the system, its reaction to the external changes.

PLACE OF THE ENTERPRISES IN THE ECONOMY OF RUSSIA AND THE REGION

The economic difficulties into which the two enterprises were suddenly plunged were matched by a loss of the political influence that had been so important in determining their earlier prosperity. There are several enterprises in Russia with very similar product ranges to those of Prokat and Kol'tso, each of which is the pocket factory of an aircraft building factory, in the first case, or linked to particular military engineering plants, in the second. With the collapse of the ministerial system each of these production complexes competed for increasingly scarce resources.

Prokat is now a member of the Altima concern, which unites all aluminium supplying and producing enterprises in Russia, but the functions of the concern are largely limited to intermediary operations, particularly in the area of foreign trade, for which it receives a commission. Its other main function is to lobby for the industry with the government. Prokat is also under the jurisdiction of the State Metallurgy Committee of the Council of Ministers of the Russian Federation. However, according to the Prokat management, the committee only carries out an overall monitoring function. Accounting documents are regularly sent to the Committee, the fate of which is unknown. It appears that the State Committee has no regulatory function and does not have any financial levers of influence. Centralised budget allocations from the Conversion Fund are channelled through the committee, but this is not a significant contribution to the resources of the enterprise. The committee performs some intermediary functions and until recently issued export quotas.

In the context of competition for scarce resources the standing of an enterprise in Moscow depends to a considerable extent on its ability to secure the support of the regional authorities. In this respect the military-industrial enterprises which dominate the city of Samara have not been in an advantageous position because of distinctive political and economic features of the region. On the one hand, the regional governor is one of the most loyal supporters of Yeltsin and reform, while the managers of the military-industrial complex were deeply implicated in the most conservative political structures of the Soviet system. The 'democratic revolution' left the industrial managers with few friends in the regional administration. On the other hand, Samara region is also home to two other powerful industrial lobbies, whose star has risen with the transition to an export-oriented market economy: the automobile giant VAZ, in nearby Tol'yatti (which has always had its contacts directly in Moscow, standing aloof from the regional authorities); and the powerful oil and gas complex, with its equally powerful financial and political connections. Moreover, Samara also has a large and potentially highly productive agricultural sector, which is a strong claimant for regional and national support.

Until the beginning of the 1990s, the military-industrial complex determined the policy of the regional authorities, which were only just beginning to establish their independence. However, the main source of the might of these enterprises, which have such an impact on the well-being of the region as a whole, was the subsidies and centralised financing which they received from the Moscow ministries and departments. With the slackening of conversion the position of the military-industrial complex has weakened significantly. Meanwhile, the oil producers, flourishing as a result of their export orientation, also dominate politically, and the regional administration is clearly oriented to their interests first of all, ensuring that they enjoy the most favourable conditions.[7] Prokat received some assistance from the regional administration in securing an order for 1,000 tons of aluminium rods from Cyprus but, although the two enterprises play an important part in the economy of the region and continue to lobby the regional administration, they do not expect to receive much other

7 Prime Minister Chernomyrdin, the king of oil and gas, was himself a graduate of the Kuibyshev Poytechnical Institute.

support from the regional authorities.

In the vacuum that has arisen in the absence of any serious support from local or central authorities, the administration of the enterprise has tried to use its own personal connections, built up over a long period of time, to get itself out of the crisis.

PRIVATISATION

Prokat

The privatisation of Prokat was initiated under order 780 of 14 July 1992 establishing a working commission on privatisation. The members of the commission were the director, his deputy for economics and finance, the chief accountant and the head of the legal department, with the labour collective represented by the chairman of the trade union committee, who was also head of the STK. The commission drew up the requisite documents and worked with various departments of the factory, including the personnel department, trade union, STK and some of the staff of the department of labour and wages. From outside the enterprise it consulted independent specialists such as lawyers and auditors. Various bureaucrats from the federal anti-monopoly committee were also involved in the preparations for privatisation and were inclined at one stage to veto the privatisation plan, particularly because the management insisted on privatising the bulk of the social and welfare apparatus along with the factory, although all their objections were eventually overcome.

Initially the commission was inclined towards the first variant of privatisation, as it seemed cheaper and more advantageous for the labour collective, while providing the chance of raising outside investment funds. However, on further consideration they changed their mind and favoured the second variant, primarily because the first variant carried the risk of outsiders assuming control by buying up shares at auction.

During August and September 1992 an intensive propaganda campaign was organised throughout the factory, using posters, the factory newspaper, factory radio and shop meetings, to persuade workers to adopt the second variant, primarily on the grounds that it left control of the enterprise in the hands of the labour force – 'we will remain the owners of our native factory' – preventing either the former ministry or outside investors from gaining control.

A labour collective meeting on 29 September 1992 voted in favour of the second option by 92 to 2 per cent, with 6 per cent abstaining, despite the fact that this option was more expensive for the workers. Workers interviewed about the reasons for their choice of the second variant uniformly responded that they voted this way because this had been the recommendation of management, that they had seen the posters and attended or heard of the meetings, that this was a matter to be decided by management, not by ordinary workers, that they did not really understand the issues involved.

The second reason for voting this way was fear of losing their jobs. Production was already falling and the labour market in the city becoming much tighter, especially for engineering workers, while the pressure of the administration on the workers was increasing, and there were widespread rumours of imminent mass redundancies. Workers knew that the administration favoured the second variant, and were required to sign openly in support of one variant or the other, so were afraid that if they did not support the administration they would be the first in line for dismissal.

The third reason for choosing the second variant was that workers had the vague idea that if they held the controlling interest they would have some control over their own fate, particularly in relation to redundancy. The administration had propagandised hard on this theme, presenting the choice as that between being owners of the enterprise and being no more than hired hands. This idea of 'we, the owners' provided some ideological continuity with the old system, 'we, the factory', 'we, the working class', 'we solve', however much at variance with reality it might have been both before and after privatisation. The linking of the individual to the general in this way, however false in reality, continues to play an important role in taking the edge off problems and difficulties in the life of the individual.

On 3 February 1993 Prokat was registered as an open type joint-stock company in the Kirov *raion* of Samara, with a temporary board of directors appointed by the regional property committee comprising the deputy director for finance, the deputy director for economics (as representative of the labour collective), a representative of the regional property committee, and a representative of the local legislative body.

On 12 February 1993 the closed subscription for worker shares began with an intensive campaign in the plant. According to various decisions, ratified at meetings of the labour collective in September and October 1992, 630,461 voting shares were available for closed subscription, three per cent of which were reserved for share options for senior management. All employees and pensioners of the enterprise, including those working in all its subsidiary activities and including former workers (men with ten years, women with 7.5 years service), were entitled to subscribe for shares. The maximum permitted shareholding was determined by the length of a worker's service and, in the case of senior managers' share options, the level of their post. This defined a coefficient of between 2 and 5 on the basis of which the senior managers were divided into four groups. The first group comprised the general director alone, with a coefficient of 5. The second group comprised the chief engineer, deputies of the director, chief accountant, chairman of the trade union, deputy chief engineer and chairman of the STK. The third group comprised the chief specialists and chiefs of the basic shops, with a coefficient of 3. The fourth group comprised the chiefs of auxiliary shops and main services, deputies of the chief specialists and several other managers with a coefficient of 2. It is worth noting that the trade union president was ranked with the top managers.

In the course of the subscription a technical problem arose with the legal requirement that half the cost of the share purchase had to be covered by privatisation vouchers, denominated at 10,000 roubles. For example, a worker might be qualified to buy 29 shares, which at the purchase price of 1,700 roubles would cost 49,300 roubles. Some of the cash came from the enterprise's privatisation fund which had been established for the purpose in 1992. However, this left the worker with the choice of subscribing two vouchers, and receiving less than his or her share allocation, or 'over-subscribing' by putting in three vouchers. Many workers did not have enough vouchers, and so would have had to buy vouchers to subscribe to their full share allocation. The majority of workers chose not to buy additional vouchers, and many did not want to put in any cash, so that many chose to buy less than their quota of shares. Virtually nobody believed that these pieces of paper would ever be worth anything, so they were very reluctant to put up 'real money'. As a result a large number of shares were left over and were distributed in a supplementary subscription, allowing those who wanted to buy more than their initial allocation to do so.

The privatisation campaign at Prokat lasted a full year. The working commission on privatisation worked every day, although these issues only concerned the labour collective from time to time, when the administration referred issues to the labour collective for its decision. This happened on three occasions. The first was the choice of variant of privatisation. The second was the closed subscription for shares in Prokat, and the third was the election of delegates to the shareholders' meeting. It is interesting to note that the workers took a different attitude to these three events. The workers took a purely formal view of the first issue, 'the administration proposed that we choose the second variant, so we voted for it…', but their attitude to the selection of delegates was very different.

The working commission of the factory proposed a temporary resolution, endorsed by a decision of the board of directors of Prokat on 14 May 1993, concerning the mechanism for the transfer of voting rights from the shareholders to their authorised representatives, on the basis of one representative per one thousand shares for employees, or one representative per two thousand shares for outside shareholders, the representatives being appointed either permanently or for a term of up to three years. A document circulated around all the shops 'recommended shareholders in large structural subdivisions to transfer their voting rights to their chiefs'. By this means the administration tried to transfer the management structure of the factory into the highest management organ of the shareholding company, the shareholders' meeting.

The shop management took this document as a guide to action, drawing up its own list of nominees comprising shop managers of various levels. The chief of the labour and wages bureau of shop 3 was asked in an interview, 'did the nominees proposed by the shop administration to the meetings of the labour collectives get through?', and replied 'they were elected almost unanimously'. However, the very same day we were at a meeting of the shop mechanics (3 June 1993) attended by 72 people who owned 4,269 shares, and so eligible to elect four representatives, chaired by the same chief of the wages bureau. The administration proposed the deputy shop chief, senior mechanic, and the deputy chief of shop for mechanical equipment. However, the workers were opposed to all of these candidates and in their place elected two repair-fitters, both brigadiers, a mechanic and the chief of the labour and wages bureau. At the meeting the workers reacted very negatively to the suggestion that they should elect their shop managers as their representatives.

After the meeting the chief of the bureau commented to us, 'it is better to see once than to hear one hundred times'. This enigmatic remark was made in the context of the fact that workers reacted in a similar negative way to the nomination of their managers at all the shop meetings. Workers have always distrusted management, but today this has become the dominant and most significant feature of their attitude to the administration.

The process of privatisation was imposed on Prokat from above, and the main aim of all the parties to the process was to preserve their status as far as they could. The management was on the whole more successful in this than the rest of the labour collective. Their main ambition was to maintain their right to manage the enterprise. They attained this ambition and moreover they managed to accumulate large shareholdings so that the higher management has in essence become legally and in practice the owner of the enterprise. Despite the fact that the majority of workers are shareowners, in practice they are merely in the position of executors of management's decisions. In the course of privatisation the workers were not able to resolve the main problem facing them, that of securing guaranteed employment, which was their way of seeking to preserve their status.

Management used sticks and carrots to get its way in the process of privatisation. During the summer and autumn of 1992, when the issue was the choice of privatisation variant, the administration was very active (even demagogic) in turning to the labour collective for support. The idea of being the owners of the enterprise, of being able to participate in the resolution of the problems facing the factory, including the question of redundancy, was strongly promoted. Once the choice had been made and privatisation had gone through, from February 1993, the management became much less active, only turning to the labour collective over particular issues, for example the question of the share subscription or the selection of delegates to the shareholders' meeting.

It was at precisely this time that the process of redundancy began. The Russian privatisation law forbids any declaration of redundancy before the process of privatisation is complete, i.e. before the first shareholders' meeting. Redundancies were not in fact declared immediately, but there was an increasingly strong expectation that redundancies were imminent through the winter and spring of 1993. This was the stick laid on the workers which eroded people's confidence in the future. In the summer and autumn of 1992 workers had still been under some illusion that the ownership of shares would provide protection against redundancy but already by the spring of 1993 these illusions were being undermined and destroyed. Through the summer and winter of 1992–3 the workers loyally supported the measures taken by management to try to maintain jobs in the factory. But during the spring and summer of 1993 distrust in the activities of the management increased rapidly. It was at this point that we could observe the beginnings of the workers' attempts to struggle to resolve their problems for themselves, with their nomination of their own candidates in the election of representatives to the shareholders' meeting. However, this initiative was unsuccessful since, immediately after the shareholders' meeting, redundancies began and people began to be sent on administrative vacation. The workers were not successful in resolving their principal problem, the preservation of their status by preserving their jobs, in the process of privatisation.

Kol'tso

All the main interest groups in the factory were involved in the privatisation process, which proceeded in a very similar way to that described in Prokat. Preparation for privatisation only began after the appearance of the privatisation decree in July 1992. The administration at first vacillated in choosing between the two variants, and in general felt rather uncertain about the issue. However, it rejected the recommendation of a working group of consultants from the local economic institute which was inclined towards the first variant. Within a month an internal factory privatisation commission had been established, which proposed the second variant, on the grounds that the second variant protected the enterprise from interference from outside interests so that the administration would keep control of the situation.

The administration and trade union carried out intensive propaganda work in support of the second variant in all shops and subdivisions. There were meetings of shop chiefs with the director, of shop trade union presidents with the fabkom (factory trade union committee), shop trade union meetings and section meetings attended by management representatives. The list for signatures in support of one or another variant was headed 'In support of the choice of the second variant of privileged privatisation of state property'. The second alternative failed to attract the necessary two-thirds support in only three collectives, but this amounted to an insignificant proportion of the labour force. The second alternative was adopted by a meeting of the labour collective on 23 September 1992.

The subscription for shares took place between 25 May and 10 June 1993: those who failed to sign up in this period lost all rights to buy shares. However, there were few such people since the administration had waged an intensive propaganda campaign to persuade workers to sign up, for fear that the necessary 51 per cent would not be subscribed. Foremen sent people to visit workers who were off sick or on administrative leave, sometimes even giving their workers time off to give them the opportunity to sign up. Shop chiefs constantly whipped up the theme of privatisation at planning meetings, conducting a propaganda campaign warning that 'we have to buy the factory so that it will not be closed'

According to the regulations on privatisation, all employees, regardless of length of service, privileges and so on were treated equally. Everyone had the right to receive two shares free of charge (paid for by the enterprise privatisation fund, amounting to 3,600 roubles per person), then 6 shares in exchange for vouchers, and on top of this any number of shares could be bought for 1,700 roubles each. Pensioners and all those who had worked at Kol'tso for a defined period (men more than ten years, women more than 7) could also participate, according to the law.

The results of the subscription demonstrated the different views of the workers. Thus, in one of the shops the majority of the workers signed for 12 shares, a couple of workers and a couple of ITR subscribed for 100, and the maximum subscribed for was 200. In another shop, 229 of the 508 people bought 8 shares, 270 wanted more than 8 and 6 more than 90. There was no clear social differentiation among those who subscribed for different quantities of shares at this stage: for example, an electrical fitter subscribed for 80 shares, a machine operator for 90, a fitter for 50, the foreman for 30–35, the majority of machine operators for 10–20. However, the privatisation commission did not provide precise information on the maximum number of shares which one person could buy, nor in general why it was advantageous to subscribe for a large number of shares. It is therefore not surprising that two divisions subscribed for the largest number of shares: the factory management and the ball shop, where the chairman of the independent trade union was a member of the privatisation commission and explained to the workers the advantage of buying a large number of shares.

Although the subscription was secret, it is interesting that the general director found it necessary to announce publicly that he had personally subscribed for 14 shares and that the whole factory administration including his deputies, had limited themselves to subscribing for a maximum of fourteen shares.

The result was that one of the largest shareholders turned out to be the director of another ball-bearing factory in the city, who had worked at Kol'tso in the past and had the necessary qualifying length of service and who subscribed for the maximum permitted number of shares, as did several other employees of his factory who qualified on the basis of an earlier period working at Kol'tso. This had not entered the plans of the Kol'tso management. They went through the fine print of the law to try to find a way of disqualifying them: they found that subscribers for a large number of shares were obliged to provide proof that their income was sufficient to buy the requested number of shares. On this basis only the general director of the second factory could prove that he personally had the 1.5 million roubles needed, and his other employees were refused.

The most interesting feature of privatisation was the activity of the commercial bank Nika, the headquarters of which was in another Volga city, which was involved on the initiative of the factory administration. A representative of Nika was included on the commission by order of the director 'to provide consultancy services' (this person subsequently became finance director of the factory). Nika offered three alternative deals to the factory's employees: workers who did not want to acquire six shares for vouchers (in practice, those who had not held on to their vouchers) could sell their right to buy to Nika for 1,000 roubles. Second, they could sell the right to buy these six and the two free shares for 3,000 roubles. Third, Nika would buy the right to subscribe for a minimum of 100 shares for 300 roubles each. It is typical that the 29 per cent of shares which passed to the state property fund were then valued at approximately 17–20 thousand each, although it is true that subsequently they were sold at the rate of 3–4 shares per voucher. Nika's offer met with a different response in different shops. In the precision bearing shop 6–7 people responded, 20–22 in the automatic rod machine shop and in the ball shop 72 people. The main motivation of the workers was the fear that because of their low pay they would not have the money to buy the shares for themselves.

Nika had the right to buy up to 15 per cent of the shares not bought by the workers, in accordance with its agreement with the administration of the factory, and to keep them for two years, after which the bank had to sell them back to the administration at the original price plus an allowance for inflation. The administration explained the need for Nika's participation in privatisation by the fact that it was afraid that the share issue would be under-subscribed so that the company would lose the controlling interest. But in fact nothing like this happened and the issue was heavily oversubscribed. With the rationale for Nika's involvement gone, it was obvious that this was only a means for the administration to acquire control over a maximum number of shares. It is notable that Kol'tso subsequently also bought the shares sold at auction by the state property committee and invested in the company's funds.

The share subscription proceeded quietly and without conflict. The workers were mainly interested in the size and frequency of dividend payments, although the general director had warned that because of the bad economic position they could not expect any dividend payments in the next two years. It was announced that because of the substantial over-subscription the maximum holding would be 14 shares, including the 8 to which everybody was entitled in exchange for vouchers, coincidentally just the amount which the general director and his deputies had declared that they would purchase. However, at the next stage of privatisation, when purchasers had to come up with the money and vouchers, workers were 'unobtrusively' persuaded to limit themselves to 8 shares, 'so as not to pay too much'.

Nika had been given special premises within the factory for the duration of the subscription campaign, but with its ending they suddenly disappeared. The over-subscription raised the question of the fate of the shares which Nika had managed to buy. The administration claimed that nothing could be done since a contract had been signed, so that there was no way in which any of the shares allocated to Nika could be got back. When a delegation from the independent trade union, Yedinstvo, asked to see the contract it was explained that this was not possible since, as the president of the fabkom of the official trade union explained to them, nobody at all had seen it. However, this did not lead to any conflict since the workers were still much more concerned about the low level of their wages than who had ended up with how many shares. Moreover, all these events took place over the summer, while the leader of Yedinstvo was on vacation and just after his deputy had left the factory completely.[8] The general view was that since the subscription was closed the administration must in fact have received far more than the declared 14 shares each, although this would be impossible to prove. Moreover, the workers had little understanding of the essence of these machinations.

In October preparations began for the first shareholders' meeting, which took place on 26 November 1993. The administration chose not to adopt the traditional form of organisation for the meeting. No norm was announced for the selection of representatives, and it was announced that in principle any shareholder could participate. However, the administration then appealed to the workers' reason, noting that there was no room which could hold 23,000 people, so that it would be better if most shareholders entrusted their voting rights to representatives. The administration opened a special lawyer's office in the administration building in which workers could register their proxies. Then production meetings began at which workers were encouraged to delegate their voting rights to management of shops, sections, divisions, to the general director himself or to his deputies or the directors of production divisions. Thus, for example, at their general meeting, the foremen-inspectors were encouraged to hand their votes and those of their workers to the deputy general director for quality, 'since he cares for us and makes money for us'. Similar propaganda took place in all divisions, openly exploiting the lack of knowledge of the workers. The inspectors were told that they could only vote for the deputy director for quality, and that no other candidates were allowed. The majority of the workers took this at face value and signed the requisite documents. In general the mass of workers took no interest in this meeting.

The only exception was the members of the independent trade union, who explained to the workers that it was better to participate in the meeting personally in order to control the situation in the factory. Many of them entrusted their proxies to their leader.

8 For an account of the independent trade union see Irina Tartakovskaya, 'The Trade Union Solidarity: A Case Study', in Simon Clarke, ed., *Conflict and Change in the Russian Industrial Enterprise*, op. cit.

SUMMER 1994 TO SUMMER 1995 HOPES RISE – AND FALL

The first stage of the privatisation process in both enterprises was complete by the end of 1993, with the management of the state enterprise having comfortably consolidated its position by transforming itself into the management of a joint-stock company. However, the economic position of both enterprises had not improved at all. Indeed, by the beginning of 1994 both enterprises were on the verge of bankruptcy. They appeared to be typical Soviet dinosaur enterprises which had been unable to adapt to the new conditions of the market economy, failing to reduce the labour force with the collapse of demand, burdened with the cost of supporting an enormous social and welfare apparatus, building up enormous debts. Privatisation and a half-hearted management restructuring had done nothing to stem the tide of decline.

However, in the event 1994 turned out to be, at least temporarily, a turning point in the fortunes of Prokat, marking a parting of the ways between the two companies. The management of both companies had priced themselves out of domestic markets by failing to reduce costs or cut employment and by borrowing on a large scale to continue to pay wages. Both pinned their hopes on breaking into world markets through 1994.

Kol'tso

Kol'tso had some success in this respect, continuing the expansion in export sales, although not on the scale achieved in 1993. Export sales in 1994 amounted to 38 million bearings, a small increase over 1993, and sales for 1995 amounted to around 43 million bearings. By 1995 it was selling to 28 countries, its main customers being the USA, Germany and India, the latter buying precision and special bearings. Production was still restricted by shortages of metal, and supplies were only allocated to production for internal and CIS orders once all the needs for export production had been met. Thus sales on the domestic market in 1994 amounted to only 25 million bearings, against the target of 98 million, with exports amounting to 60 per cent of sales, rising above 70 per cent at the beginning of 1995. This meant that Kol'tso's domestic sales in 1994 had fallen to one-eighth of those of only four years before. Despite the quadrupling of its export sales (from a low base), in 1994 it was working at less than one-third capacity, although management estimated that it could produce profitably even at only 50 per cent capacity production.

The collapse of production meant that in 1994 the price of Kol'tso's product was not even covering its operating costs – expenditure per rouble of sales amounted to 1.12 roubles, against a planned 0.86. The company made a profit for the year, amounting to a derisory 405 million roubles (against a planned 7.7 billion) on sales of 61.3 billion roubles, but this was only because of income from other activities (13.4 billion) and the sale of some of its stocks of finished products (10.4 billion). Wages also continued to fall behind, the average for the year amounting to 106,257 roubles per month, against a planned 150,992 (the figure for 1993 had been 34,845). With wages continuing to fall behind other employers in the city the number of employees continued to fall, from 21,245 in 1993 to 17,022 at the end of 1994, a fall of almost 20 per cent.

By the end of 1994 the company owed 39.4 billion roubles, 7 billion of which had been raised to meet the cost of maintaining the social facilities for 1994, and its debt interest payments had increased from 2.3 billion roubles in 1993 to 26.7 billion in 1994. It owed a further 40 billion roubles to its suppliers. The result was that no dividend was paid for 1994.

1995 saw some stabilisation of production but no significant improvement of the economic position of the enterprise. Indeed the freezing of the exchange rate of the rouble against the dollar meant that exports rapidly became unprofitable, the price of exports falling steadily against domestic prices so that export sales in 1995, which still amounted to around 43 per cent by volume, only amounted to about 30 per cent by value.

Prokat's success in Western markets was on an altogether different scale, raising hopes for the salvation of the enterprise, not least by arousing the growing interest of outside investors.

Prokat

Western partners had become a priority for Prokat with the collapse in the home market in 1992, but sales to the West only really took off in 1994: in 1992 the factory sold 5,000 tonnes to the West, in 1993 it sold 14,300 tonnes, but in 1994 it sold 82,500 tonnes and in 1995 it hoped to sell 200,000 tonnes on the Western market. Joint ventures were set up with Italy and Spain, the company was planning to open offices in Germany and the USA and was even talking of investing in the West.

At the shareholders' meeting in March 1994 the director said of Western contacts that they 'are vitally necessary, it is only due to them that the factory now has export orders for 107,000 tons of rollings … We live thanks to them'. While domestic orders continued to stagnate, export sales boomed, overhauling domestic sales in the course of 1994, up from 5 per cent in 1992 to almost 60 per cent in 1994, as domestic demand fell by a further half over the year. This trend continued into the first quarter of 1995.

A series of factors explain the problems with exporting before 1994. First, both western industrialists and the relevant department of the government's committee on metallurgy believed that it was not possible to produce high quality rollings in Russia. Therefore, while it was more profitable to sell rollings than raw materials, they sold raw materials to the west. However, the general director insisted that:

> After travelling around the world's aluminium factories we came to the conclusion that in principle they are no different from us. The basic problem is strict technological control. It is necessary to find in ourselves the boldness to go for these markets and the most important thing is to reorient the whole collective to the demands of export production.

In order to get access to export markets the enterprise certainly had to master new production methods, alloys, terminology, systems of measures and specifications. But the most important constraint was financial: the need for enough working capital to be able to buy raw materials. In Russia enterprises have insisted on pre-payment to overcome this problem, but nobody in the world market expects to have to pay in advance, particularly to Russia, while Western banks would not give credit for transactions within Russia because of social instability and constant changes in economic legislation and taxation.

Nevertheless, in 1994 the enterprise managed to negotiate contracts with an American dealer based on pre-payment. Contracts for 170,000 tonnes were signed in the US in December 1994, but because the price of processed aluminium fell, with no corresponding fall in the price of raw aluminium, it became unprofitable for the customers to buy the rollings at the previously agreed prices so that a lot of the contracts lapsed.

Tolling played an important role in overcoming the problem of working capital. Prokat established a tolling agreement with a Swiss firm under which the Swiss company covered all the costs of raw materials and of their delivery to the factory, then pays for the processing of the aluminium into semi-fabricated products which are delivered to affiliated firms. Of the 1,500 dollars price of rolled aluminium on the London exchange at the time, Prokat took 300 dollars as the cost of processing. This company, which deals in a wide range of metals, had been introduced to Prokat by the Russian government and decided to base all its aluminium dealing on Prokat, proposing the establishment of a joint trading firm with a view to conquering first the American and then other markets.

The recovery was not immediate, nor was it by any means complete. The first half of 1994 was as difficult as the previous years. In July 1994 34 per cent of workers were on administrative vacation as a result of the reduction of production. The whole enterprise went on to a four-day week, and there were regular difficulties in paying wages, workers waiting for hours at the cash offices to get their money. Increasing export orders only exacerbated the problem of a shortage of working capital with which to buy raw materials, since there was no practice of pre-payment.

However, steps were already under way to ease the crisis. The two largest banks in the region bought 10 per cent of the shares and, together with partner companies, invested in the first stage of a programme of technical re-equipment to rebuild the rolling mill to be able to meet world quality standards and to develop the production of aluminium sheet and strip to make cans for beer and soft drinks and painted sections used in construction. The company signed a large contract with German and Spanish companies to supply the necessary equipment. In the autumn construction work, some new and some long held-up by shortages of money, proceeded rapidly. In 1994 expenditure on technical re-equipment amounted to 2.049 billion roubles and 13.2 million dollars, financed by bank and shareholder investments and enterprise profits. After the sale at auction of 16 per cent of the shares still held by the government it was planned to spend twice as much again, amounting in 1995 to 149 billion roubles and 25.4 million dollars. A credit line was negotiated with a Moscow international bank. In July 1994, the management also signed a technology transfer and technical assistance agreement with the American giant, Reynolds International, to support the construction of its plant for the manufacture of cans, a project which was planned to start in the middle of 1995.[9]

The growth of exports meant that the volume of production increased significantly despite the fall in domestic demand, more than compensating for the fall early in the year, so that the result for 1994 as a whole exceeded that of 1993, with the management confident of doubling both sales and profits in 1995. The recovery was due to the traditional semi-finished products, the initial plans for conversion to the production of simple consumer goods having proved unwarranted. This was the simplest and least profitable route – the value added was relatively very low but in the given circumstances it was the only one open to the administration. On the other hand, the production of consumer goods, where the market remained very unstable, fell by 57 per cent and some lines fell by 68 per cent.

The expansion of production also ran into human barriers, sharpening the personnel problems of the enterprise. People talked for the first time about the principles of corporate culture, of the damage that had been incurred by the years of falling production, forced stoppages and the reduction of staff. The economic crisis was superimposed on a cultural crisis. In the view of the general director, for example, the biggest difficulty with expanding exports was the demands of quality and changing product range, new alloys and the organisation of production. People had got out of the habit of working hard, and, according to him, this problem was caused by a lot of factors, including the easing of labour discipline, loss of personnel and drunkenness on the job:

> Since October we have not once fulfilled the plan as a result of the poor work of collectives and supply departments. We have put many sections onto a continuous work schedule, set them to work the whole week, but the volume of production is only increasing slowly, although there is a tendency for production to increase. (Deputy director for working conditions)

Following a sharp growth of production in the last months of 1994, growth rates fell at the beginning of 1995. For example, in January 1995, only 18,000 tons were produced instead of the planned 20,000 tons and this was not only a result of the new year holidays, but also of

[9] One advantage of the deal for Reynolds, one of the world's largest producers, was that it would expand Russian aluminium consumption and so take the pressure off the world market by helping to 'reduce the world-wide aluminium supply and demand imbalance' (*Wall Street Journal*, 6 July 1994).

various social barriers in the labour force. In the first ten days of February not one subdivision made the plan.

> Apart from organisational miscalculations, among other reasons for the extremely mediocre, weak work in the first ten days one can point to the extremely low level of labour discipline. Recently in the company there has been literally a wave of drunkenness in the factory ... For some reasons people are reconciled to this in the shops. (From an appeal of the director to the factory's employees)

According to the disciplinary records 188 people were intercepted arriving for work drunk in 1994, against 125 in 1993.

These facts do not necessarily imply that discipline had in fact deteriorated, but can also be interpreted as a sign of a strengthening of the ideological and organisational pressure on ordinary employees on the part of the administration in a renewed attempt to increase the manageability of production. The need for this had been reduced in the years of declining production but, faced with the demands of foreign partners, increasing orders and the investment programme, such problems had come to the fore once again.

The basis of the sudden upsurge in exports in 1994 was not a sudden realisation of the hidden qualities of Russian metallurgy, but a by-product of the quotas imposed at the beginning of 1994 on the export of raw aluminium by the metallurgy committee of the Russian government as part of the anti-dumping agreements reached with the Western producers. At the same time this was a means of protecting the indigenous fabricating industry, for which a minimum of 20 per cent of the aluminium was reserved, as a result of intensive lobbying of the government by Prokat and other fabricators. This was a precarious basis on which to build hopes of prosperity and, indeed, after the Presidential decree cancelling all export quotas in March 1995 it became increasingly more profitable to sell raw aluminium directly to the West as the rouble hardened, so Prokat's export sales collapsed. After increasing slightly over the first three months of 1995 to 42,200 tonnes in the first quarter, exports fell to 30,200 tonnes in the second quarter, 21,500 tonnes in the third quarter, and were down to 4,800 tonnes in October 1995, a fall of over 85 per cent on the average monthly production in 1989. With domestic sales hovering around 4,000 tonnes per month, and not expanding to fill the gap, the total production for October 1995 was less than half that of January, with the export share down from 78 per cent of output in the first quarter to only 57 per cent in October. The only real hope was that new capacity would come on stream in 1996, which would put Prokat in a position to compete once more in the domestic and world markets, but the continued hardening of the rouble made the latter prospect increasingly remote.

PRIVATISATION – STAGE TWO

The first stage of privatisation had involved the distribution of a majority of shares to the labour collective, with a substantial holding remaining in the hands of the state property committee. However, the now privatised companies were in desperate need of working capital and for funds for their investment and conversion programmes. Having established firm control of their enterprises, the senior management team was not going to relinquish that control easily. Nevertheless, they did need to bring in outside shareholders who could inject much needed funds. This was the primary concern of the second stage of privatisation which began at the end of 1993.

Prokat

During 1994 the general director of Prokat used his personal contacts with members of the government, including prime minister Chernomyrdin, his deputy Soskovets (formerly Soviet metallurgy minister), the economics ministry and a visit to Prokat by the chairman of the metallurgy committee of the Russian Federation, hoping to receive a soft loan of 3.2 billion roubles for repayment over the period 1997–2000, plus the allocation of development funds from the government of a total of 54 billion roubles over three years, including 15 billion for 1994. But in the end the government refused even to provide the promised appropriation from the 1994 budget for development, the company receiving only 310 million roubles. The absence of support from central or regional government meant that the only source of funds for new investment was the sale of the state shareholding and of secondary share issues to outside investors, with the government being particularly keen to attract foreign investment. The first condition for this was a revaluation of the company's assets, from the absurdly low valuation on which privatisation had initially been based.

The assets of the enterprise were revalued at the end of 1993, in accordance with the resolution of the Russian government, and this led to an increase in valuation of the enterprise of 30 times in comparison with the privatisation valuation of the summer of 1992. (The authorised capital on 1 July 1992 had been 1.236 billion roubles. Revaluation set it at 7.807 billion for the same date, and at 223.816 billion roubles on 1 January 1994.)

In January 1994, after a sale of shares at a money auction, Prokat was authorised to make a secondary issue. This was important for the administration as a means of raising money. It was proposed that this issue would take account of the results of the revaluation, in order to attract investors. It was known that the administration had already lined up three potential large investors: Inkombank, Gazprom and the leading local bank, SVKB, which were ready to buy up to 10 per cent of the authorised capital at a price of not less than 3.5 times the nominal valuation.

However, this plan was thwarted by a letter of instruction from the Ministry of Finance in February. A change in authorised capital was only permitted to take account of the revaluation of fixed capital assets as of 1 January 1994. This had a major impact on the possibility of attracting additional investment. In this case 10 per cent of the authorised capital amounted to an enormous sum (now 22 billion, as against the anticipated 780 million) so it became more than problematic to attract large outside investors. Few of those who had originally expressed interest could come up with such money. It also became uncertain what would be the sale price of the shares and how much would be received as a result of the issue, and the amount of tax increased sharply. The directors' council proposed a figure of 11.1 billion for the authorised capital and submitted to the Ministry of Finance a proposed prospectus for the issue which would satisfy the outside investors. Experts in the administration hoped to use the old contacts and personal connections of the director and senior administration in the corridors of power to get a positive response to this request.

For the second issue they expected to sell more than 2 million nominal 1,000 rouble shares at a price of 3,500 roubles. Existing shareholders had the first call on the new shares, up to the level of their original holdings in the authorised capital at that time. However it was clear that, since shares had to be subscribed for in cash, this issue would significantly alter the distribution of shareownership.

At the board meeting on 11 March 1994, a 100 per cent dividend was declared, and a schedule for payment laid down. (First, the 20 per cent due to the state had to be paid. In April 247 million roubles would be paid to the federal budget, 79 million to pensioners and former workers and 3 million to ordinary individuals. In May they would pay 612 million to employees, 263 million to corporate shareholders.) However, the general director proposed that this year no dividend should be paid, but the money allocated to the development of the enterprise. As he announced in the factory newspaper, he owned 342 shares and 'would set an example in this matter'.

On 18 March 1994 the results of the first financial year were announced at the annual shareholders' meeting. Profits for 1993 were 32.9 billion roubles, of which 20.6 billion had been spent for various purposes. But the factory owed 43.5 billion roubles.

The shares had by now been distributed by closed subscription and voucher and money auctions. There were 24,000 individual shareholders, of whom 20,000 were employees, and 12 corporate shareholders. Twenty per cent of shares were still held by the state property fund, 15 per cent by two commercial enterprises and about 9 per cent by two local banks. One of the commercial companies, owning about 8 per cent of the shares, is located in the former training complex of Prokat and buys up shares from workers at 2,300 roubles a share. There is some evidence that this is a pocket investment fund of Prokat which, with other commercial subsidiaries, is part of its commercial activity.

In December 1994 two prospectuses for share issues were adopted. One was linked to the sale of additional shares in view of the revaluation of the fixed assets of the company. Only the final registration of this prospectus would allow the proportional distribution of the shares. At the same time a prospectus for the third issue was authorised. The sale of the third issue of shares would be handled by an investment company which is a subsidiary of Prokat. At the same time it was proposed to exchange privileged shares for the ordinary shares of individual shareholders.

The aim of the two issues was different. The second issue was directed at acquiring additional capital and necessary investments, the third at the exchange of some of the ordinary shares for shares of other emitters, first of all banks. Thus the share of individual shareholders able to influence the policy of the enterprise would be reduced and, at the same time, investors with whom the company was interested in cooperating would be attracted.

The executive body is the directors' council, originally comprising the general director and his deputies. In December 1994 the directors' council was expanded from 7 to 9 people, adding representatives of a large bank and a Siberian intermediary firm, both of which are large shareholders. The board was originally made up of four representatives of the factory (general director, executive director for economics, chief of shop 3, chair of the trade union committee) and three from outside (manager of the local branch of the main regional bank, the chief of the regional state property committee and the president of the Altima Association). In March 1995 a representative of the Swiss firm, which has 11.3 per cent of the shares and is Prokat's partner through tolling, joined the board.[10]

At the January 1995 investment competition carried out by the regional and federal property funds 16.3 per cent of the shares were put up for sale in three packets (5, 5, and 6.3 per cent). A closed Moscow company (a trading firm) bid 35.5 million dollars for all three. However, after a fierce competitive struggle and the withdrawal of the first bidder as a result of financial difficulties, the three packages were bought by the company's regular partners, the Swiss trading company and two of the large Volga commercial banks. The money received practically completely covered the company's demand for capital investment for 1995.

In February 1995 the price of the shares rose sharply as a result of the purchase of a large number of shares by one of the largest regional banks, apparently on behalf of a large investor, the shares being the fastest growing on the local stock exchange in the first part of the year, increasing by more than 54 per cent.

At this time there were officially still 25,000 individual shareholders and 23 corporate shareholders, including three foreign firms. The administration continues to pay attention to the employees of the factory since it does not want to see an uncontrolled outflow of shares. The workers are told about the rising price of the shares which make the shares real financial securities. If workers sell their shares, the administration tries to persuade them to do so only within the enterprise. However, despite all its efforts, the share of individual shareholders was changing substantially at the expense of that of

[10] Trans-CIS was said to have offered $10 million cash for a seat on the seven-person board of Prokat, an offer which was refused.

banks and other companies, culminating in the purchase of a controlling 52 per cent interest in the company by Inkombank at the beginning of 1996. The new owners immediately made it clear that they had no sympathy for the traditional paternalism of the existing management and did not intend to maintain any of the social privileges of the collective, giving rise to expectations that at the March 1996 shareholders' meeting radical cahnges both in management policy and in the composition of the Directors' Council would be announced.

Kol'tso

From the autumn of 1993 to spring of 1994 the administration of Kol'tso continued to pursue its interest in privatisation in the face of the virtually total indifference of the workers. If the workers, who had practically no money, were very ready to sell their shares to anyone who wanted them, the administration by contrast tried to buy new shares. However, no internal redistribution of shareownership could take place until the summer of 1994 when the distribution of share certificates began. At that moment Nika, which had disappeared from the factory for a period, became very active on the premises of the factory again, buying shares from workers. The agreements to sell the shares were notarised in the factory lawyer's office, with notices to that effect appearing on the notice boards in every subdivision. The view developed in the factory that this commercial structure had acquired the controlling interest, or at least much the largest number of shares.

As the workers had been promised that there would be no dividends for the first two years, they looked on the shares as worthless pieces of paper, and there were many cases of workers who, on being dismissed from the factory, demanded the return of their vouchers.

Being in a much less favourable economic position than Prokat in the crucial period following the distribution of shares, Kol'tso was not able to attract the attention of powerful banks or commercial structures as an investment prospect. Nevertheless, Kol'tso management built on its existing connections, the outcome of which was quite radical changes in the personnel and structure of the management apparatus.

MANAGEMENT RESTRUCTURING IN A MARKET ECONOMY

As flagship enterprises of the military-industrial complex management in Prokat and Kol'tso had been closely monitored by and integrated into the structures of the Party-state. Party representatives were vigilant in monitoring the ideological purity of managers, membership of the Party was a necessary condition for promotion, and all managers combined their immediate responsibilities with Party work, while Party functionaries were regularly drawn from the ranks of the factory managers. The military-industrial character of the enterprise underpinned the strictly hierarchical structure and the authoritarian style of management. However, the strategic importance of the factories also meant that professional skills and competence, within the framework of the administrative-command system, were equally important features of management.

The management team of Prokat had been formed primarily through the upward mobility of employees who had begun their careers in Prokat in the 1950s and 1960s, leading to the creation of a fairly monolithic, tight-knit factory administrative team, linked together by the experience of working together for many years. Kol'tso was an older established enterprise, with a more conservative and ossified management. However, the essential feature of both was their orientation to expanding gross output, meeting plan targets by any means.

The transition to market conditions gave increased weight to the economic services of the factory, and new departments with a market orientation were created (marketing, foreign economic relations and so on). However, these changes unrolled slowly and on the basis of the traditional system of management. The management strategy was to balance the need for fundamental innovation with a desire to maintain the existing situation, retaining the 'authoritarian paternalism' of the traditional management system. The general director retained his traditional plenipotentiary powers: with an undefined range of responsibilities no important issue could be resolved without his intervention. The deputy executive director for economics of Prokat said in an interview:

> You have to understand that the planned structure of Soviet enterprises, with strict economic management from above, meant that patriarchal relationships

> developed in the factory. ... If one manages to speak one-to-one with the general director, then it is easy to resolve any matter.

The senior management team tried to carry this traditional structure over into the management of the joint-stock company. In Prokat, 620 delegates were to be elected to the shareholders' council representing all sections of the enterprise, including the social and welfare apparatus. As noted above, many departments rejected the advice of senior management to elect their heads as their representatives at shop meetings, but when the results were announced officially all but a dozen or so of the management nominees were declared successful. In Kol'tso too, the overwhelming majority of votes at the first shareholders' meeting were in the hands of senior or middle management. Correspondingly those elected to the directors' council exactly reproduced the administration of the factory, and the general director was elected president. The leader of Yedinstvo was virtually the only person to vote against, with the few dozen votes entrusted to him. He then posted a short statement in the shop, in which he explained his view that the old director could not provide effective leadership for the factory in market conditions.

The first stage of management restructuring in both enterprises had been relatively restrained, the traditional management structure being transferred to the newly privatised company, with few changes in management of the factory beyond the creation of new commercial and marketing departments. However, once management had established its uncontested control of the enterprise, and with the economic crisis showing no signs of abating, both companies undertook a more radical restructuring of management of the factory and of the joint-stock company.

Prokat

At the end of 1993 the general director of Prokat proposed a radical structural reorganisation based on the decentralisation of management as the basis for a more effective use of resources and search for new sources of income. A new service for marketing, production and sales was established to deal with all external economic relationships and a new technical service to monitor quality, both with predominantly young staff. A trading subsidiary was also set up to earn additional money for the company. As financial and economic operations have become decisive for the fate of the factory, people with calculators have replaced technicians and engineers. However, although there are some talented and flexible managers who are able to absorb new knowledge and who learn quickly from their mistakes, it is more usual to find the same engineers in the new departments, without any special knowledge or skills and with rigid views of how things should be done. The marketing department, for example, has become the talk of the whole factory, subject to constant criticism, but it is difficult to find trained experts in this sphere in Russia, so it has to develop gradually by trial and error.

In April 1994 the management of the production divisions was decentralised with the creation of separate factories based on the foundry, the rolling shop and the press-stamp shop, although many people doubted their independent viability, especially the last, which includes both strip and tube production.[11] This was not so much a strategic decision as a response to the need for decentralisation and a strengthening of shop management in the face of the inability of the central factory services to solve the growing crisis. At the same time, such a strengthening of line management, including the addition of shop chiefs to the group of those who received additional shares on privatisation, served to produce a stronger and more cohesive management team in the face of growing discontent on the shop-floor.[12]

Over 1994–5 these tendencies converged with the emergence of a definite new ideology of management, based on the idea of creating a western type of firm by turning the company into a holding company and putting technologically-related production units into separate functional units of a new type:

> Discussions about creating factories according to types of production have been going on for a long time, but a decision was only taken after studying the structure of foreign firms. There are no such giant factories as ours in the West. Normally 1,000–1,200 people work in a factory. The factories produce one kind of product and deal only with production problems. Supply, finance, trading, this is the firm's business. We will have approximately the same kind of structure. The factories will resolve the problems of production, economics and technology (interview with deputy director).

11 Earlier the general director had decisively rejected the aspirations of some of the shop chiefs to declare their independence, commenting: 'I will not allow a Nagorno-Karabakh in my enterprise!'

12 On the changing character of middle management see Pavel Romanov, 'Middle Management in Industrial Production in the Transition to the Market', in Simon Clarke, ed., *Management and Industry in Russia*, op. cit.

By the spring of 1995 the first stage in the transformation had been completed with the formation of semi-independent units on the basis of the various production departments. According to the official declaration, this work was conducted

> with the purpose of increasing the independence of the structural divisions of the company, in particular to resolve the problems of improving technology, preparation of production, conduct of technical policy, rational allocation of equipment and labour, certification of quality, especially of export production, and also to increase in this respect the responsibility of all divisions for the resolution of the above questions and for the final result of their financial and economic activity.

In practice one can regard this as a small revolution from above, widening and deepening the status and powers of shop chiefs. And although the real shifts in the distribution of power within the hierarchy of the factory proceeds more slowly than might appear from the formal orders of the administration, they are forging ahead.

One expression of this is the changing status relations inside the shop. It would be a mistake to imagine that shop management had ever been united, but now real divisions are appearing. The shop chiefs, now that they have real managerial powers and are able to have an independent influence on the situation, are distancing themselves more and more from the lower levels of the hierarchical ladder, the foremen and section heads. The latter, although their traditional levers of authority – such as monetary incentives, dismissal of disciplinary violators and the distribution of tasks – have been considerably strengthened, are more and more pushed aside from management; and the character of their work, responsibility and place in the management system means that they become more and more mere executors.

Kol'tso

Kol'tso had moved towards a divisional structure earlier than Prokat. The production divisions, which combined several shops which produced similar products or were linked in a technological cycle, had been set up in the autumn of 1992. However, they were created not as part of a strategy of innovation, but to free senior management from their functions of direct production management so that they could concentrate on the new tasks which had emerged of overcoming the crisis, preparing for privatisation and so on.

From about autumn 1993 the management strategy began to change, although it continued to be marked by a dualism. On the one hand, significant elements of the strategy of balancing conservatism were retained. On the other, there were some new tendencies leading to change in the status quo.

This dualism can be exemplified by the strategy adopted in relation to the production division which formerly produced special bearings for military use (PSP), which was in a particularly difficult position as demand for its products had fallen seven-fold since 1991. Its management eventually decided to remove some of the equipment which had been used to make special bearings and to replace it with new automatic lines to produce bearings for the electrical industry. However, at the same time most of the old equipment was preserved in the hope of the adoption by the Russian government of a programme of military construction which would 'from 1994, maybe, at last resolve the problems with the production of special bearings' (interview with director of PSP). In March 1994 the general director went to Moscow in the hope of securing investment for the factory as 'a victim of conversion', discussing the issue with the president of the Duma's committee on industry, transport, energy and construction: despite the fact that the enterprise was by that time privatised, it continued to try to get help from the state.

However, apart from the traditional attempts to drag money out of Moscow while waiting for the restoration of state orders, the senior management of the factory now undertook a series of measures in a fundamentally different direction.

First, there was a significant change in personnel. In the autumn of 1993 the deputy general director for economics retired and was replaced by a 29-year old academic economist. This was a staggering innovation for Kol'tso, where the average age of senior management had always been 50–55, even more so since the young man had worked in commercial structures but had no industrial experience. However, he just happened to have been a member of the board of the local bank Nika, and was rumoured to have played a key role in the privatisation of Kol'tso.

At the same time the general director appointed a 39-year old deputy to head the newly created marketing department (this man was not new to the factory, he had earlier been director of the experimental factory which was part of the association Kol'tso). At the first shareholders' meeting, on 26 November 1993, the deputy for marketing was officially appointed as first deputy general director, and so a member of the board, a position normally reserved for the deputy for production, traditionally the second person in the factory. This was not simply a demonstration of new priorities – there were many signs that he really had become the number two: he gives all the interviews in the name of the board of directors, personally takes on the most difficult and tricky situations (for example, a strike in the ball shop that was accompanied by charges of management corruption). This process reached its logical conclusion eighteen months later, in the spring of 1995, when the deputy for marketing became the new general director. In 1994 the chief accountant was also replaced and the new one was again a young person, 35 years old, from outside with no previous connections with the factory.

Apart from personnel changes, new structures were also created. The new marketing department included three specialised trade departments, one of which was for export. The new department got the complete list of former customers, 3,500 of them, from Gosplan, and began to set up a network of twelve agencies to sell ball bearings, of which six have been created so far (including in St Petersburg, Moscow and Udmurt). This has considerably eased the problem of locating customers, the problems now being primarily those of the solvency of the customers and the availability of metal.

Apart from subdivisions oriented to the market, on 31 March 1994 a new research and production centre was established, an Engineering centre, comprising the design department, the technologist's department, the metallurgist's department and the design-technological department for plastics and packaging.

Another feature of the new stage in the management strategy was the absolute priority given to exports as this was the only obvious way to sell to solvent customers, who would pay in hard currency not so subject to devaluation by inflation. However, as we have seen, Kol'tso did not enjoy the success of Prokat in this respect.

To resolve the problem of non-payment the factory created an interesting commercial structure in November 1994 – a closed joint stock company 'trading house Alternative'. Alternative was created by the new deputy for economics (on privatisation the post was re-titled finance director), and was closely connected to the investment bank Nika, from which both he and the director of Alternative came. Only 14 people work for Alternative, but many of the factory's employees are involved in its various activities.

Alternative co-ordinates the settlement of barter accounts with Kol'tso's insolvent customers and so, in one way or another, helps the factory reduce its indebtedness. If a debtor enterprise has no money, but has some commodity products which it is willing to hand over to liquidate its debt, Alternative tries to sell the barter goods or to exchange them for consumer goods with some other enterprise. In November 1994 these operations contributed 400 million roubles. Alternative also developed a system of partial payment of the workers in kind, giving them goods on short-term credit which the workers can then sell independently (this suits the workers since the barter goods are 30–40 per cent cheaper than in the shops). A member of the Board said in an interview that this was more convenient than Alternative selling the goods and transferring the money to the wage fund as 'the market is overstocked and the creation of a commercial network is difficult and would create all sorts of problems'. However, Alternative is not only involved in the exchange and resale of barter without which, the management of Alternative claims, 'the factory would have come to a standstill long ago'. It is also involved in a wide range of commercial and financial operations, not all of which are legal.

The creation of such structures in privatised enterprises is a fairly typical feature of the current strategy of senior management – a very similar firm was created in Prokat. However, in conditions of economic crisis such commercial activity undertaken by the administration, even if it is motivated by the good of the factory, arouses strong discontent on the part of the workers who suspect, not without foundation, that it is all directed to the personal enrichment of the bosses. Thus it can serve as an additional factor in conflict.

One operation carried out in collaboration with the factory administration was widely publicised. The essence of the operation was that the factory administration, its metal stocks virtually exhausted, took a six month credit from Gosreserv, a state structure responsible for reserves in case of war or other extreme situations, for the purchase of metal. Instead of buying the metal immediately the management transferred 4.3 billion roubles to the account of Alternative to recycle the money. The leaders of the independent trade union, Yedinstvo, were enraged by news of this deal, in a situation in which the workers had not been paid for almost two months. The leader of the union complained to the deputy head of the regional administration and then, following his advice, to the Prosecutor, who sent a letter confirming the allegations, which was posted at every entrance to the factory the following day. This episode coincided with a strike and was widely publicised in the local press. Attempts of the chairman of Alternative to reach an amicable agreement with the head of Yedinstvo were unsuccessful.

It seems that the trade union leader's letter fell on fertile ground since at the time the management of the factory, and the general director in particular, was in growing conflict with the regional administration, the real basis of which was the redistribution of property in the process of privatisation. The immediate result of the letter was the establishment of a joint commission made up of representatives of the procurator, the auditing department (KRU), tax inspectorate and tax police, which spent several months working permanently in the factory. At the same time the disastrous financial situation meant that the director had become extremely unpopular with the ordinary workers. At the end of 1994 Solidarity organised a mass meeting of the workers in front of the company's administration building demanding the payment of wages, a meeting in which members of the official trade union also participated. The workers demanded in particular a meeting with the general director, which did not take place. Thus a whole series of circumstances condensed around the general director, resulting in a kind of 'palace revolution' supported by external forces in the form of the regional administration. The result was that the case did not come to court, but it was decided that the director would be thrown out on his ear, officially resigning on grounds of 'ill health' in March 1995, to be replaced by his first deputy. In the view of one insider 'the general director had served his purpose, and was no longer needed' – through the privatisation process share ownership had been concentrated in the hands of Nika, which was controlled by several members of the senior management of Kol'tso, above all the finance director. However, the general director was now seriously compromised for having done everything he could to promote the activity of Nika in the factory.

With the departure of the general director only five representatives of the factory remained on the board of directors, including the new general director and his first deputy, the finance director, the technical director and the director of an independent affiliated factory which had been a part of the company, but which subsequently separated from it. The technical director provided the principal link with the old management apparatus, having been in his post for many years and smoothly passed into the new management team, in contrast to the former deputy general director for production who had previously been the real number two in the factory.

Although the crisis had provoked growing conflict within the senior management of Kol'tso, leading to the removal of the general director, it would be inaccurate to characterise this as a 'conflict between new and old managers', conflicts over covert property interests, culminating in the Alternative scandal, apparently being much more significant in what was in reality an extremely complex and confused situation. Conflicts over management strategy had certainly arisen, but only over particular, though important, questions: first in the field of the disposition of the social and welfare apparatus, second in relation to employment policy, which will be discussed later. Strictly speaking the only representative of 'new management' among the senior management team was the young finance director, who was firmly committed to the adoption of a rigid financial policy, demanding above all that the company refuse to support the social sphere and that it reduce the number of workers. However, his initiatives had not provoked any serious objections (to be more precise, the heads of the corresponding services – deputy directors for the social sphere and for work with personnel – offered limp opposition). The general director had supported him without hesitation, but the decisions taken in practice were based more on compromise than on a radical agenda: of the social and welfare apparatus he had only been able to dump the kindergartens and, by gradually cutting its financing, the health services. There were periodic cuts in personnel, but they regularly turned out to amount to only half the number originally proposed.

At a pinch one could also describe the other two new members of the senior management team, who took over as general director and first deputy in spring 1995, as 'new management'. However, they were both long-term employees of the company, former heads of large 'factories within the factory': the new general director had been promoted from the post of first deputy, and had previously been head of the experimental factory, while the new first deputy had been director of the special bearings factory before becoming commercial director. Although younger than the norm, both had made their careers under the old regime and been promoted by the former general director, fusing with the old hands into a uniform management team.

The activity of the 'semi-new' management team had been marked by the proclamation of a greater market tendency and a declared willingness to take unpopular measures (above all, employment reductions). But in practice it did not really contain any managerial innovations (even in relation to the anti-crisis programme), apart from another round of structural reorganisation involving a tentative reversal of the previous decentralisation (the factories created by the unification of several shops under the former general director were liquidated) and the replacement of the chiefs of some subdivisions. The situation in the factory continued to deteriorate.

Nevertheless, it transpired that the 'palace revolution' of March 1995 was only the first step in a more radical change in management of the enterprise. Once more it is not easy to fathom the complexities of a conflict which proceeds behind tightly closed doors, but it seems clear that in this new stage it was not internal forces but the regional administration that played the leading role. Having first exploited internal divisions to remove the established general director, the regional administration now mobilised its resources to bring in a new outsider in the person of the director of the other Samara bearing factory.

In the past this factory had been considered less prestigious and solid than Kol'tso. However, since 1991 the situation had reversed. The other factory produced bearings that were more marketable than those of Kol'tso. Moreover, the general director had carried out a vigorous transformation of his plant with a significant reduction of personnel, strict disciplinary measures to increase the quality of production and a rapid reorientation to the external market. Although his enterprise, which privatised early as a closed joint-stock company, is not prosperous, it is considered stable.

The director of this plant had previously worked for a long time at Kol'tso and as a result had been entitled to participate in the privileged share distribution on privatisation. As noted above, he acquired five per cent of the shares in the first distribution, in addition to which a further five per cent was entrusted to him by the State Property Committee, under the influence of the regional administration, so that he emerged as the largest shareholder in Kol'tso. In May 1995 he was elected president of the board of directors of Kol'tso. At one level, the unexpected arrival at the head of Kol'tso of an outsider, director of another enterprise, marked the introduction of external management to a dying enterprise (the role of Fortinbras in the last scene of Hamlet). However, there is no doubt that this situation was set up by the regional administration (which supported him with the shares under its control and gave him all possible support in the election).

The interest of the regional administration in the fate of Kol'tso, as one of the largest enterprises in the region, was obvious: on the one hand, Kol'tso provided employment and a wide range of social and welfare benefits and facilities for a large number of local residents; on the other hand, Kol'tso was a vital source of tax revenue. The question of declaring Kol'tso bankrupt had been on the agenda for a long time, and was repeatedly raised through 1995, but bankruptcy in Russia has to be a carefully controlled exercise because of the social and fiscal costs imposed on the region and its administration (bankrupt enterprises are relieved of the obligation to pay overdue tax and are freed of tax for a period of two years).[13] It may be that the regional administration sought changes in the management of Kol'tso in order to avoid this fate, but it may yet turn out that the changes in Kol'tso are only the prelude to a 'managed bankruptcy'.

In fact for the first six months the new president of the board hardly interfered at all in the management of the factory, giving the new general director the chance to realise his plans. However, since there was no significance improvement in the situation, in November 1995 there was a major redistribution of administrative functions according to which the outsider became the real chief of the enterprise. Nobody from the general director's team dared openly protest at the latest revolution. It was enough for them to try to influence public opinion by spreading rumours that the new president was trampling on everybody and that it would turn out badly. However, the new president, known as a very firm leader, announced publicly at a meeting on the culture of production that he knew perfectly well who was spreading the rumours and it would not turn out well for that person. After this the whispering campaign ended.

The key feature of the new president's programme is a reduction of employment from 12,000 to a maximum of 8,000. This will hit engineers, technicians and white collar employees much harder than workers (the proportion of the former has increased sharply as a result of the higher turnover of the latter). It is planned to liquidate machine-tool-building and other auxiliary production. Apart from this a regime of strict economy has been proclaimed. The question of creating its

[13] The neighbouring aircraft factory, Prokat's principal traditional customer, was the first large enterprise in Russia to be put into bankruptcy, under the firm control of the regional administration (Pavel Romanov, 'The Regional Elite in the Epoch of Bankruptcy', in Simon Clarke, ed., *Conflict and Change in the Russian Industrial Enterprise*, op. cit.).

own heating plant and purchasing an electric generator to avoid paying for energy and electricity is being discussed.[14] There are also plans to economise in water consumption by recycling. However, all these measures (apart from redundancies) are planned for 1996. In the meantime, the factory had stopped in mid-October 1995, with no plans to reopen before mid-January 1996, the majority of shops in December having still not received their pay for August.

EMPLOYMENT POLICY

Despite the considerable differences between our two enterprises, the general outlines of their strategic development are remarkably similar, moulded by the same structural, institutional and ideological pressures. In both cases there have been frequent managerial reorganisations, alternately centralising and decentralising authority. In both cases external structural and institutional pressures have elevated the status of marketing and financial departments and gradually compelled the enterprises to live within the limits of their scant resources. Both enterprises have faced unstable markets with very limited working capital and even less investment funds. There has, therefore, been relatively limited investment in new production facilities, with virtually all changes in the sphere of production being devolved to shop-level initiatives, where they have been motivated by the demands of immediate survival. While the technical basis of production has been very little changed, we have to ask to what extent has senior management attempted a restructuring of the social relations of the workplace through its policies in the areas of employment, wages and payment systems, and welfare provision?

Employment policy is regarded as a key indicator of the willingness of senior management to ditch the traditional social guarantees and subject the enterprise to purely financial rationality. Both of our enterprises pursued passive employment policies for as long as they could, in contrast to the 'pioneers of privatisation' described in previous chapters, and represented in Samara by the other bearing factory, which actively sought to restructure the labour force by cutting jobs in order to maintain or increase wages. Both of our

14 Another striking example of the reinforcement of the autarchic tendencies of Soviet production by the transition to a market economy.

enterprises were eventually forced by economic constraints to launch redundancy programmes, although, very significantly, they do not undertake such programmes until the process of privatisation was complete and managerial control secure. Moreover, as in the pioneers of privatisation, the motivation for employment reductions was not primarily to cut costs to the immediate benefit of profits, but to maintain or increase wages in order to stem the drain of skilled labour. However much employment reductions may have been demanded by the accountants, it proved to be the shop chiefs who continued to play the decisive role in determining the real outcomes.

Prokat

Total number of personnel in Prokat, 1989–94 (end year)

Year	Employees	Employment	Production
		Percent of 1989	
1989	22,315		
1990	22,583	101	95
1991	22,253	100	78
1992	21,345	96	45
1993	19,412	87	23
1994	17,877	80	25

The average age of the labour force in 1994 was 41 years and the average length of service was 10.3 years. Despite a policy of rejuvenation, in fact the workforce continued to get older, mainly because of the lack of recruitment and the much higher turnover of young workers. Thus, over 1992–3 the proportion of employees under 30 fell from 27.1 per cent to 19.4 per cent, while there was a big increase in the proportion of those over 51: from 19 to 25 per cent.

In the Soviet period Prokat, like all large enterprises, had to maintain a significant surplus of labour so that it could respond to the various demands of the local authorities for the construction of housing, of urban facilities such as the metro, city diagnostic centre, agricultural work and routine maintenance, without this disrupting production. Similarly wages of the management in those days depended on the size of the labour force. As usual, in a situation of labour shortage there was a high labour turnover of low-skilled workers. The administration could punish violations of discipline with transfer to low-skilled low-paid low-prestige work, and this was used widely since dismissal in those days was a very complicated process. Workers could always expect to find a new job if they left or were dismissed. High-skilled workers and specialists could not only find a job elsewhere, but also get additional privileges and bonuses. When production began to fall this was first seen as a temporary phenomenon, so that it was felt to be necessary to hold on to labour for the recovery to come. But by the beginning of 1991 it was already clear that no recovery was in sight and open recruitment ceased.

A central feature of 'balancing conservatism' is an employment policy directed at avoiding reductions in the number of employees. This was achieved in Kol'tso by distributing scarce metal between the various shops according to a uniform quota so that work could be equally distributed – until exports took priority, something which angered the workers who did not work on export orders and found themselves starved of work by being denied raw materials. Administrative vacation was widespread, with workers being sent on leave in turn, or sent to carry out repair and construction work. The preservation of jobs proved to be one of the most powerful and significant levers of management used by the administration at all levels of production. Nevertheless, redundancy could not be postponed for ever.[15]

In 1991–2 the staff reduction only affected vacancies, but in 1993, after privatisation, the administration announced the end of a policy of guaranteed employment in favour of a policy based on economic feasibility. Production and employment needs for 1993 were defined by a management group headed by the executive director for economics. This planned to cut 2,880 people by the end of the year, one purpose being to increase the pay of those who remained. The plan was to 'rejuvenate' the enterprise by offering incentives to workers to retire (at the beginning of 1993 the enterprise had 2,500 working pensioners), to clear out drunks and disciplinary violators and to reduce the number of women. The number sacked for disciplinary violations in fact did double in 1993 over 1992, a year in which discipline had already been strict. But the latter aspect of the policy achieved little success, the proportion of women in 1994 being 47.5 per cent, exactly the same as in 1993. This did not mean that women were protected. They were under considerable pressure and in growing

[15] Tanya Metalina, 'Employment Policy in an Industrial Enterprise', in Simon Clarke, ed., *Labour in Transition*, op. cit.

fear of losing their jobs. It was largely because men were far more likely than women to quite their jobs voluntarily.

Targets for redundancy were passed down to shop level, where they were determined by the shop redundancy commission, which was composed of the shop chief, chief of the bureau of labour and wages, president of the shop trade union committee and the manager of the relevant subdivision in which redundancies were being considered. The commission interviewed all those to be considered for redundancy, taking all personal circumstances into account. In shop 3:

> First of all we have sacked discipline violators, second in turn are the pensioners, although this has not yet affected the pensioners with privileges, that is, those who qualify for a pension early as a result of harmful working conditions, and finally, women.

The plan to cut the labour force was extremely unpopular among the workers, and among the shop chiefs who wanted to retain their flexibility. At shop level, therefore, cuts were made more with regard to personal circumstances than to skill levels, while everything was done to avoid the need for redundancies by reclassification and transfer of employees from one shop to another within the enterprise. In practice there were few compulsory redundancies: numbers kept on falling as a result of voluntary severances, although some of these, and in particular retirements, were certainly under pressure. In July 1993 the shareholders' meeting resolved a stricter redundancy policy, but the following month the administration issued an order to withdraw from all contracts with small enterprises and co-operatives working with the enterprise (of which by then there were more than 100) with the aim of transferring redundant workers to this work. In September a new order was issued, to lay off an additional 1,170 people within the space of two months, on top of the target of 2,880 declared for the end of the year. However, in practice more than 300 people were retrained and redeployed in the course of the year, while 500 new jobs were created in connection with the expansion in the range of consumer goods produced and the growth of production for export, as a result of which only 533 were actually sacked in the course of the year.

The alternative to redundancy was 'administrative leave', under which employees remained on the books of the enterprise while receiving low or no wages, and delays in the payment of wages. This avoided the need for redundancy with its social and financial costs, the enterprise being liable to redundancy payment, while the enterprise could retain a flexible reserve of labour. While workers were universally enraged by non-payment of wages, they were not necessarily opposed to administrative leave, which enabled them to retain the privileges attached to their employment while having the opportunity to earn money on the side, in the 'second economy' – it was not unusual for workers to be able to earn more while on leave than when at their regular job. Apart from those who positively want to be sent on leave to take advantage of such opportunities, people tended to be selected for leave, as for redundancy, on the basis of considerations of social justice:

> Everyone takes it in turn, apart from those who have very difficult circumstances – single mothers, those who have alcoholic husbands.

But the workers get angry that management is never sent on leave.

Over this period the atmosphere in the shops changed fundamentally. With production in many shops almost at a standstill there is little noise and almost no activity. The shops were now extremely clean, like a doctor's surgery. There were no more mountains of shavings, piles of old boxes, heaps of metal off-cuts, pools of grease, the machines are newly painted. All the workers show much greater fear. The women especially are afraid to talk freely. The men joke, but their jokes are hollow and betray their uncertainty about the future.

This is in complete contrast to life in the administration buildings, which teem with people running to and fro, some magnificently dressed. But now, in stark contrast to the situation when we began our research, the managers are not willing to talk, everything is a commercial secret, and even shop chiefs have now become wary. The former first department (KGB) has been reconstituted, now to protect trade rather than military secrets, and security has been considerably tightened.

The unevenness of production, and the priority demands of export orders, meant that shop chiefs were keen to keep as many people on the books as they could, redeploying key workers to repair, maintenance and cleaning up rather than sending them on leave. Those sent on leave were sent for a maximum of two weeks at a time, and had to report in every two days in case they were needed. Nevertheless, despite all this, the recovery of production for export in the middle of 1994 soon ran into the problem of labour shortage, with growing complaints from senior management at the claimed sharp deterioration in labour discipline.

The relieving of the pressure on the enterprise through the second half of 1994 and the beginning of 1995 reduced the pressure to seek reductions in the labour force. Although the enterprise remained committed to maintaining a labour force in line with its planned level of production, which implied targets for significant further reductions, it did not take active steps to reduce numbers even when output began to fall sharply in the second half of 1995. However, it was most unlikely that such a policy would be sustained. From the autumn of 1995 Prokat went onto a four-day week, and stopped completely for the first time for two weeks in December 1995 and January 1996. A reduction of 450 people was announced in October 1995 and in February 1996, following the change of ownership, the general director announced deep cuts, with a plan to cut 2,000 jobs in the space of three months aimed primarily at the production shops whose output had fallen the most. The response of the chiefs of production shops was that such reductions would cut deep into the reserves of skilled labour that they had managed to retain in the hope of recovery.

Kol'tso

The number employed at Kol'tso has been falling for the past ten years, although the fall was gradual from 1985 to 1989 (from 31,045 to 29,959), accelerating somewhat from 1989 to 1992, since when it has been precipitous. The scale of this reduction was not significantly affected by the reduction and divestiture of social and welfare facilities: the rate of reduction of industrial personnel was exactly the same as that of non-industrial.

Year	Employees	Employment	Production
		Percent of 1989	
1989	29,959		
1990	28,784	96	
1991	27,942	93	99
1992	27,014	90	75
1993	23,228	78	46
1994	15,014	50	32
1995 i-iii	12,967	43	30

Twenty years ago workers were attracted by the advanced social and welfare provision and the expectation of getting housing, but rates of housing construction slowed from the early 1980s, and there were problems with hostels and kindergartens. Over 1986–8 the Association fell to last place in the city's league table of wages paid, which were then set by ministerial bodies. This was connected with the failure to change the pay scales over a long period of time combined with the system of cranking up norms as workers overfulfilled them. Thus the workers had no incentive to increase productivity because there was no opportunity to increase pay. Arhythmical working meant that a lot of overtime was available, but this was often not paid at the increased rates stipulated by law, the workers at best being given time off in lieu. Thus there has been a fall in numbers since 1985 as workers have left, unable to increase their pay and with wages and social provision declining. The ageing of the collective goes back a long time now, while the enterprise's need predominantly for skilled specialists who are able to work its old machinery means that there are few prospects for young people.

The collapse in employment since 1992 has not corresponded to any significant change in personnel policy, but only to an enormous increase in the numbers leaving as a result of dissatisfaction with low wages, and to a reduction in the numbers taken on. In 1994 only 5 per cent of the 8,214 people who left were accounted for by compulsory redundancy (and even some of those were in fact redeployed within the factory), while those who gave a reason for leaving were almost unanimous in pointing to their dissatisfaction with the pay levels.

Those who left voluntarily were primarily the younger and more highly skilled male workers. As a result there was a substantial change in the composition of the labour force: while the number of workers fell by 63 per cent and of apprentices by 90 per cent, the number of ITR fell by only 44 per cent and the number of office workers fell by only 28 per cent. Thus the proportion of ITR rose from 15 to 23 per cent and of office workers from 3 to 6 per cent of the labour force. The biggest falls in employment over the past ten years have been amongst those working in harmful conditions (88 per cent fall), and the 'labour aristocrats' (adjusters: 75 per cent, universal turners and machine operators: 73 per cent). The number of controllers and laboratory assistants has fallen by 78 per cent, but this is primarily a result of a wave of compulsory redundancy which focused on this group in 1994–5. Voluntary redundancies were significantly less among the less skilled and female occupations, where it was harder to find alternative work. Drivers were the least likely to leave (38 per cent fall) because they had plenty of opportunities to use their vehicles to earn money on the side.

The result of this voluntary redundancy was that the factory was losing workers from precisely those occupations that it could ill afford to lose: the more highly skilled workers. Thus, despite the substantial cut in numbers, recruitment has continued, never falling below 1,500 a year, although now it is high-skilled workers who are taken on, while in the past the shortage was of unskilled labour. The number of apprenticeships has been cut sharply, only about 40 being taken on in 1995. In 1995 management was afraid that, despite the 70 per cent fall in production since 1989, it could not now handle an increase in orders as a result of shortages of skilled workers.

Although there was no personnel policy at the enterprise level, there was spontaneous pressure at shop level as line managers sought to persuade older and unskilled auxiliary workers to leave, so that they would be able to raise the wages of those remaining in order to hold on to skilled workers. This pressure to leave was imposed particularly on the older and female low-skilled workers. This is part of the explanation for the fact that, although managers regularly complained that the core of the labour collective, its high skilled workers, were leaving, according to the statistics the skill composition of the labour force actually improved. Between 1985 and 1995 the proportion of workers on the bottom three grades actually fell from 53 per cent to 44 per cent of the total, while those on the top three grades increased from 47 to 56 per cent.

Such a striking divergence between the statistics and managers' perception is partly because managers do not complain at the departure of the unskilled and auxiliary workers, while there is virtually no recruitment to unskilled posts because the wages are so low. But it is also explained by the fact that grading has to do as much with seniority and age as with skill. This is confirmed by the fact that, while the average grade is increasing, the average educational level is falling rapidly. Thus the statistical improvement in the average grade of the labour force is more to do with its ageing than its increasing skills: the average age of those remaining is 45 years. Forty per cent have been at the factory for more than 20 years, over half more than 15 years, and only a third less than ten years. The proportion of those over 40 years old increased from 62.5 per cent at the beginning of 1994 to 68.6 per cent at the end of 1995. So those who remain are mostly people who have been in the factory all their working lives.[16]

By 1994 it was clear that a more active employment policy was required, particularly to reduce the numbers of those categories, above all ITR and office workers, who had not been leaving voluntarily. In a document issued at the end of 1993 entitled 'Basic Tasks and Directions of Activity in 1994' one of the tasks was expressed as 'to bring the number of personnel into correspondence with the capacity working'. An order that the number should be reduced by 3,000 by the end of March 1994 was issued in November 1993, and a joint commission of the trade union and administration was set up to implement this decision in each subdivision. No figures have been published of the results of this campaign, and most of the fall in employment has continued to be accounted for by voluntary redundancy, including those taking retirement, with only 329 of the 6743 who left the factory in 1994 being officially declared redundant. This meant that, because the staff list was not being cut, the savings in pay could be retained within the subdivision to increase the pay of those who remained. Nevertheless the general results are clear: those forced out have been primarily pensioners (over 1,000 in 1994 left to take their pension), ITR (although their proportion has still increased, from 13.6 per cent to 14.4 per cent) and auxiliary workers, including high skilled auxiliary workers. Although the latter are normally considered essential, the fall in production means that the shop can save on maintenance and repair work by simply discarding broken machinery. Because the auxiliary workers are on time-wages they have to be paid even when there is no work, unlike workers on piece-rates, so their pay can be shared out among those who remain. Those ITR identified as targets for redundancy were put under heavy moral pressure, for example being repeatedly selected for unpaid administrative leave, while the basic production workers, on the whole, are left on their own and have hardly been touched by redundancy.

The chief of one of the more stable shops said in 1994:

> We cut three or four, I don't remember, foremen and one senior foreman. We invited them to retire so that we could increase the pay of those who remained. This mainly affects those on time-wages – electricians, fitters. There are hardly any pensioners working on the machines. Since the volume of production has

16 At the same time, labour turnover is at record levels, amounting to 24.3 per cent in 1993, against 8.5 per cent in 1992.

> fallen we will keep the minimum number of repair workers, you see we have not finished with cutting them. But I will not cut the basic workers under any circumstances. There are already not enough of them.

In the third quarter of 1995, following the revolution in management, a new order came out to cut numbers in half, the fulfilment of which would certainly be a radical change in policy, if it is not merely an intimidatory threat. Up to now the declared policy has been to save the collective, and on this basis there have been no serious reductions, the factory relying instead on pensioning off those over retirement age, which also avoids the need to pay redundancy and, since it does not reduce the staff list, it leaves money to be shared out among those who remain. Some of the pensioners find work elsewhere in low-paid jobs as cleaners or cloakroom attendants. But in the shops the policy is to preserve the most valuable workers and push out the least desirable.

POLICIES IN THE SPHERE OF PAYMENT AND WAGES

Unlike our pioneers of privatisation, the industrial giants have not undertaken significant initiatives in the reform of payment systems, leaving the determination of pay to the shop level, and linking general pay increases only loosely and spasmodically to inflation, with the enterprise's ability to pay, tempered by a concern to avoid industrial conflict, the main determinant of pay policy. The only significant exception is the pay which senior managers and specialists pay themselves, where differentials increased very sharply in the wake of privatisation, the benefits filtering down to the level of middle management as a means of buying the loyalty of this strategically crucial stratum in the enterprise.

Prokat

Prokat was traditionally considered a secure enterprise with a relatively high level of wages, second only to VAZ, the traditional leader in the *oblast*. The payment system in Prokat has not been radically changed, and there have not been major changes in the differentials within the shops, although senior management salaries have increased significantly.

In the shops in Prokat there are now three payment systems: piece-rates, time-wages and salaried. ITR and managers, as well as store-keepers, cleaners and cloakroom attendants, are paid salaries. The salary paid is determined by the level of salary and the hours actually spent at the workplace. Time-wages are similar to a salary, but are applied only to workers and the rate is defined by the grade of the worker.

Piece-rates are determined primarily by the average hourly output norms for each grade, which were formerly defined by the normative documents issued by the ministry in 1986, and are now worked out by the department of labour and wages of the factory and are passed down to the labour and wages bureau of the shop. Or, to be more precise, the output norms remain constant, while the rate of payment is increased on account of inflation, the increases determined not by the rate of increase of consumer prices, but by the rate of increase of the profits of the enterprise as a whole.

In addition to the basic wage there is a large number of bonuses and supplementary payments which can raise a worker's pay by half as much again, and sometimes even more. First, there is the payment for harmful conditions, which is a coefficient applied to the output norms or hourly wage rate. In shop 3 the press operators and controllers are on the highest coefficient, known as 'one-one', because it is the highest grade of the top level.

The basis of bonus payments is the worker's labour contribution. There are various bonuses defined for each occupation. For example, for the press operators there is a 10 per cent bonus for the absence of violations of technological discipline, ten per cent for the absence of withdrawals from production by the press-operator, ten per cent for the absence of violations of the culture of production. Brigade leaders get further additional payments of ten per cent on basic, while bonuses amounting to between six and fifteen per cent can be paid for high-skilled work. According to the shop rules on payment of bonuses for such work, the shift foreman establishes a list of claimants to the bonus, these are reviewed by the engineer responsible for safety precautions and the shop chief confirms it annually. The foreman can also award various bonuses, but they are not large.

Besides these various bonuses, there is additional payment for evening work, with a 20 per cent premium on basic for the second shift, and a 40 per cent premium for the third (night) shift. There is also payment for the thirteenth month, based on the results of the whole enterprise over the year, and for a fourteenth month, payable for long service, with those who have worked continuously in the factory for over fifteen years qualifying for a bonus of up to 1.5 times their basic pay. Payment for the thirteenth month is entirely at the discretion of management, and there is no basis for negotiation over it, nor any third party which can intervene in the process. Thus the third shop received nothing for the thirteenth month in 1993. Many of the workers believed that all the money was spent on the organisation of a festival for the new year holiday in the Prokat park.

There are additional allowances for certain categories of workers, for example, in 1993 workers leaving for military service received 1,000 roubles. All workers going on holiday received 10,000 roubles. 736 people received additional payment for high-skilled work. 328 people received bonuses for 'developing their skills' or performing multi-skilled work.

The piece-rate system leads to considerable pay disparities. For example some press operators may be earning 41,000 while others are only earning 12,000. This is primarily the result of the shortage of work, which makes it impossible to distribute work among all the workers, and in particular to give all the workers a share of well-paid work. Wages of piece workers are adjusted by adjusting norms, which can only be changed by 15 per cent. This leads to a lot of conflict, especially in relation to the norms for export production. The other cause of conflict is the regular allocation of workers to other lower-paid jobs, when further money is often lost because of the complexity of calculation when workers are transferred, so that days and hours are frequently 'lost' in the accounting system.

In shop 3 in spring 1994 the piece-rate workers were earning an average 203,000 roubles, those on time wages, 165,000. Production personnel averaged 165,000, auxiliary personnel 156,000, managers 280,000, specialists 253,000, service personnel 111,000. But these average figures are very misleading: in fact auxiliary workers earned from 72,000 for a cleaner and cloakroom attendant to 230,000 for a high-skilled fitter; production workers earned from 160,000 to 280,000 for a press operator, depending on the grade and the nature of the work. The shift foremen got about 300,000, the senior foreman about 350,000. In practice the calculation of bonus was subject to principles of 'social justice'.[17] The maximum bonus was 45–50 per

[17] The concept of 'social justice' is contrasted to the principle of 'levelling': it means increasing differentials to provide managers and specialists with their 'just' rewards.

cent, which is what the bosses got. Press operators got about 40 per cent, controllers and annealers 25 per cent, cleaners 15 per cent.

Many workers expressed their dissatisfaction with the system of payment, often expressing doubts about the accuracy with which their wages were calculated. As an elderly engraver put it during a group discussion:

> I do not know whether those responsible calculate the wages honestly or not ... We have a points system for calculating wages. We work on piece-rates. The more you produce the more points you get and the more you earn. But the fact is that the 'weight' of the point depends on what was produced the day before. Yesterday this operation might have paid five roubles, but today it only pays 3.5. They cut the rate. The points depend to a great extent on the particular job, which can vary a great deal.

A forty-year-old worker joins the conversation:

> Nikiforov, he is on the other shift, is the only person who can understand this cunning, confusing system. He is cunning himself, he knows the system inside out. But nobody else even tries to understand it. Some people doubted the correctness of the calculation of their wages and went to ask the foreman to explain, and then to the department of labour and wages. But there they confused them with all sorts of figures which they did not understand, so they went away dissatisfied. Most people don't even try to understand.

When these workers are able to compare their earnings with those of other categories of workers, they are dissatisfied.[18] It seems that it is comparison rather than the absolute level of wages that is the basic cause of protest.

Opposition in principle to the system of piece-rates has also been increasing. In the conversation with workers on piece-rates just quoted, one exclaimed

> Look, you know how they work in the West. There they don't have piece-work, they have a fixed scale, but if you cannot cope with the work, at first you are sent to sweep the floor of the shop for lower wages, and then, if you don't pull your weight, it is straight out on the street.

One can hear similar things said by the press operators:

[18] Such comparison is less common nowadays than it was when it was accepted 'to count the money in someone else's pocket'. Many of those interviewed are unable or unwilling to answer questions about their colleagues' salaries, referring us to the department of labour and wages.

Work in non-ferrous metallurgy, on the presses, should not have anything in common with piece-work. (Thirty-seven-year-old fifth grade press operator).

Prokat's wage policy was to pay gradual monthly increases, which enabled it to continue paying wages, unlike other enterprises in the city which gave big increases and then could not pay. Thus the only delay was of two weeks in February 1994, while most plants could not pay anything from January to March. In the ball-bearing factory this led to a strike, in the aircraft factory to a spontaneous meeting which resulted in the resignation of the director. Regularity of payments has contributed to a stable social-psychological climate, substantially reducing the level of conflict, and supports the authority of the administration in the city.

Although pay is constantly being increased, the increases are not paid simultaneously to all the workers. In January 1993 the basic pay of workers in the core production shops was increased by 15 per cent, workers in auxiliary shops, managers, specialists, technicians and white collar workers received 10 per cent, non-productive shops got only 5 per cent. In February workers, managers, specialists and white-collar workers in production shops received 25 per cent, in non-production shops 20 per cent. In March all wages and salaries were increased by 10 per cent. In April the wage scales of all workers were increased by between 20 and 70 per cent over the February figure, while salaries were increased by 20–25 per cent. In May wages were increased by between 15 and 25 per cent, while salaries were increased by 25 per cent. In June everybody received 20 per cent. The net result for the half year was that wages increased between 2.1 and 3.7 times, while salaries rose between 2.4 and 2.6 times. The average wage on 1 July 1993 was 44,621 roubles. In July wages and salaries were increased by 30 per cent and again by 30 per cent in November.

From July 1993 a system of payments to compensate for inflation was introduced, covering 80 per cent of workers' basic pay and 70 per cent of the salary of ITR and managers. In October this covered workers 100 per cent and managers 90 per cent, in November it covered workers 130 per cent and managers to 120 per cent, and then the growth of wages stopped. For 1993 management had planned to increase pay to an average 40,000 by the end of the year. In fact it increased 8 times over the year, reaching an average of 137,687 at the year end. The enterprise had to pay 1,080,108,000 roubles excess wages tax for the year.

Kol'tso

It is impossible to get information on the pay of senior levels of the administration, but at shop level there have been very few changes in the area of pay. The traditional pay hierarchy, with main production workers at the top, largely persists in the shops, with revision of the pay system only just beginning at the end of 1995. Pay is the main source of all conflicts and discontent.

Workers in auxiliary occupations earn only half to three-quarters of the pay of main production workers. Foremen as a rule earn a little less than the workers in their section, although in 1994 an amalgamation of sections and reduction in the number of foremen made it possible to raise the pay of those who remained. There has been some tendency for chiefs and ITR to raise their pay to the level of the workers. Office staff are on a level with auxiliary production workers. The ITR in the factory-wide services seem to get a little less than those in the shops. Although ITR are still paid less than the workers, the workers think of them as parasites. MOP ('Junior Service Personnel' cleaners and so on – few of them, almost all pensioners) and apprentices at the bottom, but differentials vary considerable from one month to the next:

Average earnings in TsPA: Fourth quarter 1992 and April 1993

	1992	%	1993	%
Main production workers	15,000	100	38,600	100
Auxiliary production workers	9,700	65	19,792	51
Managers and ITR	14,000	93	29,600	77
MOP	5,600	37	7,900	20
Apprentices	2,400	16	5,000	13

The main change in the pay hierarchy has been in the increased differentials between workers, on the one hand, and senior managers and specialists, on the other. This change was closely connected with the process of privatisation. In July 1993, soon after the privatisation process had been completed, the average salary of managers was 92,500, of specialists 85,000, while workers were earning an average 60,300 roubles a month.

Until December 1992 pay was still dominated by scale pay, but now bonuses have become a very significant part of pay, from 40–70 per cent for various categories of employee, so that the bonus is an integral part of the salary.

Some of the piece-rate workers are on the brigade system. Within the brigade a levelling system continues. From time to time workers express an unwillingness to work 'for the common pot' and come into conflict with the shop administration, since it is easier for the normsetter to maintain accounts and keep strict control of additional payments in the brigade system. There is no guaranteed minimum for those on piece rates.

Pay is increased on the initiative of the administration, usually every quarter to take account of inflation, although in 1994, faced with growing unrest from the workers and even a strike at delays in increasing wages, the management tried to avoid confrontation by increasing pay ahead of time. The general director decides the level of pay for forced stoppages himself, taking account of both the economic situation and the mood of the collective. Orders about the mechanism for revising tariffs are sent down to the shops by the factory department of labour and wages.

The shop bureau of labour and wages has a lot of independence in working out the piece rates for new forms of production. In this case they agree the norms not with the enterprise department of labour and wages but with an intermediate group of normsetters and economists which has been created in most of the production subdivisions. Thus some of the authority of the enterprise department of labour and wages has been passed downwards.

The system for calculating wages is very complex and fraught with conflict. There are differences in rates for the same kind of product, because some are 'old' types and some are 'new'. Big problems arise when the shop is not working at full capacity since piece rate production workers lose out in comparison with time rate ITR and auxiliary workers. Normsetters are often the object of pressure from the workers, although this is usually resolved by the normsetters explaining why the workers have been paid such and such.

Foremen try to exert pressure on behalf of the workers when the tariff for new kinds of work is set, as the normsetter has to negotiate every rate with the foreman for each operation, although the chief of shop or director of the production subdivision has the last word. He can block a significant increase for a particular group of workers and redistribute the money at his own discretion. Normsetters claim that they have to beat out money for the workers of the shop in the factory labour and wages department.

The shop trade union does not participate in setting norms and pay rates at all. Conflicts may be addressed to it, but it plays a conciliatory role, explaining the reason for the situation or correcting errors in the calculation of pay.

Kol'tso remains the lowest paid of the large enterprises in the city, with growing discontent at extended delays in payment: at the end of 1994 the delay was two to three months. With the change of management a big effort was made to reduce the backlog, which was cut to one month, but by the end of 1995 the situation was worse than ever. At the beginning of December the workers were told that they would only receive their pay for August and September in February 1996.

SOCIAL SPHERE OF THE ENTERPRISE

The policy of 'balancing conservatism' has been followed in relation to the social sphere as much as in the spheres of wages and employment, with the enterprise trying to hold on to its social sphere, one of the pillars of the system of paternalistic management, for as long as possible, only bowing to the legal and financial onslaught relatively recently, and still, even with major changes in managerial strategy and personnel, maintaining at least a token commitment to the social sphere. The other side of the equation, that we do not consider here, is the crisis which divestiture of social assets imposes on the municipality, which has even fewer resources than does the enterprise to support the social sphere.

Prokat

The enterprise embraced not only production, but all aspects of the life of its workers, providing virtually all the housing and social, medical and welfare facilities in the district. It had the biggest social sphere in the city, used by local inhabitants, not only its own workers. Practically the whole housing stock and all establishments were built near to the enterprise, close to the workplace. It was not uncommon for all adult members of a family to work in Prokat or in the sphere of its social and welfare apparatus. The staff of all establishments were paid for by the factory, although their rates of pay were set by the regional trade union and the health and cultural administration. The factory's workers had a whole series of privileges in the use of the social and welfare apparatus.

With privatisation the whole of the social and welfare apparatus became the factory's property, although this violated the privatisation decrees. The housing stock of 500,000 square metres and medical facilities were legally transferred to the municipality but, because it had no funds to maintain them, in practice they continued to be supported by the factory as in the past.

In 1994 an agreement was reached for the gradual transfer of facilities over a five-year period. However, it was only in the summer of 1995 that the first money to cover the cost of housing maintenance in preparation for the winter, the repair of lifts and the removal of garbage was transferred to the factory's account, and this only covered 20 per cent of the real costs. The financial support of the city for medical establishments amounts to no more than the payment of salaries, with miserly means being provided for the rest. All the buildings and equipment remain the property of the factory. The employees still receive a whole series of other free medical services, at a cost to the enterprise of 80–100 million roubles a month. At the beginning of 1995 the enterprise allocated 300 million roubles for the repair of the buildings and proposed a 30 per cent pay rise for the staff of these facilities, which had been cancelled after privatisation.

Traditionally all the social and welfare establishments were considered to be subdivisions of the factory, each of which was combined with a particular shop and all distributed around the unproductive sphere of the factory, which employed a total of 4,500 people. Although each one had its own accountant, its accounts were subordinate to or simply duplicated the central accounts. All employees were employees of the factory, receiving factory bonuses and premia and sharing all the privileges of employees of the productive sphere.

All enterprises supporting social and welfare apparatus get tax privileges in that a certain amount of expenditure is tax deductible. But the norms governing the costs of such facilities are so out of date that these privileges cover only about one third of expenditure, so that tax privileges are not much help in maintaining the facilities. Nor is there any support from the city budget, apart from occasional small payments for those facilities which serve the city as a whole (organisation of new year celebrations, Victory Day, the City Day and so on). Negotiations continue with the municipality about support for the park of rest, stadium, children's and youth clubs (which were long ago closed to the city, but the factory maintains six extremely expensive establishments).

In the recent past, when the enterprise was prosperous, it financed the whole social and welfare apparatus unconditionally, with the last of its five-year social development plans being that of 1991. Now it is financed out of profits, but the size of the profits and the allocation to finance the social and welfare sphere is a commercial secret. However, the costs are huge, and managers of all establishments are pressed to earn money to augment their declining allocations from the factory administration.

In the past the factory met all the costs based on the chief of each establishment's estimate of current costs. Since 1993 each chief has had to submit a quarterly budget, reporting results and projections for the next quarter of costs and income and requesting a particular level of subsidy. If the estimates were not adequately justified the grant would be cut, within the general framework of a regular reduction of subsidy and increase in earned incomes. All this has led to a substantial reduction in social and welfare provision and a decline in the social privileges and guarantees of employees.

In 1994 subsidies still covered about 77 per cent of real costs. Charges had been introduced for most things, but they were still far below cost. All the establishments were trying to increase their revenues by renting out part of their premises (the palace of culture now houses branches of four banks, allowing the factory to cut the subsidy in January 1994 by 20 per cent; the stadium has opened a car park under the stands and so on) and to develop new earning services (a sauna in the pool, massage and various water treatments in the banya, charges for use of the library and so on). One of the employees of the social and welfare apparatus commented:

> One cannot increase indefinitely the payment for use of the swimming pool, the cost of banya tickets, payment for the use of studios or for children's creative workshops, or people will simply stop coming.

The bulk of the factory administration remained committed to maintaining social and welfare facilities as part of the apparatus of paternalistic management. However, continuing economic difficulties made it increasingly difficult to justify the cost of supporting these facilities, while the outside shareholders were particularly indignant at the drain on the enterprise's profits. In 1995 the new shareholders on the board of directors began to complain about the cost of the social and welfare apparatus, and it was decided to make all the facilities independent, a proposal which had been regularly discussed since 1992 with nothing having actually been done. All premises and equipment will remain the property of the factory and they will be rented to the new enterprises for a symbolic payment. The factory will pay taxes on the land and buildings, and all other taxes will be paid by the enterprises themselves. All the new enterprises had to submit their constitutions and budget documents by the autumn of 1995, with 12 billion roubles allocated for their establishment.

The executive director for the social and welfare sphere was no defender of the subsidisation of the social and welfare apparatus. As he said in an interview:

> The company has absolutely no obligation to support the social sphere, it should provide its employees with high incomes so that they can pay for everything that they need. Sooner or later the shareholders will have to decide either to use the company's profits to support the whole of the social sphere, and pay only symbolic dividends to the shareholders, or to pay the shareholders, so that they themselves can pay for what they need.

In addition to extensive social and welfare facilities, there has been a system of distribution of consumer goods and groceries at the factory since the times of general shortages. The administration has actively used this system as a tool of regulation and management of the labour collective. The distribution of material benefits was not the main function of the trade union, but it gave meaning to its existence in the years of stagnation and the early years of perestroika. The increase in the scale and diversity of barter at the end of the 1980s exceeded the organisational capacities of the trade union apparatus and in 1990 the management set up a special division of the factory which concentrates the main distributive functions. This decision to establish a department for goods and services (UPITU) was taken through the STK. The UPITU sells commodities acquired by purchase, barter or provided by departments and services of the factory itself. Having paid into an account in UPITU, an employee can order an iron door, corrugated aluminium sheet, shoe repairs by the factory shoemakers and so on. The main suppliers of goods for distribution are:

1. Large trade organisations and shops. Small intermediary organisations are not usually allowed to trade in the enterprise. However, in fact many small dealers have penetrated the factory and trade boldly in the shops. Nevertheless, officially preference is given to large partners who sell in the premises of UPITU and its trading points spread around the shops. A specialised building for trading is now being built, but so far all trading has taken placed in rapidly converted but unsuitable premises. Contracts with these large shops force them to sell at prices between 10 and 30 per cent lower than outside the factory, at the expense of their margins. Officially, UPITU does not take any commission.
2. Industrial partners. Although the scale of barter has fallen sharply, goods are still received in exchange for products of the factory supplied earlier. Negotiations are carried out by the production department which finds out what is available, but there is no organised system, it is largely a spontaneous process. Sometimes it is not a matter of barter, but simply the supply of goods at cost prices which are then sold to employees, with a mark up for transport and other necessary costs. The final word on what to take in payment and what not rests with the higher management of the factory.

   As a result of the crisis of non-payment a specialised group of employees of the administration was created, which still works today, and whose job was to speed the payment of debts to the factory. These debts are often paid off in products of various kinds – washing machines, fridges etc.
3. Subsidiary farms. Food products, most of which are produced by subsidiary farms, make up a large proportion of goods sold in the factory. About ten years ago the enterprise established a farm on agricultural land that it rented, which is now a regular subdivision of the factory. The present director has taken this activity under his personal control and has supervised its construction and development. Experienced cheese-makers were recruited, cheese-making equipment installed, the herds of cows were completely renewed and an abattoir and sausage factory constructed.

   In the period of food shortage Prokat was the only factory in the city able to supply every worker with 4 kg. of meat a month and at this time this was an important way of attracting labour. Rations are still distributed, but meat, cheese and butter are no longer scarce and prices are comparable to those in the shops, although the subsidiary agriculture still loses money. Over the years the distribution system has become complex and efficient.

All information about the goods arriving in the factory was provided through UPITU. The distribution of automobiles was especially complicated. Here a queue was established which took account of length of service, awards, incentives and so on. The trade union system still plays a part in the distribution of subsidiary agricultural products and is responsible for maintaining the lists. The factory trade union committee includes a post with responsibility for co-ordination with UPITU.

The paternalistic system of social guarantees had important functions for the management of the enterprise. On the one hand, it served to instil pride in the enterprise, to give a sense of its power and create the impression of a caring management. On the other hand, it was one of the methods of management of the collective and a means of attracting labour. This is why the enterprise has tried by every means to maintain the social sphere created over long years. Privatisation has led to a reduction in such social guarantees, with the creation of independent enterprises for the social and welfare facilities as an early stage of this process, but distribution retains its symbolic significance, even if its material importance is much reduced.

Kol'tso

The situation in Kol'tso is similar to that of Prokat. The factory has an enormous social sphere which it still owns. This includes a culture palace and affiliated club, food combine and shopping centre on the territory of the enterprise, 'Stone Island' holiday centre, sports facilities (small stadium, sport, water and sky bases), three summer labour and rest camps for schoolchildren, two profilaktories, 'Dream' pioneer camp, seven hostels, hunting facilities, subsidiary agriculture (2131 hectares in total, including 1314 hectares of arable farming, 300 head of cattle, 800 pigs, seven blocks of flats, a shop and mechanical workshops in the village of Mar'evka, as well as an asphalt road leading to it). The enterprise still also manages a medical centre, and a large housing stock built with its own funds (177 blocks), all but two of which are legally now municipal property, although they are still supported by the enterprise. Until spring 1994 it also had 15 kindergartens for 3,500 children.

This detail brings out the fact that the fate of an enterprise like Kol'tso cannot be reduced to the fate of its direct workers. There is a whole empire, a huge social organism, on which people depend. Thousands of local residents live in its flats and use its facilities although they have no connection with the enterprise.

For a long time the enterprise managed to maintain its social facilities despite all its difficulties, although it was the third largest category of expenditure after taxes and wages (18 per cent of net profits in the first half of 1993). The commercialisation of the social infrastructure proceeded very slowly and unevenly in the period of balancing conservatism, amounting to no more than vague plans for the future or clumsy individual initiatives (for example, an attempt to lease a labour and rest camp for schoolchildren) and it is still undertaking new initiatives in the area, for example, the purchase of imported meat-processing equipment. Kol'tso was a typical paternalistic enterprise whose administration aspired to retain the image not of a manager but of a *khozyain* on whom practically all of the workers' lives depended.

Management and the trade union complained more and more about the cost of provision, but they did not want to cease to provide these benefits because, with low wages and many workers on administrative vacation, they still provided a significant lever of influence over the workers (for example, a foreman in the shop in which the independent trade union is active is afraid to leave the official union because he is waiting for an apartment) and fear of labour conflicts, a fear which is significant despite the lack of workers' rights. Moreover, some of the facilities are considered to be valuable commercial property which can be leased (this became very clear in the course of privatisation, just as in the case of Prokat, which was delayed by a conflict with the state property committee over the desire of the administration to privatise the whole welfare infrastructure). Apart from this, preservation of social privileges serves as an argument in bargaining with the regional administration for tax, credit and other privileges.

The social policy of Kol'tso has a perfectly rational basis as it helps the enterprise to hold onto workers, especially women (who now make up more than half the labour force), and provides additional levers of management influence, indeed it is now the only lever of the trade union. Moves towards commercialisation are, nevertheless, forced on the administration by the enormous cost of provision so that social policy has gradually acquired a dual character, with a slow commercialisation of social services (for example, free holiday vouchers were no longer distributed to all employees, the price of commodities was equalised to market prices).

The crunch came as the crisis deepened from the middle of 1993, and heated discussions began over the fate of the welfare apparatus. The new financial director insisted at a meeting of the board of directors in March 1994 that the enterprise should cease to support its kindergartens, which were already juridically in municipal ownership. Experienced managers insisted that kindergartens were important to attract young workers to the factory, but the young finance director replied that if orders were forthcoming there would be no problem in recruiting labour. One shop chief argued that newcomers would not have the training and experience needed, so it was better to hold on to the existing workers. No decision was taken at that meeting, but the economic position continued to deteriorate, wages were delayed and a wave of strikes broke out. A couple of weeks later the board came back to the question, and this time the issue of transfer was not in doubt, the discussion was about the mechanism and timing of the transfer. The head of the social and welfare department proposed to transfer some of the kindergartens but to keep the best. He also pointed out that if they disposed of all the housing and kindergartens they became liable to a 1.5 per cent tax on turnover paid by enterprises without a social and welfare apparatus, but the financial department reported that the maintenance costs already amounted to about 1.5 per cent of turnover. Thus, with the support of the new managers, it was decided to transfer all the kindergartens to the municipality, with no conditions attached, not even priority for the factory's employees for which they would have had to continue to contribute to maintenance. Kol'tso was one of the first enterprises in the city to transfer its kindergartens fully to the municipality because the crisis had reached the point at which there was not even the money to feed the children. Subsequently other enterprises faced more problems with such a transfer, since the municipality was not willing to take them as it did not have the resources itself

The remaining facilities are still owned by the factory, but are slowly decaying as there is no money to maintain them. The administration considered the sale of its profilaktory-sanatorium, but this move was successfully resisted by the Veterans' Council, in this case with the support of the trade union, whose president argued that 'it is prestigious for a factory like ours', although it cannot cover its costs.

Despite these changes, the enterprise has not completely rejected its paternalistic image and policy. At the first meeting reporting to the shareholders on 14 May 1994, the new general director turned to Nika and asked it to allocate its dividends to the development of the social sphere, the director of Nika assuring the meeting that it would do so.

The story of Kol'tso and Prokat is typical. In former state enterprises the first bits of the social sphere to be cut are those which are not profitable – kindergartens, medical centre, housing – and the enterprise tries to transfer these to the municipal budget, the initiative typically coming from new managers who are not committed to the older paternalistic traditions.

The second tendency is for the more or less resolute commercialisation of those objects which remain in factory ownership in the hope of making them self-financing. This is enforced through a reduction of subsidies and increases in charges. Third, those facilities which remain in factory ownership but are not commercially viable just decay (stadia, sports facilities). Some facilities are turned over to subsidiary companies for which outside investors are sought, although this is quite unrealistic. The official position of the administration in 1995 is that 'the management of AO Kol'tso considers that the transition to the market implies the break-up of the old system under which it financed those objects which were not directly related to production' (from the minutes of a meeting of the general director and marketing director with chiefs of non-productive subdivision).

CONCLUSION

Despite considerable differences between them, our two case study enterprises turn out to have followed a very similar pattern of development over the four years of radical reform. The initial priority of both enterprises, not surprisingly, was to try to hold on to what they had in the face of a massive reduction in demand for their products and dislocation of economic, political and financial relationships. The overwhelming priority in the first phase was to secure supplies of raw materials and find outlets for their products. Relations with traditional suppliers proved most reliable, because here they could trade on informal connections to secure supplies on credit, similarly supplying their traditional customers. New connections could be established on the basis of barter and, in the last resort, with the use of scarce cash.

Responsibility for adjustment in the first instance was devolved to the level of the shops, which were encouraged to seek their own sources of supply, to develop their own products and to seek their own customers. This was reflected in tendencies to the decentralisation of management, with many functions being devolved to the shops. Although the traditional systems of control of the shops through plan targets and allocated funds were retained, shop management had much more flexibility in the use of its resources than it had had in the past, even if it was not set on a formal self-financing basis. The factory administration, meanwhile, concentrated on establishing relationships with financial and commercial intermediaries, with lobbying state bodies and with drawing up its privatisation plans. Privatisation provided the means by which senior management was able to seal its control of the enterprise and consolidate its links with its outside associates, which in the first instance in both cases were local financial and commercial structures.

Both enterprises faced a dramatic collapse of demand and correspondingly of levels of production. The principal cash expense of the enterprises was their wage bill, with raw materials largely being drawn from stock or purchased on credit, so that pressures of falling revenues were transmitted to the shops in the form of limited resources with which to pay wages. Economies could in principle be made by holding down or delaying the payment of wages or by laying workers off temporarily or permanently. In general initiatives from the centre, in particular to declare redundancies, were much less significant than the spontaneous initiatives of shop management in determining their wages and employment strategy, because it was only at shop level that the various considerations which had to be taken into account could be weighed up. These considerations involved a balance between the values and aspirations of the workers, on the one hand, and the concern of shop management to retain the shop's production capacity intact, on the other. This implied a growing priority being given by management to the retention of skilled labour by maintaining wages, if necessary at the expense of employment levels. Similar, but even more acute, financial pressures on the enterprise social and welfare services could only be met with increased charges and cuts in services.

In both cases, despite the depth of the financial crisis and the very substantial employment reductions, there has been very little change on the shop floor of the enterprise. This is hardly surprising, given the fact that production continues to be based on Soviet technology, it continues to be impeded by shortages and sporadic delivery of supplies, now compounded by uncertainties and irregularities of demand, it continues to be faced with shortages of skilled labour. With a massive surplus capacity, extremely low labour costs, energy supplies which are not paid for, raw materials which are acquired on credit, there is little incentive to restructure production in order to increase efficiency.

Following privatisation there has been some tendency to the reversal of the decentralising forces which marked the first phase of reform as management in both enterprises has sought to consolidate its links with external bodies which, it is hoped, can be a source of finance for the survival and future development of the enterprise. Here there is the principal contrast between the two enterprises, as a result of the export opportunities that opened up before Prokat in the middle of 1994, on the basis of which it established connections with multinational companies and with powerful national and regional banks which acquired substantial shareholdings. Kol'tso, by contrast, had no such attractions to offer, and was integrated into the local economic and political power structures, orchestrated by the regional administration.

The precise connections between these various different centres of political, commercial and financial power are extremely difficult to identify and to pin down. Thus it is very difficult to assess the real significance of the management changes which took place in both enterprises in the course of 1995. Although the new management in both cases has declared a new course for 1996, with substantial reductions in social and welfare provision for employees and very sharp cuts in employment, it remains to be seen whether these programmes can be implemented any more successfully than such radical programmes have been in the past. Both enterprises may appear to be hopeless cases, with huge debts, production at a standstill and wages unpaid. However, both enterprises continue to have significant regional and national importance as strategic producers and as sources of national and local tax revenue, as well as providing employment and social and welfare services to the locality. It remains to be seen whether political priorities will continue to prevail over the ruthless logic of capital.

5. On the Buses: Management Dynamics in a Passenger Transport Enterprise

Vladimir Ilyin and Marina Ilyina

PATP is a passenger transport enterprise in a northern city in one of the republics of the Russian Federation. The research in PATP was begun by a group of sociologists from Syktyvkar State University in 1989 (Vladimir Ilyin (director), V. Gruznov and Yu. Popova). The research at that time was commissioned by the Party committee of the enterprise and financed by the trade union committee, while the administration maintained a cautious neutrality. This was a pretty accurate reflection of the balance of forces of these groups in the declining years of perestroika. The research was resumed by Vladimir Ilyin and Marina Ilyina within our collaborative project in 1992, with the consent and support of the trade union committee and the administration. This research has been conducted alongside extensive comparative research in a wide range of enterprises in the Komi Republic and beyond. This makes it possible to relate the findings of our case study research to the wider tendencies of restructuring in the Republic and in Russia as a whole.

Particular aspects of PATP have been discussed at length in previously published papers.[1] These aspects will not be duplicated in this case study report, which is concerned primarily with the system of stratification in its relation with the structure of management of the enterprise and with the changes which take place as a state enterprise breaks free of administrative control with the breakdown of the system of state monopoly socialism.

[1] See, in particular, Vladimir Ilyin, 'Social Contradictions and Conflicts in State Enterprises in the Transition Period', in Simon Clarke, ed., *Conflict and Change in the Russian Industrial Enterprise*, Edward Elgar, Cheltenham, 1996 and Marina Ilyina, 'Foremen: An Ethnographic Investigation', in Simon Clarke, ed., *Labour Relations in Transition: Wages, Employment and Industrial Conflict in Russia*, Edward Elgar, Cheltenham, 1996, which concentrates on the Repair-Mechanical Workshop.

THE ENTERPRISE AND THE EXTERNAL ENVIRONMENT

In state-socialist society the enterprise was an administrative subsystem which acted according to the norms imposed on it by the state and its various administrative bodies. Perestroika, and then the collapse of the political-administrative system of the CPSU, opened up the possibility of the enterprise leaving the administrative system for the sphere of the market and its transformation into an economic organisation. Many enterprises took this opportunity. For some, immersion in the market ended in collapse, others mastered the new environment. However, there were limits to the possibility of leaving the administrative sphere for the market, despite the absence of formal restrictions. As a result, after a period of illusions and hot air, many enterprises began, willingly or unwillingly, to turn back to the administrative system. PATP is an example of the latter development.

PATP in the system of state administrative power

PATP is a passenger transport enterprise which, at the beginning of the period, provided all transport services for a city of more than 200,000 people and, even after the transformation of one bus column into an independent enterprise, still provides the rest of the city's transport needs. PATP is vital to the everyday life of the city, which is also the administrative centre of a large region of more than 400,000 square kilometres.

It is the specific features of the functions of the enterprise which determined its position in the administrative system and the failure of its attempt to leave this system. Initially, like all Soviet enterprises, it was part of a departmental structure, in this case of the Russian transport ministry. On the other hand, its key position in the infrastructure of the region required its parallel inclusion in the territorial management system. But this inclusion had a dual and inconsistent character. First, PATP was part of a large regional association, Avtotrans, which combined and organised all twenty-one specialised passenger and freight enterprises of the region and entered as a regional subsystem into the Russian ministerial structure, employing in total more than 10,000 people. In 1987 the Russian Ministry of Auto Transport transferred its rights over the centralised distribution of profits arising from central funds to the association. The freight transport enterprises which belonged to the association provided steady profits, while passenger transport enterprises, with the exception of the taxis, were planned loss-makers. The association therefore supported passenger transport enterprises by redistributing profits at the expense of freight enterprises.

Secondly, PATP was subject to regional Party and state bodies. In the latter case the administrative contacts were based on powerful mutual interests: the local bodies were very interested in the normal working of PATP, as a condition of the functioning of the administrative centre as a whole, and the administration of PATP used this interest to get additional money and to lobby in the Russian ministry.

At the end of the 1980s a drift of Soviet enterprises towards independence began. Everywhere the authority of the state was weakening, including that of the associations which stood over the enterprises, while the latter acquired more and more independence in dealing with economic questions, turning away from administrative relations towards commodity-money relations. PATP was no exception.

During the late 1980s the functions of Avtotrans gradually narrowed. At the beginning of the 1990s it had lost virtually all its power over the region's transport enterprises, preserving only some of its traditional symbolic privileges, for example, the right to approve the appointment of enterprise directors. The majority of enterprises which left Avtotrans remained state enterprises or were transferred to municipal ownership, but five freight enterprises were privatised as joint-stock companies. Having lost its administrative authority, the association tried to transform itself into an economic force. The management of the association, using its connections with the Moscow supply organisations and organs of state power, its experience of lobbying and supply (its cultural capital), set out to transform Avtotrans into a commercial organisation. At first it remained formally a state structure, but in 1992 it was turned into a joint-stock company. The regional State Property Committee held the largest packet of shares, with the remainder being allocated to transport enterprises (the wider distribution of shares was not anticipated). The general director of the association was then elected as general director of the joint-stock company. The new company comprised one head enterprise and two daughter firms and began to work with the now-independent transport enterprises on a contractual basis. The chiefs of the company negotiated with the government and purchased equipment, parts, fuel and so on behalf of the transport enterprises. Speaking in 1996, the general director of Avtotrans described the situation at that time thus:

> The decree on privatisation appeared, but nobody knew how we should be privatised. They explained to us in the State Property Committee: 'Don't worry. The main thing is to survive.' So the situation was incomprehensible: formally the heads of the enterprises remained under our wing, but without any legal basis.

However, the management of PATP at the beginning of the 1990s had its own plans and illusions. Despite the radical step of transforming the association into a joint-stock company, it was still seen as a parasite which only wanted to live at the expense of the enterprises, but which was not able to be of any use to them. As a counterweight to the ambitious plan of the former association, the administration of PATP decided to carry out all the functions of supply and administrative lobbying independently. However, it did not break its contacts with Avtotrans, which continued to sell spare parts to PATP.

It took two to three years for the local transport enterprises to understand that to buy their spare parts and fuel, to try to beat out financial support and privileges independently, was more expensive and less effective. During 1994–5 there was a tendency to the reintegration of enterprises into large territorial associations in various branches of the economy. The interests of enterprises in such a reintegration were not uniform, but depended on the power of the enterprise and its ability to exist independently and profitably. The more effective the enterprise, the less its interest in a deep integration, with the association performing only some functions of co-ordination, supply and so on. Unprofitable enterprises realised that only administrative reintegration, the restoration of associations as full administrative bodies standing over the enterprises, would enable them to survive in conditions of economic crisis and market formation. At the same time it was obvious that the motivation of attempts of weak (whether for subjective or objective reasons) enterprises was above all to secure the redistribution of money within the association in their favour, by limiting the incomes of the strong. Since these weak, sinking enterprises constituted the majority, and their interests coincided with that of the association, which still existed in a more or less transformed form, their pressure turned out to be the more successful. The tendency to the reconstitution of associations appeared simultaneously almost everywhere: the fate of Avtotrans is typical.

At the end of the 1980s the process of breaking up state property began. With the collapse of centralised administrative management the concept of state property had become almost an abstraction: enterprises were considered state enterprises, but many of them had left the sphere of state management and paid the same taxes as private enterprises. Only after 1992 was the ownership of the objects of state property defined concretely, some passing to ownership of the Federal government, others to regional bodies (republican, *oblast*) or to municipal authorities. After a period of confusion when nobody knew who owned PATP, it fell into the hands of the Committee for the Management of State Property. The regional authorities took on themselves the functions of strategic control of the activity of the enterprise.

At the end of 1994, under pressure from the weak passenger transport enterprises in the region and from Avtotrans itself, the local power and management bodies decided to unite virtually all the transport enterprises which had not become joint stock companies into a single association with one bank account and a centralised strategic management. The general director of Avtotrans presented the question point-blank to a meeting at that time: 'Either we unite, or we disintegrate'. All the directors of the state transport enterprises, with the sole exception of the director of PATP, supported this proposition. For this purpose the state body, Avtotrans, was recreated, which was joined by the managers and apparatus of the joint-stock company Avtotrans, which in effect transformed itself back into a state company. Avtotrans has been headed through this entire evolutionary process by the same person.

After a long and at times conflictual process the co-ordinating role of the association in relation to all the enterprises was re-established, but not in the same form as before. Nine enterprises entered the association as daughter companies, maintaining their independent accounts but becoming accountable to the association. All the property of the transport enterprises which joined the association belonged to the Republican ministry for the management of state property and privatisation. However, it was contractually assigned to the association, which in turn concluded contracts with the enterprises concerning the transfer of this property to their management. This meant that they had the right freely to use this property, but could not sell it or lease it out without the agreement of the association. At the same time the re-establishment of the association did not restore the situation which had existed before perestroika, when the association interfered in the most trivial activities of the enterprises and appropriated all their profits, not least because its administrative apparatus was much reduced, from 120 people then to only 25 today. A further fifty people are employed in two enterprises which come directly under the association: its automobile column, with 30 automobiles, and a repair enterprise. The privatised transport enterprises remain outside the association, but still retain close connections with it, working on a contractual basis. However, according to the general director of the association:

> S—v, the director of one of the privatised freight transport enterprises, is free in relation to me, but following tradition I remain a boss for him. But this is not strange: they have already elected me general director six times. So, if he has to go somewhere for a few days, he phones and asks my permission, although formally there is no need to do this. The directors of the privatised companies give me the list of people responsible for keeping order during holidays.

The enterprise in the market sphere

At the end of the 1980s it seemed that there was not one enterprise director who did not dream of pulling himself out from under strict administrative control to enter the free market. One could often hear them promise that if this happened then they would show that they could work. The administration of PATP was no exception. The question of leasing the work of the bus drivers and repair workers had already been discussed at the end of the 1980s, and the taxi drivers did transfer their automobiles to leasehold.

When privatisation began, the question of including PATP in the process of privatisation was discussed among the managers of the enterprise and its employees. The then-director of the enterprise, Yu—n, declared that in the right conditions the privatisation of a passenger enterprise was possible. For example, PATP could conclude an agreement with the local authorities to provide passenger services and, as long as they observed all the conditions of the contract, they would receive sufficient payment to cover all their costs and make a profit. The question of the price of tickets and the level of subsidy would then be a matter for the local authority. The management of the association Avtotrans also proposed the privatisation of the enterprises which remained members of the association. However, the majority of workers and employees were very sceptical about the idea of privatisation. Thus the question of the privatisation of PATP as a whole enterprise was abandoned. However, the taxi column was privatised as a separate collective of the enterprise (see further below).

At the same time there was a parallel struggle of the enterprise to reduce the level of its losses, if not to eliminate them entirely. A key element of this strategy was a rapid increase in the price of tickets: from the classic 5 kopeks of the socialist epoch, to 1000 roubles from 1 September 1995, an increase of 20,000 times. However, the market gave a cool reception to this attempt of the administration of PATP to make a profit: as the price of tickets rose, the number of fare-dodgers rose in step. For every action there is a reaction: in 1993–4 the number of inspectors on the bus routes was increased sharply, and on some of the routes conductors were introduced, which further increased the costs of the enterprise. Nevertheless, these measures met with some success. Although PATP did not become profitable, by the end of 1995 the proportion of costs covered by revenues had significantly increased.

The main buses used by PATP are Hungarian Ikarus buses. In the 1980s they arrived in the region on the basis of inter-governmental agreements between Hungary and the Soviet Union as members of the Council of Mutual Economic Assistance. With the collapse of the CMEA economic transactions between the two countries were transferred to convertible currency. This led to a sharp fall in trade since neither side had enough hard currency to buy the other's commodities. The losers from the break in East European co-operative links in this instance were Ikarus and Russian passenger transport, including PATP. The very high price of the Ikarus put it beyond the reach of the enterprise.

Even if PATP can see the light at the end of the tunnel in terms of its recovery of its operating costs, there are absolutely no prospects of it being able independently to re-equip itself. This would only be possible with public funds. In the first half of the 1990s two distinct, but closely connected, processes coincided: more and more of PATP's buses wore out and the poverty of the state budget became more and more obvious. Both these processes pushed PATP to the bottom, making it impossible for it to survive independently in the sphere of the market. There was only one way out, to return to the bosom of the administrative system.

Of course, not all enterprises found themselves in such a hopeless situation. In many spheres it was quite possible to work without any financial support from the state. In particular, motor vehicle enterprises could enter the market with a view to more than survival. Thus, lorry transport enterprises, carrying high value goods, have been able to take advantage of the new conditions, to privatise and turn themselves into profitable economic organisations. In small towns there are often mixed enterprises, carrying both goods and passengers. In these cases unprofitable passenger transport is compensated by the high earnings on the carriage of goods, quite apart from the provision of grants from the local authorities to cover passenger losses.

The labour collective as a means of lobbying

In state socialist society the status of an enterprise depended almost completely on its relations with higher Party and Soviet bodies. The overall performance of the enterprise was measured first of all by the degree of plan fulfilment, which was a result of the negotiations of the enterprise administration with higher planning bodies: a low plan could easily be overfulfilled and secure the status of 'leading workers' for the labour collective. The possibility of fulfilling the plan also depended on the supply of equipment and materials to the given enterprise, which also depended on the higher leadership's attitude to it. Finally, the objective significance of the enterprise for the country, region or city, was taken into account, as were the informal relations with the enterprise director and other of its representatives.

The work of PATP in the command economy was assessed by the percentage of its plan fulfilment, which included a large number of indicators (from the volume of passengers carried to economies in the use of fuel). Plan fulfilment determined whether or not the collective received its bonus, whether the management received moral encouragement or was reprimanded for deviating from the Party or administrative line, whether the director was promoted or removed from his job. Success in securing a good plan and in maintaining the conditions of its fulfilment (receiving new buses, money and material resources for fuel and for the construction of the garage and repair shops, which was begun in the 1980s) depended mainly on the diplomatic skills of the director and, particularly, the Party secretary, on their ability to convince the management of Avtotrans and the regional and city executive committees of the justice of their demands. PATP was successful in these terms, as shown by the fact that at the end of the 1980s it occupied spacious industrial premises, had new buses, and its workers regularly received their bonuses.

A characteristic feature of the enterprise in the administrative system was the existence of a 'labour collective', which is a completely real social phenomenon, and not simply a creature of the propaganda apparatus of the CPSU. Its essence consists in the fact that external contradictions completely dominate internal ones. In other words, the level of pay of the workers, their working conditions, the amount of housing construction and other key problems affecting the employees of the enterprise are determined not within the enterprise, but by higher administrative bodies. Thus it is pointless entering into conflict with the foreman or director over a serious question when it hardly depends on them. In the event of conflict the director would simply spread his arms and say: 'What can I do about it? It is outside my sphere of competence'. Thus all demands got passed up the administrative hierarchy. Under the strict political regime of state socialism to put pressure on the upper echelons of power amounted to a crime against the state, and entailed all the consequences appropriate to such a crime. Such an outcome could only result from an irrational outburst of rage, as at Novocherkassk in 1962. Expressions of dissatisfaction could provoke the ominous response: 'What is this? Are you against the policies of the CPSU? Are you against Soviet power?' Only the most foolhardy courage could motivate a positive answer.

Certainly, the employees of the enterprise would evaluate their chiefs in terms of their ability to go into the necessary offices and 'beat out' a low plan and abundant resources for the enterprise. Of course, not all bosses could do this, in which case the question arose 'But why are things better at that other enterprise?', a question which was not seditious from the point of view of the system as a whole, but was very threatening from the point of view of the administration of the enterprise. And this brought into play another mechanism of the social contract: 'If you don't like it, go to the other enterprise', and indeed those who were not satisfied had no trouble in finding a job elsewhere. They left, and calm was restored. It was only in the countryside and small towns that workers really had nowhere else to go. Elsewhere, Soviet workers traded low pay and bad working conditions for a freedom to choose their work which is unheard of in a market economy. Thus the shortage of labour, itself the unintended result of the extensive pattern of economic development, provided an important basis for social stability.

Despite all, sometimes tensions arose in the social relations between managers and workers, the administrative responsibilities of the former being in direct contradiction to the interests of the latter. In a capitalist society such tension would lead to a strike, but under state monopoly socialism both sides were, in the end, hired labourers, and both typically perceived state property as nobody's. So, in the case of conflict the workers could easily ask their foreman or shop chief: 'What is it to you – why should you be so bothered?' And if the boss at that moment is fed up with fighting, remembers his health and thinks about the fact that he is fed up with this damned work, that nobody has a good word to say to him, he might silently agree. Concessions on the part of managers towards workers are a kind of compromise between hired labourers who agree to swindle their common owner for their mutual satisfaction. The most widespread forms of such a social contract between the two groups of hired labourers are the inflation of the amount of work carried out, the acceptance of defective or broken products, inflating grades, turning a blind eye to disciplinary violations and so on.

At the same time a significant proportion of stoppages are the result of the inefficiency of management. Their inefficiency deprives them of the moral right to put pressure on the workers, who can simply reply: 'So whose fault is that?' Moreover, if there is a serious conflict it will be the senior management which will take the blame. Thus there was a strong objective basis for the mutual regard of managers and workers. For many enterprises which, like PATP, could not leave the administrative system, the situation today remains as it was before, although the internal independence of the administration has increased significantly.

The changing political situation in the country at the end of the 1980s removed much of the external pressure from the administration, but it did not necessarily undermine the 'social contract' between management and workers. Like many other enterprises, PATP was inspired by the example of the miners, beginning in the summer of 1989, whose strikes allowed the administration of the mines and associations and the coal ministry literally to force essential additional resources out of the government. The success of the miners showed that the workers' strike was a highly efficient means of lobbying higher administrative and political bodies. 1989 put the idea of a strike as a legitimate means of pressure into the minds of the workers and employees of PATP. The weakening of the ability of the state to respond with serious measures of political repression considerably widened the arsenal of the struggle for social self-assertion within the framework of the administrative system.

In the course of economic reform in the first half of the 1990s many enterprises pulled out from the vice of the administrative system to enter the market, where success is determined by quite different factors. PATP, as we have seen, was not one of these. Thus the rules of conduct accepted in the former command economy, and supplemented by the strike as a gain of perestroika, remained in the arsenal of the management of PATP in the new situation.

It is not a strike, but more the threat of a strike, which provides a means of pressuring higher bodies. Thus the management of PATP, to justify the need for increasing expenditure on wages since 1989, can refer to the growing social tension in the drivers' collective, which might erupt in a strike which would paralyse the life of the city. However, the city administration has not always been in a position to provide the money needed, in which case the threat of a strike began to seem far-fetched.

In the spring of 1992 the discontent of the PATP workers at the low level of their wages was growing. The administration spread out its hands: 'so, we cannot do anything, because neither the city nor the region give us any money, ask them'. The administration attempted to direct the workers' discontent into channels favourable for the enterprise. A strike committee was elected at a meeting of the labour collective. It is remarkable that they elected the deputy director for operations as its president, a man who had previously been the chief of the first column, where he had had good relations with the drivers. One person from his former column had called out his name, and others, not having anything against him, supported his nomination, although, according to the president of the trade union committee:

> Power has spoiled him. It was easy to be close to the workers in the auto column. In his post as deputy director he depends on his chief and will be thrown out of his post immediately if his actions conflict with the actions and plans of the director.

The deputy director tried to refuse nomination. But either he did this too weakly, or the workers were too persistent, so he took the position. And the director, judging by all that happened, had no objections.

However, the strike committee also included opponents of the director. As a result the demands that it worked out were also directed against the director, Yu—n. The first group of demands, for a doubling of pay and fulfilment of the tariff agreement, were completely acceptable to the administration of PATP and corresponded to its interests (the administration also lives on its pay). However, the second group of demands introduced dissonance into the unity of the labour collective: to replace the director of the enterprise and implement the collective agreement.

The packet of demands turned out to be too radical for the deputy director, and he refused to press them. The director and all the management of the enterprise had nothing against a strike which pressed demands on the local authorities, but under pressure from the trade union committee the workers had gone much further, turning the strike weapon against the director himself. Thus it was quite natural that the president of the strike committee should put the brakes on everything, the strike was called off on the grounds that some of the demands had been met, and the strike committee quietly stopped its activity.

Serious internal contradictions between the director and the president of the trade union committee prevented the wide use of the strategy of using the workers' movement in the general interest of all the employees of the enterprise. In an interview in 1993 the director of PATP, Yu—n, complained that with a normal trade union committee it would be possible to achieve much: the administration could press on the local management bodies through their channels, but the trade union could threaten to strike. The new director of PATP M—v subsequently acknowledged with complete conviction that the previous chief, his deputy and various other members of the administration had urged the workers to strike in order to resolve the financial problems of the enterprise.

M—v rejected such a tactic and relied on negotiation with the chiefs of the sitting and the region, using his informal connections, his authority and, if these were not enough, win them over. This worked for almost two years. However, at the end of 1994, despite his objections, the managers of a number of other passenger enterprises in the region decided to re-establish a single association Avtotrans, including state enterprises. The regional administration quickly supported their initiative and issued the appropriate decree. According to this document PATP loses the right of a legal subject and its own bank account. This did not suit the new director M—v at all. All his attempts to reach an agreement with the administration about preserving the independence of PATP had come to nothing. And so in the summer of

1995 a conference of the labour collective of PATP was convened, which was attended by press and TV journalists. The delegates gathered. The director appeared at the table on the platform and opened the proceedings. They immediately elected him president of the meeting. The enterprise lawyer explained the danger of losing independence. The director reinforced the arguments, and added some details. Then several workers and employees spoke. It became clear from their speeches that only one form of struggle remained, the strike. It was also obvious from the behaviour of the director that even if he had not been the initiator of the strike, he supported it completely. As president of the meeting he organised the vote on this question, not having said one critical word against the proposal. The conference unanimously called for the use of the strike threat, and a strike committee was elected. They proposed including the enterprise lawyer on the committee, but he explained that, as a representative of the administration, formally he could not be a member of the strike committee, but unofficially, of course, he would give all the help he could. Several subsequent interviews with leaders of the administration and of the trade union committee (the president of which had refused to organise the strike) did not leave any doubts: the real organiser of the strike action was the administration headed by the director.

SOCIAL STRUCTURE OF THE ENTERPRISE

Social-technological structure and its contradictions

Organisational structure and its dynamics

One of the foundations of the enterprise as an organisation is its functional-technical division of labour, logically following from the differentiation of productive functions and their assignment to particular subdivisions and to groups of employees with special knowledge, skills and experience of work in the particular social position. The technological division of labour entails social consequences, for the specialised subdivisions necessarily acquire specific interests (methods of social self-assertion), various groups of workers are distinguished by their wage levels, conditions and intensity of labour, their prestige and their influence on the process of administrative decision-making. As a result, the social-technological structure acquires the features of a hierarchy of ordered social disparity of status positions and groups of employees occupying those positions, whose interests are simultaneously united (the enterprise as a whole) and contradictory (the methods of social self-assertion do not coincide, sometimes competition in the distribution of resources arises).

The social-technological structure takes different forms in different enterprises, the differences depending on the branch and scale of production. However, its universal elements are:

- An administrative-managerial apparatus (management is not only a social but also a technological function, so the apparatus as a multidimensional group retains its privileges in both systems of stratification)
- Main production
- Auxiliary production

Table One: Organisational Structure of PATP (1 October, 1994)

Subdivision	Number of workers
Bus Column 1	172
Bus Column 2	169
Bus Column 3	63
Bus Column 4	89
Repair Mechanical Workshops	232
Administration	n.a.
Main power department	13
Construction section	39
Repair workers	3
Security	19
Bus station	12
Conductors	168
Fuel-lubricant materials department	13
Cash department	12
Hostel	1
Canteen	14
Communications Department	2
Central dispatching service	19

In PATP all the elements of this structure are present. All the bus columns and the taxi column are main production, the repair-mechanical workshops (RMM) are auxiliary.[2] In addition there aare a number of small auxiliary subdivisions (the canteen, the fuel-lubrication materials department and so on).

The character and scale of the enterprise determines a particular structure. From the end of the 1980s, when enterprises acquired a high degree of independence, their managements began to create structures corresponding to their idea of its optimal form although, certainly, they also had to take into account the position of bodies on which the enterprise depended financially. For PATP, these were the association and the city executive committee (later the city administration).

During the period of research there were some changes. In July 1990 column 5, servicing a suburban region 18 kilometres from the city, was made into an independent enterprise. In 1993 three columns were merged into two. In the course of privatisation the taxi drivers bought their column and set up an independent enterprise.

The administration of PATP retained its functional structure almost unchanged throughout the research period, its structure comprising the following elements:

- Director and his deputies
- Personnel department
- Accountant's department
- Planning department
- Wages department
- Operations department
- Production-technical department
- Material-technical supply department

In 1993–4 the new director, M—v, introduced some modifications in the organisation of the administration. He introduced the posts of shift foreman, technician for accounting for work time, technician for workshops, deputy head of the security department, deputy chief of column, technician for ecology (a job created for his daughter-in-law), production line foreman, engineer for servicing and introducing computers, and deputy directors for capital construction, for economics and commercial activity and for production. The posts of deputy

[2] For a detailed account of the structure of the Mechanical Repair Workshop see Marina Ilyina, op. cit.

director for social questions, for traffic safety and for operations were abolished.

Being part of one organisation, and having different status positions and interests, the functional subdivisions find themselves in contradictory relations to one another. They regularly run into the problem of having to share in the division of a single pie (the wages and materials funds, financial benefits and so on). In contemporary conditions, when delays in the payment of wages have become almost systematic and universal, contradictions and conflicts have begun to arise around the need to take turns to receive payment of wages, something unheard of in the past.

Contradictory relationships arise at the level of the subdivision as a whole and at the level of particular jobs. Economy of time and effort for one subdivision may turn out to cause problems and headaches for others (for example, poor quality repair), increasing demands from one side imply an intensification of labour and reduction of earnings for the other. Thus any enterprise has a whole bouquet of contradictions between its subdivisions, which in appropriate circumstances can turn into conflicts and lead to the disintegration of the enterprise (also a specially new phenomenon, connected with the fact that the fate of the enterprise and its subdivisions has come to be decided largely within the enterprise, and not in the Moscow ministries).

Table Two: Changes in total employment in the PATP collective

1.04.89	1490
1.01.92	1205
1.01.93	1207
1.10.94	1153
1995	1317

The main factor underlying the changing numbers employed has been changes in the organisational structure of PATP, particularly the departure of two large columns (a bus and the taxi column). The second factor is changing forms of work, so in 1994 the management sharply increased the number of conductors. In 1989 there were 36 conductors, January 1993 – 65, January 1994 – 57, January 1995 – 168. The introduction into the RMM of a new repair line led to an increase in the number of workers there from 195 in January 1994 to 232 by October of that year.

Some fluctuations in the number of bus drivers are caused by fluctuations in the number of working buses. The number of drivers fell as buses had to be taken out of service. However, nobody was sacked on these grounds. In the taxi column between 1991 and 1992 there was a sharp reduction in the number of automobiles (scrapping of old ones, resale of new ones) and the number of taxi drivers fell from 150 to 80 over the year.

Labour turnover increased substantially in the 1990s. In 1989 the turnover was 7 per cent, but even then 23 per cent of the labour force as a whole, and 50 per cent of the most highly qualified employees, expressed a desire to find another job, the main grievances being injustices in payment (24 per cent), dissatisfaction with the level of pay (20 per cent), bad working conditions (16 per cent), inconvenient work schedules (11 per cent), lack of prospects for improved living standards (10 per cent) and fluctuations in pay (10 per cent).

Labour turnover peaked in 1993 at 41 per cent, over half of the departures being accounted for, according to the official figures, by voluntary severance, and 10 per cent for disciplinary reasons. However, many workers who are induced to leave following disciplinary violations are recorded as voluntary severance. The deepening economic crisis has meant that work in passenger transport appears more secure than work in many other industries, so the personnel department can be more choosy whom it employs. As the chief of the personnel department explained in 1994:

> In the past we would take on almost anyone. Now there is almost a competition for jobs. Now people with high skill grades come to us from other factories, there are quite a few people with middle and higher special education.

The highest levels of turnover are found amongst the lower-paid categories of workers: especially the repair workers and conductors. Many people are attracted to the latter job from low-paid jobs in other enterprises, but soon find that they cannot stand the high level of stress involved in the work. Forty-five per cent of the repair workers and over 90 per cent of the conductors left over 1993, while only 16 per cent of the elite drivers in column one left, as against almost a third in columns two and four. With such a high level of turnover the reduction in the number of drivers is regulated by reductions in the recruitment of new workers to vacant posts.

Main and auxiliary production

The division of production into main and auxiliary has not only a technological but also a social character. The management of an enterprise, and in the past the chiefs of the central departments, when thinking about the structure of the enterprise, always proceeded from the idea that the fate of the enterprise is decided by its main production. As a result there is an administrative hierarchy of production, which is manifested in levels of payment, working conditions, prestige and personnel selection.

In PATP there are several levels of social-technological stratification. At the same time each of these blocks has an internal stratification. Thus the main indicator of stratification is the degree of significance of the subdivision for the fulfilment of the functions of the enterprise. As a result of this the various departments of the administration do not have a uniform social status.

The functions of the bus columns are attached to the routes that they serve. The routes are distinguished by their degree of importance for the city. So, the routes which carry the largest number of passengers and are most important for the population of the city are those to which the city authorities pay the most attention. This work imposes the greatest pressure on the driver, with the largest number of passengers on the busiest streets in the city. Therefore the management of the enterprise puts the most productive buses on these routes, the Ikarus buses imported from Hungary. These buses are much more comfortable for the driver, but on the other hand they are much more capacious, longer, requiring more care and attention and more experience on the part of the driver. All the new equipment is directed first of all to these routes, which improve working conditions and efficiency. These drivers are the best paid and enjoy the highest prestige. Thus column one, working on the most responsible routes with the best equipment, was always the elite column, and was universally recognised as such. On less responsible routes, with fewer passengers, the work is easier, but the equipment is worse and productivity lower, so the pay of the columns working these routes is lower and their work less prestigious. In 1989 the scale pay of an Ikarus driver was 1.04 roubles an hour, but a driver of a LIAZ bus (a smaller and less comfortable Soviet bus) received 0.96 roubles. These differences were not large, but they had great symbolic significance. The proportions remained in subsequent years, despite rapid inflation.

The RMM is at the bottom of the social-technological hierarchy.

Here the workers appear contradictory. The repair worker is a person who understands how to repair various types of bus, who has higher technical skills than the bus driver (it is obviously easier to learn to drive a bus than to repair it), and who works in more harmful conditions (the fumes are bad). But nobody is in a hurry to work here and every attempt to work out a payment system which would force the repairmen to run around in circles has come to nothing. It is not uncommon for the workers to be tipsy. Here is the largest concentration of drunkards and absentees. This is where drivers are banished for a shorter or longer period of time as a punishment for disciplinary offences. In PATP there is even an expression, 'to be put on the broom', which means to send a driver for a certain period to do auxiliary work, including cleaning, in the repair mechanical workshops where the pay and prestige are lower.

The different status positions of the workers of main and auxiliary production give rise to social tension. The repair workers, whose work is no less heavy and responsible than that of the drivers, grumble amongst themselves about the injustice of their position. They secretly envy the drivers, who work in white shirts and rake in the money. These complaints are not usually expressed face to face (what is the point of saying anything to the drivers? They cannot do anything about it). However, whenever the drivers take their buses in for repair they are given every opportunity of sensing on whom the fate of the enterprise and their own pay depends. Here the situation forces him to smile at the mechanic, even if he is in the hands of a drunken layabout. Even the dashing taxi drivers, who show no fear in expressing their opinions to the director, instinctively speak about the repairmen in a lowered voice, and some simply walk away from the conversation. However, amongst themselves the drivers have no doubt about their superiority as an elite over the repair workers. Only occasionally do they express their feelings openly in an emotional exchange of views, expressed in obscene language, if their repair is unduly delayed.

The social tension between workers in main and auxiliary production is directly derived from the distinction in their status (working conditions, pay and so on). But the main, the deepest, reason is that their objective interests are distinct and frequently contrary. A piece-rate worker tries to complete the repair in the shortest time possible, neglecting the quality of the repair, since his pay depends on it, but a worker on time-wages has an objectively different point of view of the situation. In many enterprises they try to connect the pay of repair workers with the speed and the quality of their work (for example, the pay of a fitter is related to the percentage of time the buses or trucks are operational). However, it is far from always possible to do this. Sometimes achieving a uniformity of interests in one section leads to a complete difference of interests with another.

The market within the enterprise

Total state appropriation of the means of production and the pervasiveness of state control are the main features of production in state socialist society. However, any totality is closer to utopia than to reality. Extensive and deep control turned out to be impossible. While the system of motivation of labour was based on the idea of total control (Lenin: 'socialism is record-keeping and control'), there were no internal motives to work better. Therefore private interests penetrated every pore of state socialism, introducing an essentially different logic into production, the anarchy of the shadow economy. One of the most important manifestations of this process has become the covert privatisation of the state means of production.

The participation of hired workers in covert privatisation was determined by their place in the stratification of administrative power, their membership of this or that industrial group. At each layer there were opportunities to participate in covert privatisation. One of the forms of covert privatisation was the temporary use of public means of production for private use, for example the production of goods or services on the side. This phenomenon was widespread in motor transport enterprises. On the one hand, the drivers would covertly use the vehicle assigned to them for work on the side for a part of the working day. In PATP this was only really possible for the taxi drivers, but the pay of the bus drivers was related to the work done, so they were also interested in minimising the stoppages, although the force of this interest was not so strong as that of the taxi drivers. Naturally, the taxi drivers behaved as though they were the real owners of their vehicles, so their private interest had a clear and direct manifestation.

In the repair shops a connection was established between the half-free driver and the repair mechanic paid a salary according to the normal system of the public sector. The mechanic did not have, and could not have, as great an interest in the rapid and high quality repair of the automobile as did the driver, who was in a hurry to get back on the job. Thus, inside the state enterprise there was a contradictory connection between the state and the private sector. The private shadow sector resolved this contradiction by drawing the workers of the state system into shadow economic relations. The drivers paid from their own pockets for the repairs to be carried out speedily and to a high quality.

Such market relationships were very highly developed in the taxi park, one of the most market-oriented parts of the Soviet economy. 'Would it be possible to get an automobile repaired without paying extra, and how large were these extortions?' we asked a veteran taxi driver:

> I do not think that these were extortions, he replied. In our state we live as we can. In the 1980s the drivers earned 220 roubles and the repair workers altogether earned only 70. But the repair worker's job is much more difficult ... Well, the result was that people earned a bit extra. Everybody did it. We understood this and so no real conflicts arose. We always used to hand over a few kopecks. Well, if you don't like it – then you just have to wait your turn.
> Of course, you could get it done without paying extra, confirmed another veteran, well you knew all the lads. But you sometimes give them a bit extra, and everything is OK.

> Maybe, added the taxi driver Mikhail, if you had a lot of time and were in no hurry to get anywhere. But really – wait your turn! You do not want to wait – so you reach an agreement with the repair worker yourself.

In especially market-oriented parts of the state sector (such as the taxi park) the interests of the workers in the results of their labour were so great that they invested their own money in obtaining tools and parts. As a result covert privatisation acquired a new colouring: in practice a mixed form of property arose.

We asked several experienced taxi drivers whether they had had to buy parts themselves before the transfer to leasehold. 'Of course', said Nikolai, 'I always bought them myself, who else would do so? Who apart from me was concerned?'

'Yes', says Viktor, 'I regularly bought parts myself. You could never find them in our enterprise. Nobody was interested in your problems.'

In the period of perestroika leasehold relations began to be introduced into some areas of production. This partially legalised the market mechanism in the workplace. Money-commodity relations began to penetrate deeper into the links in the technological chain. 'How did the transfer to leasehold affect the relations between the drivers and the repair service?' 'Very much', answered Nikolai.

> In the first place the behaviour of the drivers themselves changed. You see, in the past, if a particular part was worn out, the driver threw it away and took a new one from the warehouse. With leasing we had to pay for everything, and the driver thought one hundred times: is it worth changing the part, or would it be better to pay a bit to get it repaired.

'So how much did you invest in your automobile from your own pocket? Did the enterprise compensate you for these payments?'

'It is difficult to say how much I have invested in it', answered Nikolai:

> According to the agreements in 1989 and 1992 the administration was obliged to ensure that the machines were technically serviceable and to ensure their maintenance. But who is concerned about our problems, apart from us? In practice the administration partially compensated us for our expenses. After you had bought a part in a state shop you could present the receipt and they would pay you. But by no means everything could be found in the state trading system, so you had to buy things privately, and then, obviously, you did not have a receipt.

'How many roubles did I invest? Well I feel that it is completely mine', asserted Viktor, 'only the bare body belongs to the enterprise.'

'Yes', confirmed Mikhail, 'the whole thing, apart from the body, has been bought with my money.'

The attitude of the workers to official privatisation was determined to a considerable degree by the extent to which covert privatisation had taken place. When the taxi column was put up for sale by auction the taxi drivers took an unequivocal position: 'We will not allow anybody to buy us out.' 'How will you be able to prevent it, if competitors pay more?' 'We have already invested so much money in these automobiles that they are almost ours. But if it happens as you say, then we would do better to pour acid all over the Volga. But we simply will not allow it', said one of the drivers.

At a deeper level the privatisation of the drivers' jobs provoked as a corresponding reaction a strengthening of the undeclared process of privatisation of the fitters' jobs. This led to a further crystallisation of market contradictions between these two categories of worker. As in the Soviet market as a whole, here an enormous role was played by the factor of monopolism: if the repair workers monopolise the local market for parts and servicing, then their market situation in relation to the driver-customers would be considerably strengthened. With the appearance of competitive repair services the market situation of the taxi drivers would be considerably strengthened.

The relationship to this internal market does not by any means always develop simply, but the drivers try not to wash their dirty linen in public and speak about their strongly felt dependence on the repair workers as something they are used to. Certainly there are other repair workshops in the city where the automobiles can be taken for small repairs. But these workshops are not serious competitors in the repair of the Volgas, so the drivers have no choice but to accept the fitters' terms, terms which are often nothing less than extortionate.

The relation of the taxi drivers and the bus drivers to the repair workers has always been different. While the taxi drivers have always had a personal and vital interest in minimising the time their automobiles are off the road, the bus drivers have never had such a strong material interest, since they only have a chance to work on the side outside the city. Thus they have a more cool attitude to the pace of repair and do not have a high market demand for the services of the repair workers. Certainly they sometimes pay for a speedy repair with a bottle of vodka, but only if speed is necessary.

Separatism of the most profitable divisions

The social system is made up of elements of various degrees of vitality and efficiency. Their contribution to the reproduction and development of the system is not identical. Apart from this, the insertion of an element into the system implies that it works not only for itself, but also for the system of which it is a part. The functioning of any system includes the process of redistribution of resources, in two main directions. First, for the general needs of the system, to maintain systemic qualities (for example, management bodies). Second, to maintain the weaker elements, since the reliability of the system is determined by the reliability of its weakest link, so that the failure of a weak but important element can lead to the breakdown of the whole system. For example, an enterprise may be brought to a standstill as a result of a stoppage of one part of the technological cycle. Since the weak elements of a social system usually carry out dependent functions, the burden of maintaining the system falls on its strongest elements.

This raises the problem of maintaining the interest of the strong elements in remaining a part of the system. In an authoritarian system this can be resolved simply by the force of compulsion, when objective interests are simply ignored. Moreover, the strong element may be interested in this system if it is given a controlling position and subordinates the activity of the whole social system to its own needs. In the opposite situation, the objective interests of the most effective element are increasingly clearly expressed in separatist tendencies.

In a passenger transport enterprise the taxi column was always the only profitable subdivision. All the other columns were planned lossmakers, depending on regular subsidies. Only the taxi drivers brought in profits. This gave them the feeling that they supported everything, that they were exploited, that if they separated then their life would be much better. Even during our first research in the enterprise in 1989 the taxi drivers were already clearly inclined to separatism, although it is more than likely that they had been so inclined from the very beginning, from the moment at the beginning of the 1970s when the taxi park lost its independence and became part of the larger passenger transport enterprise.

The form of the taxi drivers' separatism changes with the situation. They struggled for leasehold, for transforming the column into an independent municipal enterprise. When mass privatisation began, the taxi drivers decided that the best way out was to buy their enterprise. In 1993 the taxi drivers' collective bought their enterprise at auction against competition from two other firms and left PATP, although they retain a leasehold relationship with the latter, leasing part of the garage, workshops and offices.

STRATIFICATION OF ADMINISTRATIVE POWER

Contradictory interests

The basis of any social organisation is the stratification of administrative power. In other words, the organisation is divided into managers and managed, who are in turn divided internally into strata which have different degrees of authority.

The status positions of workers and management employees are not only different, but are in general counterposed to one another. This cannot but lead to contradictory interests and social tensions. The immediate functions of many management employees are related to their monitoring the observance by the workers of a large number, sometimes an indefinite number, of norms. The observation of these norms is inconvenient for the workers, it leads to an additional burden of work, so it is quite natural that they should prefer to ignore them. The management employees identify these violations and punish the workers, primarily by depriving them of a part of their bonus.

Role of education

The stratification of administrative power is to a considerable extent correlated with stratification by level of education, although it does not completely coincide. There are quite a few people in the administration without higher education (although not so many in key posts). At the same time, quite a few of the drivers are graduates of institutes of middle special education (*tekhnikum*), which gives them the right to occupy a position as an ITR.

Table Three: Stratification and education (per cent, 1 April 1989)

	Number	Higher	Middle	Middle Special	Incomplete Middle Special
ITR and office workers	162	12.3	27.2	35.2	25.3
Workers	1328	0.4	51.3	8.6	39.8

These figures were last collected in 1989. In the past they were collected on the orders of the territorial Party bodies, monitoring the growth of the educational level of the labour force. At the level of middle management there is not much difference between workers and managers in the level of education, since both section chiefs and quite a few workers have middle special education. Chiefs of columns are usually former drivers, and the experienced drivers know that they are qualified to be a chief of column, so relate to the latter on the basis of some equality. The relatively high educational level of the labour force equally underpins its scepticism regarding management as a whole, especially as the transition to a market economy has devalued much of the training, especially in the sphere of economics, which managers had obtained before 1990.

Pay as an indicator of the stratification of administrative power

One of the most important indicators of social status is the level of pay. In state-monopoly socialist society the official ideology in this sphere propagated the principle 'from each according to his ability, to each according to his labour'. Thus it was explained that the labour of the manager is more complex, so he needs a higher salary. However, at the same time distribution took account of the demands of the classics (Marx, Lenin), connecting the pay of managers and the pay of skilled workers and emphasising that they must be equal. And externally this approach was adhered to. The salary of the secretary of the local Party committee or the director of the factory was comparable to the pay of a skilled worker. PATP could not be an exception to this.

However, there were a lot of ruses to be found in the system of payment. Inspection of records in the department of labour and wages in 1989 allowed us to see evidence of some of them (such an opportunity did not recur).

The main hidden mechanism of pay differentiation was the bonus. The bonuses of the workers and the apparatus were basically drawn from different sources. Thus, the workers received theirs from the wages fund, made up of 51 per cent of the enterprise's income. The apparatus received its bonus from the material incentive fund.

The most solid bonuses, unrelated to the performance of the enterprise, were those received by the director and his deputies. Thus, in 1988 the director received 1,373 roubles in various bonuses, and his four deputies received 1,694, 1,243, 1,023 and 1,186 roubles, while the remaining ITR received 812 roubles. The head of the department of labour and wages could not explain what these bonuses had been awarded for.

The payment system for the workers was constantly being modified in its details, but always remained extremely confused. As a result most of the workers had little idea of the reason for fluctuations in their wages, and this caused much barely concealed irritation. Our survey in 1989 found that only 19 per cent of the workers felt that they had a good understanding of how pay was calculated. Thirty two per cent considered the level of their information to be satisfactory, and 49 per cent as bad. Alongside this, we found fundamental differences in the understanding of the system on the part of workers and of the apparatus. Thus 87 per cent of managers and an identical proportion of specialists considered their information to be good or satisfactory, while only 42 per cent of drivers and 37 per cent of those in auxiliary departments felt the same.

The complex and confused system of calculating wages and bonuses included a mass of indicators according to which the workers' labour was evaluated. To keep an eye on all of them was extraordinarily difficult. Every oversight meant a reduction by a particular percentage or loss of bonus. Thus, in March 1989 a 'quality system' was introduced. Experts openly recognised that the main aim was to save money from the wages fund. The secretary of the Party committee explained: 'It is only necessary for the accounts department, where they have a bonus for reducing expenditure on wages'. The head of the department of labour and wages added that the enterprise was overspending its wage bill and the quality system had been introduced to prevent this. It aroused discontent on the part of the workers. Informal leaders ('trouble makers', in the words of the administration) incited the workers to put their complaints to the court.

Since then, changes in the system of payment and bonuses have been introduced repeatedly. Their general aim remains always the same, to reduce expenditure on wages. From time to time this provokes renewed friction between workers and management.

Any system of pay is a lever of power. Power is the ability of the subject of managerial relations to take decisions which the objects of management have obligatorily to carry out, regardless of their own wishes. The administration exerts its authority over the collective by influencing the level of pay, which is closely related to the willingness of the drivers to be subject to orders. The more confused is the system of pay, the more complicated it is, the more levers the administration has to punish the undisciplined and the disobedient. Thus, what is really important is not the observation of all of the large number of norms, but the general willingness of the drivers to be subject to them. With so many norms virtually every driver violates them to a greater or lesser extent, but the administration can take careful note and react with retaliatory sanctions, or can close its eyes to small and casual infringements. The carefulness of control also appears as a lever of power.

Commercial secrets

Political freedom has made the workers less compliant than in the years of 'developed socialism', and the economic crisis has angered them. As a result the game of self-management became dangerous for the administration. The orientation to self-management was thrown out at the same time as the liquidation of the leading role of the CPSU in the political system of the country.[3] A course was steered for the creation of a capitalist economy, resting on a class of owners who had emerged from the technocrats. The winding up of all those bodies which bore the imprint of ideas of self-management has naturally resulted in a radical change in the dissemination of information in enterprises. Meetings of workers have almost everywhere ceased to take place, while shareholders' meetings in privatised companies happen rarely and are carefully organised. The collectives find themselves in an information vacuum. A new concept, the 'commercial secret', never heard of before, has universally entered everyday use.

The interests of the bosses, pushing for the monopolisation of managerial information, are diverse. The most important group of reasons are related to a desire to increase the manageability of the collective. In other words, it puts the worker in a situation in which he cannot 'interfere in his own affairs', 'swing his rights' before management.

Interest in such a monopolisation significantly increases if the bosses have something to conceal. Most frequently this is a distribution of pay which is unjust and difficult to explain. Commercial secrets are especially important where management is engaged in the *prikhvatisatsia* ['grabbing'] of state property, trying to enrich themselves by every legal and illegal method. Then superfluous ears and eyes are completely undesirable.

PATP is much less secretive than many other enterprises. Management is very ready to describe the production situation to outsiders. The trade union committee has always had good access to management information. However, this is the result of several factors. First, PATP has not been through privatisation, and property has not been divided (a process which is the strongest stimulus to secrecy). Attempts of the administration between 1990 and 1993 to impose secrecy on information concerning the salary of chiefs and sales of the property of the enterprise met with a powerful reaction from the

[3] In 1989 well over three quarters of those questioned in the collective of PATP who had a view on the matter believed that all managers from the director to brigadiers should be elected. Nevertheless, the official organ of self-management, the Labour Collective Council (STK) was already moribund when the new director arrived in 1990.

collective and the trade union committee. The main difference between PATP and the majority of enterprises, the presence of a militant collective and trade union committee, is a specific feature of this enterprise excluding it from the process of imposing secrecy.

Relation of workers to the administration

Workers and the administration in any enterprise execute rather different social roles so that their interests in many respects appear opposed. The main function of management, the control of the work of the workers, contradicts the interests of the latter and meets if not hostile at least negative reactions. Ever since we first visited PATP we have had the impression of an administration on the 3rd and 4th floors of the four storey main building of PATP, sitting as in a besieged fortress, surrounded by an unfriendly and often almost hostile mass of workers living in the garages and workshops around.

The strongest of these contradictions was encountered in the first phase of the research. Subsequently the emotionally negative attitude of workers to the administration began to change gradually into a sober appreciation of the need for managers. Our monitoring of other enterprises in various branches of production shows the same tendency. This can be most clearly observed in the coal mining industry, where the antagonism between workers and the administration was extremely strong at the end of the 1980s. What was, and is, the strongest reproach addressed by the workers to the administration?

> Up there, says a bus driver, there are an awful lot of people. They sit and do nothing. … I think the situation in the departments is bad, but in the accounts department there are far too many people. We could keep only half of them.

> There are too many ITR. They all sit around and drink tea.

> If you get rid of 70 per cent of the administration, the rest will work better … Ten years ago there were half as many.

> – There are too many people up there.
> – Where in particular?
> – I don't know. I hardly ever go there.

Middle management

Middle management comprises the heads of columns, chiefs of workshops and foremen. This link in the management chain has a particular status: the management of the enterprise puts pressure on them from above, demanding a strengthening of discipline, increase in labour productivity and so on, while the workers press them from the opposite direction. As a result, management decisions undergo a significant deformation in the immediate contact between management and workers in the shop: their fulfilment depends on the results of a social struggle and a process of negotiation between the workers and middle management.

As a result of this the workers are interested above all in seeing a person with whom they can find a common language in the post of chief of column. The higher levels of the administration understand that in reality the fate of management is decided at this level and try to put in these positions people who will not be pliable in the face of pressure from the workers.

Column one is headed by G—ko, a former driver in this column. He easily found a common language with the drivers, and they with him. The most obstinate drivers are to be found in this column, causing a lot of anxiety on the part of the administration. In the opinion of the director, the chief of the column spoiled his drivers and was not able to impose normal discipline. Eventually the director ordered the merger of the first and third columns, and offered the post of chief to the head of the small third column. The drivers of the first column demanded the return of their chief, and threatened to strike. However, G – to, having been offered a quieter but just as well-paid post in the administration, refused to return to his former post and the conflict was settled. The drivers were still dissatisfied, but there was already no way out.

Workers and the lower levels of the administration

The lowest layer of the administration of the enterprise includes two main categories: 1) auxiliary technical staff (typists, couriers and so on); and 2) status positions connected with the monitoring of the activity of the workers and the taking of the simplest management decisions at the operational level (dispatchers, account-keepers, time-keepers and so on). The first category has little to do with the workers, so direct contradictions do not arise in their work. However, there is a widespread psychological alienation, distrust, and sometimes hostility towards them among the workers.

The second category is located on the hottest line of the relationship between the workers and the management apparatus. On the one hand, their status position gives them a definite power over the workers, allowing them to influence the intensity of their labour and their pay. The conditions of their labour are more comfortable, which is an important factor in forming the psychological alienation, the division into 'us' (eternally dirty, working in dirt and cold) and 'them' (clean, drinking tea in warmth and cosiness). But at the same time the pay of this category of management is usually significantly lower than that of the workers. Psychologically their labour is often clearly more uncomfortable, for the work involves constant nervous tension, forcing the workers to do what they do not want, but having only the minimum of power to do this.

Objectively the function of this level of management employees puts them in a contradictory relation to the interests of the workers. Since their power and authority is very limited, the pressure from below on the dispatchers and various controllers is very significant. This is considerably reinforced by the fact that these posts are filled, as a rule, by women. Traditional male arrogance in relation to women is transferred into the sphere of service relationships. In turn the woman, having acquired her cultural norms in childhood, impregnated with ideas of male domination, does not feel comfortable in a position in which she has to give orders to men. All this creates a cultural environment in which pressure from below on the lowest level of the management apparatus proves to be very successful. Here rough pressure, supplemented with threats, is interwoven with flirtation and the presentation of gifts. This leads to a situation in which the accounting and control function is deformed into the mere collection of information. This happens particularly clearly in those spheres of production in which it is difficult to control the controller.

The lowest level of the apparatus is between the hammer and the anvil. Middle and higher management demand that they carry out their functions diligently, but they are not in a position to resist the pressure from below. As a consequence at the intersection of the two groups of the labour collective a sphere of compromise is formed, in which both sides negotiate, moving towards one another. Thus, in the end, the process of negotiation comes down to personal interests. The demands on the workers are reduced.

Since it is extremely difficult to combine the responsibilities of the post of controlling the workers with the desire to live in peace and friendship with the object of control, the sphere of relations between workers and this stratum of the apparatus is marked by conflict. Here the dispatcher or controller has constantly to balance the risk of falling into disfavour in the face of his or her own superior and the fear of engaging in conflict with the workers.

As an example of the problems of this group we can take the case of the dispatchers. There is a central dispatching service, whose function is to control the observation of the schedule by the buses. Thus the dispatcher not only gathers information concerning the passage of each bus past the control points, but also has power over the driver: reporting upwards information about infringements of the schedule entails negative sanctions. Moreover, the dispatcher, in the case of any kind of interruption to the schedule (for example, the breakdown of a bus), can assign a driver from another route to this line, that is an available power function. In such cases it is not uncommon to have to overcome the resistance of the driver, who may not want to take over the offered route for one reason or another.

If the dispatcher identifies an infringement by the driver, and reports this to management, the driver can lose his bonus. But if the dispatcher conceals such information, and this becomes known to management, the dispatcher becomes subject to similar sanctions. Thus the status positions of the dispatcher and the driver are such that in the process of control they are counterposed if the driver violates the regulations. Such an antagonistic opposition of objective interests arises only in the case of a serious incident which it is impossible to conceal.

In the normal course of her work the dispatcher has all kinds of ways of covering up the violations of the drivers. Thus her actions are not dictated rigidly by the regulations which prescribe her duties, but are largely the result of the personal relations which exist between her and a particular driver. These official-personal relations, in the last analysis, derive from the status positions. Thus, from time to time a dispatcher may have to assign a driver to another route which is not attractive to him. The driver has all sorts of ways of getting out of this, aggravating the situation, using the roughest language. Thus one driver, a veteran of the Afghan war, was rather free in his choice of language and was so resolute in rejecting every encroachment of the dispatchers on his freedom, that he even had to be sacked. The authority of the dispatcher is much too limited to be able to demand unquestioning subordination. However, such a situational (short-term) conflict is remembered. And if one fine day the driver commits even a trivial violation, what will happen depends on the dispatcher: whether she strictly follows the letter of the regulations, or acts humanely. What the dispatcher chooses to do will depend on how that particular driver has used such freedom in his relations with the dispatcher in the past. Thus the dispatcher may assign an unpleasant or intractable driver to the difficult routes more often than others, provoking him into conflict and disciplinary violations. The clever driver tries to maintain good relations with the dispatcher. That is not very difficult, and it makes life easier.

The dispatchers are mostly women between 30 and 40 years old, although there are also some girls straight out of school and some pensioners. Their pay is substantially less than that of the drivers. The work requires no special education or even much training on the job. Its prestige is very low. At the same time the control functions of the dispatcher make the position an important one for the drivers. As a result the dispatcher becomes an object of pressure from their side. Some, using the fact that the dispatchers are women, try to negotiate with them from a position of strength. Others try to find a common language with them, or at least to establish good relations with them. On the various holidays the dispatchers receive small presents, one from one driver, another from another. The young women become the object of particularly close attention from the drivers. Naturally relationships sometimes extend beyond work, even from time to time resulting in marriage. Such an interweaving of family and work relations cannot but have an impact on work: the husband is in a privileged position, and under the protection of his wife the dispatcher. One conflict even arose on this basis: one driver, whose wife was a dispatcher, violated the regulations and another dispatcher reported him, provoking a very strong negative reaction on the part of his wife.

When the drivers touch on the popular theme of the surplus of managers, they specify first of all the lowest level of the administration, since these are the people whose work they know best, which is carried out in their full view:

> There is no point in having controllers. They only need to keep 3–4 people.
>
> Who is surplus here? The controllers on the line. I myself worked in their service as a driver of 'Rafik'. They sit in the car, they loaf about, fishing out stopped buses … I cannot say anything about the work of the department – I have had nothing to do with it.

Leasing of jobs

A logical continuation of the tendency to covert privatisation in a small number of enterprises at the end of the 1980s was the leasing by workers of their jobs. This happened in the clearest form in motor transport enterprises. Having understood that it was pointless and extremely costly in time and effort to struggle against covert privatisation, the enterprise administration grabbed at the opportunity opened by perestroika to abandon the detailed control of their employees and to confine themselves to collecting rent from them.

In the taxi column the drivers had waged a long struggle with the chiefs of the enterprise to transfer to leasehold. In 1989 one taxi driver described the situation thus:

> We have literally been at war over leasehold. But the head of the planning department said 'No!' She is the most important person here. The director is more concerned with his pig-sties and building housing. Everything that we proposed was rejected. At last we reached agreement. From 1 March 1989 we transferred to leasehold on their crushing terms.
>
> The project was developed by one of the managers of the association on the basis of a proposal which he had worked out by a Leningrad economist. The taxi drivers had a plan: to bring in 911 roubles per month. The rent payment was 571 roubles.
>
> The rest was supposedly mine, said the indignant taxi driver, but from that 93 roubles goes for fuel, 23 roubles for rubber; plus check-ups, repairs, 20–30 roubles. That leaves 204 roubles. But this is less than I got under the previous system. We have to work on the price-list: 5 roubles per hour.

'So why did you agree to leave the old system and transfer to the new one?', we asked him.

> In the new conditions I preserve my nerves and my health. There is not the old race for the plan. You have paid back the money, and you work as you want. There is no compulsory regime: you work when you want.

The taxi drivers were indignant at having to pay such high rent. According to their calculations the old leased automobiles cost far less than they were paying. Then the management of PATP explained that, apart from the rent, this sum included overhead charges for the support of the apparatus of the enterprise. This argument only poured oil on the flames:

> With the transition to leasehold I drive into the garage once in a month,

> complained one driver. We do not need the apparatus for our work. It should be cut. They do nothing for us. I do not use their services. It is enough for us to have a director, chief accountant and good supply storekeeper. We do not need any more. Now there is a mass of people in the offices, but for even the most trifling matter you have to spend all day, when my job is to earn money.

Twenty-six drivers with 14 Volga automobiles transferred to leasehold from 1 March 1989. The rest were afraid ('you have to pay for everything, it is terrible') and decided to bide their time.

With the transfer to leasehold in the taxi column the taxi drivers received one Volga automobile between two drivers put at their complete disposal. They had received the freedom of which they had always dreamed. Their relations to PATP were reduced to the payment of rent. At the end of November 1992, in the final stage of the existence of this column, each driver had to pay the enterprise 7,469 roubles a month, of which 3,544 roubles was value-added tax; 101 roubles amortisation; 1,468 roubles overhead charges (to pay for management services); 504 roubles target profit of the enterprise; 450 roubles reserve for vacations. On top of this the drivers had to pay from their own pockets for fuel and to buy spare parts.

This has transformed the drivers in practice into the owners of the means of production. This was clearly reflected in their attitudes to everything which concerned the rights to control and manage their activity. Any encroachment on their freedom and right to dispose of production assets has provoked a pained response.

Autonomy of the administration and '*prikhvatisatsia*'

The delegation of administrative authority to the managers of the enterprise led to their virtually complete economic independence from state bodies. This gave rise to a paradox: a state enterprise, independent of a state which had lost the means of managing its property. This sharply strengthened the process of growing chaos in the economy.

The delegation of administrative rights from above did not coincide with privatisation. The directors received uncontrolled power, but remained salaried employees, with no interest in increasing the assets of the enterprise. Thus they used their freedom from control to enrich themselves rapidly by means of *prikhvatisatsia* and increase their salaries up to a level restricted only by the tax system. This gave rise to a new paradox: enterprises were destroyed, managed by rapidly enriched directors. The resale of the assets of the enterprise at knock-down prices to their own commercial structures became a universal phenomenon. Thus the analysis of *prikhvatisatsia* is first an object of crime detection, and only then of sociological research.

Since the law enforcement agencies have never shown any special interest in these phenomena, many facts about *prikhvatisatsia* can only be interpreted as hypotheses. Thus, many workers in the motor transport enterprise are convinced that their former director was actively engaged in *prikhvatisatsia*. They accuse him of having sold a large number of Volgas at give away prices into the private hands of outsiders, that he also sold a motorised cafe for a song and so on. He had done nothing illegal: he had sold equipment for the proper price, its residual cost, but nothing was said in the relevant legislation about rampant inflation which made such a price ridiculous. The director's opponents powerlessly asked:

> Do you suppose that an intelligent person would simply sell the equipment to outsiders at a knock-down price, way below the market price? Of course not. He clearly had something to do with it, but if there is no crime there is no thief.

But the director also had a convincing argument. These deals were conducted in conditions in which the rouble had already ceased to function, but when it was still impossible to sell any of the assets for market prices. The enterprise had to build, to modernise, and it did so through barter deals: the automobiles at residual cost in exchange for construction services at state prices.

> Who was going to build the repair shop at that time with their own materials? (Said the director in an interview.) I had to sell the automobiles to give an incentive to the builders... You cannot judge actions in 1991 from the situation in 1992, when the rouble was already working and you could buy and sell what you wanted at market prices.

It is already impossible to prove what really happened, although in this research, where the enterprise is anonymous, it is not so important. The main thing is that such a mode of activity of the director was potentially possible, and if the director's own account is true, his thoughtful action would have only been for moral reasons, in contradiction with the director's own material interests. And once such a means of enrichment of the director becomes possible (as was confirmed, without any fingers being pointed, by various experts, including the director himself), then it cannot but be put into practice.

Rational economic behaviour cannot, as practice shows, be restrained on a significant scale by moral restrictions. Moreover, in many enterprises one can hear similar stories, supported by a large amount of evidence.

The reaction of the collective to the director's initiative was as varied as it could be, covering the spectrum from complete calm and indifference, on the one hand, to the organisation of a vote of confidence with a view to dismissing the director, on the other. The choice of variant depended on a series of factors. For the alienated worker: 'to hell with it all'; 'they haven't stolen anything of mine'. But if the director infringes the rights of a collective with a real chance of privatisation, such as the taxi drivers, the reaction is very sharp. The other factor determining the reaction is the character of the organised representation of the collective. If the trade union committee is an appendage of the administration, then a collective reaction is improbable. But if the trade union committee has become an accurate expression of the interests of the workers and organiser of their activity, then an organised and active opposition to *prikhvatisatsia* is very likely. Then even the suspicion of its existence can play a fatal role for the director.

Workers – co-owners of state property and the director's *prikhvatisatsia*

In the course of *prikhvatisatsia* the workers, having really or spontaneously become co-owners of their jobs, can no longer react to the director's arbitrariness as apathetically as alienated workers. In a number of cases, nobody's state property became the object of a struggle between management and workers. Precisely this type of conflict was seen in the case of the taxi column. In PATP the director, leaning on the support of the chief of the taxi column, began quietly to sell off the Volgas, reducing the number in the column from 80 to 42. Some of these were written off as worn out, but a significant proportion were sold on the side. The taxi drivers were extremely interested in buying these automobiles at reduced prices. Three of the drivers managed to buy their automobiles at prices which were, for those times, rather high: 68,000, 40,000 and 38,000 roubles. But most of them were sold to outsiders at ridiculously low prices, 1,500 to 2,000 roubles. This led to extreme indignation on the part of the taxi drivers, who saw the actions of the director as an encroachment on their rights.

The chief of the column at first tried to convince the workers that he had nothing to do with these deals, but witnesses were found who had seen him taking the numbers off the automobiles which had been sold. The drivers collected the evidence which, from their point of view, proved the wrong-doing of the director and handed it over to the investigators. But the investigation revealed nothing criminal. This did not surprise the drivers, since some of the spare parts had been sold by one of the managers to the city police.

The re-sale by the director of PATP of the taxi column's automobiles with the knowledge and participation of their chief aroused open indignation on the part of the taxi drivers. On 7 September 1992 all the automobiles of the column were driven to the main square of the city, and drawn up in front of the building of the Council of Ministers and the Supreme Soviet. The drivers insisted that they would stay there until the sale of the automobiles by the director was stopped. It is very difficult to discover precisely how this strike took place. All those who were interviewed insisted that it was a common spontaneous action, which was only given organisational form by the shop committee of the trade union.

Representatives of the republican bodies of power entered into negotiations with representatives of the taxi drivers. The remaining strikers waited on the square for the outcome of the negotiations, sitting in their Volgas. In the end the republican chiefs agreed that the demands of the taxi drivers were legitimate. The director was forced to cancel the orders to sell the automobiles.

This was a victory for the taxi drivers. However, after the conclusion of the negotiations they were approached by the police, who accused them of breaking the traffic regulations (there is a no entry sign at the entrance to the square). The drivers were fined.

GENDER STRUCTURE

In PATP there is a clear gender division of labour, with a sharp division between men's and women's jobs. Certainly, one can observe movement across the established limits of gender differentiation throughout the period of our research, but only as an exception.

At the beginning of 1994, 298 women worked in PATP, but in October there were around 400. Such a sharp increase was related to the recruitment of a large number of conductors. This profession was always considered in the USSR to be especially female. However, recently in PATP the salary of conductors has increased considerably, reflecting the aspiration of management to attract people to this difficult job through which they hope to increase the revenue from the buses. The parallel fall of real wages in other enterprises in the city led some men to ignore the traditionally female character of this occupation. A small number of male conductors has appeared.

In the view of the head of the personnel department, men are less suited to this work, which requires a high degree of diplomacy and persistence. A man, in her opinion, lacks these qualities and loses his temper easily. Not long ago a male conductor got into a conflict with a group of drunken passengers trying to travel without tickets. When he went to call the police he was thrown into the street.

The job of controller-dispatcher, checking that the drivers keep to their schedules, was also, and remains, an especially female job. Women were traditionally controllers on the routes, checking the tickets. As a rule this job was done by women between 30 and 50 years old with a manifestly militant disposition, able to force those without a ticket to pay a fine and ready to enter conflicts by the hour. Their female status in the Soviet period gave them some protection from male aggression (only the most demoralised man was able to show physical aggression to a woman – at least in public). However, more recently public standards have changed, as has the scale of ticket prices and fines. In this situation the work of the controllers on the lines has become more dangerous. Passengers increasingly frequently refuse to recognise the conductor's authority. It is obviously for this reason that they have begun more actively to recruit men for the job of controller, as in many analogous enterprises in the country. A significant number of young men, between 20 and 25 years old, many of them students, have appeared among the controllers during the 1990s.

The bus station, serving passengers on the suburban and inter-city lines, is a women's collective (dispatchers, cashiers, cleaners and so on), and only women work in the canteen.

There is a very clear gender division of labour within the administration, according to type of education and content of the job. Thus most engineering posts are held by men, while women dominate the economic services. This division appears primarily to be a hangover from the old system, when the economic departments had low prestige and were poorly paid. In those days women dominated economics faculties in higher education, which determined the female dominance of the economic service in enterprises. During the 90s the situation has changed rapidly. The transition to a market economy has sharply increased the status of the economist. In economics faculties competition has increased and now there are a lot of young men. However, the change in the gender structure among economists as a whole has only just begun. Young male economists are keenly sought by the most profitable enterprises and organisations (banks, commercial enterprises and so on). Therefore in old state and recently privatised enterprises, where the skeleton of the administration has been preserved over the years, women still predominate in the economic departments.

When a new director came to PATP in May 1993, he introduced the post of deputy for economics and commercial questions. Within the established gender structure of the collective he had no choice: this post could only be filled by a woman. And the chief accountant of PATP became the deputy director, a young woman who had graduated as a correspondence student from the economics faculty of the university a couple of years before. However, she did not work in this post for long: it soon turned out that she had been involved in some frauds involving petrol, a criminal case was opened and she had to leave the enterprise. For a long time the post remained vacant. In PATP the accounts department is a purely female collective, as is the planning department and the personnel department.

Such a gender division of labour coincides with the functional division on the level of departmental managers. Thus, women head the personnel department, planning department, accountant's department, bus station, central dispatching service, incomes department and the canteen. These are all women's collectives, and each is headed by a woman.

However, untypical situations have also arisen: a woman at the head of a man's collective. Thus, a woman headed the motor department in a local centre a couple of hundred kilometres from the city. There the collective was basically male, but for a long time neither the management of PATP nor the local authorities could find a man who would fill this post, although this was what they wanted. Every likely applicant, once he got to know more about the job, refused it. Therefore at the head of the collective, in the post of temporary director of the department, is a woman, having agreed to such an extraordinary step.

The mechanical repair workshops were always purely male collectives. But the new director, suddenly deciding to strengthen discipline, ran into a problem, the resolution of which turned about to be the appearance of a woman in a responsible post in the workshops. N— had worked as a conductor and had become famous for her battling character, her persistence and her refusal to compromise. This had led to complaints from passengers. The director, being very sensitive to the public reputation of the enterprise in the city, never failed to take appropriate steps in response to such complaints. This time he took an extraordinary decision: he transferred the woman to the repair mechanical workshops where, in his opinion, the foremen suffered from excessive liberalism. A special post was created for her, with responsibility for controlling labour discipline.

The new director also used a woman in another area where, in his opinion, discipline had to be strengthened. He introduced the post of 'technician for the control of working time'. A young woman sits at the entrance to the garage and notes the time at which every worker in the enterprise arrives and leaves. The workers initially greeted this innovation with sabotage and, arriving at the enterprise, demonstratively tried to come in through the traffic entrance, rather than the entrance where the woman sat. However, the administration compelled them to recognise the new post and new boss.

Traditionally the central dispatching service is predominantly female. This lowest level of the administration is at the forefront of the contradiction between workers and the apparatus, taking on the high nervous costs of this social conflict for modest payment.

The tactic of using women in the lowest controllers' posts in men's collectives turns out not to be accidental. Having put women in that position, the administration gives them power over a large number of men, who have much higher levels of skill than these women. This clearly flatters the vanity of the women and stimulates their eagerness to serve. Such a situation restrains the male vanity of the drivers and fitters. They try either to ignore the controllers, or subject them to pressure. The semi-hostile attitude of the male workers to the lowest level of the administration pushes the women into a more intransigent position. The circle is closed. Deals between controllers and controlled become much less likely. Thus, the conscious interweaving of the administrative power and gender stratifications makes the watershed along the line worker-administration more sharp, which improves the quality of control.

INSTITUTIONALISATION OF SOCIAL INTERESTS

The enterprise and social interests

An enterprise is a social organisation created to satisfy the economic and industrial interests of this or that subject. All enterprises in the USSR were state enterprises (collective farms were pseudo-collective enterprises). Thus the enterprise was constituted with the aim of realising the interests of the state. The labour collective is formed as a means of realising these interests. At first sight the social measures implemented in the enterprise had the purpose of meeting the interests of the workers themselves (stable employment, improved working conditions, development of the social infrastructure and so on). However, these interests were considered to be secondary to the interests of the state. Care for the workers was a care for the means of realisation of state interests, and was implemented only to the extent that it did not contradict those interests.

An important indicator of the social content of an organisation is the criteria according to which it is evaluated, the basis for the encouragement or penalisation of its employees. The most superficial analysis of enterprises in state monopoly socialist society shows that the main criterion was the ability of the enterprise to carry out state tasks. For this they gave bonuses, certificates, banners, promotions or dismissals. 'All for the state, all in the name of the state!' was the unwritten motto of every enterprise.

A whole system of Party and state bodies checked that the enterprise pursued first of all state rather than group interests. Both Party control and superior industry bodies, above all associations, were directed at this task. Within the enterprise, Party criticism and self-criticism were encouraged with a view to revealing and suppressing private interests. However, despite all this, private interests forced a way through for themselves. The contradiction between the nationwide interest pressed by the system and the private interests of employees of the enterprise was the basic contradiction in the development of the Soviet and post-Soviet enterprise at all stages in its history.

The primary Party organisation

The presence of the primary organisation of the CPSU as the nucleus of the system of social management of the collective was a feature of the structure of the enterprise in the society of state monopoly socialism. Its main official task was to subordinate the activity of the enterprise to the satisfaction of the general state interest. Thus questions of the management of production were at the centre of its attention.

Our content analysis of the minutes of Party bureaux and committees in ten enterprises in the Komi Republic over the years 1966–75 showed that 47.9 per cent of the points on the agendas concerned concrete technical-organisational matters; 11.4 per cent concerned the selection and appointment of staff; 10 per cent concerned the results of plan fulfilment; 7.9 per cent concerned the organisation of socialist competition; 7 per cent concerned labour discipline; and 16 per cent concerned other questions of production organisation. The work of Party meetings was organised in the same way. On average, in the Party organisations studied, questions of production management occupied 62.4 per cent of the meetings.

The inclusion in membership of the primary Party organisation of key figures in the administration made its decisions extremely significant for the process of management. The director was almost always a member of the Party committee. Exceptions only arose for a short period of time, for example when changes of director did not coincide with changes in the structure of the Party committee. But in any case the director played a key role in the work of the primary Party organisation.

The Party organisation was, above all, an instrument of the administration, allowing it to mobilise the most skilled and disciplined part of the labour collective for the fulfilment of the economic tasks presented to the enterprise. The city Party bodies, monitoring and directing the activity of the primary groups, closely checked that the enterprise executed its functions and that the primary Party organisation 'struggled' for this (in the Party lexicon the word 'struggle' was usually used in place of the word 'act'). Participation of a wide circle of workers in the work of Party organisations gave legitimacy to the Party's decisions, duplicating the orders of the administration: they had voted for this decision themselves, which means that they must carry it out.

At the same time the Party organisation, incorporating a significant proportion of the employees of the enterprise, had the right to control the economic activity of the administration. Usually this right was reduced to regular information from the chiefs of the enterprise concerning the fulfilment of plans and the new tasks confronting it. However, in tactical questions ordinary members of the Party organisation could correct the actions of the administration, indicating some errors in its work. This to some extent ameliorated the technocratic approach of the administration, forcing it to think of the social aspects of the decisions it adopted. Thus, through the Party organisation, the labour collective could, even if only to a limited extent, influence the work of the administration.

By virtue of the contradictory role of the primary organisation in the system of social management of the enterprise, workers were not unanimous in answer to the question put to them in a survey in 1989, 'Whose interests does the Party organisation defend?' The answers were distributed as follows: society as a whole 2 per cent; the state 2 per cent; the whole labour collective 15 per cent; specialists and office workers 4 per cent; workers 7 per cent; the administration 27 per cent; nobody's 9 per cent; difficult to answer 32 per cent.

However, alongside the indeterminacy of the employees of PATP, everybody was inclined to the view that the Party organisation did not express the interests of the collective. In the eyes of the workers the Party organisation was merged with the administration.

A key figure in the Party organisation was the secretary of the Party committee. As he was the only member of the Party organisation who did this work in a professional capacity, the lion's share of the work of the Party organisation was reduced to the activity of its secretary. He came to the enterprise at the beginning of the working day and left at the end, as often as not having to stay on for an hour or so after work. Officially his working day was considered to be unlimited. The work of other members of the Party organisation was reduced to the monthly payment of membership dues and monthly attendance at Party meetings. A few members of the Party committee participated another one or two times a month in meetings of the Party committee, or periodically looked into this or that question prepared by the Party meeting. However, as a rule their Party activity had an episodic character and was easily manipulated by the Party secretary.

Usually the Party secretary and the director of the enterprise worked together, carefully avoiding disagreements and, if they occurred, tried to smooth them over to reach a compromise and conceal them from the eyes of outsiders. Open conflicts between them happened extremely rarely. The Party organisation of PATP was no exception. How did this unity come about?

The city Party committee recognised that the director was the main figure in the enterprise, and the main function of the Party organisation was to ensure the fulfilment of the plan tasks. This automatically made the Party secretary the second figure in the enterprise. And the secretary, understanding this very well, was cautious in his relations with the director. He understood that in the event of a conflict he had little chance of securing the support of the city Party committee.

Moreover, usually the director of a reasonably significant enterprise was elected to the city Party committee, which gave him a solid weight in the Party hierarchy as well.

The secretary of the Party committee of the enterprise was much less often a member of the city committee. The secretary of the Party committee was a professional Party worker, paid by the city Party committee. However, in most cases he was appointed from among the engineers in the enterprise, so that traditionally he continued to look at the director from below. Moreover, for most Party secretaries their professional Party work was a temporary occupation: at the next conference they had a very real chance of returning to the ranks of the engineers. This also ensured that they were very cautious in their relations with the administration.

The PATP Party secretary, Y—n, was elected from among the engineers of the enterprise. His activism and initiative had also been noticed at the city level. As a result he was elected a member of the city Party committee. However, he regarded his Party activity as a very temporary part of his own biography. The decline in the authority of the Party and the falling prestige of Party workers at the end of the 1980s clearly encouraged such an attitude.

He obviously noticed the deficiencies in the work of the administration. From his replies to questions it became clear that he did not agree with the administration's recourse to authoritarian methods and its neglect of the interests of the workers. However, he had decided not to state his criticisms openly. At the same time, the secretary clearly followed the popular line of that period of the democratisation of enterprise management, pushing the workers to assert their rights more boldly. He regularly went to the shops and columns, talked to workers about their problems and kept in contact with the most militant members of the collective, whom the administration saw as trouble-makers. It was he who commissioned our research in 1989.

The independent position of the secretary of the Party committee and his attempt to find a common language with the workers allowed him to attain a singularly high level of authority within the labour collective. In 1989 the ratings, out of 5, were: director of PATP 2.8; president of trade union committee 2.2; trade union committee 2.1; Party committee 2.8; secretary of the Party committee 3.0.

In interviews conducted at that time workers approved the Party secretary with the following phrases: 'he has his own position', 'he knows people pretty well', 'he comes to the shops'; 'you can talk to him man to man', 'not a bad bloke', 'I know him through playing sports with him' and so on.

However, the influence of the Party organisation was irresistibly extinguished together with the influence of the CPSU as a whole, and a single person could not alter the situation. The influence of the Party committee and its secretary on the administration was appreciably greater than among the workers. Moreover, the Party organisation acted in such a way that those who were not members had only the vaguest impression of its activities (even most Party meetings were closed). For this reason only 12.5 per cent of the collective of PATP questioned answered that the Party organisation had an appreciable influence on the life of the collective. Forty per cent answered categorically that it did not, while 47 per cent did not or could not answer. Once it became obvious that the CPSU had no future Y—n handed over his Party post to another engineer and returned to his profession to work in another enterprise.

M—i was elected as the new secretary, but he soon had to leave his post when in 1991 Yeltsin prohibited the activity of Party primary organisations in enterprises, and after the putsch of August 1991 Yeltsin dissolved the Party altogether.

The primary Party group of PATP disappeared quietly and without a sound. Nobody openly objected to its dissolution. There was an impression that its members had only been waiting for the moment when they could stop paying their Party dues.

The consequences of the liquidation of the primary Party organisation was far from unambiguous. If at the level of the country as a whole the liquidation of the CPSU was a great leap forward in the democratisation of the country, in enterprises the liquidation of the primary Party organisation meant the liquidation of the sole effective form of control of the activity of the administration on the part of the labour collective. With the disappearance of the Party organisation opportunities have opened for the establishment of a more rigid authoritarian regime: now the administration can act safely, without looking over its shoulder at the Party organisation. The trade unions, even in those rare cases such as in the coal-mining industry or in PATP where they have been militant and independent, have never had the rights to control the administration which the Party organisation had had since the end of the 1930s.

At the same time, with the removal of the primary Party organisation, the administration has also lost a relatively effective means of controlling the labour collective. As a result of its departure the gap which had always divided workers from the administration became obvious, for the small bridge, in the form of the Soviet type of labour aristocracy represented by the worker-communists, had disappeared.

The director of PATP who held the post from 1990 to 1993 had previously worked in a similar enterprise in a polar city. There he had been secretary of the Party committee, deputy director, and then director and so was very well placed to judge the role of the Party organisation. In his retrospective evaluation, given in an interview in 1993, he argued that the Party organisation not only was not a handicap to the director, but also helped him to resolve many production problems and to strengthen labour discipline. In those years it was easier for him to operate the enterprise with the Party organisation alongside him, as the worker-communists to a significant extent supported the process of management. Now the director has lost this support. Thus he recalled nostalgically how, when the nights were very cold, the Party organisation called in the worker-communists and they kept the engines warm all night so that in the morning the buses could leave for their routes without any problems.

The administration as a bearer of social interests

The administration is the main subject of authority in the enterprise. Everywhere and always it is called on to express and to protect the interests of the owner. In a state enterprise, as PATP was and remained, it was supposed to protect the interests of the state. In conditions of state-monopoly socialism there was a complex and strict system monitoring the activity of the administration, directed at preventing deviations from state interests. PATP received its plans for the carriage of passengers from above. State and Party bodies checked on their fulfilment, taking the director strictly to task for deviations from the plan.

However, private interests found a way through. Thus the planning process took the form of constant negotiations between the director and the association. The essence of these negotiations was simple: he always fought to reduce the plan and to increase his material and technical supplies. In other words, the main interest of the director was to reduce the efficiency of production. If he was successful, the enterprise could work quietly and everyone could earn as much or more, since earnings depended strictly on plan fulfilment. Correspondingly, the lower the plan, the easier it is to fulfil, and the higher are the bonuses.

Moreover, the administration in state-monopoly socialism is a part of the labour collective: they too are hired labourers, like the workers, although endowed with more rights and responsibilities. Thus the majority of directors to a greater or lesser degree tried to defend the social interests of their collective, which facilitated the management of the collective and expanded the opportunities for realising their own interests.

The director of PATP at the end of the 1980s was especially attentive to the subsidiary agricultural activity of the enterprise. In the view of some of the workers he spent more time in the pig sties than maintaining passenger transport.

In the Gorbachev period of perestroika a process of decentralisation of management began, with the aim of increasing its efficiency, but this led to an interesting metamorphosis of the Soviet enterprise.

The organisation was created for the realisation of definite interests. It was subordinate to those interests. However, the transformation of the organisational structure often leads to a rebirth of the organisation, usually unplanned and unexpected: it begins to work for other interests. The transformation of the form also deforms its content.

In the process of decentralisation the dominance of general state interests over the interests of the labour collective and its separate parts, particularly the administration, began to weaken. Carefully suppressed interests began to emerge more and more obviously in the economic activity of enterprises, and then in general came to the fore. Decentralisation meant the delegation of authority to the subjects of management of the enterprise, above all the administration and, particularly, the director as the one-man-manager. As a result of this process the interests of the administration began to define the content of management. The phenomenon of *prikhvatisatsia* was the clearest expression of this. The interests of the collective were taken into account only to the extent that they coincided with those of the bosses of the enterprise, or were protected by the development of self-management.

The enterprise and social policy

The main economic law of the state mode of production is the increase of the power of the state – deliberately and rationally to do everything that makes the state stronger and more stable. This is fundamentally different from capitalist rationality. Therefore the same action is evaluated completely differently in the context of different modes of production. This is completely the case with regard to the regulation of social relations. The main purpose of their regulation in a capitalist enterprise is the creation of the most favourable conditions for the intensification of production. In state monopoly socialist society the enterprise is an element of a uniform management system, therefore its social policy was evaluated only from the point of view of its consequence for the stability of the state as a whole. Economic rationality inevitably played a minor role in this process.

To be stable, the state requires a social base: a mass of citizens who support it, or are at least ready to tolerate it. In conditions of shortages of resources it is necessary to think carefully about their distribution.

One of the laws of cybernetics states: the reliability of a system is measured by the reliability of its weakest element. In society the least reserves of patience and loyalty are usually found in the lowest layers of the population, whose consumption level is the closest to the subsistence minimum. Therefore the first problem of social policy is to prevent hunger riots. In state monopoly socialist society one of the key directions of social policy has been the support of the lowest layer through the principle of compulsory employment. The surplus of jobs permitted any able-bodied person to find work without special problems. Therefore the problem of extreme poverty was removed: the available work was associated with a guaranteed minimum wage which, with low prices for basic food and clothing, was enough to survive. The widely developed system of hostels in principle ensured that everybody had somewhere to live.

Those who did not want to work in such miserable conditions were considered delinquent and could be involved in forced labour. Thus, the stabilisation of society through the compulsory employment and minimum payment of the lowest layers of society was one of the leading principles of social policy in state monopoly socialist society.

Of course the apparatus could not be expected not to think of itself. Social policy was modified in its interests, for increasing the power of the state naturally entailed improving the living and working conditions of the administrative elite, however much that contradicted its loudly proclaimed ideological principles. This was the other leading direction of social policy.

With the gross inefficiency of production, which was also overloaded by the burden of militarism, once these two social problems had been resolved there were very limited resources to be distributed among the ordinary population. Thus the egalitarianism of Soviet society is caused not by Marxist–Leninist ideology, but by the iron logic of the state method of production. As for egalitarian ideological principles, it is well-known that the Soviet Party-state discarded without hesitation those principles of Marxist theory which contradicted its interests of increasing the power of the state and the social self-affirmation of its apparatus. Fate would soon have disposed of egalitarianism if it had not corresponded to the logic of the social policy of the state mode of production.

The key role in the realisation of this direction of social policy was played by the enterprises. It was they which provided universal employment. If this direction of social policy had contradicted the interests of the administrative apparatus, it would have remained only on paper. Soviet history provides ample proof that, even in conditions of terror, policies would not be carried out if there were not groups in the population with whose interests those policies coincided. The policy of social guarantees through compulsory employment corresponded to the interests of the chiefs of the enterprises.

Within enterprises, as already noted above, there were ample opportunities to not work, only to simulate work. This was an expression of one side of the social contract between the workers and the administration, but at the same time it corresponded to the social policy of the Party-state. Moreover, production was organised in such a way that the enterprise was interested in having plentiful stocks of every kind of resource: raw materials, fuel, machinery and workers.

These reserves made it possible to survive in the face of an increase in the plan tasks, in conditions of permanent storming at the end of the month, quarter and year. A reserve of labour made it possible to increase the productivity of labour without difficulty by sacking a certain number of superfluous workers.

The enterprises were incorporated in two different control systems: the branch system, under the ministry, and the territorial system, under the city and regional committees of the Party. The latter demanded that the enterprise should provide labour to help out collective and state farms in weeding, harvesting, preparation of forage and sometimes even in feeding of cattle, in construction of villages, in delivering goods, in the 'shock' construction of buildings for the city or region, to help out comrades lagging behind in socialist competition, to sort out vegetables in the warehouses, to participate in *subbotniks* to clean the streets and so on, almost indefinitely. At the same time, the enterprise had to perform all these tasks without falling behind for one moment in its production plan.

It was much more difficult to escape the all-seeing eye of the local Party bodies than to twist the far-away Moscow ministry around one's little finger. Therefore the enterprise had to maintain substantial reserves of labour to cover its participation in the regional economy. The availability of plentiful cheap labour also relieved the directors of a major headache when it came to technical re-equipment: it was much easier and was cheaper to employ twenty loaders than to automate or to mechanise the work of loading and unloading. Moreover, as against the narrow specialisation of expensive equipment requiring skilled maintenance and repair, the unskilled ancillary workers could carry out a much wider range of work, and could be thrown into the hot spots.

One of the most important elements of social policy is the system of social protection for those who are not able to support themselves by their own labour. In Soviet society the enterprise played a special place in this system of social protection as the principal framework for the redistribution of material goods and services. However, at the level of the enterprise the initial idea of the system of social protection was substantially transformed and it became primarily a system of non-monetary benefits which recognised labour and administrative status and served to increase rather than reduce inequality.[4]

4 See V. Ilyin and Yu. Popova, 'Workers of the Management Apparatus: Specific Character of their Status Position in the Light of Empirical Sociological Research', *Bureaucratism and Self-Management*, Syktyvkar, 1990.

The social policy of the enterprise plays a double role. On the one hand, it makes it possible to increase the standard of living of the workers, supplementing low pay and reducing the likelihood of conflict. On the other hand, it aggravates social inequality among the employees of the enterprise, first of all on the basis of their status in the system of administrative-power, contradicting the most widespread conception of social justice and increasing the likelihood of conflict around distribution.

The purpose of this discussion of the past is not to indulge in an historical excursion, but because the essential features of state monopoly socialist society remain, even though we are now enduring the painful process of its dismantling. It is impossible to understand the transition process without an understanding of the specific form of society on which it is based.

Trade union organisation

Trade union organisations played an important role in the system of the Soviet social contract. Since 1921 they had been assigned their function of being 'schools of communism': their tasks being mainly to mobilise the masses for the fulfilment of the production plan (socialist competition, the rationalisation movement and so on). At the same time the trade unions, having become in practice appendages of state bodies, were an important link in social policy, providing support for the social contract in the enterprises. Although an appendage of the administration, they at the same time limited its ability to adopt strict management methods, to clean out the enterprise of drunks and absentees (it is well-known how difficult it was to sack bad employees, since in the majority of cases the trade union committee came to their defence). The trade unions held in their hands the distribution of a whole range of social benefits: vacation vouchers, apartments. Together with the administration they participated in the distribution of the bonus fund.

Thus, although the trade unions were an appendage of the administration, they were also a buffer in the relationship between the administration and the workers, constraining management enthusiasm for technocratic methods of management, fraught with the risk of worsening social relations in the enterprise. Some independence of the trade union from the administration was secured by law, and by the political line of the CPSU which acted as the patron of the trade unions at all levels. In the enterprise the trade union committee acted on the basis of the support of the Party committee. The directors were afraid to ignore the trade union committee, for this smelt of deviating from the Party line.

The trade union organisation of PATP at the end of the 1980s was completely typical. Its president avoided excessive independence, always listened to the opinion of the administration and leaned on it for support. This led to the growing alienation of the trade union leadership from the ordinary members of the trade union.

When the workers were asked in the summer of 1989, 'whose interests does your trade union organisation express?', 11 per cent replied the interests of workers; 38 per cent the interests of the administration; nobody's interests 16 per cent; would not or could not answer 9 per cent.

In the eyes of the enterprise's employees the trade union appeared to be even further from being a defender of the workers' interests than was the Party organisation. Its subordination to the administration was even more obvious than in the case of the Party organisation. Thus, in assessing the role of the trade union there was a sharp difference between workers and administration. Forty five per cent of the drivers and 61 per cent of the repair workers thought that the trade union expressed the interests of the administration, but only 13 per cent each of the managers and ITR expressed the same view.

The trade union had clearly lost control of its members. The influence of informal leaders in the collective was growing ever stronger. Discontent with the administration was increasing. All of this was very reminiscent of the processes unfolding on a larger scale and in a clearer form in the coal-mining industry at that time. Realising the danger of such a tendency, the secretary of the Party committee called in our sociological team. His action also had a hidden aim: to use independent outside researchers to prove the necessity of renewing the trade union leadership. Our data put objective arguments into his hands. It is remarkable that the money for the research was provided by the trade union committee, which had no idea that it would undermine its own position. Following our research not only the trade union committee, but also the absentee director of the enterprise, was removed.[5]

[5] A comfortable and well-paid position was found for the former director in the regional transport administration. When asked later whether he would be willing to return to his old job, he replied categorically that he would never go down that road again.

In conditions of political and social crisis after 1989 the Soviet trade unions found themselves at the cross-roads. They developed in different directions in different enterprises and different industries. In the coal mining industry the workers' movement split: alongside the traditional state trade union appeared a new independent miners' union. Soon after, a similar split arose in the air transport industry. In some places, particularly in the private sector, the trade union was liquidated completely. In many enterprises the trade union committee became an even more obedient appendage of the administration than it had been in the past.

The fate of the trade union in PATP illustrates another, and much rarer, variant of development: the transformation of a Soviet trade union organisation into a militant body defending the interests of the workers.

In September 1989 the VIth Plenum of the Soviet trade union organisation, the VTsSPS, having recognised that the trade unions faced a crisis of confidence, proclaimed their main function to be the defence of the interests of the workers. It also for the first time declared the independence of the trade unions. The traditional Soviet trade unions would have to set off on the road of radical transformation: in time they distanced themselves from the CPSU and significantly renewed their apparatus, although the influence of the old nomenklatura was not extinguished and the unions appeared independent not only in name, but also in their position in relation to both enterprise administration and the government.

The same quiet revolution took place in a small number of primary trade union organisations. In a completely legal way, as a result of a trade union conference, the most radical leaders of the labour collective were elected to leadership of the trade union. They set themselves the task of removing the trade union from the pocket of the administration and converting it into an independent organisation, asserting the interests first of all of the workers as a part of the labour collective. This led to a radical change in the relations between the trade union committee and the administration.

This was just the way in which events developed at PATP. In October 1989 the trade union conference took place. There were three candidates for the post of president, including the former president, who received only two votes. The second candidate received four votes. Everyone else voted for N – v, who had worked as a driver for 19 years and was president of the shop trade union committee of his column. The membership of the committee was also changed, and almost all its new members were workers. Several workers who joined the trade union committee had previously been in serious conflicts with the administration, including V – m, a driver who had a reputation as a battler for justice, who had been sacked illegally but, thanks to his determination, had taken the administration to court and secured his reinstatement.

The new trade union committee did not take the most radical step of declaring itself the basis of a new independent trade union, but set out to transform its primary organisation into an independent force while remaining within the structure of the official trade union. Thus a social revolution took place: a trade union committee became a defender of the workers instead of a defender of the interests, above all, of the administration.

From October 1989 the position of the workers in the trade union at PATP began to strengthen all the more obviously. The trade union increasingly asserted the workers' interests above all. The influence of the administration was in constant decline. This is shown clearly by the changes which the trade union committee managed to introduce in the collective agreement. In the 1989 agreement the rights of the trade union were traditionally delimited, the trade union having the right to monitor management decisions only in the areas of health and safety and the training of workers. In the 1992 agreement the trade union had a substantially expanded sphere of influence:

> The administration agrees, in accordance with the law, to inform the trade union committee of all significant organisational changes in the activity of the enterprise, of the distribution of income, of current plans and long-term proposals and about construction of new facilities. ... The administration must agree with the labour collective, trade union committee and STK of the enterprise any decision to lease or sell the enterprise's equipment to any other parties, organisations or individuals.

The trade union had the right to resolve conflicts between the administration and the labour collective. A special section on the rights, guarantees and privileges of trade union activists protected the independence of the trade union, protected their pay and bonuses and gave them privileged access to housing. 'Black Saturdays', on which workers were compelled to work without additional pay, were abolished; a five-day working work was guaranteed; women with children under twelve secured additional privileges; work breaks were increased; a minimum wage was established; overtime rates were increased; the trade union was to be consulted over managerial salaries; workers approaching pension age were protected from dismissal; the trade union was to be consulted in relation to all production stoppages, redundancies or deterioration in working conditions; vacation entitlements were improved; privileges for pensioners were improved.

Such a beneficial collective agreement was not in itself a remarkable phenomenon. Many collective agreements provided for a wide range of benefits and rights for the workers. However, normally the collective agreement was merely a formal document which was signed annually and put in the bottom drawer. What was remarkable in this case was that the trade union pressed for the implementation of the collective agreement. In PATP the director signed the 1992 collective agreement on the traditional understanding, never expecting that he would implement it. Indeed, it was only after the agreement had been accepted by the labour collective and signed by the director that he sat down to read it properly and decided that he had been tricked by the trade union president. The administration drew up a memorandum of disagreements, specifying the points in the collective agreement which could not be fulfilled, which the trade union president simply ignored.

The trade union kept quiet for several months, but then took the director to court for failure to meet the terms of the collective agreement. The court ruled that the director had indeed violated the collective agreement, but recognised that he was unable to implement it because of a shortage of money. This allowed both the director and the trade union president to claim victory. The formal decision of the court did not arrive for several weeks. In the meantime, stiff negotiations were under way for the 1993 collective agreement, the key point for the administration not being the substantial concessions on pay and working conditions, but the right of the trade union to be consulted over the sale and leasing of the enterprise's property. In the event these negotiations were overtaken by the removal of the director and changes in the personnel of the trade union committee.

As soon as it became clear that the trade union committee was determined to pursue an independent course, and even to oppose the administration, the director of the enterprise responded: he publicly left the trade union and at the trade union conference called for others to leave with him, initiating an open struggle with the union. He was followed by a significant proportion of management employees. The chief engineer hesitated, but decided to stay in the union.

The director decided that the management employees needed their own trade union and began to take steps to establish such an organisation. The same idea was becoming popular at a republican level within the trade union. In 1993 the Komi republican committee of the trade union of motor transport employees prepared a draft of a new constitution in which it was envisaged that those who fulfilled the functions of hiring, firing and punishing would be excluded from membership. Several directors left the union, joining an association of directors. However, some of the directors ignored these hints and stayed in the trade unions, aiming to keep control of them from within.

Social delimitation in the collective is not limited to the division between management and the rest of the collective. Workers, ITR and office workers have different interests, and there are differences among the workers themselves. These differences were also reflected in proposals for the reorganisation of the trade union. Thus, the road transport union experimented with the introduction of sections for bus drivers, taxi drivers, repair workers. However, in practice it turned out that their common interests outweighed the differences and the experiment was abandoned.

Social differentiation in the trade union organisation regularly leads to the escalation of objective contradictions in the intense atmosphere involved in conflict. The administration begins to perceive a disobedient trade union as a completely unnecessary obstacle to its work. Both sides, administration and trade union, begin to take offensive action.

This was how events developed at PATP. The administration took a series of steps to weaken the trade union organisation, turning it into its opponent. They demanded that the trade union should pay rent for its premises. The president of the trade union committee managed to provoke the administration into taking illegal actions, putting the law on his side. An important role in this struggle was played by the lawyer of the enterprise. He gathered all the information about those changes in legal and administrative norms which could be used to undermine the position of the trade union and drew them to the attention of the collective. Thus, in 1992 he posted a newspaper cutting on the notice board, with the hand-written instruction, ‘read’. The cutting explained that failure to pay trade union dues was not a ground for depriving a worker of the right to financial assistance or to access to the sanatorium and so on. Another cutting explained that, according to a ministerial order, trade unions have no right to collect dues without a written application from each member. It was also announced that the director and chief accountant had already stopped paying their dues. Somebody had written on this notice, 'good riddance!'.

According to the president of the trade union committee, management planning meetings were regularly littered with attacks on the trade union, with statements such as 'What do you expect of this trade union?' 'Paying fees is a complete waste of money'.

Under these influences many management employees and some workers left the trade union. However, by the end of 1992 around 90 per cent of the members had confirmed their membership by signing individual applications and submitting them to the accounts department with a request to check their membership dues off from their salary. By the middle of 1993 only about 40 per cent of ITR and office workers remained in the union, and almost all the chiefs had left.

The administration began to boycott the trade union committee, which made the trade union's work more difficult since most of it is connected with distributive functions on behalf of the administration. Thus the accountant of the trade union committee had to make a list of the children to be given holiday gifts. She did not have much time and could not make the chiefs of columns give her the information, so she turned for help to the director, who answered, 'look for your contacts yourself'. After this episode the accountant reached the conclusion that there was no point in looking to him for co-operation.

The struggle between the trade union committee and the administration extended to all spheres of trade union activity, including the determination of wages and the collective agreement. At the beginning of 1993 the director tried to move to a contract system, the purpose of which was seen by the trade union president as being to conceal the salaries of senior managers from the rest of the employees. The trade union president responded by publishing details of managerial salaries just before the spring 1993 conference of the labour collective. The administration conceded: the trade union was invited to participate in the commission established to determine the salaries of ITR and managers.

The trade union committee decided to try to remove the director. Following its failure to have him removed for violations of the law in connection with the sale of taxis, the trade union proposed a vote of no confidence at the 1992 labour collective conference. However, the trade union committee was too complacent and the administration prepared carefully for the meeting by controlling the selection of delegates, to such an extent that even the president of the trade union committee was not selected as a delegate and the no confidence motion did not receive a single supporting vote. The trade union then began to collect signatures for a petition demanding the resignation of the director, but this also came to nothing.

The trade union committee prepared much more carefully for the 1993 labour collective conference. The director, probably realising that he was destined to lose the struggle, not only failed to prepare adequately for the meeting, but went on sick leave just before, and the meeting voted its lack of confidence in the director, a decision that was supported by the regional state property committee. The director resigned, and in May 1993 a new director, M—v, who had worked previously in a similar enterprise in the region, came to PATP. He was nominated by the regional transport association and the city administration, after consultation with the president of the trade union committee. His candidature suited everybody in every respect. The information presented about him made him appear to be a boss who was able to organise the work of the enterprise well, which suited the administration of the city and the association, and able to secure a stable standard of living for his collective, which suited the trade union committee.

M—v, having agreed to become director of PATP, knew the sad history of his predecessor. However, in his view this had arisen as a result of serious errors in economic and social policy. Seeing them, he hoped to change both the economic and the social situation with the help of a different management strategy.

The new model of social relations was announced by M—v on his arrival, when he declared to the most active leaders of the trade union, 'You have broken up the firewood. Now let us get out of this difficult position together … It is easy to criticise, but I am proposing that we work together.' The approach was extremely specific: he offered the newly created post of first deputy director for production to the trade union president, who had just completed his higher education in engineering by correspondence, having earlier been a driver. The president accepted. One of the leaders of the trade union committee accepted a post as chief of column, another rejected such an offer on the grounds of his age. As a result, the most militant members of the trade union committee were absorbed into the administration. The administration, together with the trade union committee, then considered the question of suitable replacements for those who had left. The director offered the vacant post of president of the trade union committee to the deputy director for social questions, who is responsible for the administration of the social and welfare facilities. It is said that just before the trade union conference the director said to him, 'I am cutting your post. If you want to remain in the enterprise, fight for the trade union'. The trade union committee, whose leaders had already decided to join the administration, supported his candidature.

At the conference one of the most militant members of the trade union committee, who had been actively struggling with the administration for years, was unexpectedly nominated. However, to the surprise of many people he attracted only two votes, including his own. This was a clear expression of the willingness of the collective to support the strategy of the new director for a strong social contract.

The new director, now in close alliance with the former president of the trade union, made substantial personnel changes, removing many managers and replacing them through internal promotion. At the same time he threw out various private enterprises which had been established on the premises of PATP on the basis of leasehold agreements with the former director, including the now independent taxi enterprise which had leased a part of the garage space. Now without any internal opposition, the new director was able to restore the traditional methods of one-man-management.

However, at the beginning of 1995 a new conflict began between the new director and the new president of the trade union committee, who had refused to struggle together with the director against the reformation of the regional association. The director had not forgiven this treachery, and his relations with the trade union rapidly deteriorated. Meanwhile, the previous president of the trade union committee, now deputy director, took the side of his boss without question. The history of the new conflict shows clearly that it is not connected to personalities, but has a structural character, the roots of which, we hope to have shown, lie in the position of the administration within the social structure of the enterprise and in the interaction between administrative and market structures in the period of transition.

Index